FOUNDATIONS FOR YOUTH JUSTICE

Positive approaches to practice

Anne Robinson

First published in Great Britain in 2014 by

Policy Press
University of Bristol
6th Floor
Howard House
Queen's Avenue
Clifton
Bristol BS8 1SD
UK
t: +44 (0)117 331 5020
f: +44 (0)117 331 5367
pp-info@bristol.ac.uk
www.policypress.co.uk

North America office:
Policy Press
c/o The University of Chicago Press
1427 East 60th Street
Chicago, IL 60637, USA
t: +1 773 702 7700
f: +1 773 702 9756
sales@press.uchicago.edu
www.press.uchicago.edu

© Policy Press 2014

British Library Cataloguing in Publication Data
A catalogue record for this book is available from the British Library.

Library of Congress Cataloging-in-Publication Data
A catalog record for this book has been requested.

ISBN: 978 144730 699 3 hardcover
ISBN: 978 144730 698 6 paperback

Cover design by Policy Press
Printed and bound in Great Britain by TJ International, Padstow
Policy Press uses environmentally responsible print partners.

Contents

List of tables and figures

Tables

Figures

List of abbreviations and acronyms

ADHD	attention deficit hyperactivity disorder
AL	adolescent-limited
ASBO	anti-social behaviour order
BME	black and minority ethnic
CAMHS	Child and Adolescent Mental Health Services
CCTV	closed circuit television
CDA 1998	Crime and Disorder Act 1998
CAF	Common Assessment Framework
CJA	Criminal Justice Act 1948, 1991, 2003
CJ&IA 2008	Criminal Justice and Immigration Act 2008
COSR	court ordered secure remand
C&YPA	Children and Young Persons Act 1933, 1963, 1969, 2008
DCSF	Department for Children, Schools and Families
DfE	Department for Education
ECHR	European Convention on Human Rights
ESPAD	European School Project on Alcohol and Other Drugs
ESRC	Economic and Social Research Council
ESYTC	Edinburgh Study of Youth Transitions and Crime
FTE	first-time entrant (to the youth justice system)
GP	general (medical) practitioner
HBSC	Health Behaviours in School-Age Children
HMIP	Her Majesty's Inspectorate of Prisons
HRA 1998	Human Rights Act 1998
ICT	information and communication technology
IOM	Integrated Offender Management
ISS	Intensive Supervision and Surveillance
ISSP	Intensive Supervision and Surveillance Programme
LAC	looked-after child
LASCH	Local Authority Secure Children's Home
LASPO 2012	Legal Aid, Sentencing and Punishment of Offenders Act 2012
LCP	life course-persistent
LSCB	Local Safeguarding Children's Board
MAPPA	Multi-agency Public Protection Arrangements
MATCh	Multi-agency Teams in Children's Services (project)
MUD	moral underclass discourse
NDYP	New Deal for Young People
NEET	not in education, employment or training
NTA	National Treatment Agency
NYA	National Youth Association
ONS	Office for National Statistics
PA	personal adviser

PAYP Positive Activities for Young People
PYO persistent young offender
RED redistributionist discourse
RFPP risk factor prevention paradigm
RJ restorative justice
SEU Social Exclusion Unit
SID social integrationist discourse
STC secure training centre
UNCRC United Nations Convention on the Rights of the Child
YCAP *Youth crime action plan*
YIP Youth Inclusion Project
YISP Youth Inclusion and Support Project
YJB Youth Justice Board
YJS youth justice system
YOI young offender institution
YOP youth offender panel
YOT youth offending team
YRO youth rehabilitation order

Introduction

For me this book is intensely personal. My career as a probation officer was mostly spent working with young people. In 2000, I was keen to join a newly formed youth offending team (YOT), and over the next five years was a practitioner and later a manager in teams coping, first, with unfamiliar professional configurations, and then, with the challenges of the referral order and Intensive Supervision and Surveillance Programme (ISSP) initiatives. The New Labour reforms recreated working relationships and the day-to-day routines of practice, unsettling the values and beliefs that previous practice had rested on. Being intimately involved with these reforms, my analysis here of policy and the changes it has brought to practice is informed as much by my own experience as by academic reading. And of course, it is most apparent from the inside how key aspects of practice – whatever the intentions of politicians and policy-makers – are slow to change or stubbornly resistant (and sometimes rightly so) to outside pressures.

Practitioners are directed to work within the frameworks established by the laws and policies that govern their professional terrain and have obligations to do so. For youth justice in England and Wales, these include the structure of YOTs, their governance arrangements, their organisational requirements and their relationships with courts and other agencies for the purposes of public protection and safeguarding. However, practitioners are not automatons and so must foster a critical awareness that they work at a particular place and time, and that their practice is shaped both by the social and political climate and by reactions to events. The youth justice system (YJS) and youth justice practice existing in any given place and time are not inevitable; they have been produced through a series of decisions, responses to political pressures, lobbying from interested parties and reactions to critical moments.

Under New Labour the level of youth justice activity expanded considerably and not without controversy in relation to children's rights, freedoms and the risks involved in trying to predict and prevent involvement in offending. The net result was a much higher profile within the network of services for children, at strategic and operational levels, for a group of young people who had been previously relatively neglected and viewed as 'troublesome' rather than 'troubled'. But the downside was a regrettable increase for most of the time New Labour were in office in both the numbers of young people entering the YJS and those held in custody. I have charted the rapid changes in the youth justice landscape and offer a balanced critique of these developments and the subsequent changes under the coalition government operating in a climate of austerity and with different ideological imperatives at play. Thankfully the expansion of the YJS and its criminalising effects has been halted, but other concerns are now starting to impinge.

Whatever the systemic challenges, responsive youth justice practice relies on a body of knowledge and understanding of young people's development in the current social context. The concept of 'youth' is often treated by adults with suspicion; it has a certain nebulous quality, leaving behind the associations of childhood and innocence but not yet anchored to stable adult characteristics and responsibilities. Yet the very uncertainties of 'youth' mean that it is full of possibilities (admittedly negative as well as positive) as young people move towards adulthood. It is now almost a commonplace to refer to the many different routes to adulthood and the complex choices that young people must make along their way. Certainly there are continuities with previous generations of young people, but some markedly altered social circumstances as well, most strikingly in the labour market but also in housing, patterns of family and intimate relationships and use of technology. Youth justice faces a huge challenge in working with a constituency of young people who typically have fewer realistic choices and more limited personal and social resources to draw on than many of their peers, as well as the impact of being identified as anti-social or as 'young offenders'; a huge challenge indeed, but for me always stimulating and full of interest, because these young people's lives were not fixed and could – and demonstrably did – take so many different directions.

The young people who enter the YJS are not always easy to engage, but they are rarely dull. I always enjoyed my relationships with them and I am sure I learnt from them quite as much as they learnt from me. The habit of listening and trying to enter young people's worlds is very much reflected in this book in the way that I have drawn on qualitative research to introduce their voices as much as possible. This is unusual in the youth justice literature, but there is a huge volume of research, not least in the field of youth studies, that helps illuminate how young people see their life choices and how they actively construct their journeys towards various adult (or more adult-like) destinations. The main study used here is the major Inventing Adulthoods project by Henderson and colleagues (2007), introduced in Chapter One and referred to in later chapters along with other smaller studies relating to the topic of each chapter. Some of these come from limited, yet still insightful, qualitative research projects, so it is necessary to be cautious about taking these views as representative. I have been guided by the extent to which they resonate with the types of experiences and narratives that young people related to me over the years, and I have selected views and voices that seem to fit with what I know of young people and the themes of (lack of) power and agency so vital to them.

Throughout the book, I mainly refer to those under 18 in the YJS as *young people*; this is also intended to refer to those children brought before the courts who may be as young as 10 and even younger children who may be engaged in prevention projects. Conversely, in relation to human rights and other legal provisions that define a *child* as anyone under the age of 18, there are occasions where this terminology is reflected in the discussion.

The book is structured into three sections. The first, *Theories and concepts of youth and justice*, examines the experiences of young people and their transitions in modern society. The first two chapters argue that young people are active in creating their own worlds and are 'strivers' and 'survivors' rather than passive victims of circumstances and life events. This suggests different perspectives on, and understandings of, anti-social and offending behaviours and their attractions for young people. Chapters Three and Four outline the YJS in England and Wales and its historical development, but the latter part of Chapter Four moves on to develop a youth justice approach that is more responsive to young people and attentive to their rights and needs for recognition and for access to social capital, as well as to risks.

The second section, *Issues for young people*, comprises six chapters exploring areas of personal development and social life that each play a part in young people's progress towards adulthood, these being: the transition from school to work; social and intimate relationships; mental health and well-being; growing up in public care; alcohol and drugs; and anti-social behaviour (actual or perceived). Taking a broad sociological approach to each area, the chapters highlight key issues and concepts, relating these to current policy and implications for what I call youth-centred practice.

The third section, *Issues for youth justice practice*, focuses on specific areas of youth justice practice, starting with the broader concerns about risk and harm, safeguarding and collaborative and multi-agency working. The chapters then move successively through the youth justice process, looking at prevention and pre-court intervention, then the workings of the court through to the use of custody for young people. There is a discussion of practice informed by the ideas and insights introduced in the earlier chapters and the model of youth-centred practice.

Critically reflective practice entails a great deal of understanding and knowledge applied thoughtfully to the assessments, decisions, actions and interactions that constitute day-to-day practice. I have written this book as a contribution to improved practice and to provoke thinking about how we might 'do youth justice differently'. Working with young people and appreciating their perspectives and experiences seems obvious on the one hand, but a long way on the other from the official versions of youth justice under New Labour and the present coalition government. I truly hope this can change, and for the better.

Section 1

THEORIES AND CONCEPTS OF YOUTH AND JUSTICE

ONE

Growing up in the modern world

What is it like growing up in the UK today? Some aspects of moving towards adulthood are constant over time and place, but others are highly contingent, depending on social attitudes and conditions. This chapter explores how transitions have changed, becoming more individualised and more complex towards the end of the 20th and into the 21st century. Drawing on young people's own accounts of their journeys towards adulthood, it questions common assumptions about the experience of adolescence and growing up. In this chapter and throughout this book, young people are shown as gradually exercising more agency and choice as they move from states of dependence (social, financial and domestic) to greater independence, testing out and seeking recognition for their growing competence. Yet experiences are not the same for all young people, who have varying access to opportunities, resources and support. These differences are explored using Bourdieu's (1986) notions of social, economic, cultural and symbolic forms of capital (see Table 1.1 later in this chapter).

Whose problem is it anyway?

Something about young people troubles society intensely. The period between childhood and adulthood seems inherently unsettling. However, although a significant minority of young people do experience difficulties, empirical evidence suggests that most get on well with their parents and cope adequately with adjustments throughout adolescence (Coleman, 2011). Consequently, some have argued that views of adolescence or youth as essentially problematic may well originate from adults rather than young people themselves (Brown, 2005; Muncie, 2009), the majority of whom successfully survive the experience intact and move relatively painlessly into adulthood.

Various terms are used to describe this 'middle phase', including 'puberty', 'adolescence', 'teenage years' and 'youth'. They refer to different aspects of growing up, some more focused on the physical changes, others on social status, but they all share one feature in that they carry more negative than positive associations. Furthermore, as Philip Graham remarks, in a society where discrimination against women, older people and minority ethnic groups is now less tolerated, 'the teens have become the last group whose disempowerment is invisible because it is so much taken for granted' (2004, p 1). This rather amorphous life stage can be approached from biological, psychological or social perspectives. These each contribute understandings and insights, but no single one presents the entire picture. This chapter presents key themes from these three perspectives before introducing a different view of young people as social actors, which is developed as a central motif throughout this book.

Developing bodies and minds

While the period of youth or adolescence has no precise start and end points, there may be general consensus that the early stages coincide with the physical changes brought about by puberty. This involves increases in height and weight, sexual maturation and brain development. Although experienced by all young people, the chronological age at which they occur can vary from one individual to another and may be affected by broad social trends, such as improvements in general health and nutrition. For example, recent research in the US has shown links between obesity and early menarche (Walvoord, 2010), which may become a cause of future concern for the UK.

Whereas physical change and sexual development are common to all young people, the psychological impact may differ significantly. This is particularly so when growth and development is either early or late compared to others in the same peer group. Coleman (2011) highlights difficulties when there is a lack of 'goodness of fit' between the social context of the individual and his or her behavioural and physical characteristics. Interestingly, he cites research by Brooks-Gunn and Warren (1985) comparing a group of girls in dance school with a group in regular school. Within the dancing cohort, low body weight associated with late maturation was considered an advantage. Girls who may otherwise have been disadvantaged by being 'off-time' in their physical development tended not to experience difficulties, whereas those who developed at a more conventional rate showed more personality problems and eating disorders.

The brain continues to develop during adolescence, improving its ability to process and store information. This involves more than just increasing cognitive skills because, alongside this, the quality of thinking changes and, specifically, the aptitude for abstract reasoning. Piaget (1958) differentiated between the concrete thinking skills of the younger child and the ability of young people from roughly 11 years to engage in what he called 'formal operations' (Sylva and Lunt, 1982), developing the capacity to hypothesise and to test out propositions that go beyond simple, observable facts. This effectively represents a shift in emphasis from 'the real' to thinking about 'the possible' (Coleman, 2011), although the shift may happen more gradually (Donaldson, 1978) and may be less universally applicable than Piaget suggested (Jones, 2009).

In adolescence, young people also acquire more complex skills in reasoning and moral judgements. Piaget's early work in this area (1932) was later progressed by Kohlberg (1981) whose model of moral development proposes that the individual moves from a simple, ego-centric viewpoint through a series of stages towards a more complex understanding of principles, interrelationships and different perspectives. In response, Gilligan (1982) has argued that women are more likely to emphasise relational factors in their reasoning. The contrasting 'ethic of care', she proposes, is intuitively attractive and suggests why some individuals might not make a linear progression through Kohlberg's six stages. The evidence is certainly not clear-cut (Coleman, 2011), particularly on the question of gender

(McLaughlin, 2003), but both propositions give insights into the basis of moral reasoning and how it might develop.

Graham (2004) also gives attention to moral thinking, arguing that adolescents are more able cognitively than is commonly recognised. He distinguishes between *fluid intelligence*, which involves the processes of thinking and reasoning, and *crystallised intelligence*, which relates to the individual's accumulated knowledge. While young people do not have the same knowledge base as adults, many are highly competent in their thinking and reasoning at a surprisingly young age. In contrast, research suggests that emotional and social maturity may lag behind, although there may be considerable variation from one young person to another (for a summary, see Prior et al, 2011).

One US study by Cauffman and Steinberg (2000) looked at what they termed 'maturity of judgement' and how the process of decision-making is affected by psychosocial development as well as cognitive ability. They examined three key categories of psychosocial factors: *responsibility* (including self-reliance, clarity of identity and independence); *perspective* (being able to consider situations from different viewpoints and appreciating wider social and temporal contexts); and *temperance* (involving impulse control, the ability to defer gratification and to stand back and evaluate situations). They tested a sample of over 1,000 individuals in five different age cohorts, including young adults and adults over 21, asking them to respond to a series of hypothetical scenarios. Socially responsible decision-making was found more commonly in the older age groups who scored higher in terms of *responsibility, perspective* and *temperance,* but did not appear to increase appreciably after the age of 19. There was much greater variation between the three adolescent age cohorts, leading the authors to suggest that the period between 16-19 years is important for psychosocial development and also, in relation to risk-taking, that 'it is adolescents' deficiencies in the psychosocial domain, not the cognitive domain, that lead them to take more chances and get into more trouble' (2000, p 757). And such psychosocial immaturity may be more pronounced for young people who face barriers to their development, affecting their ability to refrain from delinquent acts (see the discussions in Bryan-Hancock and Casey, 2010, 2011). This then starts to beg questions about the social context in which young people make their decisions, pro-social or anti-social.

Historically, the overriding influence on thinking about psychosocial development has been the work of G.S. Hall (1904), an early psychologist who famously characterised the adolescent period as one of 'storm and stress' in which instability and turbulence is normal and to be expected (Hopkins-Burke, 2008). Current writers on adolescence are sceptical of the idea that young people are inherently at the mercy of raging hormones and dramatic mood swings (Graham, 2004; Coleman, 2011). Instead, they point to challenging behaviour often arising from frustration at restricted opportunities and lack of recognition, particularly in the light of current social trends that impose extended periods of semi-dependence on young people. Transitions to adulthood are not as certain as in previous decades as employment, education, housing markets and family structures have changed. In this scenario, young people present more problems than ever. But are these society's problems rather than young people themselves being problematic? If biological and psychological perspectives only take us so far, what insights are gained from looking at 'youth' through a sociological lens?

Socially constructing 'youth'

It has already been noted that childhood, adolescence and 'youth' are not fixed concepts. Beliefs and assumptions about these life stages are influenced by the prevailing social conditions and norms. The qualities or characteristics attributed to each life stage are largely a product of social and cultural processes. As Brown explains,

> The only "truth" we have is that we are born, we grow older and we die. The attributes attached to the intervening years ("childhood", "youth", "adolescence", "middle age", "elderly" etc) are largely social. By this we mean that the expectations attached to age are culturally produced and sustained. (2005, p 5)

Looking back in time, the transition between childhood and adulthood in the UK was often rapid, with children frequently entering the labour market at very young ages or living away from parents. However, with the growth of the middles classes in the Victorian period and the expansion of education, the teenage years assumed greater significance. This was unproblematic for those young people whose behaviour was regulated through schools and other institutions, but working-class children (and later adolescents) were regarded as a threat to the established order and received a different, less benevolent response (Hendrick, 2006).

The late 1800s saw the establishment of institutions with clear disciplinary purposes such as reformatories and industrial schools. The subsequent period of rapid social change immediately before the First World War produced the beginnings of the welfare state and more community-based responses to the 'problem' of young people, both those construed as 'depraved' and those seen as 'deprived'. These included the new juvenile courts established by the Children Act 1908 and the birth of the probation service. This period also saw the beginnings of youthwork, located in networks of boys and girls clubs, as well as the scouting movement (Muncie, 2009). Together, these acted to socialise young people into a dominant middle-class template of acceptable childhood (Hopkins-Burke, 2008), and inevitably these organisations and activities were more accessible, economically and culturally, to the children of the middle or skilled working classes than to young people from poorer backgrounds (Muncie, 2009). Interestingly, Muncie notes that 'by the turn of the century, the model adolescent became the organised youth, dependent but secure from temptation, while the independent and precocious young were stigmatised as delinquent' (2009, p 72). The behaviours and attitudes of working-class young people were fast becoming the focus of (middle-class) adult anxieties, which were used to legitimise the greater use of social and penal measures (Brown, 2005) over the next three decades.

The period after the Second World War was more socially liberal, reflected in a relatively benign approach to young people within the context of the new welfare state. Undoubtedly punishment still had its advocates, but many at the time viewed young people breaking the law as socially needy rather than morally deficient. However, a change of administration in 1970 brought a rapid end to progressive plans to decriminalise youth justice and, over the next decade, welfare approaches fell distinctly out of official favour. The attitude towards young people in the 30 years since is markedly more comparable with the early part of the 20th century. We are again in a period of social transformation; adult anxieties and insecurities are coalescing once more around young people, particularly those detached from the labour market. Worryingly, the current apparatus of the state is much more developed than it was 100 years ago, and the measures that can be employed to seek to re-engage young people and to penalise them when they fail to do so are more varied and sophisticated.

Attitudes to juvenile misdemeanours had already been hardening during the 1980s and early 1990s, with concerns about 'feral youth' and incorrigible young offenders. But the critical moment came in February 1993 with the murder of the toddler, James Bulger, by Robert Thompson and John Venables, triggering widespread moral outrage and deep questioning of the nature of childhood and its capacity for 'evil':

> The Bulger case had at least three related consequences. First, it initiated a reconsideration of the social construction of 10 year olds as "demons" rather than as "innocents". Second, it coalesced with, and helped to mobilise, adult fear and moral panic about the moral degeneracy of youth in general. Third, it recast child offenders as "devils" and legitimised a series of tough law and order responses to young offenders, which came to characterise the following decade. (Muncie, 2009, p 5)

This underpinned a climate unsympathetic at best, and deeply antagonistic at worst, to young people, particularly those who conformed least to conventional notions of acceptable childhood, for instance, young people who committed crimes, who used drugs, who were homeless or in care. Present-day society is highly individualised and exclusive, and the social processes of *othering*, that is, treating groups of young people as strange, threatening and 'not one of us', are extremely powerful (Brown, 2005).

Reflections on late modern society

Part of the background to these altered perceptions of young people lies in late modern concerns about the place of young people in society, and specifically about their transitions into adulthood. Changes in the structure of society, especially the labour market, have resulted in extended periods of adolescence or 'youth' for many young people. Typically, young people now spend longer in a kind of limbo state, unable to take up adult responsibilities (and to receive recognition of adult status). There may be positives in this; certainly writers such as Arnett (2004), talking about a new phase of *emerging adulthood*, are optimistic about the possibilities of taking time to try out different roles and identities before 'settling down'. However, the biographical details from young people involved in the Inventing Adulthoods study (Henderson et al, 2007), discussed later in this chapter, show that experiences are highly variable according to the support and resources available to young people, as well as their location.

Theorists have conventionally talked about three main areas marking the transition from adolescent or youthful dependence to adult independence (see Furlong and Cartmel, 2007):

School/education   → work
Family of origin   → family of destination
Family home   → independent housing

These transitions have become less straightforward as the nature of employment has changed and access to private rented and social housing has become more restricted. The mores around relationships have also changed, and for many young people commitment to one long-term sexual partner and the prospect of parenting is deferred. Consequently, young people are involved in negotiating their lives and their life choices in a way that would be unfamiliar to previous generations. Young people's routes to adulthood have therefore become more diverse, but in a context where collective social provision and sense of community has declined in favour of individualised solutions, creating risks as well as freedoms and opportunities. Beck encapsulates this notion: 'In the individualised society the individual must therefore learn, on pain of permanent disadvantage, to conceive of him or herself as the centre of action, as the planning office with respect to his/ her own biography, abilities, orientations, relationships and so on' (1992, p 135, cited in Thomson, 2007a, p 79).

The social conditions in which young people are making these choices and creating what Beck calls an 'elective or DIY biography' (Woodman, 2009) are paramount. The certainties and belief in rational thinking and scientific knowledge that characterised the modern era are giving way to a sense of insecurity, danger and unpredictability in what has been termed a *risk society* (Beck, 1992). This is a more pluralist society where opportunities are opened up as traditional restrictions, for instance, associated with class and gender roles, are relaxed. But it is also a society whose institutions and collective consciousness are preoccupied with risk and the distribution of ills, rather than goods (Hudson, 2003). What is thus created is a context where the lack of solidarity breeds feelings of threat, the exaggerated fear of crime and of young people being symptomatic of this.

The implications for young people are threefold. First, there is an implicit expectation that they will take responsibility for shaping their own lives, using their individual agency to mobilise resources and to move forward. Young people may be more conscious of the agency that they exercise than the constraints and the social conditions that limit their choices and the actions available to them (Furlong and Cartmel, 2007). In some senses this is a consumerist orientation, focusing on the choices and actions of the individual, rather than collective responsibility for ensuring that opportunities and pathways are opened up. It therefore follows that where a young person is not successful materially or in terms of acquiring work-related skills, for instance, that it is construed as an individual rather than a systemic failure. Indeed, evidence suggests that this is internalised by young people (Henderson et al, 2007). It is certainly reinforced by explicitly negative attitudes to young people who are unable or unwilling to risk pursuing specific educational or other opportunities in order to progress. Yet, in reality, a young person from a relatively disadvantaged community whose family has no history of educational achievement may feel more threatened and fearful of the prospect of going away to university than a child of middle-class professionals. Similarly, for some young people without secure systems of support, even an entry-level course at college may seem a risky choice.

Second, responsibility for avoiding negative risks also falls to individuals through their decision-making and the exercise of prudential choice (Kemshall, 2009a). Both are facets of responsibilisation, shifting a heavy burden of responsibility and accountability on to the individual rather than the onus being shared by the individual, the community and state institutions.

Third, the breaking down of conventional class, gender and other roles in a more democratised late modern society does not mean that inequalities have been eroded. In significant ways they have been remade and reinforced within the *risk society*. Furlong and Cartmel (2007) note that an emphasis on individual responsibility and accountability, combined with vulnerability and lack of control, create a heightened sense of risk and insecurity. Those young people whose family relationships or financial and social circumstances are less stable are likely to experience risk and insecurity in more acute ways and may well have fewer resources to draw on to help withstand them.

Fresh insights, new analyses

So far this chapter has given a relatively conventional account of adolescence and youth as a life stage, referencing historical and more recent academic thinking. Certainly the risk society and individualisation theses and their impact on young people have been extensively analysed (France, 2007; Furlong and Cartmel, 2007; Kemshall, 2009a). The notions of the *elective biography* and of young people negotiating risks and opportunities, however, point to debates that feature little in the youth justice literature but are active in childhood and youth studies. These debates reject the idea of young people as either passively subject to their social circumstances or responding in any obvious or pre-determined way to those circumstances. Rather, young people are acting on and interacting with their social world and the key players in it. In Coleman's terms, 'individuals are agents of their own development' (2011, p 16), capable of constructing aspects of their childhood and adolescent experiences in important ways (with positive and negative effects).

The question of agency is interesting and it is useful to contrast two schools of thought. The first is that the child is 'becoming'; this future-orientated view sees the child as lacking competence and skills – an adult-in-the-making – and is the construction of childhood and adolescence that explicitly underpins most youth-related policy in the UK. The second perspective sees the child as an actor in his or her own right, already possessing skills and competencies, and with views and experiences of being a child (Uprichard, 2008) which should be recognised as valid.

Uprichard argues that separating these two discourses is not necessarily helpful: while young people are social actors in the present, they are also in a process of growing up and becoming adult, so the two aspects are present simultaneously. In her research interviews in York and Dijon, the children (aged 4-12) reflected on change:

> The children articulated what they thought the changes around them would be, and they also spoke about how they themselves may or may not change. They also showed a reflexive awareness about the ways in which changing perceptions of the changing environment may affect their perceptions of themselves. All the children in both cities voiced that perceptions and attitudes to change are relative to the tastes of the individual, where in the life course the individual was, as well as the general cultural fashion of the time. (2008, p 309)

This shows a sophisticated awareness of growth and change, as well as thoughts on how self-image or identity shifts over time. It is perhaps a surprising level of reflection and reflexivity, but consistent with the findings of the Inventing Adulthoods study and other research.

The idea of young people as simultaneously in a state of 'being' and 'becoming' is central to the orientation to practice developed in this book. The book also recognises young people's capacity for reflexivity, indeed the necessity for engaging in reflexivity as they grow up in late modern society. Giddens' (1992) notion of the *reflexive project of self* is significant here, referring to the way that identities and self-narratives are constantly being constructed and reworked. Within the current social context, this suggests it is necessary to respond to changes in work, education and engagement with other aspects of public life, which are not fixed and constant, requiring adaptation to different circumstances and settings as individuals perhaps move from one job to another, engage in politics or voluntary work, and pursue courses of different types and from different disciplines over time. Thomson (2007a) also argues that work on self-identity takes place within personal relationships, in conversations with friends, partners and family members, as well as through activities such as consulting natal charts or reading to increase insight and self-awareness.

Biographies, then, are not fixed, and young people are effectively engaged in their own *biographical project*. The Inventing Adulthoods study is aptly named, as the young people involved demonstrated again and again how they were approaching adulthood in a relatively piecemeal way and had to work to achieve a sense of adult identity. The researchers illustrate a variety of life paths created by participants in the study, with an impressive diversity of work, education, leisure and other activities involved in building a secure sense of self and moving towards the transition to adulthood.

A simplistic view of both *elective biographies* and the notion of the *reflexive project of self* might suggest that the late modern scenario is positive, with a plethora of choices available. However, both Beck (1992) and Giddens (1992) are conscious that a more diverse and pluralistic society does not necessarily mean greater equality, although superficially it may appear that this is the case. Opportunities and the ability to exploit them is very much dependent on where the young person is located socially, in terms of class, gender, ethnicity (Furlong and Cartmel, 2007) and location (Henderson et al, 2007), as well as access to different forms of capital.

Forms of capital

The analysis of the Inventing Adulthoods research draws on the thinking about the *risk society* and the concept of the reflexive project of self. It also employs a second conceptual framework taken from the work of Pierre Bourdieu (Henderson et al, 2007). In Bourdieu's (1986) account, the complexity of social life, power relations and inequalities can be illuminated by thinking in terms of capital. Although a word most associated with economics, he applies it in a wider sense to explain social relations and why there is no perfect equality of opportunity because we live in a society that is not brand new, but has a past in which networks and associations have developed. These allow individuals or organisations to accumulate advantages and social assets through their actions or social practices. This may happen to greater or lesser degrees, so the net effect is that these assets – or in Bourdieu's terms, forms of capital – are unevenly distributed throughout society and are incorporated into its structures (see Table 1.1).

These forms of capital are a potential resource for young people, but it is apparent that individuals have different amounts and types of capital available to them, according to their social position and location. A study of working-class young people in four sites in Finland (Tolonen, 2005) shows how cultural and social capital is used in different ways, influenced by the young person's sense of agency and, for the young women, awareness of 'respectability'. Their connections to their community and the extent to which they felt they had social support was also important in how they mobilised their sources of capital and were able to make progress. The young people's choices and practices exemplified further

Table 1.1: Forms of capital

Type of capital	Definition
Social	Associated with relationships and social networks. Social capital is strongest where networks are wide, characterised by mutuality and trust, and includes individuals who are rich in other forms of capital. Networks of relationships and membership of social groups are not fixed, but need constant investment
Economic	Refers to material resources, such as money and property rights
Cultural	Is possibly the least transparent except where institutionalised, for example, in the form of educational qualifications. It involves cultural competence and status. This may be connected to possession and use of cultural goods (books, pictures, machines) but is also less tangibly present in terms of individual tastes and dispositions. It takes time to accumulate, so is a long-term rather than an immediate source of capital, and is perhaps less easily transmitted from one individual to another than other forms of capital
Symbolic	This comes into play when other forms of capital receive authorisation and recognition. This may happen in institutional ways through the awarding of a title, honorary degree or peerage, for instance, but may also occur through more informal rituals and processes

Source: Adapted from Bourdieu (1986)

concepts of capital developed by Putnam (2000): *bonding capital* is focused on building and consolidating local or community networks and social supports; *bridging capital* is concerned with accessing and accumulating capital that can be traded in the wider world and eases passage into new areas, educationally, geographically or otherwise. This latter is more typically associated with the more outward-looking and 'cosmopolitan' middle classes (Thomson and Taylor, 2005).

Within the Inventing Adulthood study, the researchers go beyond Bourdieu's concepts of social capital in suggesting that young people are not just passive recipients of their parents' capital, but are active producers and consumers of capital in their own right (Holland et al, 2007). Relatedly, Raffo and Reeves (2000) describe each young person having an individualised system of social capital, which is dynamic and at the same time able to support and constrain the individual's actions and agency. In their research with young people in Manchester, they found that their biographies suggested four specific and yet broad types of individual systems of social capital – weak, strong, changing and fluid. Significantly, while young people in more disadvantaged circumstances typically have access to fewer resources to increase social capital, nevertheless they are still able to exercise degrees of choice and agency in order to develop helpful social relations over time.

Listening to young people

The Inventing Adulthoods study has already been referred to throughout this chapter and will also feature in later chapters. So it is helpful at this point to pause to discuss the detail of the study, its approach and its characteristics.

Most of the qualitative research cited in this book is retrospective in that it asks young people to reflect over their lives. In contrast, Inventing Adulthoods adopted a biographical approach that was prospective, following a sample of young people over a 10-year period, using repeat individual interviews, focus groups, questionnaires and personal diaries (memory books) (Thomson, 2007b). Interviews invited young people to look back on their lives and at the same time to look forward into their possible futures, discussing life plans and where they envisaged they might be in terms of family, work and domestic or other circumstances (Henderson et al, 2007).

The original mixed method research started as an Economic and Social Research Council (ESRC) project, 'Youth Values: Identity, Diversity and Social Change', between 1996 and 1999, involving 1,800 young people in five geographical locations. When further ESRC funds were secured, 121 young people were selected from the Youth Values cohort for a new study, 'Inventing Adulthoods: Young People's Strategies for Transition', which ran between 1999 and 2001, allowing for three in-depth interviews with each participant. A further two rounds of interviews was made possible through a continuation project, 'Youth Transitions and Social Change', lasting from 2002-06 (Thomson, 2011).

In all, 62 young people were retained in the project and followed through a 10-year period, providing a rich source of data about their lives and how they negotiated changes and transitions. The research was conducted in five contrasting geographical locations, described by the research team (Henderson et al, 2007) as:

- the isolated rural area
- the disadvantaged estate (in the North of England)
- Northern Ireland
- the 'leafy suburb', an affluent area near a commuter belt town
- the inner-city site (in the South of England).

The research team engaged in cross-sectional analysis of data, identifying themes and both common and divergent experiences across the cohort at each wave of interviews. Increasingly, as the project developed, the team created longitudinal case histories, following the paths of individuals and tracing themes over time (Thomson, 2007b).

What is striking is how the voices of young people express concerns distinct from those of adults:

> Seen through the eyes of the adult world, drugs, violence, health and education were perceived to be the areas of relevance to young people, but it was mobility, belonging, home and sociality that emerged as most meaningful to young people themselves. These are the things that young people value, that motivate their actions and characterise their sense of self. (Henderson et al, 2007, p 99)

Clearly youth policy has focused on these adult concerns, not what is important to young people, and this is reflected in the priorities set for children's services and youth justice.

Two other messages from Inventing Adulthood clearly stand out. One is the significance of *critical moments* in young people's lives. A critical moment is defined as an event described in an interview that either the researcher or the young person identifies as having important consequences for his or her life or identity. Some were common experiences relating to educational transitions, relationships and family. Others tended to cluster in particular locations. For instance, more descriptions of chronic illness and death came from young people from the disadvantaged estate (Thomson et al, 2002). Leisure and consumption also featured as critical moments, as did rites of passage such as 'coming out' as gay or lesbian. Some were clearly external events, whereas others were internal changes, for example, recovering from depression or the impact of a friendship or intimate relationship breaking down (Henderson et al, 2007). Critical moments can be categorised in terms of the extent to which (a) the event is within the control of the young person and (b) the young person was subsequently able to respond to the event (Thomson et al, 2002). This links back to questions of agency and resources available to the young person to capitalise on, to resolve, or at least to survive situations.

The second message is the significance of competence for young people – the sense of mastery or the pleasure of doing something well – and of that competence being acknowledged and given legitimacy:

> As we sought to understand how young people invent adulthood over time, we realised that they felt adult in different ways and different contexts, and thinking of themselves as adult was related to their feelings of competence and the recognition they received for that competence. (Henderson et al, 2007, p 29)

This can be connected to the previous discussion of capital and the importance to young people of being recognised as possessing capital as they seek adult status. In some senses it also resonates with Graham's (2004) notion of young people as 'young, though inexperienced adults', more able and competent than adult society routinely acknowledges. Inventing Adulthood shows that young people are motivated to invest in areas of life where they receive recognition for their capabilities (Thomson, et al, 2004), and are unwilling to engage where they feel either incompetent or where their competence goes unrecognised.

Being mobile

Location and mobility were consistently highlighted as key concerns for young people involved with Inventing Adulthoods (and in research elsewhere). This can be broken down into:

- physical mobility, being able to move around
- attitudes to the local environment and to thoughts of moving away
- social mobility.

Ability to move around their home environment was important for young people and was seen as linked to independence and autonomy. This manifested itself in different ways across the sites, with driving and car ownership more significant for those in the 'leafy suburb' and the rural site. This opened up opportunities for socialising and leisure but also, in the rural site, employment. In contrast, the young people in the inner-city site had greater access to public transport and so less need for their own transport (Henderson et al, 2007). These young people talked less about moving away than those from the rural site, the 'leafy suburb' and Northern Ireland, suggesting to the researchers that localities each have their own economy of mobility, operating at the level of material, cultural and fantasy (Thomson and Taylor, 2005). For instance, in Northern Ireland, young people had to negotiate how they moved physically and socially within and between communities on either side of the sectarian divide. Attempting to transcend those divisions, Karin, a young Catholic woman, joined a youth club in the inner city in order to find a religiously mixed social group (see Thomson, 2011). Significantly, the young people in Northern Ireland had access to friends and relatives who had moved to England, Scotland and the US, providing role models and resources as young people contemplated life plans, which often included migration for educational or work purposes (Henderson et al, 2007).

Mobility had practical and aspirational dimensions. There were degrees of choice and necessity in young people's discussions of migration and mobility. The 'cosmopolitan' is characterised by ease of movement and competence, whereas the 'local' does not have the same outward-looking orientation and the 'exile' is displaced and rootless (Henderson, et al, 2007). Jamieson's (2000) research with young people in the Scottish borders sheds further light on young people and migration, distinguishing between 'leavers' and 'stayers' as well as those who are 'attached' and those who are 'detached'. Significantly, in terms of the 'detached stayers':

> Embitterment about entrapment and strong negative feelings for their locality were most forcefully expressed by Jean, Rosanne and Richard, "stayers" who crossed class boundaries or had ambiguous class positions and had negative experiences at work, but who also lacked emotional and social support through a network of social relationships. (2000, p 214)

Access to social capital is important in how young people experience their local environment; certainly, within Inventing Adulthoods, there were examples of young people choosing to stay in localities despite more restricted opportunities there because of the bonding social capital available through networks of family and friends. For instance, Lauren, a bright young woman from the disadvantaged Northern estate, dropped out of college where she was taking A-levels that would have given her entry to university. With parental encouragement she then pursued a course in hair and beauty but later enrolled to train as a nurse, an option that did not involve leaving the local area (Henderson et al, 2007). In a different way, Stan, from the 'leafy suburb', had professional parents but also rejected his original plans for university, training as a cabinet maker (his grandfather's trade) and staying in his local area. However, he still had the resources needed to retain a 'cosmopolitan' identity, played out in his involvement with snowboarding and other high-risk sports. Interestingly, this also enabled him to pursue a kind of middle-class version of masculinity through a culture of consumption (Thomson and Taylor, 2005) alongside a more working-class male identity as an artisan (Thomson, 2011).

Stan is perhaps one example of downward social mobility, although this is not necessarily so: in the present economic times, the cultivation of cosmopolitanism may be an important resource for holding on to privilege or accessing opportunity (Henderson et al, 2007). However, for this generation, upward social mobility has become more difficult as inequalities in society deepen. Individualised life plans hold inherent risks that are more easily negotiated by those with access to greater and more flexible sources of capital (often bridging rather than bonding capital). Discussing the educational pathways of three young women from the disadvantaged Northern estate, Thomson et al conclude that:

> First, resources are distributed very unequally and there is no easy distinction between material resources and those more usually attributed to the individual. Second, an individualised "can do" discourse exists across differences of class, gender and ethnicity, yet beneath it can be detected other powerful discourses of loyalty to locality and not getting above yourself. (2003, p 45)

Young people's agency and choices are constrained by the opportunities open to them and what they can realistically pursue, given the resources and support they can mobilise. There are cultural pressures as well that may bind young people to their immediate environment or push them out of it, and clearly class, enduring expectations of gender roles and geographical location all continue to have an impact on young people's transitions and mobility. Structural position and individual agency both play their part, and so should receive recognition accordingly.

Implications for practice

'Youth' is a complicated life stage involving physical and psychological change. Its ambiguous social status between child and adult perhaps accounts for the feelings often expressed of uncertainty, even fear, about young people and their potential (frequently seen in negative rather than positive terms). Young people occupy a precarious position in society: the tendency is for adults to treat them as a problem, judging them to be either risky or 'at risk', a view that permeates youth-related policy.

According to the *risk society* thesis (Beck, 1992), young people are growing up in a world that offers more choice and fewer restrictions on the one hand, but places more responsibility on individuals for making 'good' choices and deploying their resources on the other. Yet opportunities are not open equally to all young people, and support and resources to pursue opportunities are distributed unevenly across society. For a significant minority the net result is increased exclusion and alienation: these young people are disproportionately present in the youth justice system.

Young people are not passive in the face of their social and economic circumstances. Rather, they actively seek to make sense of their world and to exercise choice and personal agency, even where their options are limited. Youth-centred practice appreciates the way that young people view their worlds and seeks to understand their choices and decisions. Too often it is assumed that young people are deficient in thinking and reasoning – it may be that the deficiencies lie in the paucity of appealing choices open to them or the particular factors that matter to young people. Inventing Adulthoods (Henderson et al, 2007) highlights that young people value mobility, belonging, home and sociality – very different from what adults feel is important for their lives and the assumptions that have formed the basis of social and youth justice policy.

Bourdieu's (1986) notion of capital provokes thinking how young people weigh up diverse options and the costs and benefits they might bring. This framework is used to explore young people's accounts of their transitions within Inventing Adulthoods (Henderson et al, 2007). Passage into adulthood is now more complex than it was for previous generations, and feelings of competence and recognition for competence are critical in progressing through the transition. This is a significant insight for youth justice that has fixated on problems and deficits rather than strengths and competences, and suggests a new and very different orientation for future practice, which is fleshed out in the chapters of this book.

Further reading

Coleman, J.C. (2011) *The nature of adolescence* (4th edn), Hove: Routledge.

France, A. (2007) *Understanding youth in late modernity*, Maidenhead: Open University Press.

Henderson, S., Holland, J., McGrellis, S., Sharpe, S. and Thomson, R. (2007) *Inventing adulthoods: A biographical approach to youth transitions*, London: Sage Publications.

Jones, G. (2009) *Youth*, Cambridge: Polity Press.

TWO

Young people at the margins

The previous chapter discussed adolescence and transitions to adulthood in general terms, highlighting commonalities and diversity in young people's experiences of growing up. Most reach adulthood without causing any great concern, but some encounter difficulties and, of these, a small minority are deeply disturbed in ways that endure into adult life (Graham, 2004). But why is this? And why do these young people appear disproportionately in the youth justice system (YJS)?

These are key questions for youth justice practitioners seeking to develop insight into the possible links between young people's behaviours and experiences such as poor family relationships, abuse, mental ill health and chronic poverty, without assuming direct and simplistic causal links and denying young people the agency that they are able to exercise in even the most adverse circumstances. This chapter explores the utility of different models for understanding young people's behaviours and looks critically at the evidence from research on young people, crime and the life course. Building on the notions of social capital, competence and recognition introduced in Chapter One, it questions the dominant approach to young people who do not follow a 'normal' pathway through adolescence, an approach overly concerned with problems, deficits and risks. It ends by starting to sketch out an alternative practice paradigm based on a different analysis of the motivations and to search for meanings behind young people's life choices and behaviours.

In or out of mainstream society?

It has already been noted that we are now living in a more individualised and, in many ways, a less tolerant and inclusive society. In its first term, the New Labour government was greatly exercised by social exclusion, manifested in the creation of the Social Exclusion Unit and a commitment to evidence-based social policy (Cook, 2006). What such evidence seemed to suggest was that negative life outcomes were associated with a range of factors including child poverty, disengagement from education, worklessness and lone parenting. These became the focus of subsequent policy within a broad philosophy of social integration, largely through promoting re-entry into the workforce (Rodger, 2008). Although undoubtedly well intentioned, over time the justification for many social policy and urban regeneration initiatives focused down on narrower instrumental concerns about crime reduction, thus further blurring the boundaries between social and criminal justice policy (Cook, 2006). This move was clearly associated with the 'youth problem' (Muncie, 2009) and has generated specific provisions that, paradoxically, threaten to increase marginalisation if young people do not comply or if they make 'unacceptable' life choices (early pregnancy, dropping out of school, leaving a training programme, and so on). In this context, citizenship and inclusion must be earned (Cook, 2006), and failure or inability to do so risks being relegated to the status of moral underclass (Levitas, 2005; Rodger, 2008).

Later chapters will explore in more detail what this focus on risks, problems and social exclusion means for the YJS and for young people. The challenge for youth justice practitioners is to resist blaming or disciplinary modes of practice and to be supportive of young people and their families, while reinforcing pro-social values and behaviours. This means developing an approach to young people and their involvement in anti-social or criminal behaviours that appreciates their motivations and perspectives, and makes explicit use of conceptual models to help analyse what young people are doing and why.

From the beginning of the formal study of crime, theorists have considered psychological and sociological explanations for deviance or offending, some within a quasi-scientific positivist framework, some from critical or other perspectives. The intention is not to go through the range of theories that are fully presented elsewhere (for instance, Downes and Rock, 2003; Tierney, 2006), but to concentrate on evidence and theoretical explanations derived from evidence of offending patterns that might provide more useful guides to how best to develop intervention.

So what do we know?

Collection and analysis of accurate information about offending is notoriously difficult and depends on the source of the data, how crimes are categorised and what sub-criminal behaviour is included (aspects of anti-social behaviour and minor incivilities). Briefly, there are three principal ways of gathering quantitative data:

- official records, for example, concerning arrests, charges and convictions
- victimisation surveys such as the British Crime Survey (now called The Crime Survey for England and Wales)
- self-report studies.

There are issues affecting the reliability of each of these sources of data, however. Police records do not include offences that are not reported, and surveys of young people and their involvement in offending are typically based on school samples or, as in the 1998/99 Youth Lifestyles Survey, young people in private households, so they do not include those in residential care or other non-family accommodation (Graham and Bowling, 1995: Flood-Page et al, 2000). Nevertheless, one of the most robust findings across different sources of data, and at various periods and locations, is that offending behaviour tends to peak in the teenage years and to decline in frequency with age. This trend – known as the *age-crime curve* – has been consistently evident in empirical research, yet it is not well understood (Whyte, 2009). Various explanations have been offered and later sections will explore their merits and limitations after first looking at illustrations of the age-crime curve based on police data from England and Wales, then from two different self-report surveys.

The age-crime curve: three illustrations of offending by age

There are consistencies and divergences between these three graphs constructed from two different types of data sets (see Figures 2.1, 2.2 and 2.3). Broadly speaking, all three show less offending for individuals entering adulthood (note that in Figure 2.2 the time periods are not equal, which seems to indicate a second peak in offending and masks the steepness of decline). Offending activity for females is closest to males at 12–13 years, but peaks earlier and is significantly lower overall.

Figure 2.1: Official data for those found guilty at all courts or cautioned for indictable offences per 100,000 population during 2009

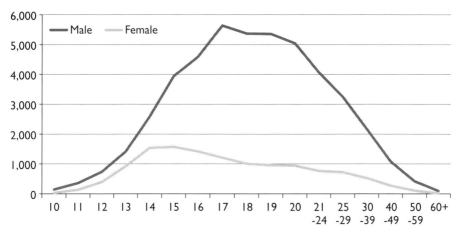

Source: Ministry of Justice (2010a)

Figure 2.2: Percentage of young people admitting offending once or more in the 12 months prior to interview (1998/99 Youth Lifestyles Survey)

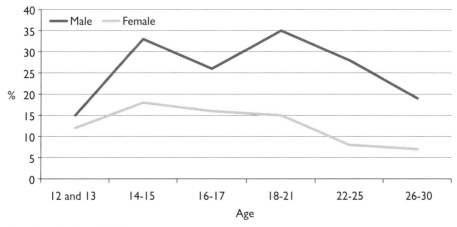

Note: Sample size = 4,848.
Source: Flood-Page et al (2000)

Figure 2.3: Percentage of young people reporting one or more of 20 core offences in the 12 months prior to interview (2006 Offending, Crime and Justice Survey)

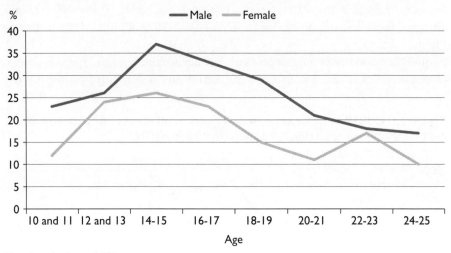

Note: Sample size = 4,901.
Source: Roe and Ashe (2008)

McVie (2004), among others, challenges the unquestioning acceptance of the age–crime curve and argues that the ubiquitous curve illustrated from various data sets does show variations worthy of analysis. For example, the curve may peak at slightly different ages and more or less sharply. It may also vary according to specific crime type, both in terms of the proportion of young people committing that crime (prevalence) and the number of such offences (incidence). Examining data from the longitudinal Edinburgh Study of Youth Transitions and Crime (ESYTC), McVie identified different trajectories up to the age of 16 for fare dodging (an increase in both prevalence and incidence), fighting (a decrease in both prevalence and incidence after 14 years) and possession of weapons. In this latter case prevalence increased sharply between 12 and 14 years, then steadily declined, whereas incidence continued to increase until age 16, showing that a smaller number of young people were carrying weapons more frequently.

In a much earlier article, Farrington (1986) identified that some crime types peak in later adulthood – drink-driving being one example – and opportunity or social position affect other offences, such as child neglect or white collar crime. Looking at data over several decades, he argued that the steepness and the peak of the age-crime curve could also be influenced by particular historical factors (the 'period effect') or by the characteristics of a specific age cohort (the 'cohort effect'). Nevertheless, overall the relationship between age and crime still holds (Farrington, 1986).

The critical debate about the age-crime curve concerns the evidence and the interpretations of prevalence versus incidence and how they contribute to the increase and decline in offending as young people move through adolescence towards adulthood. The following sections discuss the main arguments and the sources of data used to develop explanations.

Developmental explanations

Gottfredson and Hirshi's *A general theory of crime* (1990) proposed a form of control theory which suggests that all individuals share the same propensity for crime, but vary in how they have been socialised and their degree of self-control. Earlier work by Hirschi had discussed how the social bonds that individuals develop are influenced by attachment to others as well as commitment to, and involvement in, conventional behaviours or activities. He also argued that the extent to which individuals believe they should obey the rules of society differs, even though offenders and non-offenders may well share the same basic value system and accept the same social norms (Hirschi, 1969, cited in Downes and Rock, 2003).

Looking at the age-crime curve some two decades later, Gottfredson and Hirschi (1990) gave more prominence to the role of low self-control and associated characteristics such as impulsivity, risk-taking and commitment to immediate gratification (Tierney, 2006). Further, they contended that low self-control is a stable personality trait that does not vary over time. However, this is not a genetic predisposition, but is dependent on early parenting, and is largely fixed from around the age of eight. What follows from this is that later interventions are inevitably ineffectual and efforts should be focused on parenting in the early years (Soothill et al, 2009). Although a simple association between low self-control and ineffective parenting has been questioned (Hopkins-Burke, 2008), this notion has been taken up by policy-makers and seems to have popular appeal, being more manageable and less challenging as a proposition for practice than more radical social interventions (Soothill et al, 2009).

According to Gottfredson and Hirschi's (1990) analysis, involvement in offending later in life can be reliably predicted in childhood, a contentious claim at odds with perspectives focused on change over the life course (Wortley, 2011). In terms of the prevalence versus incidence debate, their view is that prevalence – the number of offenders – remains constant, and that it is the frequency of their offending that decreases with ageing but also associated reductions in opportunities to offend. The research implications of this are significant, because if it is believed that the propensity for criminality is stable over time, there is no need to follow populations and to trace patterns of offending over long periods of, perhaps, 30-40 years (Soothill et al, 2009).

Of course, researchers adopting sociological approaches are committed to examining offending over the life course. However, there is one interesting strand within the developmental field that incorporates aspects of sociological understandings within a broadly psychological analysis. This is the research by Moffitt and colleagues based on a sample of 1,037 young people born in Dunedin, New Zealand in 1972-73 (1993).

Moffitt's characterisation of two distinct offending trajectories has been highly influential and does offer new insights into the age–crime curve. The patterns of offending are identified as:

• adolescent-limited (AL)
• life course-persistent (LCP).

This suggests that a higher proportion of young people are involved in anti-social or offending behaviours during adolescent years, but that most of these desist as they move towards adulthood. So there is a greater prevalence of young people engaged in anti-social and offending behaviour during adolescence. However, a smaller constituency of young people continue offending into adulthood, so maintaining their frequency of offending (although the anti-social acts themselves typically change). This explains why offending peaks in the teenage years and then declines, but with some individuals still showing an anti-social disposition into adult life, representing the continuity that Gottfredson and Hirschi suggest (Soothill et al, 2009).

Moffitt (1993) was interested in a wide spectrum of behaviours, not just those officially identified as criminal. The Dunedin Multidisciplinary Health and Development Study (also known as the Dunedin Study) examined the cohort members throughout their childhood and found that individuals within the LCP offender group were more likely to experience neurological difficulties affecting social and cognitive development and to display anti-social behaviours from a young age (Moffitt, 1993). However, Moffitt also argues that problems do not arise purely from genetics or biology, but are mediated by the environment (Wortley, 2011). She notes that vulnerable children are disproportionately found in families experiencing stress and disadvantage. Problematic parent–child interactions may also compound difficulties and influence later transactions with other adults and peers or within the school environment:

> If the child who "steps off on the wrong foot" remains on an ill-starred path, subsequent stepping-stone experiences may culminate in life-course persistent anti-social behaviour. For life-course-persistent anti-social individuals, deviant behaviour patterns later in life may thus reflect early individual differences that are perpetuated or exacerbated by interactions with the social environment: first at home, and later at school. (Moffitt, 1993, p 25)

Essentially, this suggests that there is a cumulative social disadvantage resulting from neuro-psychological problems (Wright et al, 2001). A further cohort study in Pittsburg, US (Raine et al, 2005) and a retrospective review of data from a Philadelphia cohort (Piquero, 2001) seem to confirm Moffitt's initial findings, pointing to deficits in memory and spatial and verbal functions as significant. Other longitudinal research programmes, such as the Cambridge Study in

Delinquent Development, have also noted that small numbers of offenders commit disproportionate numbers of offences (Farrington, 1986), thus offering support for the LCP offender thesis.

Compared to LCP offenders, individuals whose offending is limited to the adolescent period have fewer entrenched problems. Their anti-social behaviours tend to start later and are more susceptible to social influences. Specifically, at this period in history, biological maturation is taking place earlier, but social transitions into adulthood are increasingly delayed, creating a tension that Moffitt refers to as the 'maturity gap' (1993). In addition, in adolescence, AL offenders may begin to mimic the behaviours of their LCP offender peers. However, the attractions and gains from offending for AL offenders diminish as they access adult privileges and resolve the 'maturity gap'.

Moffitt's taxonomy is not universally accepted, and the sharp delineation of the offender groups she describes has not been evident in later research, such as the Sheffield Desistance Study (Bottoms and Shapland, 2011, and see the discussion in D.J. Smith, 2007). Nevertheless, it is a simple, clear explanatory model suggesting that behavioural patterns and anti-social disposition are more fixed for LCP offenders than for AL offenders where there is greater dynamism and change. Interestingly, further research on the Dunedin cohort has suggested that individuals with low self-control are more affected by pro-social bonds (education, employment, family ties) which deter crime and, conversely, by anti-social ties (for instance, commitment to a delinquent peer group) (Wright et al, 2001). Thus, depending on the nature of social bonds, individuals may experience either a social protection or social amplification effect, deterring them from anti-social behaviours or pushing them further towards them. It may be that accumulative negative experiences and social reactions mean that LCP offenders are less likely to build positive social bonds that influence in a pro-social direction.

Life course perspectives

Alternative explanations of crime over the life course come from research on criminal careers. Prominent among these research studies is the work of Laub and Sampson, who have re-examined data from an early pioneering study by Sheldon and Eleanor Glueck, *Unravelling juvenile delinquency* (1950; see also *Delinquents and non-delinquents in perspective*, 1968). The Gluecks had taken a sample of 500 young men remanded to reform school during their adolescence and a matched sample of 500 'non-delinquent' young men. They contacted this sample at the ages of 14, 25 and 32, establishing for the first time the strong messages reinforced by later research about the relationship between age and crime (that individual rates of offending declined with age) and that early age of onset was associated with a longer criminal career (Soothill et al, 2009).

Sampson and Laub (1993) re-analysed the Gluecks' data and found the same patterns of stability in criminal behaviour, but alongside this they also identified change caused by life events (such as marriage) and the strengthening of positive social bonds. From these findings they developed a theory of age-graded informal social control that superficially appears similar to Gottfredson and Hirschi's (1990) propositions. However, they do not start with the same assumptions about human nature and the fixed propensity for criminality. Also, they specifically challenge Moffitt's AL and LCP offender taxonomy (1993) and are sceptical of the ability to predict future criminality:

> Developmental criminology, in practice if not in theory, tends to emphasise the notion that people get "locked" into certain trajectories. One of the lessons of prospective longitudinal research is that there is considerable heterogeneity in adult outcomes that cannot be predicted in advance. (Sampson and Laub, 2005, p 14)

In their later work, although not denying the importance of childhood factors, they are keen to emphasise the role of human agency in grasping opportunities or making changes in adult life that can transform or redirect a trajectory (Laub and Sampson, 2001). This approach is therefore more optimistic about rehabilitative prospects.

Re-interviewing 52 of the original Glueck sample in their later years, they found that certain turning points had been significant in the lives of these individuals, including moving house, entering military service and marriage. However, it was not these changes in themselves but the way they have an impact on social bonds and informal social controls that was important (Sampson and Laub, 2005). They also realised that the influence of turning points may be gradual rather than immediate (this seems to bear similarities to the critical moments identified in the Inventing Adulthoods study introduced in Chapter One; see Henderson et al, 2007).

Prospective long-term studies

It is interesting to note that the life course perspectives being proposed by Sampson and Laub (for example, 1993, 2005) and other developments in research into why offenders desist, stand at odds with another major and internationally renowned longitudinal research project that has been most influential in the UK. In 1961, the Cambridge Study in Delinquency Development identified 411 boys living in an inner-city area of South London at the age of 8-9, and followed the sample through to approximately 50 years of age.

Although limited by a relatively homogeneous male sample, the Cambridge Study has generated a considerable amount of empirical data, and its findings underpin the *risk factor prevention paradigm* that came to dominate youth justice practice in England and Wales under New Labour. The significance of this paradigm is explored in later chapters; in essence, it pinpoints characteristics associated with offending which have been adopted in practice as a means of identifying young people 'at risk' who are then targeted for intervention (see Stephenson et al, 2011). These include:

- impulsivity
- intelligence or attainment
- poor parenting
- criminal family
- socioeconomic deprivation
- child anti-social behaviour (Soothill et al, 2009).

Unlike other long-term studies, the Cambridge Study is not underpinned by explicit theoretical frameworks (Soothill at al, 2009). It does not articulate a model for understanding the patterns it observes, particularly in relation to broader social rather than individual person and family-specific influences (Muncie, 2009). However, it does provide a rational basis for decision-making about actions and prioritising resources. Together these qualities made it exceptionally attractive to policy-makers wanting to develop pragmatic responses to young people's behaviours and to justify public expenditure.

What is more promising in revealing social processes is the evidence generated by the ESYTC. Again, using a prospective design, this research has tracked a single cohort of young people starting secondary school in Edinburgh in 1998 through adolescence, a sample of approximately 4,300. The ESYTC has published findings on a range of issues relating to young people, such as smoking, drinking and drug use during adolescence (later chapters will draw on these and the journal articles produced by the research team). Overall, however, its findings can be summarised as follows:

- Persistent serious offending is associated with victimisation and social adversity;
- Early identification of at-risk children is not a water-tight process and runs the risk of labelling and stigmatising;
- Critical moments in the early teenage years are key to pathways out of offending; and
- Diversionary strategies facilitate the desistence process. (Adapted from McAra and McVie, 2010)

In relation to the focus on social systems and structures, the ESYTC has also highlighted how agencies tend to label young people and to keep recycling the 'usual suspects' (McAra and McVie, 2005, 2007). This opens another insight into the age-crime curve in suggesting that, for specific groups of young people, being targeted by official agencies and receiving continued attention (whether social care or criminal justice) may hamper movement towards pro-social identities and desistance.

Looking further at routes into offending

Young people inhabit an anomalous position in society as they engage with key transitions in adolescence and youth. Their status in terms of citizenship and rights is ambiguous and, as outlined in Chapter One, sources of capital and of social recognition are not straightforward or as readily available as they are for most adults. What might this mean for their involvement in offending and the points at which they may desist?

This and the following section of this chapter examine insights from qualitative research into the onset of offending, maintenance or persistence, then processes of desistance, bringing these together in a framework of understanding around change and development during transition. Bourdieu's concept of capital (social, economic, cultural and symbolic) is a useful analytical tool in looking at the gains and losses that young people perceive from offending. As Barry persuasively argues, 'The temporary nature of youth transitions and the lack of legitimate, longer-term capital during that transitional period are important factors in better understanding how, when and why offending and desistance occur' (2006, p 6).

Furthermore, in situations where there are limited opportunities to access lasting forms of capital, young people may use offending as a strategy to create a valuable source of identity, status and recognition during a period of their lives when they are potentially marginalised (Barry, 2006). These may not be viable choices in the long term and may have negative impacts, but the immediate gains may seem compelling.

Interviews with young people reveal how much this is the case. Consider, for example, the experiences of young men involved in stealing cars:

> 'You'd never do it on your own, what'd be the point? It'd be pointless not showing your mates what you'd done ... you play games like how many of one make you can get. We change the games all the time, it's just one big game ... your mates are important and you need to see that they respect you.' (quoted in Stephen and Squires, 2003, p 152)

> 'I'm the driver ... I always drive the car, they all know I am the top one there so they let me drive it mostly. It feels good, you feel more important, in charge, on the road.' (quoted in Stephen and Squires, 2003, p 155)

In Barry's research with 40 young people who had been heavily involved in offending, relational factors were often highlighted as influential in onset. The two following accounts from her interviews illustrate two different ways this might work; the first example is after 'Pete' had moved to a rural community and a new school:

'I was looking for, I suppose in a way, folk to look at me in a different light. For folk to think of me differently – to fit in, in a way ... I had to make friends because I was alone in a strange countryside village with no one that I knew about me and it was like, how – what can I do? Where am I going to turn, you know? And to me [offending] was my only escape.' ('Pete', 19, quoted in Barry, 2006, p 50)

'All my friends were going into town to shoplift and dressing smart with the clothes that they'd stole and at first I was always saying "how could they do that? I wish I could do that." And then ... I was in town with my friend and she was a bit older than I was and she stole herself a big shiny necklace. She said "Just do it ... it's easy," and I did, and it was easy.' ('Helen', 20, quoted in Barry, 2006, p 49)

Relational factors seemed particularly important for young women and, in contrast to young men, some reported the impetus to start offending coming from their partners, often associated with drug use. Interestingly, for young men offending tended to precede drug use but it came after for young women (this is also the case in McIvor et al, 2004). Material gain was an attraction linked to consumption and, for young women, their appearance and enhancement of their symbolic and cultural capital (see also Sharpe, 2012). Eight of the 20 young women interviewed by Barry also cited anger and depression caused by bereavement or abuse as significant. On the other hand, boredom and the quest for excitement were almost exclusively mentioned by young men, and this is replicated in research elsewhere:

'It's the adrenaline rush, you know what it's like on a roller coaster, well, it's exactly the same feeling.' (quoted in Stephen and Squires, 2003, p 157)

The search for recognition and for meaning is especially important for young people in the context of a changing society and labour market conditions (MacDonald et al, 2010). In Stephen and Squires' research the young men were not just reacting to the social circumstances they found themselves in but were actively trying to make sense of the protracted limbo between childhood dependency and the independence and status they associated with conventional male adulthood without the means of moving from school into paid employment:

The acquisition of status through group support and identity, a sense of belonging in a consumer society from which they recognised their own marginalisation, provided a normative context for being proactive in manufacturing their own forms of leisure, if not also employment. (2003, p 160)

Furthermore, although vehicle taking is a risky activity, the authors comment that, for young men like this at the margins of society, it nevertheless generates positives in terms of self-expression, skills and peer group bonding, paradoxically offering a sense of security in the face of a risk society characterised by insecurity and inequalities.

In Barry's study interviewees described offending after the onset phase becoming routine, even mundane. However, there was an element of habit for some and, for others, the desire to keep consuming (and therefore to maintain the benefits of the cultural and symbolic capital gains from material goods). For instance, Cathy, aged 23, described herself as,

> '[U]sed to having things ... used to having everything ... the money and everything that comes with it.' (quoted in Barry, 2006, p 89)

This is reflected in Sharpe's (2012) research with younger women, and she comments that,

> Girl's shoplifting can be understood as an inclusionary strategy which enables them to participate in a consumer-driven society, as well as being status-enhancing through the bodily display of clothes, make-up, false nails and other such symbols of glamour. (2012, p 94)

Research further shows that drugs and alcohol are a major trapping factor, and often the associated lifestyle isolates young people from non-offending friends and family, meaning they were less accessible as a resource (Barry, 2006).

Among the 12 interviewees in Barry's sample who were still offending, there was greater awareness in this maintenance phase of the disadvantages of offending and the risks associated with it. However, Barry argues that greater calculation of risk does not increase with age per se, but is connected with the process of becoming an adult and the rights, status and responsibilities that come with it (Barry, 2006). This may include the risks to the role of parent – certainly two of her interviewees still offending were expressing a desire to stop because of their children and the fear of imprisonment. In general, Barry's research, in line with others, suggests that 'involvement in crime moves offenders beyond the point at which they find it enjoyable to the point at which it is debilitating and anxiety-provoking' (Sommers et al, 1994, p 146, cited in Barry, 2006, p 101). Finally, as an illustration, one young woman in another Scottish study reflected that,

> 'I used to feel really guilty and I used to think that everyone knew. Every time anyone looked at me I thought 'They know what's happened, they know what I have done'.... I went through a lot, a lot of guilt.' (quoted in McIvor et al, 2004, p 188)

Looking further at routes out of crime

Desistance is not a clearly defined concept and research studies have used different means of identifying 'desisters'. Nevertheless, common themes emerge from the accounts of young people who have ceased offending (or at least identify themselves as doing so). Some of these are negative, associated with stigma and hassle as well as the practical consequence of offending and involvement with the CJS (Graham and Bowling, 1995; Barry, 2006). Others are more positive in terms of assuming adult roles and responsibilities, including parenting (although this is a more accessible route to adulthood for young women) (Graham and Bowling, 1995).

Other social factors, such as moving out of the family home, may be either positive or negative, depending on the circumstances and social supports or influences available in the new environment. Changes in friendship groups are also significant and may involve conscious decisions to break away from previous associates or natural changes as a result of moving neighbourhood, changing college or school or starting a relationship (with a non-offending partner).

Research by Jamieson et al (1999) indicates that influences on desistance are similar for young men and young women, but they may work in different ways and vary in their salience. While young men and young women both spoke of growing up and becoming more mature and circumspect in their attitudes, young men employed more utilitarian and individualistic explanations whereas young women referred more often to relational or moral dimensions. Desistance for young women is also more frequently associated with actual commitment to others, particularly children, compared to young men's potential commitment to work and family (Barry, 2007). One young woman cited in McIvor et al encapsulated this when she said, 'I realised I've got the wean [child] to think about. I cannae just think about myself all the time. I've got to put him in front of me' (2004, p 191).

Despite these differences, McIvor et al (2004) suggest that age may be more significant in terms of the influences on desistance and the processes involved. In an earlier research study (Jamieson et al, 1999), 276 young people were interviewed. There were equal numbers of young men and young women in three age cohorts (14-15, 18-19 and 22-25). Young people were characterised as *resisters* (non-offenders), *desisters* (with a past history of offending but not in the past 12 months), and *persisters* (with at least one serious or several less serious offences in the past 12 months). The research explored the experiences, view and attitudes of the young people and found considerable consistency within each of the groups. Significantly, the *desisters* tended to be located between the other two groups in most dimensions. For instance, many of their habits and routines – drinking or taking drugs, 'hanging out' – were more similar to persisters, but they resembled resisters more closely in terms of seeing offending in broad terms as immoral or futile (McIvor et al, 2004).

What is notable is that the reasons given for desisting varied between the age groups: the 14- to 15-year-olds were more likely to cite the consequences of offending (actual or perceived) or growing awareness of the pointlessness or immorality of offending as reasons for desistance; the 18- to 19-year-olds also referred to growing maturity but, for this group, more often linked to factors associated with the transition to adulthood, such as employment, starting college or university, establishing a relationship or leaving home; the 22- to 25-year-olds more frequently reported taking on family and other responsibilities or making conscious lifestyle changes (McIvor et al, 2004).

This is an interesting finding, certainly in terms of desistance and young people in the YJS. The developing literature on desistance among adults emphasises the role of cognitive transformation and a re-structuring of self-narratives (see, for instance, Maruna, 2001) associated with the move from *primary desistance* – stopping offending – to a more sustained form of *secondary desistance* and the adoption of a non-offending identity (Maruna and Farrall, 2004). But is this process the same for young people who are inherently in a process of forming their identity and their sense of self? McNeill explains that,

> Desistance resides somewhere in the interfaces between developing personal maturity, forming new or stronger social bonds associated with certain life transitions, and individual subjective narrative constructions which offenders build around key events and changes. It is not just the events and changes that matter; it is what these events and changes mean to the people involved. (2003, p 151)

The balance between these three elements may be significantly different for young people under the age of 18 compared to adults (see Figures 2.4 and 2.5). It may be that to develop opportunities to build and to expend social and other forms of capital (Barry, 2012) and to overcome obstacles (Bottoms and Shapland, 2011) is more salient for this age group. It is not that internal narratives are unimportant for young people; as suggested in the Inventing Adulthoods study (Henderson et al, 2007), they can be highly creative in their construction of self and able to reflect on that process. But the significance of the three elements seen as important for desistance may vary, with the development of psychosocial maturity featuring prominently for young people (see Chapter One).

This chapter has shown that there are a variety of ways of understanding young people's involvement in offending and the social and psychological processes that mean that the majority cease offending and reduce associated behaviours, such as drinking and drug use, as they approach adulthood. There are also different ways of understanding and responding to the smaller constituency of young people whose behaviour is much more entrenched and whose social circumstances may be so much less supportive of positive change.

Figure 2.4: Relative impact of influences on desistance for a young person under the age of 18

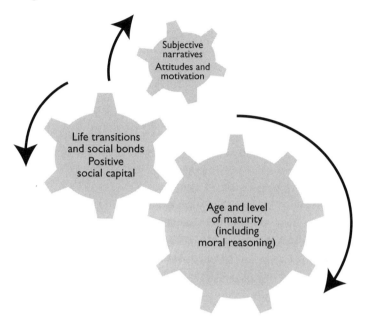

Figure 2.5: Relative impact of influences on desistance for an adult (over the age of 21)

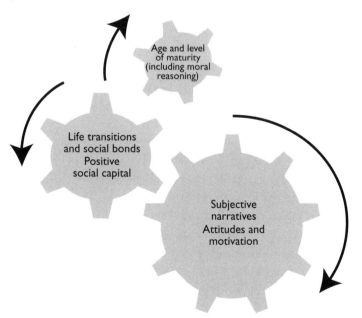

Implications for practice

The fundamental effort of the practice model proposed in this book is to understand young people and their behaviours. Official statistics on offending differ from self-reports by young people, yet both over time and across multiple studies, show that offending peaks in the teenage years and declines thereafter. But explanations and analyses are complex and contested. They also raise awkward questions about what society considers and formally responds to as deviant, and how social actions and reactions themselves contribute to delinquency.

Recent youth justice practice has been dominated by developmental criminology and the risk factor prevention paradigm. Although useful as a basis for decision-making and interventions, it does not offer any great insights into the behaviours and motivations of individual young people, and has left practice woefully uninformed about key aspects of transitions and the wider social and structural systems and processes that impinge on growth and development. In the New Labour era, this also included an almost wilful neglect of thought about the impact of the YJS itself and its procedures, as it absorbed more resources and expanded its activities. Sensitivity to the effects of the system itself – and the interactions of each individual practitioner – is essential to properly reflective and reflexive youth justice practice.

Life course perspectives on offending shed more light on the effect of different life stages and the social roles and bonds that develop with growing maturity and adult responsibilities. They also show the impact of life events and the choices that individuals make, challenging the developmental criminological view that individual pathways are very largely determined from early in life.

Further insights into youthful behaviours can be gained by using the notion of capital. As social actors, young people make choices based on the capital and resources available to them and the opportunities they can access to accumulate more capital. They may also choose to avoid situations that deplete their capital and where they risk receiving negative rather than positive recognition. Looked at in this light, decisions such as dropping out of school, involvement with drugs and starting to commit offences are rendered more understandable, although perhaps giving only short-term gains.

The notion of capital further assists youth justice practice in considering why and how young people desist from crime. Access to adult roles, such as parenting, may be important for some in leaving behind an offending identity. Also significant are opportunities to receive positive social recognition and acknowledgement of competence as young people take on adult-like responsibilities and commitments.

Further reading

Barry, M. (2006) *Youth offending in transition: The search for social recognition*, Abingdon: Routledge.

Sharpe, G. (2012) *Offending girls: Young women and youth justice*, Abingdon: Routledge.

Soothill, K., Fitzpatrick, C. and Francis, B. (2009) *Understanding criminal careers*, Cullompton: Willan.

THREE

Youth justice histories

This chapter opens discussion of society's response to young people, particularly those 'on the margins'. The YJS has always recognised that challenging and anti-social behaviours are often present at the same time as need and vulnerability. Indeed, needs and vulnerability may be directly linked to presenting behaviours. In this sense, youth justice has historically encompassed both the 'deprived' and 'depraved', although the emphasis shifts and is reflected in the legal and structural arrangements in place at any given time. Essentially, the pendulum has swung between more welfare-orientated and more punishment-led approaches, but both have always been evident. New Labour, coming into office in 1997, sought to change the terms of the traditional penal welfare debate. Reforms to the YJS were prominent in their modernisation agenda, bringing in restorative and actuarial practices alongside punishment and welfare-based interventions. The extent to which they successfully established a coherent new youth justice philosophy for England and Wales is debatable (Muncie, 2009), but the framework in which practice exists changed dramatically with the introduction of the Youth Justice Board (YJB) at a national level and multi-agency youth offending teams (YOTs) locally, the expansion of early interventions focused on crime prevention and the greater integration of children's services under the Every Child Matters initiative.

This chapter takes a broadly historical view before detailing New Labour's reforms to the YJS and exploring young people's views and experiences of youth justice.

Early beginnings

The belief that young people breaking the law should be treated differently to adults is relatively new, developing as ideas about childhood and, more recently, adolescence as distinct life stages became established. Two hundred years ago the age of criminal responsibility in England was seven. Criminal proceedings did not distinguish on the basis of age and children could be hanged, transported or sent to prison where they would be held alongside adults. It was a time that was markedly more punitive physically. Shockingly, in 1814 it is recorded that on one day five children between the ages of 8 and 12 were hanged alongside each other for petty theft (Pinchbeck and Hewitt, 1973, p 352, cited in Hopkins-Burke, 2008, p 47).

Punishment, however, was beginning to take a different form with the growth of the prison system premised on repentance and reform of prisoners (see Foucault, 1977). As criminal law also expanded and changed its focus from the question of sin to a preoccupation with delinquency and property crime (Muncie, 2009), young people were singled out for attention, particularly within the rapidly expanding urban areas. The Factory Acts of 1819 and 1833 were intended to prevent children under the age of nine working in mills and factories and to restrict the hours that older children could work, but paradoxically may have created more hardship for families already struggling to survive and increased the number of children who were vagrant, destitute or eking out a living on the streets (Muncie, 2009).

Early developments in the prison system did not differentiate between prisoners according to their age, but it was not long before concerns were raised about the potential for children to be morally contaminated through contact with adult prisoners. The first separate prison for juveniles was opened in 1838 at Parkhurst amidst debates about how to recognise childhood in social and penal policy. The central dilemma concerned the fundamental conception of childhood at the heart of policy, and whether these children should be viewed as victims or as threats (Hendrick, 2006). The Youthful Offenders Act 1854 was the first piece of legislation explicitly to address juvenile delinquency by creating reformatories for children convicted in the courts (that is, those seen as a threat). Then, only three years later, the Industrial Schools Act 1857 established schools for 'neglected' children (that is, those seen as victims), so reinforcing an uneasy conceptual divide.

Reformatories and industrial schools gradually became the main official responses to children offending or viewed as 'at risk' replacing bodily punishments with a structure of institutionalised surveillance and control (Hendrick, 2006). Intervention was justified on moral grounds, in terms of prevention of criminality in young men and sexual transgressions in young women (Muncie, 2009). By the turn of the century, more than 30,000 children and young people were being held in one or other type of establishment (Radzinowicz and Hood, 1986).

Of course, penal affairs never stand still, and towards the end of the Victorian era rescue and reform came even more significantly to the fore. The Gladstone Report (Home Office, 1895) concluded that the prison service should have two aims: punishment with the aim of deterring criminals, and reform with the aim of rehabilitation. These two aims are not easily compatible and constitute a longstanding tension at the core of prison provision (Coyle, 2005), particularly evident at that time in relation to children and adolescents (the latter just beginning to attract official attention). The Gladstone Report argued that young people should be dealt with separately from adults, extending this to the age of 21. The Liberal government in 1908 thus created a new custodial sentence for 16- to 21-year-olds and opened a series of new establishments for young people, the first in Borstal in Kent, giving rise to the term 'Borstal training'.

Even this short account is enough to demonstrate how competing rationales and discourses shaped the beginnings of youth justice, with no one clear overriding purpose. (This is reflected in later developments outlined in this chapter.) Hopkins-Burke in fact comments that, 'From the nineteenth century, when the troubled and troublesome among the youth population was first thought to require a different response to that afforded adults, the history of youth justice has been riddled with confusion, ambiguity and unintended consequences' (2008, p 64).

Reaching into the community

In the Victorian era, institutions of various kinds proliferated, dealing with social groups deemed to be a problem for society. These included workhouses, asylums, prisons and orphanages as well as reformatories and industrial schools. As the state apparatus developed at the beginning of the new century, the broad architecture (McAra, 2010) of the YJS in England and Wales was put in place, extending its reach into the community.

First, the Children Act 1908 created the juvenile court, dealing with young people aged 16 and under and having jurisdiction over civil as well as criminal matters. The court attempted to reconcile the twin demands of welfare and justice by dealing with the socially needy alongside the delinquent (Hendrick, 2006), but in fact the expectation that the court would seek to 'rescue' as well as to punish children created inherent conflict and ambivalence in its workings from its very beginnings (Gelsthorpe and Morris, 1994). Moreover, the juvenile court was established (and still exists as the present-day youth court) within an adversarial justice system, which necessarily affects the potential for young people to actively participate in proceedings (McAra, 2010).

Second, the probation service came fully into being with the Probation of Offenders Act 1907. The origins of the service as Police Court missionaries points to the moral endeavour that early probation officers engaged with and their 'hard-headed and practical Christianity' (Canton, 2011, p 20). Some accounts of the probation service refer to this as the missionary phase (Chui and Nellis, 2003), while others acknowledge different motivations more connected with social control and anxieties about working-class young people (Vanstone, 2004). Certainly, even in its infancy the service was able to collaborate with other professional groups and to use new understandings of adolescence such as G.S. Hall's (1904) 'storm and stress' model to establish its standing in the emergent welfare state.

Third, while adult crime had been reducing, there appeared to be an upward trend in recorded juvenile crime, mainly summary offences such as drunkenness, begging and loitering, exacerbated by aggressive enforcement actions by the police and courts (Hendrick, 2006). This was a period of intense insecurity immediately before the First World War, with growing tensions in Europe, unrest in Ireland and antagonism between the classes at home. Once again, adult anxieties gathered around young people and the threat of disorder, made still worse by a moral panic about hooliganism – at that time a new term, but one that carried great resonance (Brown, 2005; Muncie, 2009). This created a climate that called for the greater regulation of young people and their activities. Organisations duly sprung up to fulfil this demand. The probation service clearly had legislative backing; others rose from similar roots in the community or the church, but found their support locally. Rixon (2007), for example, cites the Sunderland Waifs Rescue Agency and Street Vendors Club, the St Christopher's Working Boys Club and the Cambridge Association for the Care of Girls.

These organisations and their aims engendered the welfare ideology that in a later form underpinned the developing social work profession. Although benevolent in certain respects, it nevertheless permitted significant state intervention into the lives of working-class young people considered to be unruly or immoral (Hopkins-Burke, 2008). The traditional notions of punishment were fast being replaced by welfare and new discourses around reclamation and treatment (Muncie, 2009).

The welfare paradigm

During the interwar period the understanding of delinquency as connected to psychological and social conditions developed further, assuming a significant overlap between offending and welfare concerns. These assumptions were ultimately enshrined in the Children and Young Persons Act (C&YPA) 1933 which allowed juvenile courts to act in loco parentis as a closer link was forged between delinquent and neglected children (Hendrick, 2006). The wider use of probation, approved schools and other forms of social care for young people that was part and parcel of this approach was not necessarily popular with sentencers and the police. Nevertheless, the 1933 Act still retains a significant foothold in today's youth justice, most importantly through the welfare principle contained in Section 44 and the provisions relating to reporting restrictions of cases in youth court.

> **Section 44: Children and Young Persons Act 1933**
> Every court in dealing with a child or young person who is brought before it either as an offender or otherwise, shall have regard to the welfare of the child or young person and shall in proper cases take steps for removing him from undesirable surroundings and for securing that proper provision is made for his education and training.

The dominance of the welfare ideology continued after the Second World War as the new welfare state was being constructed and the social work profession was further establishing itself. However, enthusiasm for punishment never entirely disappeared (Morgan and Newburn, 2007); the Criminal Justice Act (CJA) 1948, for instance, established detention centres with an explicitly punitive regime (Muncie, 2009). An extra element of tension was introduced to the mix as youth or teen cultures and patterns of consumption began to develop and to distinguish themselves from adults (Brown, 2005).

The 1960s saw serious questions and doubts raised yet again about youth justice, particularly given the rise in offending even in the face of increased affluence, plentiful employment and the developing welfare state, all of which, from a liberal point of view, might have been expected to reduce criminality. In 1960, the Ingleby Report (Home Office, 1960) identified conflicts in the YJS between the dual expectations of punishment within a court-based system and promoting the welfare of young people (Hendrick, 2006; Hopkins-Burke, 2008). These contradictions were also reflected in the C&YPA 1963 which raised the age of criminal responsibility to 10 in England and Wales and empowered local authorities to engage in preventative social work with families, while still maintaining the view of young people both as a threat and as victims (Hendrick, 2006).

It was during the 1960s that youth justice policy north and south of the Scottish border began to diverge. In Scotland, the Kilbrandon Report (Kilbrandon Committee, 1964) strongly advocated a welfare-based system for dealing with young people up to the age of 16. The Social Work (Scotland) Act 1968 subsequently established the Children's Hearing System, involving lay members of the community in what are effectively welfare tribunals, and creating a more central role for social workers (Muncie, 2009). Children's hearings still operate today and the original welfare philosophy has retained a much stronger hold than elsewhere in the UK, although from the 1990s philosophies and practices have tended to converge (McAra and McVie, 2010).

In England and Wales, the fortunes of welfare have followed a different trajectory. The 1968 White Paper, *Children in trouble*, introduced by the Labour Party, argued from a similar perspective to Kilbrandon that very few children grow up without ever having broken the law, and that often such behaviour represents little more than an incident in the pattern of a child's normal development (Home Office, 1968, cited in Muncie, 2009). The White Paper led to the controversial C&YPA 1969, which proposed to drastically reduce the use of custody in favour of community disposals and residential provision, to raise the age of criminal responsibility from 10 to 14 and to shift decision-making away from the judicial arena of courts towards social services departments. It sought to focus attention on the role of the family and its circumstances as a cause of delinquency, promoting social work intervention in the family in line with this (Hopkins-Burke, 2008). The Act allowed the courts to make a care order as a response to offending rather than imposing a punitive sentence. It also created supervision orders which were the primary disposal for young people until the introduction of the youth rehabilitation order in 2009.

However, with a new Conservative government in power in 1970, the more radical parts of the 1969 Act were never implemented. So, instead of social welfare replacing custody, intermediate treatment and other interventions existed alongside it, widening the youth justice net and drawing increasing numbers of children and young people into it:

> Rather than replacing the old structures of juvenile justice, the new welfarist principles were grafted on to them. The treatment-punishment continuum was merely extended ... in practice, traditional principles of punitive justice were never seriously undermined by the 1969 Act. (Muncie, 2009, pp 278-9)

The fundamental welfare principle of the C&YPA 1933 is still in place, but the YJS has since been refocused on criminal matters rather than broader social concerns. The Children Act 1989 created the family court and removed care-related cases from the juvenile court, leaving it to deal with criminal offences only. Two years later the CJA 1991 repealed the powers to make criminal care orders and raised the age range for the juvenile court to include 17-year-olds, with the court being rebranded as the youth court. Section 37 of the Crime and Disorder Act (CDA) 1998 established a statutory aim for the YJS of prevention of crime by children and young people. That same Act also – and controversially – abolished *doli incapax*, a legal presumption dating from the 14th century that children between the ages of 10 and 13 do not know right from wrong, and are therefore incapable of criminal intent.

Yet welfare has not disappeared as a central concern for practice. The UK is signed up to the 1989 United Nations Convention on the Rights of the Child (UNCRC), which contains sections relating to children (in this case, any person under the age of 18) in the justice system. UK legislation and youth justice agencies are thus required to comply with the principles of the Convention. Finding an appropriate balance has not been easy for practitioners expected to have regard to different, sometimes conflicting, purposes and aims of the YJS. New Labour's White Paper, *No more excuses*, which preceded the CDA 1998, attempted to clarify but in fact muddied the water even more:

> The Government believes that there has been confusion about the purpose of the youth justice system and the principles that should govern the way in which young people are dealt with by youth justice agencies. Concerns about the welfare of the child have too often been seen as in conflict with the aims of protecting the public, punishing offences and preventing offending. This confusion causes practical difficulties for practitioners and has contributed to the loss of public confidence in the youth justice system.
>
> Children need protection as appropriate from the full rigours of the criminal law. Under the UN Convention on the Rights of the Child and the European Convention on Human Rights, the UK is committed to protecting the welfare of children and young people who come into contact with the criminal justice process. The Government does not accept that there is any conflict between protecting the welfare of a young offender and preventing that individual from offending again. Preventing offending promotes the welfare of the individual young offender and protects the public. (Home Office, 1997, p 6)

The shift to 'just deserts'

In the 1970s, welfarism was under attack from Conservatives for being 'soft on crime', but it also found itself criticised from liberal perspectives. Although apparently progressive, welfare approaches placed decision-making in the hands of social workers, rather than young people themselves, doing little to encourage their active participation and empowerment (Brown, 2005). Concerns were increasingly voiced about the denial of young people's rights through the lack of due process, the wide use of (social workers') discretion and the ability to impose greater intervention than the behaviour itself actually warranted on the basis of perceived need (Muncie, 2009). Moreover, the definition of what constitutes 'need' was, and still is, highly problematic, and the links between needs and delinquency can be understood in a variety of ways.

The Conservative government elected in 1979 had taken an overtly politicised stance towards law and order issues during the election campaign (Hopkins-Burke, 2008). Nevertheless, policy development during the 1980s was not as straightforward as might have been expected from their punitive rhetoric, the promise of 'short, sharp shocks' for young offenders and the focus on individual responsibility. Certainly, the belief in welfare and welfare interventions was explicitly abandoned in the light of the 'Nothing Works' messages of Martinson (1974) and others. However, government policy had two strands, one strengthening and toughening custodial and community sentences, the other seeking to reduce intervention and to create cost savings where possible (R. Smith, 2007). The system therefore bifurcated: young people with more serious or persistent patterns of offending were singled out for punitive measures while other young people were diverted out of the YJS, primarily through the use of cautions and informal action by the police. This created the opportunity for a progressive 'back to justice' movement to take hold at a grassroots level as the decade progressed. Although apprehensive about the Conservatives' punishment orientation, this movement acknowledged the merits of firmer boundaries around sentencing and changes such as the replacement of the indeterminate Borstal regime with determinate sentences of youth custody (R. Smith, 2007).

Ironically, the 1970s, which should have seen a reduction in the use of custody with the C&YPA 1969 in place, experienced a significant increase. Conversely, the Conservative government presided over a period of decarceration, with a drop in the numbers of 14- to 17-year-old males sentenced to immediate custody, from 13,500 in 1983 to 3,300 in 1993. The numbers of young people cautioned or convicted also fell from 204,600 to 129,500 over that same period (Muncie, 2009). Although partly explained by the smaller juvenile population, youth justice practices had a significant impact (R. Smith, 2007), including:

- crime prevention initiatives;
- diversion from prosecution – by the 1990s approximately 60 per cent of young people were dealt with by means of cautions or informal action by the police rather than court proceedings, a practice bolstered by Home Office Circular 14/1985;
- diversion from custody – the DHSS Intermediate Treatment Initiative in 1983 funded 110 alternative to custody schemes in 62 local authority areas;
- local systems management, bringing relevant agencies together in problem-solving groups. (Adapted from Muncie, 2009, pp 291-3)

The trend was on the whole positive, and characterised by a high degree of consistency and consensus among the criminal justice stakeholders. Policy was unusually driven by principles in the period prior to the CJA 1991 (Brown, 2005), and its explicit framework based on proportionality and thresholds that must be met before either community sentences or custody could be imposed. This was about punishment and 'just deserts', but delivered in a measured way and with an eye to cost-effectiveness and managerial efficiency. However, the success in reducing the numbers of young people caught up in the YJS was not matched by success in reducing offending which was continuing to rise (across all age groups). The bifurcated youth justice policy adopted by the Conservatives had in any case favoured retribution towards serious and persistent offenders. This group was disproportionately made up of working-class young people who were casualties of the laissez-faire economic and social policy of the 1980s, excluded from the labour market and constructed as the 'underclass' (Hopkins-Burke, 2008).

Sadly, under systems management and minimum intervention, political analysis of such social and economic factors affecting crime had been subsumed by pragmatic responses. The youth justice profession really had no answer to the re-politicisation of youth justice under Michael Howard as Home Secretary, or to the moral panic around persistent offenders, such as the mythical 'Ratboy'. The fragile consensus was further strained by judges' and magistrates' dissatisfaction with the constraints that the CJA 1991 put on their sentencing decisions. Against this backdrop, the murder of the toddler James Bulger in 1993 served to escalate fears and provide justification for a harsher rhetoric around young offenders (Muncie, 2009). The strict proportionality principle of the CJA 1991 was soon watered down and new legislation, such as the Criminal Justice and Public Order Act 1994, was distinctly more retributive, bringing in a range of new offences dealing with disorder and expanding custodial options, including the secure training order (STC) for 12- to 14-year-olds. At the same time, Home Office Circular 18/1994 stopped the practice of repeat cautioning (R. Smith, 2007), and in this way the hard-fought gains of the previous decade were rapidly reversed.

What about the Labour Party?

The climate in the mid-1990s had turned increasingly hostile towards young people: clearly there was a political will for something to be demonstrably 'done' about young offenders. The Labour Party – with Tony Blair as leader and freshly branded as New Labour – joined their Conservative opponents in talking tough about youth offending. Both picked up the messages from a highly critical Audit Commission report (1996): *Misspent youth* found the YJS to be expensive, slow and inefficient, with limited impact on offenders. It was particularly concerned about how little intervention most young people received, and how little of what they did receive related to their offending. It highlighted the problems and delays in court proceedings, particularly for persistent young offenders. *Misspent youth* also authoritatively and comprehensively challenged the practices of minimum intervention and diversion associated with the 1980s, advocating more intervention, including preventative work based on the findings of the Cambridge

Study in Delinquent Development (Farrington, 1989, 1994) and Graham and Bowling (1995) among others (see Chapter Two, this volume).

Although New Labour presented their policy proposals on coming into office as radical and new, in reality there was significant continuity with the previous regime in terms of reliance on the messages from developmental criminology, the emphasis on personal responsibility and the willingness to use technologies such as electronic monitoring (R. Smith, 2007). The promotion of partnership working was also an element that both political parties had in common. New Labour busily set about establishing partnerships at strategic and operational levels, although to some extent they were taking the benefits of partnership working on trust because at the time there was no substantial body of evidence to support their enthusiasm (Rumgay, 2003). However, another philosophical element distinct to New Labour came into play and informed a new approach to the oversight and delivery of services, in the guise of the Third Way.

The experience of the previous decades had undermined the belief in the previous 'grand narratives' used to explain social, political and economic life. Large-scale welfare programmes and state intervention had been discredited, with its underpinning notions of class and social structure. Similarly the forces of the market and neoliberal politics had proved inadequate to the challenges of complex society in late modernity. The Third Way approach adopted by New Labour in its early days in office sought to find new solutions to 'wicked problems' such as youth crime and drugs, moving beyond both the state (that is, the public sector) and the market and focusing on modernisation and new 'joined-up' forms of governance (Cook, 2006). This was most explicitly embodied in their reforms to the YJS.

New Labour quickly produced a White Paper, *No more excuses* (Home Office, 1997), referring simultaneously to a more rigorous approach to young offenders and higher expectations of youth justice professionals. The White Paper was followed soon after by the CDA 1998. The Act stated for the first time a clear purpose for the YJA:

Section 37

(1) It shall be the principal aim of the youth justice system to prevent offending by children and young persons.

This is a collective responsibility for all the agencies involved with young people, who should have regard to this aim of preventing their involvement in offending. At a national level, the YJB was established as a non-departmental public body to oversee the reformed system and to provide strategic direction. Section 38 placed specific responsibilities on local authorities to provide a range of youth justice services and on the police, probation and health to cooperate in the management and delivery of services.

Multi-agency (or more properly, *inter*agency) YOTs were introduced by Section 39 as the operational arm of the new system, involving at a minimum:

- the police
- probation
- children's social care
- education
- health.

Other agencies such as Connexions are not statutory partners but were often included due to a common interest in re-engaging young people in education and reducing the NEET (not in education, employment or training) population. Additional services could also be involved by virtue of contractual arrangements or service level agreements. So YOTs developed as complex beasts and, with a basis of required elements, were shaped according to local need and circumstances. Governance and leadership was provided through the Crime and Disorder Reduction Partnership and, currently, Community Safety Partnership structures, but YOTs also have links to the strategic body overseeing children's services within the local authority.

As part of the multi-agency approach, the different agencies were expected to work to common objectives within the broad youth crime reduction agenda. These common objectives included:

- the swift administration of justice so that every young person accused of breaking the law has the matter resolved without delay;
- confronting young offenders with the consequences of their offending, for themselves and their family, their victims and their community;
- punishment proportionate to the seriousness and persistence of offending;
- encouraging reparation to victims by young offenders;
- reinforcing the responsibilities of parents; and
- helping young offenders to tackle problems associated with their offending and to develop a sense of personal responsibility (Home Office, 1997).

The structural and cultural changes associated with 'joined-up justice' were made more complex by the introduction of intensive schemes for young people with persistent or serious patterns of offending. The ISSP, involving surveillance and a requirement for 25 hours contact each week, was indicative of a markedly more interventionist YJS. The reforms also brought in actuarial practices in the form of structured assessment tools, Asset and Onset (for young people in the pre-offending stage). Furthermore, in 2002, the referral order initiative came into operation, representing the most explicit embodiment of restoration as a key principle for the YJS (see Chapter Sixteen, this volume). However, the new aims such as restoration, reintegration, crime prevention and surveillance were incorporated without replacing the more long-standing concerns about welfare, retribution and rights, adding to the complexities and contradictions already inherent in the system (Muncie, 2009). (The impacts and the implications of New Labour's reforms are explored in the next chapter.)

Girls and young women in the youth justice system

Youth justice has always been a highly gendered domain, with male norms dominant and limited understanding of young women who break the law, especially black young women and those from other minority groups. Muncie insightfully comments that 'while cultural codes of masculinity, toughness and sexual predation are the norm for young men, there is little or no conception of "normal" exuberant delinquency for young women' (2009, p 286). Historically, relatively few young women have committed criminal acts, and criminological concern and policy development has focused on young men. Even within judicial processes, the courts seem to regard male offenders as 'normal' and females as 'special', so 'reinforcing the notion that criminality is a male preserve and that female criminality is a very peculiar phenomenon indeed' (Brown, 2005, p 134).

Although feminist criminologists have ensured that more is now known about women's offending, there has been little empirical research specifically on young female offenders (Brown, 2005). The assumption has been that the views and experiences of young women will be similar to those of adult women, and their distinctive age-related needs and development have been neglected (Burman and Batchelor, 2009).

Young women have experienced a greater degree of informal social controls, such as parental surveillance, than young men, and have been less visible on the streets. However, a smaller number have also attracted more formal responses to their behaviours. Throughout the history of youth justice, girls and young women have been disproportionately subject to state intervention for welfare or moral reasons (Gelsthorpe and Sharpe, 2006), or for status, rather than criminal offences. As Gelsthorpe and Worrall note,

> Until the late 1960s at least, girls and young women were often more likely to be caught up in the juvenile justice system as a consequence of gender inappropriate behaviours such as running away, wilfulness and unsanctified sexual activity – behaviours that undermine stereotypes of feminine passivity, chastity and submissiveness. (2009, p 209)

In terms of court processes, young women have tended to feature at the lower end of intervention, reflecting the less serious nature of their offending, greater likelihood of admitting guilt and a generally paternalistic attitude on behalf of (mainly male) criminal justice professionals. In the 'old' YJS, young women were more likely to be cautioned than young men and, in the reformed system, to receive a reprimand or final warning (Feilzer and Hood, 2004). However, the apparently benign nature of sentencing often resulted in young women being made subject to relatively intrusive welfare disposals, such as supervision orders, rather than the full range of disposals, including financial penalties, reparation and attendance centre orders, used for young men.

Of course, not all young women are treated leniently by the courts, and critics have argued that those who do not fit accepted gender stereotypes are dealt with more harshly, a process known as 'double deviance' or 'double jeopardy' (Hudson, 1988). These might include young women who are in the care system and outwith conventional family controls; young women who display aggressive rather than submissive behaviours; young women who are not remorseful; and young women who are black or lesbian. The double jeopardy thesis suggests that these young women are being punished twice – once for offending against the law and a second time for offending against accepted notions of femininity.

Attitudes to young women are also changing as they increasingly claim the public sphere and are demonstrably drinking more heavily in social situations (Gelsthorpe and Sharpe, 2006). However, the moral panics around female intoxication and aggression are disproportionate – and disproportionately condemning – to the actual increase in anti-social behaviours (Burman and Batchelor, 2009), which are tolerated more readily in young men.

Coming into the 2000s, youth justice policy attempted explicitly to move away from welfarist assumptions towards young women and to adopt a more gender-neutral approach. However, this meant that young women lost the advantages of leniency associated with welfarism as well as the disadvantages of over-intervention. The 'search for equivalence' partly driven by feminists, partly by interests less sympathetic to women (Silvestri and Crowther-Dowey, 2008), has resulted in young women's behaviour being more readily criminalised rather than simply viewed as problematic (Sharpe, 2012). Furthermore, New Labour's youth justice reforms introduced a culture of early preventative work with troublesome boys and girls, with the result that,

> Gender-blind policies and practices legitimating criminal justice intervention into the lives of a vastly expanded population of young people because they are deemed to be "at risk of offending" have had particularly dramatic and criminalising consequences for girls and young women in the 21st century. (Gelsthorpe and Worrall, 2009, p 219)

Paradoxically, there are indications that young women are being referred to prevention projects because of their sexual behaviours, harking back to earlier practices. Sharpe, in her recent study of young women in the YJS, found that 'the policing of girls' sexuality through the YJS was still very much in evidence…. In the twenty-first century, it appears that that "pre-crime" risk assessment and referral practices are drawing young women into the youth justice system on account of not of the risks they present to others but because of their own vulnerability and "at-riskiness"' (2012, p 143). Young women also remain marginalised within YOT provision, much of which is geared towards male offending. Groupwork frequently concerns types of offending, such as car crime, where young women have typically little involvement, or the groups are mixed gender and arguably struggle to meet the needs of young women. A survey of YOTs in 2004 found that only 45 out of 113 YOTs responding (40 per cent) had specific programmes for young women, while the majority (56 per cent) catered for young women through generic mixed sex programmes (YJB, 2004a).

Young women face an iniquitous position in relation to custodial sentencing. Whereas fewer young women than young men are sent to custody, their numbers over the decade 1993-2002 rose dramatically and proportionately much more than the numbers of young men (Gelsthorpe and Sharpe, 2006). Nevertheless, the very low numbers has meant that until recently no special provision has been made for them. So young women entering prisons have been placed in establishments which accommodate the full age range, including the most serious adult women offenders, and which have not been able to offer appropriate educational and welfare services.

So what do young people think?

Most accounts of the YJS and its history are written by adults and from an adult perspective. A review by Hazel et al (2002) found little empirical research on young offenders' perceptions of their experiences in the YJS compared to studies about the onset of crime or evaluations of disposals. What literature does exist suggests that young people do not understand the YJS and are confused about procedures at court and elsewhere in the system.

The work by Hazel and colleagues also included qualitative interviews with 37 young offenders. What is noticeable from their accounts is how young people were encouraged to adopt a relatively powerless role at all stages of the YJS and that they learnt to cooperate simply to get through their sentences, whether custodial or community-based (2002). Significantly, in terms of supervision, there were differences in understandings and interpretations between young people and youth justice workers, with interviews revealing high levels of confusion, isolation and resentment, which, in the authors' view, hardly provide a useful basis for changing behaviour among young offenders. Furthermore,

> While they started out feeling in control of their actions, accounts of young offenders became striking in their lack of "agency". Giving in, submitting, becoming marginalised and losing power were central themes, quite contrary to the assumption of engagement and responsibility that the system hopes to achieve. (Hazel et al, 2002, p 14)

Feelings of powerlessness and alienation may be compounded by earlier experiences that then translate into criminal justice processing for particular groups of young people. For instance, research on African Caribbean and Asian young offenders presented in The Children's Society report, *Just justice* (Wilson and Rees, 2006), illustrates how accumulative experiences of differential treatment and suspicion in school and in the wider community provide the backdrop to their behaviours to the point that 'when they try to "keep low" but are further provoked, and when they feel that "enough is enough" and then "go mad" at the system, then it becomes increasingly likely that the law will get broken and that young black people will be criminalised' (Ofutu, 2006, p 46). Black young people in particular express negative views of the police, but antagonism to the police is also reflected in the Hazel et al research (2002) and in Sharpe's (2012) small-scale study of young women in the YJS. These are indicators from relatively small groups of young people rather than substantial and authoritative evidence, but important messages can be drawn from what they say.

Significantly, it appears that these young people experienced most court orders as punitive (Hazel et al, 2002), even where they were intended to be restorative (Sharpe, 2012). However, responses to the individual workers in YOTs and the relationships they built were markedly more positive (Hazel et al, 2002; Hill, 2006).

The role of relationships is worth considering in more depth. In a Scottish study of probationers and ex-prisoners, interviewees (all over the age of 16) discussed the qualities associated with a good relationship and identified these as trust, friendship, openness, caring and an easy-going manner. In contrast, difficult relationships tended to arise when social workers adopted authoritarian, judgemental, rigid or distant approaches (Barry, 2000). Probationers most appreciated practical help and advice, but valued social workers who also took time to get to know them as individuals. Significantly, they highlighted that they themselves needed to be involved in the process of change (Barry, 2000). This seems to resonate with research findings elsewhere (see, for instance, Rex, 1999; Batchelor and McNeill, 2005) and McNeill's conclusion that 'It is vitally important to young people that they are treated as "ordinary human beings", not just as a client (de Winter and Noom, 2003) and as whole people rather than as instances of some "problem" or "disorder"' (2006, p 133).

Barry talks about her interviewees expressing two distinct views about the purpose of supervision. The first group tended to see it as reactive, with the social workers taking the role of monitor of behaviour and compliance with requirements. The other group saw the social worker as more proactive and willing to mentor and to provide opportunity for help and advice about personal and social problems. Attending to the offender's agenda and any personal or practical concerns is important in developing relationships sufficiently close and trusting to engage the offender in the change process, rather than imposing supervision that may be experienced as top-down, alienating or irrelevant (Barry, 2000).

Implications for practice

Youth justice practitioners should be aware of the history of the system that they work in and the historical tensions still playing out in today's youth justice between justice/punishment and welfare orientations. A critical view of more recent development also recognises the impact of managerial or corporatist practices and the confused set of philosophies operating within the system.

Developing new and different approaches to youth justice must start from analyses of the past and the failures of previous attempts to respond to young people's 'problematic' behaviours. In particular, listening to young people's experiences of youth justice interventions shows how disempowering they are and how they fail in their stated intention to engage and to encourage young people to take responsibility.

Research with young people suggests they are more positive about individual practitioners than they are about the YJS. They value practitioners who treat them as individuals and display honesty, openness and willingness to work together. They stress that they must be involved in the process of change, which implies that only too often the necessity for change is experienced as something imposed on them, rather than something they accept and own themselves. This is surely a crucial point to carry into attempts to develop new orientations to practice.

Further reading

Brown, S. (2005) *Understanding youth and crime: Listening to youth?* (2nd edn), Maidenhead: Open University Press.

Muncie, J. (2009) *Youth and crime* (3rd edn), London: Sage Publications.

Smith, R. (2007) *Youth justice: Ideas, policy, practice* (2nd edn), Cullompton: Willan.

FOUR

Youth justice – present and future

The first three chapters have outlined in sequence: understandings of adolescence and youth in the context of late modernity; different ways of accounting for young people's delinquency and what might motivate both their offending behaviours and desistance from crime; and how the YJS in England and Wales has responded to young people who are 'troubled' or 'troublesome' over time. Throughout these discussions, the emphasis has been on the voices of young people and their views as well as the implications for practice, both from the general debates and from the experiences of young people revealed through research.

This chapter picks up historically where the last chapter ended, with the New Labour reforms in place. It examines the impact of these reforms for young people and youth justice practitioners, exploring developments towards the end of New Labour's period in office. It outlines how the youth justice landscape is changing under the coalition government. Despite the promise of the Every Child Matters initiative (DfES, 2004), neither administration has pursued policy responsive to children and young people engaged in offending or anti-social behaviour, continuing instead to see them as a problem to be controlled. Their gaze has also increasingly sought out children and young people 'at risk', largely premised on the much-vaunted predictive capacities of developmental criminology – in Jack Straw's infamous phrase, 'nipping youth offending in the bud' (Home Office, 1997). But how do the youth justice reforms and new legislation measure up against standards of justice, welfare and children's rights?

The final part of the chapter sketches out the principles and values that might underpin an alternative vision for youth justice. However, bearing in mind that we have to live in the real world, it also points to opportunities and possibilities for more positive and child-friendly practice within the present youth justice context, proposing a model of 'youth-centred practice' that underpins the analysis and discussions throughout the remaining chapters.

What works in youth justice

On assuming power in 1997, New Labour expressed its intention to develop policy based on evidence from research and practice rather than on unproven beliefs in the efficacy of either welfare or justice approaches. In terms of youth justice, this was separated into four distinct strands promoted by the YJB.

First, the YJB was keen to adopt and adhere to the messages from the effective practice literature and research that had increasingly influenced probation practice throughout the 1990s. This drew on the findings from meta-analyses of large numbers of research studies and evaluations of interventions with young offenders which identified the broad characteristics of programmes demonstrating a more pronounced effect in reducing the rate of re-offending. Such characteristics included matching the level and intensity of intervention to the assessed seriousness of offending and risk of re-offending; interventions focusing on factors more closely related to offending; programme content and methods that are skills-based, problem-solving and cognitive behavioural in orientation; and responsivity in terms of meeting the learning needs, styles and strategies of young people (for an overview, see McGuire, 1995).

Second, the YJB set out to generate an evidence base of its own, resulting in a substantial programme of empirical research on YJB-sponsored interventions in YOTs. These included evaluations of new court orders and initiatives introduced by New Labour, including parenting programmes, restorative justice projects and cognitive behavioural interventions, as well as referral order schemes (Newburn et al, 2002) and ISSP (YJB, 2004b). Interventions were effectively graded according to the extent and nature of evidence supporting their claims for impact in a 'hierarchy of evidence' ranging from what works, what is promising (some but less robust evidence), what evaluation shows does not work to what is unknown (Stephenson et al, 2011).

Third, in line with actuarial techniques and developments in the probation service, assessments were required to become more structured. A suite of Asset forms was introduced that had to be completed at key points in the criminal justice process, such as bail decisions, sentencing and release from custody. A simplified form, Onset, was later brought into practice in prevention projects for use at the 'pre-offending' stage. The Centre for Criminology at the University of Oxford devised these based on the correlation between psychosocial risk factors and future offending (Case, 2010) within the framework of the risk factor prevention paradigm (RFPP).

Fourth, the YJB commissioned a training programme accredited by higher education institutions, the Professional Certificate in Effective Practice, which was supported by digests of relevant research findings, 'Key Elements of Effective Practice'. These were used as the framework for quality assurance in YOTs in conjunction with key performance indicators focused on youth justice processes and outcomes such as speedy access to assessment of substance misuse, accommodation and education, employment or training placements.

The four strands are all indicative of a growing corporatism within youth justice (Pratt, 1989), with the adoption of pragmatic and managerial approaches to risk management and the sorting of offenders (and 'pre-offenders') into different risk categories. In many senses, looking for evidence from which to develop practice is a welcome development, but its positives in youth justice have been consistently subverted by the inherent tensions in trying to pursue rational decisions and policy-making and at the same time satisfying the demands of a punitive-minded public (Graham, 2010). There is also a danger of policy becoming evidence-based rather than evidence-led, and this manifested itself in what became a highly selective approach to evidence which was then used to justify policy rather than to shape and inform it (Hopkins-Burke, 2008). On this point, Muncie caustically notes that 'clearly considerations of what is deemed to "work" are as much driven by political, economic and ideological imperatives as any adherence to the application of "science"' (2009, p 324).

Phoenix further points to the utilitarian nature of the research used by the YJB and the research it commissioned, which sat largely within the scope of administrative criminology and aimed to produce findings useful to practitioners rather than questioning the nature and purpose of youth justice practice itself:

> The one piece of "evidence" that policy-makers cannot collect, the one question that "what works" research into youth justice practice and policy cannot ask, is arguably the most fundamental question: are justice interventions into young people's lives desirable? (2010a, p 78)

It is also notable that the 'evidence' rarely included the views and experiences of young people themselves (Hine, 2010); not understanding young people's perspectives on offending and what helps them desist necessarily limits the effectiveness of any interventions to reduce offending (Barry, 2009).

Whatever happened to welfare?

As indicated in Chapter Three, welfare concerns have not entirely disappeared in the face of risk management and 'joined-up justice'. The UK must still comply with the UNCRC 1989 which requires in Article 3 that,

> In all actions concerning children, whether undertaken by public or private social welfare institutions, courts of law, administrative bodies or legislative bodies, the best interests of the child shall be a primary consideration.

The UNCRC is supplemented by guidance, for instance, the Standard Minimum Rules for the Administration of Juvenile Justice (the 'Beijing Rules') 1985 and the Directing Principles for the Prevention of Juvenile Delinquency (the 'Riyadh Guidelines') 1990. These emphasise children's rights and, broadly speaking, social education as a response to young people who may be in conflict with the law or vulnerable due to abandonment, neglect, abuse or other social risks.

While the principles expressed in these international conventions and guidelines have been incorporated into children's legislation in the separate UK jurisdictions, in reality they are often superseded by criminal justice imperatives in the case of young offenders. It is significant that Article 3 of the UNCRC states that the welfare of the child should be '*a* primary consideration' rather than '*the* primary consideration' (Whyte, 2009) because this allows priority to be given to other concerns such as punishment and actions to prevent offending, even where this may be detrimental to the well-being of the child or young person. The criminalisation of young people through anti-social behaviour orders (ASBOs) and the increase in the use of custody throughout the New Labour period are obvious, but pertinent, examples (Whyte, 2009).

Practitioners are conscious of their responsibilities for public protection and reducing re-offending within the reformed YJS. This is reinforced through the emphasis on structured risk assessment and on participation in multi-agency initiatives such as Integrated Offender Management (IOM) for persistent offenders and Multi-agency Public Protection Arrangements (MAPPAs) for young people whose offending poses a serious risk of harm to others. Nevertheless, practitioners are still very aware of the welfare needs of the young people in contact with them and of the links between unmet need and being 'at risk'. This might mean being at risk of offending or other problematic behaviours, or being vulnerable to victimisation or abuse. The conflation of different types of risks and vulnerabilities is evident in research. For instance, Phoenix found in her interviews with practitioners that 'instead of assessing young people's "risks", "needs", "criminogenic risks", vulnerabilities or "protective factors", they talked about assessing young people's "at riskiness"' (2009, p 123). This generalised notion of risk underpinned the proposals that YOT workers made to court or was further used as they explained young people's offending.

The New Labour reforms to youth justice placed emphasis on intervention, which it specified should be early and targeted. Sadly, proportionality of interventions seemed to fall by the wayside. Phoenix's (2009) study found that her interviewees were calling for greater YOT involvement, variously justified on the basis of their judgements about young people's (in)ability or (un)willingness to take responsibility for managing their own risks, and on the basis of their belief that they could fill the gaps in welfare provision where the state was not fulfilling its own responsibilities. Sadly, as a consequence, 'highlighting the welfare needs of young lawbreakers can, and does, render them more not less punishable' (2009, p 114).

This may sound contradictory, but greater intervention within a criminal justice context carries with it risk of enforcement action or punitive responses for not responding 'appropriately' to help that is offered. For instance, young people subject to final warnings were referred to the YOT for assessment and intervention, which was technically voluntary, but had implications in that the young person's engagement or otherwise could be reported to a subsequent court hearing should the young person re-offend. Phoenix (2009) refers to this as a return to 'repressive welfarism' redolent of the expansion of the YJS in the 1970s that drew so many more young people into the ambit of the system.

Interestingly, Field's (2007) research into YOTs in Wales found that practitioners still stressed the importance of responding to welfare needs, if only because they were so intimately connected with risk of re-offending. Social workers had made significant accommodations to work with the expectations of what was, at the time of his fieldwork, still a new YJS, coming to terms with earlier intervention and greater use of coercive or compulsive measures, which he refers to as 'qualified voluntarism' (2007, p 316). Field suggests that welfare concerns retained a central but 'reconstituted' place in the priorities of practitioners. However, he also notes that the commitment to community intervention sharply reduced in relation to young people judged to be at the custody threshold due to the seriousness or persistence of their offending. It is inappropriate perhaps to generalise on the basis of relatively small studies, but it does appear, within the context of the reformed YJS, that support and welfare interventions may be offered on a more conditional basis.

The YJS before the New Labour reforms was largely populated by social workers. At that stage probation officers working with young people were also social work trained, so welfare principles and developmental concerns tended to be uppermost and there was a shared antipathy towards the use of custody across the youth justice workforce. Recent research, echoing Field (2007), has indicated that the value base for youth justice is much less coherent, as the workforce has diversified and many more practitioners without a specific professional background have been recruited to YOTs. The result is a markedly greater acceptance of higher rates of imprisonment and readiness to enforce orders (Bateman, 2011). The New Labour reforms may not have produced a more punitive practitioner base per se, but they do seem to have created a climate in which greater degrees of control and surveillance are tolerated, and in which failure to take advantage of opportunities and interventions offered through community disposals can result in more punitive sentencing. In this sense, the long-standing distinctions between the 'deserving' and 'undeserving' are very much alive, alongside notions of young people who can be 'rescued' or 'remoralised' and those who are 'incorrigible' and so ripe for punishment and control. The iniquities arise where the opportunities and interventions on offer are not adequate to address the complex social and personal problems that young people are facing, and they are made subject to sanctions for deficiencies in state support or provisions rather than their own failures.

The end point for New Labour

Smith states boldly that 'youth justice in England and Wales has taken a wrong turn' (2011, p 1), blaming it for being ineffective and at the same time repressive (R. Smith, 2007). Muncie further adds that 'a constellation of the managerial and the authoritarian is one of the defining fault-lines in 21st century youth justice' (2009, p 347).

The previous discussions have uncovered just some of the tensions inherent in what has become an extremely complex and contested policy domain. The YJS has one principle aim – to prevent offending and re-offending – but multiple and often contradictory subsidiary aims. Yet not all the commentary is highly critical. In 2002, for instance, Newburn pointed to the potential of the reforms to create a more coherent YJS, better placed and better funded to deliver services – a positive aspect of the managerialism that is more often regarded as problematic (2002). Hopkins-Burke (2008) later broadly endorsed New Labour's crime control strategy as a 'realistic' response to the crime affecting many communities, while accepting the legitimacy of concerns that it has been too rigorous and has placed too much emphasis on individual responsibility. The YJB itself, unsurprisingly, was up-beat about what it claims are its successes. But how successful has it been? And what terms should be used to judge success?

If we look first at the YJB's own criteria and the targets that it set for the YJS, progress has been mixed. Significant items include:

- an initial rise in first time entrants (FTEs) to the YJS, followed by a reduction between 2005-08 in line with the 5 per cent target;
- partial success in terms of reducing re-offending. This latterly was made part of the Public Service Agreement targets, requiring a reduction of 10 per cent between 2005 and 2011;
- average time from arrest to sentence for persistent young offenders halved by 2002;
- reductions in the use of secure remands but not other remands to custody;
- initial targets on reducing custodial sentencing met but not later, more stretching, targets.
- targets relating to accommodation, substance misuse and mental health assessment, and education, training or work placements proved problematic, although there was some evidence of progress. (Adapted from Graham, 2010, pp 123-5)

This appears to demonstrate improvements in criminal justice processes, but less impact on the wider range of services for young people. The interagency scenario is more complex than the targets initially set seemed to assume. YOT managers do bring their weight to bear within the strategic groups around substance misuse, child and adolescent mental health and children's services generally, but they influence rather than direct decisions and the shaping of service priorities. Moreover, the inability, until recently, to reduce the stubbornly high use of custody testifies to the difficulties of trying to meet a worthy aim in an era dominated by popular punitivism.

So in its own terms, the efficacy of the YJS overseen by the YJB is doubtful (Graham, 2010; Smith, 2011). Towards the end of New Labour's term in office there was a tentative acknowledgement of this and a loosening of the managerialist hold on the system. This was seen in the decision in 2007 to allow the newly created Department for Children, Schools and Families (DCSF) to share responsibility for the YJS with the Ministry of Justice, thus allowing greater alignment with other children's services (Graham, 2010). The proposals in the *Youth crime action plan* (YCAP) (HM Government, 2008) issued the following year, despite frequent references to punishment and enforcement, talked extensively about bringing services together and promoting coherence. The Criminal Justice and Immigration Act 2008 introduced the 'youth conditional caution', a return perhaps to previous strategies of diversion (Graham, 2010), and the youth rehabilitation order. As a generic community order, it also has potential for diversion – this time from custody – as it was intended that it could be used flexibly on multiple sentencing occasions. However, again the tensions in the YJS are apparent, as useful case management guidance supporting implementation of the youth rehabilitation order seemed on the one hand to be less technocratic while the *scaled approach* introduced alongside smacked of rigidity and reduction of practitioner discretion.

Looked at from other angles, the judgements on New Labour's reforms are harsher. The number of young people in custody increased throughout most of New Labour's period in office, approximately 80 per cent of these being young men held in prison service establishments. The population of under-18s in custody peaked in 2008 at over 3,000, but reduced in 2009/10 to an average of 2,416 (Ministry of Justice, 2012a) and has lowered since. However, this does not appear to be because of a softening of government approach but may be connected more strongly with a parallel reduction in FTEs into the YJS (Bateman, 2011). More generally, the formal part of the YJS combined with the activities around anti-social behaviour and prevention has significantly impinged on young people's rights and freedoms. And this impact has not been even, but has weighed more heavily on young people who are socially marginalised, who belong to minority groups or who are lacking in human and social capital (Smith, 2011). The ESYTC has found that young people entering the YJS tend to be 'recycled' by the agencies involved and that being known in the system is more predictive of future system contact than the individual young person's actual behaviours (McAra and McVie, 2007). In a similar vein, Smith (2011) talks about 'recruiting' young people into the YJS, primarily those labelled as socially excluded. An explicitly interventionist YJS brings greater control, surveillance and intrusion into these young people's lives, and so may be doing them an injustice, rather than offering appropriate help and support. Indeed, Smith notes that 'there is considerable evidence now available of the very real "damage" that is done to young people in the name of justice' (2011, p 142).

Youth justice under the coalition

The coalition's attention to date has clearly been on the adult criminal justice system, with proposals to restructure probation services and to open up significant areas of offender intervention to competition under the *Transforming Rehabilitation* agenda (Ministry of Justice, 2012b, 2013a). They have also brought forward sentencing reforms in the Legal Aid, Sentencing and Punishment of Offenders Act (LASPO) 2012, including changes in the provisions for dealing with 'dangerous' offenders introduced by the CJA 2003 and an increase in punitive measures. This is a significant and regrettable retrenchment on the early rhetoric about the 'rehabilitation revolution' and the promise of decarceration (Ministry of Justice, 2010b).

Youth justice reform has so far taken a secondary place, but the pace of change is now beginning to gather speed and four aspects should be noted. The first of these is decentralisation and the push for local autonomy, which allows greater freedoms to determine services at a local level. The YJB, although initially threatened with abolition, is still in place but with a reduced role within the Ministry of Justice and with considerably less autonomy.

The second development is the introduction of payment by results into the YJS, currently being piloted. Although more tentative and small scale than in the adult system, the express intention to create an enhanced role for the private and for the voluntary and community sectors is similar. That in itself could be a welcome development, bringing creativity and innovation, but it may also increase the fragmentation that could take place in any case because of decentralisation (Cavadino et al, 2013). It is also accompanied by an overall reduction of resources and, in a time of austerity that is impinging across the range of social provision, does not augur well for consistent and coherent services responding to the varied needs of young people.

The third aspect of note is the proposal to expand restorative justice (Ministry of Justice, 2010b), which could be hugely beneficial for young people if previous tendencies to use restorative practices to responsibilise young people can be avoided. There seems a reasonable prospect of an increase in restorative justice if only because of its potential for cost savings through reducing expensive court processing (Cavadino et al, 2013).

The fourth development is welcome in the sense that the coalition is keen to promote practitioner discretion and judgement, and as part of this move is replacing the overly prescriptive assessment framework and dismantling other procedures established by New Labour. This creates greater freedoms for practitioners and allows more effective prioritising and targeting of their efforts, although the benefits are inevitably limited in the light of reduced resources.

In general, the coalition has been less keen than New Labour to promote the integration of children's services, so the Every Child Matters initiative has been downgraded and the DCSF replaced with a more traditional Department for Education (DfE). There are indications that the safeguarding agenda will narrow its scope and that social care will assume the responsibility for child protection that had been shared across agencies (Solomon and Blyth, 2012). In a time of austerity, reductions in prevention activity across children's services will also have an impact on the prevention projects associated with YOTs, which under New Labour received regular injections of cash, but are now shrinking back, leaving YOTs to focus on core youth justice services. In summary, the greatest effects on youth justice under the coalition will come from its loosening of centralised controls and the considerable tightening of purse strings, which will act on youth justice services themselves and, crucially, all the other support services and agencies that YOTs rely on.

What else for youth justice?

This is not, on the whole, a hopeful scenario for change, with the Conservative side of the coalition government calling for tougher law and order policy and the prospect of a further lurch to the right. However, in the face of this, it is more important than ever to map out how an alternative YJS might look, because at the very least this opens debate about the values and principles that could be used as starting points. In the New Labour era debates of this kind tended to be buried under the rhetoric of a managerialism that sought pragmatic and technocratic solutions to presenting problems, instead of understandings of their causes.

Recent history has shown that reforming the YJS without challenging the penal–welfare nexus at its heart is likely to perpetuate, rather than resolve, its inherently contradictory and inequitable nature (Smith, 2011). New Labour's reforms introduced structural change requiring interagency cooperation and alignment of services, while still relying on an adversarial court-based model of justice. In effect, what has happened is an increase in the state apparatus for processing (and controlling) young people seen as 'troubled 'or 'troublesome'. The opportunities for them to meaningfully participate are limited: even the potential of the young offender panels (YOPs) dealing with referral orders has not been exploited. This is not to deny the good work that undoubtedly does take place, but points to the prescriptions and rules that have constrained practice and reinforced the power of professionals over young people's lives.

Moving towards a more positive YJS capable of responding to children and young people in ways appropriate to their age and development would mean as preconditions: restricting the scope of its activities; reducing the disciplinary aspects of the machinery dealing with anti-social behaviour; and a commitment to decarceration. From the messages of the previous three chapters and the discussions here about the New Labour reforms, five key principles emerge and five foundations for practice derived from them.

The principles are:

- *Children's rights:* practice, and the frameworks within which practice is developed, should be directed by the principles and standards outlined in the UNCRC (Whyte, 2009), and its affirmation that children are different from adults (Archard, 2007). This should give primacy to the child's best interests and to the promotion of positive rights, encouraging participation and developing citizenship.
- *Early help:* support and interventions should be delivered at an early age or early stage of difficulties through services that are accessible and non-stigmatising.
- *Social education:* approaches used should encourage the development of pro-social interactions and behaviours, collaborative working with young people and sensitivity to what might help them desist.

- *Inclusion and integration:* practices should focus on children and young people being positively engaged within their communities and institutions such as schools, and promote understanding and involvement of 'interested parties'.
- *Wide evidence base for practice:* practice should be informed by messages from research, including qualitative data and studies exploring the views and experiences of young people. Research findings should be regarded critically and not treated as though they are a 'formula that can be applied in any routinised way to children and young people' (Whyte, 2009, p 45). Evaluation should be an integral part of interventions and service delivery, providing a reflective learning loop.

These are broad principles that do not dictate the details of what a future youth justice system might look like, but the following five foundations for practice might begin to suggest the outlines of the basic architecture (McAra, 2010):

- *Participatory problem-solving:* conflicts should be approached in a problem-solving way at the lowest appropriate level and encourage the involvement of all 'interested parties'. This could, but would not necessarily, include restorative justice interventions and may suggest the development of different sorts of meetings or hearings as the venues for deliberations and determining future actions.
- *Diversion from the formal YJS:* wherever possible children and young people should be diverted from formal processing in the YJS. This is of particular importance for children and young people in public care. Welfare and other social needs should be addressed by appropriate services, not within the YJS, and routes to relevant services and resources should be developed.
- *Prevention not punishment:* youth justice sentencing and interventions should not have punishment as a purpose (Smith, 2011) but should be focused on working with the young people and their families to enable them to desist from crime. The YJS should also be alert to any unintended punitive impacts and take appropriate actions to redress.
- *Proportionality:* the level of intervention and of any controls and constraints put in place should be proportionate to assessed risk of harm and re-offending.
- *Community not custody:* except in exceptional circumstances, intervention should take place in community not custodial or other residential settings.

If brought into operation, these principles would have consequences not just for the YJS itself and sentencing in the courts, but would involve the span of children's services. The vision is aspirational and would involve a significant change in orientation and thinking about children and young people. Essentially it advocates for a more constructive approach that seeks to avoid labelling and criminalising young people and to work with them to access rights and to build non-offending futures.

Changes in practice

The section above has outlined what would be radical new departures for youth justice. It is critical for those working in the YJS to have a sense of what might be and how youth justice structures and practices could develop in a positive direction. The underpinning values of belief in young people, understanding them as social actors and commitment to social justice and rights, give purpose and direct how this vision might be flashed out in practice.

These values may also provide a source of resistance to the authoritarian and technocratic YJS that exists today. Certain matters are beyond the influence of the individual practitioner or operations manager – the legal provisions or multi-agency partnerships in place, for instance. However, the way that practice is conducted even within the constraints of the current YJS – a system in flux in any case – is amenable to individual approaches and professional use of discretion. And practice can be developed in ways consistent with these values and supportive of desistance.

The question for those involved in youth justice is, what sort of practice paradigm could best give expression to the values, principles and understandings laid out in this text? It may be helpful to illustrate one possible framework and then to sketch out how this might appear in practice.

The base of this triangle (see Figure 4.1) refers to rights and risks, which form the foundations of practice and sit alongside each other. This model for youth-centred practice sees young people as moral agents and the bearers of rights, not

Figure 4.1: A model for youth-centred practice

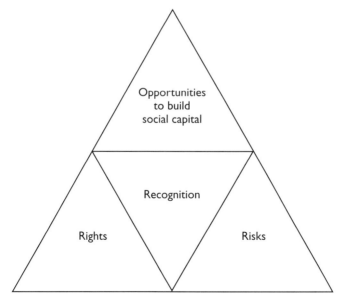

just entitlements, so it moves beyond a welfare approach focused on needs. The UNCRC sets out three related rights:

- To the provision of services;
- To protection and care; and
- To participate in society and decision-making at both political and individual level. (Bell, 2011, p 55)

Youth-centred practice should have regard to rights and should draw on advocacy and related skills to ensure that young people are able to access these rights, even – perhaps especially – in custodial settings. This is not necessarily straightforward as there may be tensions and contradictions between rights relating to protection and those relating to participation and choice (Archard, 2007). Moreover, rights and the exercise of agency are dependent on the age and maturity of the young person and are inextricably bound up with the moral rights of parents to care for and to raise their child. Relatedly, Connolly and Ward comment that:

> From a developmental perspective, it is important that young people who offend are able to engage in increasingly adult-like processes that reinforce accountability and restoration, while at the same time being protected from the full force of the law in recognition of their special status under UNCRC as young offenders with special rights (Article 17 UNCRC). Rights-based youth justice solutions have the capacity to provide social-structural resources that can accommodate a young person's maturing capacity for agency and its concomitant attribute – responsibility – while at the same time recognising that young people, by virtue of their relative immaturity, have special needs that must also be considered. (2008, p 75)

This inherently involves complex judgements and decision-making about how much responsibility a young person could appropriately take for his or her behaviours, and what sort of responsibilities and duties others have towards the young person. Making a young person overly accountable in a context where the local authority, schools and others are not being held accountable for their services or duty to care appropriately for the young person – either currently or historically – is unlikely to encourage positive change. Neither is placing undue responsibility on parents whilst denying them the economic and social structure to support them in the difficult task of parenting. That said, not enabling or encouraging a young person to take appropriate responsibility is also self-defeating and, in fact, may represent missed opportunities to grow and to receive recognition for more adult-like behaviours.

Bringing a focus on rights into practice in this way involves key skills around advocacy, brokerage and negotiation. Yet rights should not be treated as entirely separate from risks, as consideration for the rights of all parties should be integral to responses to risk. Clearly, within this framework, the young person's rights to opportunities, support and services to promote growth and development are critical and limits placed on his or her freedoms should be at the minimum level necessary to protect the rights and freedoms of others. In doing this, the experiences of victims or communities affected by crime or anti-social behaviour should not be ignored. Yet, at the same time, attending to their rights to peace, stability and so on should not mean completely negating the rights of young people in some zero-sum approach (Hudson, 2003). In fact, diminishing the rights of young people who break the law in unfair and disproportionate ways is counter-productive and, from a social learning perspective, does not model or encourage future good citizenship and respect for others.

Attention should be paid to achieving an appropriate balance between the rights of young people to protection and participation in society on the one hand, and actions to contain or to reduce risk on the other. Where possible, the reasons for decisions should be explained to the young person, although how this is approached will depend on maturity and understanding, taking into account any other factors such as learning disability or English being the young person's second language. It is important not to impose conditions and controls that the young person may experience as arbitrary and unrelated to what he or she has done. Discussions and negotiations may be carefully judged but, however this is achieved, the young person – and, where appropriate, parents or carers – should be engaged in jointly identifying and agreeing actions to reduce risk. In instances where the level of risk of harm is higher, there may be elements that are non-negotiable, such as a curfew or strict reporting restrictions imposed by the court. The practitioner should be clear about what can be flexible and what elements of negotiation the young person has, and where the practitioner's boundaries lie, in line with the principles and practices of pro-social modelling (Cherry, 2005; Trotter, 2006). The setting of a supervision plan or referral order contract, for example, should provide an opportunity for honest explanation and negotiation, and in this process 'care should be taken to ensure that a shared understanding has been reached, and in a language that is clear, explicit and accessible, with sufficient information for the task at hand' (Trevithick, 2012, p 259).

A common agreement may not be reached in every case and the young person (and parents) may not accept the conditions under which he or she is supervised. In these circumstances it is helpful to acknowledge feelings while still being firm about what is required of the young person. This is important in terms of establishing the legitimacy of the working relationship and, potentially, a basis of honesty. Whereas in the first instance, compliance may be motivated by not wanting to return to court or avoiding further sanctions, a positive supervisory relationship, over time, may encourage a more fundamental adoption of pro-social attitudes and behaviours (Seymour, 2013). This is termed *normative compliance* (Bottoms, 2001) and is associated with attachment to key individuals providing positive role models and acceptance of social norms.

Relationships, then, may be significant in terms of engagement and working towards meaningful, rather than just outward compliance. In desistance terms they also assume significance within the recognition aspect of the youth-centred practice model. In this context they might refer to recognition of:

- the young person's strengths and competences;
- the young person's achievement of change or personal goals;
- growing maturity, outlook and identity; or
- developments in social circumstances and relationships (such as a young person sustaining a work placement and becoming part of a team).

At the outset, encouraging a young person to understand and to develop his or her capacities and to build towards the future may hold more promise than focusing on past behaviours and deficits (although analysis of offending and triggers for offending have their place too). Later in the supervision process, attention may turn to endorsing or validating positive changes that a young person has made and moves to create a non-offending identity. As Barry's (2006) research (see Chapter Two, this volume) discovered, in the initial stages trying to stop offending or drug use can be extremely difficult and has few pay-offs. She talks about the amount of determination and resolve shown by the young people she interviewed. Practitioners may be well placed to support and help young people sustain their efforts to desist, recognising and praising the changes they are making, even small changes. They may also be able to help the young person appreciate that desistance is an uncertain process and that lapses are normal, not a sign of failure. Finally, practitioners may be able to facilitate opportunities for young people to gain wider social recognition through, for instance, volunteering, education or training, or involvement in creative or campaigning projects. These all provide a means of enabling young people who may be depleted in positive forms of capital to accumulate the sorts of capital that might help them progress in key transitions.

Although building capital may begin within the cluster of services and activities associated with prevention projects, YOTs or social care, the apex of the practice triangle looks outwards. Ultimately, young people moving towards a non-offending adult identity must be able to gather and to use different forms of capital and to engage with the wider institutions of society. To some extent this is a reciprocal process. The literature around desistance in adults talks about *generative activity* (see, for instance, Maruna, 2001) which enables individuals to pay back to society and to gain self-worth that feeds into the development of a reconstituted identity. Generative activity may feature in a different way for young people with less entrenched patterns of offending than the long-term offenders involved in research by Maruna and others. Nevertheless, where young people find openings that allow them to make positive contributions, to receive recognition and develop reciprocity in relationships (Jones, 2009) these can powerfully reinforce change and promote integration. These could include activities such as peer mentoring or sports coaching, or more generally involvement in a faith community, voluntary project or even assisting family members.

Social and other forms of capital are important for young people who make strategic decisions about their lives, the social groups they mix with and activities they commit to, with regard to cost and benefits in terms of capital and their sense of self. They are active in creating their own lives within the constraints that they experience. For those young people coming into the ambit of youth justice, the scope for choice and resources to allow them to pursue options are typically limited. A refreshed orientation to practice could ensure that these young people are able to envisage more positive futures and empowered to follow their chosen pathway, rather than being stuck with a decreasing range of life choices that lead to further criminalisation and exclusion.

Implications for practice

The New Labour reforms to the YJS brought benefits in terms of resources and more coherent structures for youth justice practice. However, their managerial approach and emphasis on intervention caused many more young people to be caught up in the net of justice provision for a confused range of purposes, including control, punishment, restoration, rehabilitation, reintegration, enforcement and risk management. The indications are that the reforms did not create a more coherent and unified set of values and aims for youth justice activity.

Under the coalition, the wide net of youth justice is reducing, if only because of shrinking resources. This may mean that we see less of the over-intervention that can too readily tip over into 'repressive welfarism' (Phoenix, 2009), but the direction of the present government is sadly no more child-friendly and no less punitive in practice.

In the face of developments under two administrations, those involved in the YJS need to have a sense of what the best, the most responsive, youth justice might look like – a vision that is both aspirational and inspirational. For too long, approaches have been dominated by pragmatic and technical 'what works' logics, and it is time to turn to values, principles and basic beliefs about young people and their capacities and to consider how these might shape practice.

At the same time, it is necessary to be realistic about the contexts in which youth justice operates and what practitioners and operations managers may be able to change within their sphere of influence. There is space to explore different orientations to practice, particularly as the present government is relaxing prescriptions and directives. The model for youth-centred practice is one constructive and balanced approach that recognises young people's rights, risks, strengths and search for capital, seeking to work with them through their transitions and towards meaningful desistance. This will be a theme throughout each of the chapters in this book.

Further reading

Barry, M. and McNeill, F. (eds) (2009) *Youth offending and youth justice*, London: Jessica Kingsley Publishers.

Smith, R. (2011) *Doing justice to young people: Youth crime and social justice*, Abingdon: Willan.

Whyte, B. (2009) *Youth justice in practice: Making a difference*, Bristol: The Policy Press.

Wood, J. and Hine, J. (eds) (2009) *Work with young people*, London: Sage Publications.

Section 2

ISSUES FOR YOUNG PEOPLE

FIVE

The transition from school to work

Chapter One outlined the notion of transitions – the social transformations that young people make on their journey to independence and 'adult' responsibilities. There has always been some variation, but transitions today are even less likely to take a straightforward and linear course. Young people's plans and aspirations are shaped by the labour market and, specifically in the UK, the move from manufacturing and industry to more flexible employment, for example, in the service and retail sectors. So there are now more choices, but involving greater insecurity and risks.

Tony Blair described his early priorities as Prime Minster as 'education, education, education'. In this he signalled the primacy of education and training under New Labour as a means of tackling social marginalisation and exclusion. Their initial focus was on young adults through the New Deal for Young People (NDYP) and, related to this, the New Deal for Lone Parents. However, the younger age group quickly came under the spotlight with initiatives on truancy, school exclusions and training provision for 16- and 17-year-olds, as well as a reshaping of the 14-19 Curriculum. At the same time, new forms of guidance and support – both targeted and universal – became available through the Connexions Service.

New Labour policy had two main facets: it concentrated on increasing employability rather than job creation itself and it worked to provide equality of opportunity rather than reducing social inequalities. In this respect, responsibility was again placed on the individual to actively make choices, to pursue opportunities and so to reap the benefits, particularly the benefits that were seen to accrue in terms of social inclusion. But inclusion is not inevitable: for some young people the available employment excludes even further when it is insecure, exploitative or isolating due to long or unsocial hours. The coalition government is following in much the same vein but is working in worse economic circumstances and in a climate of increased animosity towards benefit claimants, heightening geographical and social disparities.

This chapter explores aspects of the school to work transition in the present social and economic context, evaluating the impact of the New Labour and now the coalition government's responses to the changing world of work and the extension of periods in training and education.

Post-16 choices

At one time the majority of young people would leave full-time education and enter employment, but now only a small minority does so. As early as 1999, the newly formed Social Exclusion Unit (SEU) noted that the 23 per cent of 16-year-olds in full-time work in 1989 had dropped to only 7 per cent by 1997 (SEU, 1999). And the trend has continued in that direction, with more young people staying in education and often combining education and part-time employment.

This reflects the shifting nature of the labour market and is also reflected in the way that young people are thought about and discussed. Graham tellingly comments that 'the needs of the adult world change from time to time. Then the adult world changes its mind about the sort of adolescents it needs' (2004, p 41). This means that in periods where there is demand for young people's contribution to the workforce or in warfare, they are more likely to be constructed as responsible and capable, and this will be reflected in the discourse from politicians and policy-makers and in the media. Conversely, when not required in the labour market, they are more often constructed as adults-in-the-making and in need of guidance and tutelage, rather than as fully competent in the present.

The following figures illustrate the shifts in post-16 activities for 16- to 17-year-olds over the past 25 years (see www.education.gov.uk), emphasising the reduction in employment in favour of education. In Figure 5.1, the economically inactive category includes young people who are ill or who have caring responsibilities.

There has been a significant increase in the numbers in full-time education whose labour market status is classified as unemployed (these young people are seeking work and are available for work, although studying in the meantime) (see Figure 5.2).

Figure 5.1: Trends in education, employment and training, 1985-2010

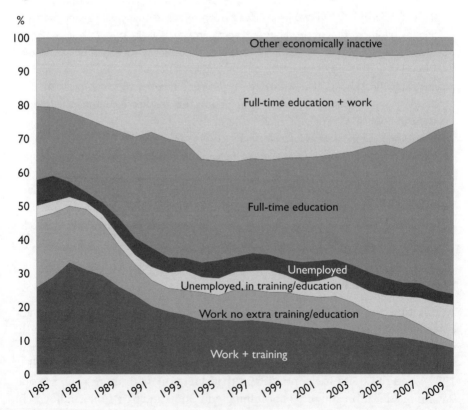

Figure 5.2: Percentage of 16- to 17-year-olds in full-time education, 1985-2010

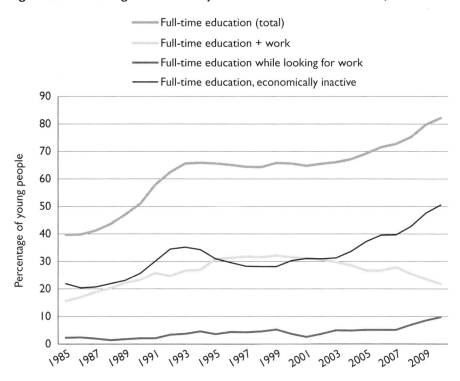

The proportion of young people in employment has dropped sharply over this 25-year period, although many are working to gain an income while in full-time education.

It is also striking that the 20.7 per cent of young people who were in employment with no additional training component in 1985 had reduced to 2 per cent by 2010 (see Figure 5.3).

Considering a wider age group of 16- to 24-year-olds, data from the Labour Force Survey covering eight quarters of 2008-09 shows that:

- the total population in this age group was 7.3 million;
- two thirds were economically active, that is, working or available for work, and of these, roughly one in six was unemployed;
- 0.934 million young people were studying full time and also working, while twice that number were studying and neither working nor looking for work (25 per cent of the age group);
- of the remaining 8.3 per cent of young people who were economically inactive, 300,000 (4.1 per cent) were carers and 100,000 (1.4 per cent) were long-term sick. (Adapted from UK Commission for Employment and Skills, 2011)

So the changes are marked and transitions are consequently lengthier and more diverse, with extended periods in education and movements between different

Figure 5.3: Percentage of 16- to 17-year-olds in employment (excluding those also in full-time education), 1985-2010

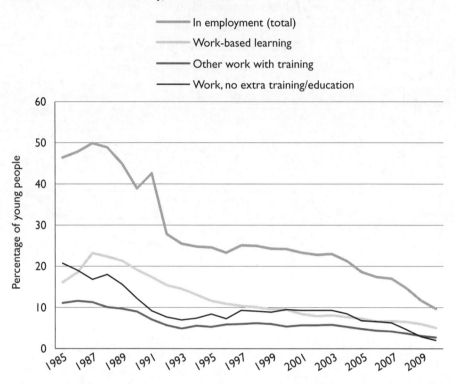

forms of employment and learning. Employment opportunities were restructured following the collapse of the youth labour market in the 1980s, and policy since has focused on expanding training, increasing flexibility and reducing labour costs (Furlong and Cartmel, 2007). But experiences are not consistent, and access to post-16 education and work-based training has remained highly stratified according to class, gender and ethnicity. Despite the expansion in education and training for young people, existing social disadvantages still persist (Furlong and Cartmel, 2007). In fact, young people from less advantaged families face a new set of disadvantages because of their position at the margins of the labour market, and may find themselves 'cycling' between insecure jobs and benefits well into adulthood (Ray et al, 2010; Shildrick et al, 2012). In contrast, the prospects for those who stay in post-16 education and gain higher level skills and qualifications are much brighter, reinforcing and deepening social divisions (Jones, 2002).

Analysts have suggested that the employment market has grown in a hour glass fashion, with expansion in jobs at the well-paid, high-skill end of the market and low-skill casualised work at the bottom, but a real squeeze in the middle-range skilled manual, trade and other jobs (Wolf, 2011). The effect is intense competition at the bottom end of the job market. One interesting study (Tunstall et al, 2012) investigated what this might mean in terms of searching for work, adopting an innovative mixed methodology that included creating fictional identities and applying in all for more than 2,000 job vacancies in three local labour markets. The jobs chosen were in sectors such as sales, security, cleaning and office administration – many part-time or with non-standard hours. The 'dummy candidates' were well qualified for the positions, but even so on average it took four applications to get a positive response (interview or request for more information); weaker candidates are likely to face even more of an uphill struggle. The research highlighted the need to be well informed about the local labour market, as vacancies are often filled in astonishingly short spaces of time, disadvantaging those without access to the internet. Significantly, employers tended to prefer experience over formal qualifications and looked for personal characteristics such as reliability and social skills – a real barrier for those who have yet to build up a work history.

Opportunities for all?

The Inventing Adulthoods study (Henderson et al, 2007) introduced in Chapter One explored the significance of work for young people in their mid teens, many of whom already had experience of part-time paid employment. The researchers found that young people attached a range of different meanings to paid work which could represent: a way to learn about the adult world and broaden social horizons; an opportunity to develop confidence and authority; increased independence; or simply a chance to make new friends. So work opportunities are important for young people in terms of mastering skills and growing socially, taking steps towards adulthood.

   Later interviews explored the sources of support they might need in relation to education and work, at that stage mainly family members, who provided financial, emotional and other sorts of help as well as access to networks and contacts. The authors' analysis is revealing:

> The examples of the well-networked in our sample tended to be middle-class young people, although in a range of circumstances. They also tended to be flexible and their networks spanned different age groups and communities – local, family, educational, work, leisure – and a range of activities from bell-ringing to volunteering. These types of networks can be theorised in terms of "weak ties" and "bridging social capital" as they enable an individual to access resources and opportunities beyond those of their immediate environment and relationships. (Henderson et al, 2007, p 53)

Many of the working-class young people were also well networked and had resources that could facilitate social mobility, but some tended to have 'strong ties' and 'bonding social capital': their networks linked them into family, community and neighbourhood, rather than creating wider contacts and opportunities for education and work, and they had fewer resources to draw on. The authors comment how some young people who are better supported – often from the middle class – could find ways of exploiting the potential of part-time work through building networks and accessing the sorts of work experience that could enhance CVs and provide opportunities for gap years and future employment. In contrast,

> Others have to be reflexive in order to survive. They are likely to have the wrong kind of part time jobs (that interfere with their ability to study) and the wrong kind of work experience that reconfirms the limits of their social worlds and those of their parents. (Henderson et al, 2007, p 54)

So it is not just participation in education or work that is important; the nature and the quality of education and work is also significant (MacDonald and Marsh, 2005). Typically the development of fixed work-related identities is postponed as young people choose pathways or navigate a course through different options on their route to adulthood (Vaughan, 2003). But the experiences they have along the way help constitute their sense of self and the possibilities open to them, and for some individuals these will reinforce negative identities and blockages.

It is worth considering the role of education in opening up opportunities. First, there is strong evidence to suggest that educational qualifications per se are not a guarantee of secure and meaningful employment (Shildrick et al, 2012). So while some young people can take the 'high road' to educational and employment success, 'for many others these extended educational transitions are now the low road to lower-quality, lower paid jobs nearer the bottom of the labour market' (Shildrick et al, 2012, p 197). Second, academic qualifications have been privileged over practical learning, with an emphasis in schools on GCSE performance and an explicit aim to get 50 per cent of young people participating in university education. Although that aim was never reached, it does clearly beg the question of what happens to 'the forgotten half' (Birdwell et al, 2011). Third, the influential Wolf report (2011) is highly critical of the provision for vocational education, which it found too confusing and complex and which offers too many young people low-level qualifications which have little currency in the job market. Moreover, the courses on offer are poorly matched to the needs of employers.

The array of options facing young people is truly bewildering. One New Zealand study (Vaughan and Roberts, 2007) analysed the interplay between the choices young people make and their identity by following 114 young people's progress in the period after leaving secondary school in the context of a structured framework of post-school pathways. They found that young people were not only interested in outcomes: indeed 'chosen pathways and career options are valued as much, and sometimes more, for what they can *do for* the young person than for what they *are* in terms of discipline or industry content' (2007, p 101). They saw that young people orientate themselves in diverse ways in relation to exploration and the desire for security, finding four distinct clusters among their interviewees:

- *Hopeful reactors:* these young people were relatively passive in terms of their choices but were generally determined to make the best of the options available to them. Their planning was largely short term, although they were motivated by the chance to succeed in a way they had been unable to do at school and by wanting to avoid a variety of negative outcomes. In this sense, they were very aware of risks.
- *Passion-honers:* the young people in this largest group had tended to engage more in planning and had drawn on their contacts and resources to help them make sense of the choices available. They actively crafted their pathways and had a clear sense of their desired destination.
- *Anxious seekers:* this was quite an apprehensive group, unsure about their options and frequently changing pathways. Security was more important than exploration and most were keen to have back-up plans and to 'bank' qualifications.
- *Confident explorers:* these young people were the most reflexive and most likely to create the 'choice biography', being bold in making 'identity investments' (Hollway and Jefferson, 2000) which were often more important than the content of their work, training or study. They were imaginative in making links between different experiences and areas of knowledge and skills. (Adapted from Vaughan and Roberts, 2007)

This illustrates how young people vary in their willingness or capacity to make choices and to be proactive in creating and pursuing options. To some extent this will depend on individual characteristics and personality traits, but it is also affected by the young person's social circumstances, resources and networks, and by the cultural influences and norms in his or her environment. Certainly in terms of education, it is clearly the case that:

> Policy only creates the opportunities. What is critical is the way that middle class parents are able to mobilise their personal and collective economic, social and cultural capital to give their children advantages within the education system. (France, 2007, p 89)

And this creates models of behaviour and expectations for young people as they reach the stage where they are increasingly beginning to take more control themselves, and to deploy their own sources of capital. Thus structural inequalities are reproduced, rather than broken down – an essential contradiction within New Labour policy that explicitly looked to education and work to reduce inequalities and social marginalisation.

Social exclusion to the fore

Why was social exclusion so important for New Labour? And why were education and employment identified as the means of tackling exclusion? Broadly speaking recent social policy had tended to follow one or another of the *grand narratives* associated with the market (neoliberalism), social redistribution (Marxism/ socialism) or social democracy in the centre ground. However, by the time New Labour came to office these were judged inadequate to deal with the varied and complex demands of late modernity (Cook, 2006). New Labour sought a more flexible and reflexive approach that they framed as the Third Way. This was an attempt to provide an invigorated form of social democracy with new forms of governance, fewer services provided directly by the state, enhanced roles for the voluntary and community sectors and a focus on civil renewal (Rodger, 2008).

In many ways the Third Way was based on pragmatism rather than ideology, and this means that it tended to talk about actions and approaches – 'what counts is what works' – not necessarily the values and assumptions that underpinned it. Nevertheless, its rhetoric was deeply value-laden, particularly in its emphasis on communitarian thinking and the coupling of *rights* and *responsibilities* (explored further in Chapters Ten and Sixteen). It also explicitly promoted a particular notion about social justice delivered through equality of opportunity rather than equality of income and resources, so brushing aside questions of redistribution (Cook, 2006). And the opportunities in question were predominantly related to work and efforts through education or training to enhance employability, which was seen to equate with social inclusion (Cook, 2006).

Social exclusion itself is a slippery concept, which perhaps explains its utility in comparison to poverty or relative disadvantage. The definition offered by the SEU describes it as:

> A shorthand label for what can happen when individuals or areas suffer from a combination of linked problems such as unemployment, poor skills, low income, poor housing, high crime environments, bad health and family breakdown. (SEU, 1998, p 1)

The concept is therefore broader than just income poverty and refers to complex and interrelated social processes that together limit participation in society, so it can be applied both to individuals and to communities or neighbourhoods. Properly used it is capable of recognising degrees of exclusion and inability to participate, rather than denoting clear divisions between the included and the excluded (MacDonald and Marsh, 2005). However, it is inherently problematic in neglecting the differences among the 'included' – not least in terms of disparities in income between the very rich and others – and in treating the 'excluded' as pathological, ignoring the real concerns about the endemic nature of inequality and poverty in our society.

Analysing the way that social inclusion/exclusion is talked about is instructive. Levitas (2005) has identified three broad discourses, each with its own understanding of exclusion and proposed solutions. The redistributionist discourse (RED) emphasises poverty as a prime cause of exclusion and inability to participate in society. It seeks to address inequalities in social, political and cultural aspects of citizenship as well as material wealth. The moral underclass discourse (MUD) in contrast sees the morals and behaviours of the socially excluded as qualitatively different from the mainstream majority. It has no interest in the structures of wider society and views reliance on state benefits and 'welfare dependency' as deeply problematic. The social integrationist discourse (SID) that was popular with New Labour sees participation in paid work as the key to social inclusion, but rather simplistically assumes that all paid work is good. It tends to neglect questions about the inequalities between paid workers and who benefits most from productivity and wealth creation. It is also ambivalent about recognising the value of unpaid work, and how parenting and volunteering, for instance, make a vital contribution to the social organisation of labour. In this respect, it is a highly gendered discourse.

In essence, the three discourses regard the socially excluded as having different problems and deficits, as Levitas summarises:

> To oversimplify, in RED they have no money, in SID they have no work, and in MUD they have no morals. (2005, p 27)

'Old' Labour tended to subscribe to a social democratic model, drawing on redistributive discourses and policy prescriptions. Seeking to distance itself from this legacy while still appealing to its traditional supporters, New Labour talked more explicitly in SID mode, and promoted the notion of the 'stakeholder society' in which everyone has an interest. But they increasingly used the language of opportunity and responsibility to shift the emphasis from the labour market and employment to the work-related skills and employability of the potential workforce. Unemployment was reconstructed not as a structural societal problem but as an individual failure on the part of those not seeking work or ensuring that they were fit for the work opportunities available (Levitas, 2005). The emphasis was thus placed firmly on the supply side of the equation, leaving aside important questions about employment and employees' rights and conditions (Ray et al, 2010).

The SEU was established early in New Labour's first term of office and given a brief to develop strands of work under a framework of four broad goals, which were:

- lower long-term unemployment and worklessness
- less crime
- better health
- better qualifications.

From the outset this evidenced a blurring of social and criminal justice policy (Cook, 2006), particularly in conflating the issues about economic marginalisation and high crime rates within neighbourhoods. Among the first priorities were truancy and school exclusion, and in this and subsequent work there started to be a drift from SID into MUD (Levitas, 2005). A similar slide also permeated New Labour rhetoric throughout its first term of office in relation to anti-social behaviour (Rodger, 2008), teenage pregnancy, parenting and homelessness (Dobrowsky, 2002). Unemployed young people and those not engaged in education or training – pejoratively referred to first as Status Zer0 and then NEETs (Furlong, 2006) – became a special focus of concern, with a consequent drive to encourage, if not to coerce, participation.

The social investment state

New Labour was strenuous in its attempts to disassociate itself from previous 'tax and spend' policies and to create a new post-welfare settlement. Within the context of the Third Way, this was framed as the 'social investment state', highly interventionist but not primarily orientated on welfare. Its spending was targeted and strategic, in relation to children and young people being focused on activities and services that would enhance their potential as future citizens, workers and consumers. And superficially this was an attractive argument, but it also contains an underlying coercive message, as Dobrowsky notes:

> It is hard to disagree with the fact that children need to get an education or work at learning skills for the market. At the same time, children reinforce parents' obligations to find paid work. Parents have a duty to their children to look after their health and welfare, to give them good quality education, and so they should be out working as providers ... the social investment state can ensure that children can avoid life on benefit because opportunities provided now will shape their life chances in the future. (2002, p 51)

Attempts to provide choices and opportunities for training and education sit firmly within a SID approach, but such offers are not unconditional, and the sanctions and social controls that are threatened in the event of non-participation are more redolent of MUD. Social investment can thus be at the same time generous, moralistic and deeply normative in its impulses.

One major social investment initiative was the creation of the Connexions Service that was rolled out from 2001 to replace a careers guidance framework that was acknowledged to be patchy and inconsistent (Yates, 2009). It had two key functions – participation in appropriate learning for all young people and a specific brief for those young people most at risk of social exclusion. The service it offered was therefore universal and targeted, aiming to 'mop up, re-engage and re-orientate those who fall by the wayside' (MacDonald and Marsh, 2005, p 215). However, balancing universal and targeted provision proved hard to manage within schools and other institutional structures where it had to establish its role and a distinct professional identity for its personal advisers (PAs) (Stephenson, 2007; Birdwell et al, 2011).

While work delivered by Connexions PAs often focused on complex areas of young people's lives, its success or failure was judged on performance indicators relating to the movement of young people from school to education, employment or training post-16 rather than 'softer' or more diverse outcomes. Connexions partnerships were given targets to reduce the population of young people in their area who were NEET, thus directing their attention in certain directions which may not have met the developmental or other needs of the young people with whom they were working (Yates, 2009). Levitas (2005, p 198) moreover criticises the PA system for its 'manipulative' approach to changing individuals' behaviours and to entry onto welfare to work schemes.

Within its targeted remit, Connexions has worked closely with YOTs to support and guide young people within the YJS. While there are benevolent aspects to these working relationships, there is also a utilitarian purpose in terms of reducing the numbers of young people offending or engaged in anti-social behaviour through their participation in education or other activities to increase employability (Rodger, 2008). From critical perspectives, the monitoring and tracking functions of Connexions could be seen as a further disciplinary and controlling mechanism for a 'problematic' population, particularly where allied to the YJS. Conversely, it could be viewed as providing individualised solutions for a diverse group of young people (Furlong, 2006). Whichever is the case, difficulties arise because of the focus on reducing the numbers of NEETs and the definition of NEET itself. Furlong (2006) argues that is, on the one hand, too wide, drawing in a heterogeneous population of young people and shifting attention from especially vulnerable groups, while on the other hand, it is too narrow in ignoring the precarious position of many young people in the labour market.

Connexions works with the 13-19 age range, originally as an independent organisation but now absorbed into local authority structures. NDYP, explored in the next section, was another early New Labour initiative for 18- to 24-year-olds out of work for at least six months, involving non-negotiable guidance and support to secure entry to work or training.

Transitions and the New Deal

A series of research studies on Teesside has examined in depth the transition experiences of young people in an area of extreme economic marginalisation. Work was once plentiful, but concentrated in the steel and chemical industries and heavy engineering; the loss of jobs in ICI and British Steel in the 1980s, alongside reductions in construction and manufacturing, was therefore devastating, particularly for young men, as the economy was inevitably – and painfully – restructured (MacDonald and Marsh, 2005). From being vibrant and economically successful, the area referred to in this research as 'East Kelby' rapidly changed character, falling into decline so that by the time the research started towards the turn of the century, it had the highest concentration of deprived wards in the country and all the interrelated problems associated with social exclusion

(MacDonald and Marsh, 2005). In the mid-1990s, East Kelby had also been highly vulnerable during the second wave of heroin outbreaks, when the social housing estates were flooded with cheap smokeable heroin (MacDonald et al, 2011).

Murray (1994), one of the chief proponents of the underclass theory, cited Teesside as support for his theory, largely on the basis of high numbers of births outside marriage, households headed by lone parents, teenage pregnancy and families reliant on welfare benefits across the area, but featuring at dramatic levels in particular neighbourhoods (MacDonald and Marsh, 2005). The Disconnected Youth? study involved participant observation and qualitative biographical interviews with a purposive sample of 88 young people between the ages of 15 and roughly 25 (at second interview). What is notable is how little of the culture of welfare dependency and asocial (if not anti-social) attitudes that the MUD discourse attributes to such communities was evident. In fact in this and the follow-up study, Poor Transitions (Webster et al, 2004), there was an enduring attachment to conventional notions of full-time secure employment. This was further reinforced when some of the same sample group were contacted again as part of a later study (Shildrick et al, 2012).

Even among those young people who had fared better at school and were closest to the labour market, there were:

> Difficult, extended transitions to paid employment. Those who had accessed jobs often described them as being poor quality, temporary and exploitative. Employment was usually intermittent and low-waged. One of our most striking findings is the durability of these informants' strong attachment to work, and the persistence of their search for it, in contexts where their aspirations were rarely met ... most recognised that their experiences had been of "dead-end" jobs that did not lead to career progression. (Webster et al, 2004, p 6)

What was seen was not detachment from the labour market but insecure attachments to it, with young people 'milling and churning' (Vaughan, 2003) round different jobs and education or training schemes, and this is similar to earlier research in the West of Scotland (Furlong and Cartmel, 2004). The jobs available in East Kelby, MacDonald and Marsh (2005) termed 'poor work', insecure and often casualised employment in which the flexibility seen as desirable by employers was problematic for the young employees who could only too easily be replaced if they found the low wages insufficient to compensate for the working conditions and the nature of the work. The most powerful example was the turkey factory: employers were not choosy about qualifications or criminal records, but the tasks involved were 'dirty, unpleasant and dull' (MacDonald and Marsh, 2005, p 116). Other young people described jobs in caring, fast food outlets, telesales and security in similarly negative terms.

It is interesting to question why work still retained such importance for these young people. Teesside has a predominantly white working-class population and the conventional route to male adulthood at least had been relatively easily attained in periods of fuller employment. The increase in service sector jobs has tended to benefit young women, bringing them more decisively into the labour market. For young people involved in the research, work was seen as a means of providing structure and purpose, relieving boredom, enabling participation in a consumer culture and allowing social contact. Over and above that, a strong moral sense about work and its social value emerged, not least in terms of its role in enabling young people to move towards adult independence. In fact, interviewees were surprisingly critical of 'dole wallahs' and welfare dependency, themselves resorting to MUD-type rhetoric in relation to others, perhaps to bolster their own sense of respectability (MacDonald and Marsh, 2005).

In areas such as Teesside or East Kelby, the nature of transitions and individual biographies are more determined by the socioeconomic situation and necessity to find strategies to 'get by' than by particular choices made by the individual (MacDonald et al, 2011). Yet the interviewees very much seemed to adopt a sense of personal responsibility for their own circumstances. This brings into relief some of the classic debate about the relative importance of structure versus agency. These young people tended to echo the New Labour (and now coalition) government emphasis on choice and individual autonomy in terms of pathways into full-time employment (and consequent adult status), although also being pragmatic about the constraints on the options available to them. MacDonald et al (2011, p 150) stress how 'overall a discourse of individual responsibility ruled', and see this as reflecting the increasing individualisation of transitions in late modernity and loss of historical and class-based perspectives. New Labour's response, through initiatives such as NDYP, was explicitly weighted towards individual agency and away from attention to the structural conditions and economic inequalities that shape local labour markets. Agency is, of course, limited by the nature of local markets, but also by the coercion involved in schemes such as NDYP and the previous Youth Training scheme:

> 'I feel forced a bit, because I didn't have no choice really. I couldn't say no because they were looking for young people 18-24 – my name came up so I had to do it, and if I didn't do it, they'd stop your benefit.' (quoted in MacDonald and Marsh, 2005, p 98)

NDYP and Connexions are both premised on the belief that jobs are available for young people who are appropriately skilled and prepared for work after education and training, and that the problem of unemployment – and therefore social exclusion – is the problem of young people who are unwilling or unable to make themselves fit for the labour market. Although the social and economic conditions in Kelby are more extreme than in other areas, the research on Teesside exposes the fallacy of these assumptions. Furthermore, experiences vary according to gender and ethnicity: one study (Escott, 2012) covering five areas identified as suffering disadvantage found that black and minority ethnic (BME) young women with poor qualifications, ill health and caring responsibilities experienced particular difficulties. However, even for those young women who had gained qualifications, appropriate opportunities were restricted, and the types of work available still insecure and within a limited range of low status sectors. So again this shows how access to employment and social mobility is not just dependent on personal characteristics or individual effort, but follows the nature and the structure of local labour markets.

Young people will typically find ways of surviving and of living with their situations of economic marginality. In Disconnected Youth? they moved around jobs and engaged in informal or 'fiddly work' (MacDonald and Marsh, 2005), finding forms of employment through contacts, rather than the job centre or NDYP. In this respect, bonding social capital was important; it also came into play in terms of social networks and friendship groups that compensated for some of the risks and problems associated with living in East Kelby. In fact, far from being socially excluded, many of the interviewees were very much part of their geographical community and were surrounded by family and friends. However, in this sense, bonding capital may be constraining rather than enabling either social or physical mobility (Holland et al, 2007), being reliant on highly localised – and quickly exhausted – networks and contacts.

Raising the participation age

The experiences of young people in East Kelby may be more difficult than in many other areas of the country, but they powerfully illustrate the lengthening and the growing complexity of transitions. Social and economic change inevitably means that social processes change, in this case the processes involved in transitions and in reinforcing the insecure and marginal status of many young people in the labour market. The response has been to increase efforts to involve young people in education or training with a view to building social and work-related skills. One key measure relates to the age to which young people are required to remain in some form of education or training, although the statutory school leaving age set at 16 in 1972 has not been extended per se.

The Education and Skills Act 2008 requires that in England young people under the age of 18 must be:

- in full-time education or training; or
- accessing training via an apprenticeship; or
- engaged full time in an occupation and also receiving sufficient 'relevant' education or training.

'Full-time' occupation can mean employment, self-employment, volunteering or holding an office for 20 or more hours per week (excluding the hours of relevant education or training). This will apply to all young people who have passed the compulsory school leaving age until their 18th birthday from 2015. The first stage of implementation requires that from the summer of 2013, young people are participating in one of those forms of education or training until the end of the academic year in which they reach the age of 17.

Although the coalition government is not a believer in large state intervention in the same way as New Labour, they are providing significant funds to support the Raising the Participation Age initiative, investing further in vocational training and options for work experience. Following the recommendation of the Wolf report (2011), opportunities for apprenticeships will be expanded. This is a welcome move, although concerns have been raised about whether the projected expansions will compromise quality (Birdwell et al, 2011). The Education Maintenance Allowance that previously supported young people from households with lower income to stay on in education has been replaced by a bursary system. Local authorities are charged with a key role in both tracking participation and ensuring that provision is available for young people with particular difficulties, such as learning disabilities. Additional provision is available through initiatives that are part of the Youth Contract arrangements predominantly aimed at 18- to 24-year-olds.

The Youth Contract is similar to the NDYP in that it offers enhanced guidance and supports targeted groups of young people identified as at risk of long-term unemployment. However, where it does differ is in looking to the private and third sectors to act as support agencies and offering contracts on the basis of payments by results, in this case how many young people have been placed in full-time education, apprenticeships or a job with training (see www.education.gov.uk). Yet these opportunities clearly do not come free of strings, particularly for the 18- to 24-year-olds, as spelt out in the White Paper, *Building engagement, building futures*:

> As we are providing more support and more opportunities for young people, we will also expect more in return. Those failing to engage positively with the Youth Contract will be considered for Mandatory Work Activity. Those who drop out of a Work Experience place or a subsidised (or other) job without good reason will lose their benefits. (DfE, 2012, p 7)

In many respects these developments continue existing trends with an emphasis on increasing employability and subsidising jobs and work experience, rather than intervening in the market in a more decisive way. Young people in the YJS are likely to be disproportionately represented in the NEET and other vulnerable populations targeted within this provision. As before, this may produce certain good outcomes mixed with less positive impacts as regulation and the threat of disciplinary measures are brought to bear. The critical factor will be the quality of the arrangements in place and whether they enhance the prospects of young people seen as problematic or simply contain them for a period. Critical too will be the fortunes of the economy and whether it is capable of generating more meaningful work opportunities for those who are keen and 'job-ready'.

Implications for practice

Young people's transitions have extended and no longer have a common linear development. This is particularly so in terms of the school to work transition as the economy and the needs of the labour market have altered. Work is often less secure and young people are finding themselves 'milling and churning' (Vaughan, 2003) around different jobs and other activities. While for some young people this is positive in providing an opportunity to experiment and to build experiences before making commitment to a particular work identity, for others it represents a series of dead-end jobs and little chance of moving out of economic marginality.

New Labour, and now the coalition government, invested in training and skills development for young people with a view to increasing their ability to enter and move around flexible education and labour markets. However, young people vary in their abilities and willingness to make choices and to negotiate risks. Moreover, a policy emphasis on increasing employability is limited if local labour markets do not have the jobs on offer or if the jobs are predominantly insecure, poorly paid or exploitative, as on Teesside. Employment of that kind may further exclude and marginalise young people, exposing the mistaken assumption that participation in the labour market necessarily equates to social inclusion.

New Labour turned away from the policy of redistribution in favour of a drive for social inclusion through participation in the labour market (and education or training to prepare for the labour market). However, this carries risks in terms of the potential to adopt a moralising attitude to those who are unable to participate, and it underplays the social value of unpaid work, such as caring. This was evident in New Labour rhetoric and the direction of policy during its term in office, and is currently apparent in initiatives such as the Youth Contract under the coalition government, despite evidence that the problem may not be wilful detachment from the labour market, but insecure attachment through inadequate forms of 'poor work'.

The priority for youth-centred practice is to help young people negotiate the difficult choices post-16, enabling them to access resources and services appropriate to their needs and to build contacts and networks that will allow them greater opportunities for the future. This is a real challenge in a time of austerity, but a necessary one. Young people need opportunities to build confidence and to demonstrate their competence and mastery of skills, whether these are practical or softer interpersonal skills. This requires sensitive work at the individual level but also proactive YOT engagement with employer and training networks ensuring that young people are not ruled out of opportunities because of their offending histories or personal circumstances, and that the options that they access allow room for development and growth.

Further reading

Cook, D. (2006) *Criminal and social justice*, London: Sage Publications.

Furlong, A. and Cartmel, F. (2007) *Young people and social change: New perspectives*, Maidenhead: Open University Press.

MacDonald, R. and Marsh. J. (2005) *Disconnected youth? Growing up in Britain's poor neighbourhoods*, Basingstoke: Palgrave Macmillan.

SIX

Sex and relationships

The previous chapter outlined the increasing diversity in pathways from school to employment; a similar diversity is also apparent in the way that young people move from their family and the family home towards increasing independence and, ultimately for most, a committed partnership. This chapter describes trends in family and household structures, and asks what they might mean, both for young people's experience of 'home' and families of origin, and for the partnerships and families they choose or create as they grow older.

The ability to relate to others, to develop a secure sense of self and to build relationships of trust and reciprocity is affected by early experiences of care and nurturing within the family. Youth justice practice focused on the precepts of the risk factor prevention paradigm recognised the importance of childrearing but did not talk in terms of attachment and relationships, although these notions are now coming back into view and are briefly explored here in terms of young people's relationships with peers and in social settings and relationships of intimacy.

'Youth' is a period of growth and experimentation. Most young people have sufficient resilience, and are able to draw on family and other supports, to be able to recover from hurts and setbacks. Others are sadly more vulnerable and may find themselves in situations that are damaging or abusive. A small but worrying number become involved in activities involving sexual exploitation or even commercial sex. The discussion here looks at the official definition of 'children abused through prostitution' who now come within child protection procedures, and highlights key assumptions in this approach which may not fit with these young people's own perspectives.

The other area where young people's sexual behaviours may cause concern is where those behaviours are abusive towards others. This chapter ends with brief thoughts on young men who commit sexually abusive acts and the sorts of understandings that might inform responses and interventions of a justice or a social care/therapeutic kind.

The family experience

Growing up inevitably involves developing autonomy or independence, which means moving away from dependence on family, but exactly how this happens depends on the nature of the family unit, its social circumstances, ethnic and cultural identities, the gender of the young person and many other factors (Coleman, 2011). Wider social changes and economic realities have also brought a generational change in the way that many young people separate from their families, as they now remain at least partly financially dependent for longer periods. Yet the tensions in extended periods of dependence are largely unrecognised in social policy, whereas the reality is that such dependence may be more acceptable to middle class than working class families, where dependence is more typically associated with failure and shame (Jones, 2009).

In addition, family structures have changed in recent decades. The majority of young people still grow up in households headed by a married couple, although a greater proportion of these are now reconstituted families. There are a growing number of children being raised by co-habiting couples and, again, in many cases, one of the adults in the couple may not be the biological parent of the children he or she is caring for. In England, Wales and Scotland the proportion of households headed by a lone parent rose from 4 per cent in 1971 to 12 per cent in 2007 (ONS, 2008) (see Figure 6.1).

This means that there are multiple permutations of caregiving and support for children and young people, sometimes involving grandparents and other members of the extended family. Social change also means that young people's expectations of their own relationships and domestic arrangements as an adult are increasingly diverse, particularly as young women are now able to be economically independent.

The Inventing Adulthoods study found that the young people interviewed,

> Valued and desired relationships and commitment, but marriage was less important (Sharpe, 2001). Many viewed the first stage of a serious relationship as involving co-habitation which might or might not lead to marriage.... It has become more a matter of identity than social structure or survival, another aspect of consumption and lifestyle choice. (Henderson et al, 2007, p 137)

Figure 6.1: Families in 2010

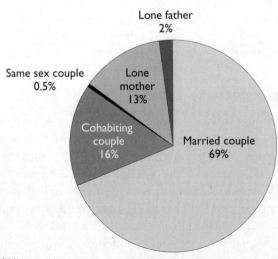

Source: ONS (2011)

Looking at the trends in housing and family arrangements, it is clear that more individuals are now choosing to live alone. In 2007 in Great Britain, 29 per cent of households comprised only one person (12 per cent of individuals). Although roughly half of these were over state pension age (ONS, 2008), reflecting an ageing demographic, this nevertheless still includes an increasing proportion of young adults in single-person households. Figure 6.2 illustrates some of these changes between 1971 and 2007, including the rise in the proportion of couples without children and the decrease by one third of couples with dependent children.

The patterns of conception and parenthood are also changing, with the average age of the mother at birth rising from 25.2 years in 1971 to 29.5 years in 2006. The average age of first giving birth also rose over that same period, from 23.6 years to 27.6 years (ONS, 2008). In 2006, 43.7 per cent of births occurred outside marriage, but an increasing proportion of these were registered by both parents, with only 6.8 per cent of the total births for that year being solely registered (ONS, 2008). Although the age of mothers at birth is typically increasing (as illustrated in Figure 6.3), in 2009 there were still 97,900 conceptions in females under 20 years. Conceptions in girls under 16 are reducing but still numbered 7,200 in that year, resulting in almost 3,000 live births (ONS, 2011).

The benefits of family and home

Family and home environments – including care arrangements outside of the immediate family – should provide warmth, shelter and physical sustenance for

Figure 6.2: Trends in how individuals live, 1971-2007

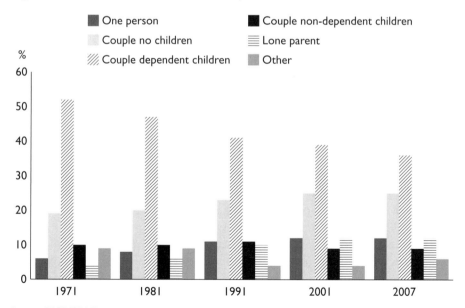

Source: ONS (2008)

Figure 6.3: Live births by age of mother

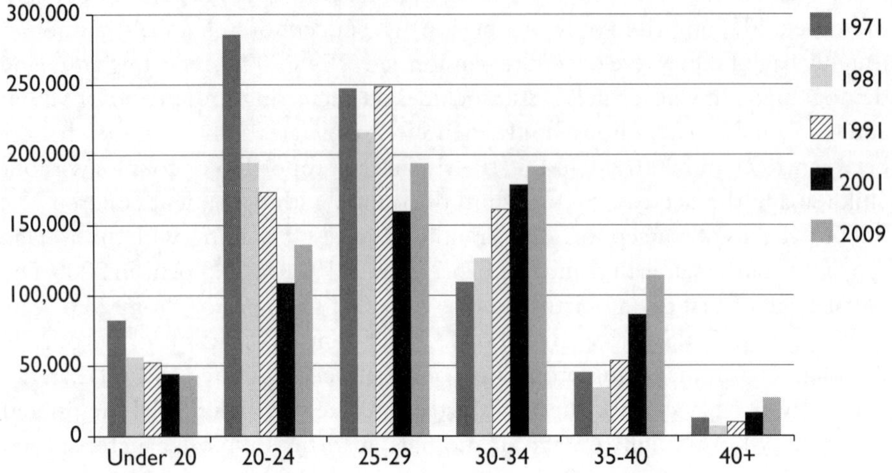

Source: ONS (2011)

children throughout all their dependent years. It is equally important that they give emotional nurturing and model relationships of care and reciprocity. The emotional and psychological needs of babies and infants are most famously conceptualised in Bowlby's (1953) notion of *attachment*. Dogra et al (2009) describe the development of attachment as an interactive process between the baby or infant and *primary caregiver* (usually, but not inevitably, the mother). If the adult is responsive to the developing infant and sensitive to his or her needs, the attachment will grow and form a secure base that allows the infant to explore but is also reliably there for the infant to return to. Many factors may affect the formation of early age attachments, including situations where a parent or carer is under stress, experiencing mental ill health or is otherwise unwell. Yet even where parenting is hostile or neglectful, the primary carer is still the child's attachment figure (Howe, 2009). Subsequent theorising has refined Bowlby's original theory and identified different patterns of attachment:

- *Secure:* the infant is able to happily explore, confident that the caregiver will be there to return to when needed. The caregiver is emotionally responsive so, as the child grows, he or she learns how to express feelings and how to deal with them. This provides a good basis for development in adolescence in terms of self-identity, constructive engagement with problems or difficulties and building relationships of reciprocity.
- *Avoidant-dismissive:* where the caregiver does not respond to the infant or responds with hostility, as he or she grows, the child learns to subdue or ignore his or her feelings in order to avoid rejection. This may become a systematic avoidance of negative experiences and memories. As a result he or she may become emotionally disengaged and perhaps overly compliant and anxious

about getting tasks 'right'. In adolescence, a young person may be reserved or excessively self-reliant, avoiding relationships and seeking detachment rather than attachment. He or she may display anxiety, agitation or anger, even aggression, on occasions.

- *Ambivalent-preoccupied:* if a caregiver responds inconsistently to the infant, then he or she may develop crying, clinging or demanding behaviours in order to provoke a response. As he or she grows, the level of demands or attention-seeking will typically increase. Where this produces a negative reaction or parental withdrawal, the child will experience still greater distress, anger and despair. Ambivalent children show poor levels of concentration. In adolescence, behaviours can be extremely difficult, perhaps also accompanied by threats and conflict, as the young person feels angry with the carer and at the same time wants his or her approval. (Adapted from Walker, 2011, pp 56-63)

The idea of *disorganised attachment* has also been proposed. This may be connected with experience of abuse or severe difficulties with parenting, such that the child responds with conflict behaviours, confusion and even fear of the caregiver (Dogra et al, 2009). Trevithick explains that 'some parents not only neglect and frighten their children but also fail to recognise their child's distress. As a result, children have to take charge of their needs and safety – a situation marked by children's need to adopt controlling strategies' (2012, p 138).

Attachments are essentially adaptive behaviours, and early experiences with parents and other caregivers provide mental models of relationships that help shape later encounters (Coleman, 2011). Dogra et al (2009) note that in the course of childhood, the characteristics of a child's attachments become more unified, so that by adolescence and adulthood the individual has established a pattern of social interaction. Having said that, there may be overlap between the categories above and young people may have degrees of difficulties, some of which can be ameliorated through later more positive experiences of relationships. Reliability and consistency are important qualities in professionals working with young people whose attachments are insecure, as well as the ability to maintain safe and clear boundaries (Harris, 2011). But positive experiences are not limited to professional roles, as Howe notes, commenting on the potential for change:

> The more significant the relationship with a key other – whether parent, partner, lover, therapist – the more radical the shift in life circumstances, the more likely it is that an individual's attachment organisation will change. Children placed with warm, loving, insightful foster carers gradually develop secure attachment. Insecure people with secure partners might begin to feel loved and valued, and with those feelings their attachment grows more secure.... (2011, p 226, cited in Trevithick, 2012, p 139)

Moving beyond the family

As children grow and move into adolescence, relationships with parents typically alter so that they become more equal and involve more discussion and negotiation. Friendships and contacts outside the family assume greater importance, but the way that young people develop their relationships and networks depends not only on the social opportunities available to them but also their patterns of attachment. As expressed by Coleman (2011, p 183) 'most of the characteristics that young people bring to their friendship and peer relationships will have their basis in what is learnt in the home.' Friendships also change during adolescence, becoming more reciprocal and frequently offering a significant source of information, guidance and feedback.

The role of peer relationships is complex, but some of the functions that they serve include: companionship; access to wider social networks; self-validation and affirmation of identity; opportunities to practice new social roles and skills; a sense of acceptance and belonging; and intimacy. They facilitate growth and development, particularly of personal identity.

For most young people, parents and peers are both significant and ongoing influences; Coleman (2011), for example, cites research that suggests that parents remain important regarding plans for the future (education and career choice) whereas friends are more influential over short-terms decisions, such as leisure and consumer choices. Although peer relationships may fill any void left by parents who are absent or disengaged or perhaps where young people experience conflict or alienation in the home, for most young people there is a balance between friends and family. Peer influences for the most part are not experienced as direct 'peer pressure' but in the form of:

- modelling (where young people emulate the behaviour of others);
- providing opportunities (for example, creating an arena for certain types of activities such as drinking or taking drugs at a party);
- normative regulation (collectively defining norms of behaviour and attitude). (Adapted from Coleman, 2011, p 180)

The latter is particularly evident in the research on same sex friendships. For example, McLeod found in her longitudinal study in Australia that 'friendships and inter-personal relations are practices for the playing out and policing of gender identities…' (2002, pp 222-3, cited in Robb, 2007, p 326). Girls, in particular, use friendships to actively work out and negotiate their identities as young women, but always in the wider social context of structural inequalities and gendered power relations (Robb, 2007). Such work on feminine and masculine identities through friendships will also intersect with the development of specific ethnic, religious and other identities.

Two particular features of contemporary friendships and social life are of note. The first is the use of new technologies for keeping in contact and extending social networks. Interestingly, the Inventing Adulthoods study (Henderson et al, 2007) took place over the period that mobile phones became commonplace, and the authors noted the different use of mobile phones and other ICT (information and communication technology) across their research sites, with the young people in the more socially advantaged areas using a wider range of computer and other technologies in addition to mobile phones to enhance their social lives and their social and cultural capital. In the less advantaged areas, such as the disadvantaged Northern estate, the value of mobile phones was initially more as a consumer item. As time went on, the researchers noted the normalisation of phone ownership and texting as a means of maintaining existing relationships and initiating new ones. For some young people whose social worlds were restricted through disability or gendered cultural practices, this was literally liberating. On the other hand, parents had also adopted the new technology and were using it as a means of monitoring and surveillance. The authors comment that,

> Viewing the use of ICT in the context of particular projects of self, allows us to see how the mobile phone, messaging and the internet together facilitate a reworking of public and private boundaries, as the individual becomes the centre of a network of communicative practices, easily accessed and able to access others. (Henderson et al, 2007, p 164)

The second area to consider is the increased importance of leisure and of consumer culture. Both are related to the growth of new technologies, and indeed the unequal access to new technologies – the 'digital divide' – reflects the general inequalities in opportunities to engage in leisure and consumption. What is interesting is the shift in the position of young people from being centrally involved in manufacturing and production, to being a critical element of the marketplace. Some young people may use their patterns of leisure and consumption creatively and as self-expression, particularly as they move from 'organised leisure', perhaps in clubs and sporting activities, to 'commercial leisure' (Furlong and Cartmel, 2007). Nevertheless, they are part of the political economy of consumption characterised by huge structural inequalities and differential access (France, 2007). Many of the young people featured in the Disconnected Youth? study (MacDonald and Marsh, 2005) discussed in Chapter Five, for example, are effectively excluded from these social and cultural sites of youth activity.

Developing intimacy

Friendships and peer networks have always contributed to growing independence and autonomy connected with transitions, but also the development of complex ties of interdependence. Interestingly, the researchers in Inventing Adulthoods (Henderson et al, 2007) found young people moving between two models of adulthood, one stressing independence and autonomy and the other relationships, interdependence and care. The latter implies a degree of maturity and a relatively formed sense of self-identity that young people may not possess at the time of early tentative one-to-one relationships. Helpfully, Brown (1999, cited in Coleman, 2011) suggests that there may be four stages in relationship development:

1. *Infatuation*, where the focus may be as much on the self as the other person.
2. *Status*, where the young person is primarily concerned about how the relationship may affect his or her reputation and/or status in the peer group.
3. *Intimacy*, where mutual interests and feelings for each other can develop and there is more sharing of emotions.
4. *Bonding*, where commitment, care and loyalty become as important as the immediate pleasures of being together, and concerns turn to the future as well as the present.

Early relationships can be intense, echoing to some degree the intimate contact between mother and child in infancy (Coleman, 2011). This is particularly so when relationships become sexual, and the nature of these relationships – and the break-up of first relationships – can be significant critical moments for young people. In any case there is a process of adjustment as young people engage with intimate relationships, but especially so when this throws up issues of sexual identity or sexual orientation. Different issues, of course, arise when the timing of sexual involvement is not of the young person's choosing, in which case the experience may be assimilated negatively rather than positively into his or her sense of self-identity.

Within Inventing Adulthoods (Henderson et al, 2007, p 136), the researchers found that 'having a couple relationship took increasing prominence in young people's narratives over time, often representing critical moments and providing motivation in their lives'. However, young people viewed relationships in different ways that were affected by individual characteristics but also by social status and location. In the more working-class areas committed relationships tended to start earlier, and setting up home with another person was more likely to take precedence over personal ambition. The research identified three different 'tendencies' or orientations towards relationships, characterised as *fusion, autonomy* and *uncommitted*, although these are not mutually exclusive and some young people moved between these tendencies over successive interviews. Young people who were uncommitted tended to opt for either no relationships or casual relationships, wishing to remain independent and without having to feel answerable to a partner. Young people favouring autonomy would typically take a more instrumental approach to relationships, unwilling to compromise personal goals and ambitions for self-realisation and perhaps being ambivalent about the investment of time and effort in a relationship. In contrast, other young people placed more value on the support and emotional security they gained from relationships and were prepared for a greater degree of fusion. Furthermore,

The biographical narratives of [these] young people demonstrated that trusting and intimate relationships enabled some of them to cope with the uncertainties of the "risk society" through providing them with a significant other who was trusting and accepting. (Henderson et al, 2007, p 139)

Elsewhere the research explored young people's perceptions of 'home' and found that they regarded home and the family unit as:

- a physical/practical resource;
- having meaning at an emotional/psychological level; and
- located in specific social/structural and community contexts.

It may be that those young people whose early life had been disrupted were more motivated to look for qualities of security and nurturing in a partnership and/or in creating a new 'home', and these are more likely to be young people from the areas facing greater social disadvantage (Henderson et al, 2007).

Moving from family to form committed partnerships is an important step towards adulthood and preparation for adult responsibilities such as parenting (although a partnership is no longer seen as a pre-requisite for parenting). However, not all young people make this transition in a smooth and painless way. The next two sections explore the issues about young people exposed to exploitative sexual relationships and young people who commit sexually abusive acts themselves.

Exploitative sexual activity

Although sexual exploitation is primarily associated with girls and young women, boys and young men may also be exploited in the sex industry and this is not an issue about sexual orientation; what evidence does exist suggests that only a minority of the young men involved in commercial sex (and their 'punters') would identify themselves as gay (Sanders et al, 2009). The risks and vulnerabilities for both genders are similar, and these are not just individual factors as it is clear that poverty, living conditions and lack of appropriate social supports all feature prominently (Pearce, 2009). Sadly, for some young women, entry into and involvement in the sex industry is connected with experiences in local authority care, which, research suggests, fails to provide them with the practical and material support they need and also fails to provide an environment that allows them to develop a healthy sense of self (Coy, 2007).

From research with young women, three categories of 'risk' of involvement in selling sex have been identified, and these are helpful in exploring what is a complex and, in many respects, largely unknown phenomenon:

Category 1, at risk: running away from home or care, prolonged periods of truanting from school/going missing, beginning to engage in emotional and sexual relationships with older, abusive men.

Category 2, swapping sex: increasing engagement in sexual relationships with older, violent men, increasing use of drugs and returns 'in kind'.

Category 3, selling sex: spending extended periods of time on the street, living in temporary accommodation or homeless, selling sex and intermittently identifying as working in prostitution. (Pearce et al, 2002, adapted by Sanders et al, 2009, p 63)

This shows how social systems and structures are important because, where they fail, they may leave young people vulnerable, but it also follows from this that providing more and better housing, social care services and other forms of support may be beneficial. Yet this runs counter to the direction of recent policy which individualises risk rather than recognising the very real risks created by failures of social systems and procedures.

All young people under 18 at risk or involved in selling sex now fall within the remit of the child protection system. The powers of prosecution are still available for young people who persistently return to prostitution, although in practice these are rarely, if ever, used (HM Government, 2009). Nevertheless, within this framework the dominant construction of young people involved in prostitution or in exploitative relationships is that they are either victims (passive) or villains (active). The current emphasis on child protection and social work intervention is in many ways a positive development (Pearce, 2009), but this is to some extent dependent on young people accepting the label of victim, and risks neglecting the needs and vulnerabilities of those young people who reject that label, who resist help and who may act in challenging or even overtly sexualised ways. As noted by Barratt and Ayre, 'aggressive, anarchic young people who steal and do drugs as well as prostitution do not conform obviously to our idealised image of a child in need' (2000, p 55, cited in Sanders et al, 2009, p 59).

Young people's perceptions of victimhood or otherwise are highly pertinent to the sorts of help and support they might accept. Pearce describes two young women she met in her research, who,

Took what they saw as positive steps in running from home, taking enormous risks in so doing. At the early stages, neither were receptive to being "rescued" from circumstances they were trying to control in their own way…. Jo saw running as a means of sorting things out in her head and Angela considered swapping sex with her "boyfriend" to be an effective way of getting a bed for the night rather than having to return home to abuse. (2006, p 205)

As Pearce powerfully expresses:

> Many of these young people do not ask to be protected. They may openly rebel against being seen as victims, may have been groomed by people they call "friends", may proclaim "love" for their abuser, may be in a complicated, inter-dependent violent relationship with an abuser, or may be purposefully swapping or selling sex for accommodation, food, drugs or money. (2009, pp 123-4)

In this scenario, the most helpful services may not be child protection services, which tend to be geared towards protection from familial child sexual abuse. Support and intervention that focuses on other aspects of their lives – education, work, friendships – may be more useful in helping professionals 'get alongside' sexually exploited young people and avoids conveying the message that they themselves are the problem. It may be that they behave in rebellious, challenging and difficult ways, but so do many other young people (Pearce, 2009). They do not want to be judged and may not accept adult views that they need protection, but they may well value supportive relationships and opportunities to develop their sense of self-determination and to move on at a point where they are ready to do so.

Abusive sexual activity

Some young people experience sexual exploitation and abuse; they may be seen as victims but may also be subject to blame and to moral censure for their behaviours. Similar ambivalence seems evident in relation to young people who commit sexually harmful acts but who are still essentially children with needs and often significant vulnerabilities. They have a kind of 'dual status', being in need of both care and control (Masson, 2007) that creates challenges at the levels of policy and of practice.

There is no inevitable link between experience of sexual abuse and becoming an abuser, either as an adolescent or as an adult, but research suggests that sexual abuse is present in the history of many adolescents who display sexually harmful behaviours (between 30 and 50 per cent, depending on the study) (Erooga and Masson, 2007b). Research that asks about their experiences of abuse suggests that it typically starts at a young age and extends over a significant period (Way, 2002). Physical abuse is even more common and, while less evidence exists in relation to neglect, it is also likely to feature in many of these young people's lives, given what we know about development (Way, 2002) and the nature of attachments.

Adolescents who engage in sexually harmful behaviours are by no means a homogeneous group (Whittle et al, 2006): although predominantly male and in the mid-teens, a small number of young women can and do display aggressive sexual behaviours (Scott and Telford, 2007), and also children under the age of criminal responsibility (Butler and Elliott, 2007). A significant proportion appear to have learning difficulties or disabilities (Erooga and Masson, 2007b) or neurological deficits. For some, offending behaviour is restricted to sexual acts, while for others the sexual offending sits within a much broader pattern of damaging and delinquent behaviours. Research shows that some young people with sexually harmful behaviours experience significant psychosocial problems, have poor cognitive skills, are isolated and impulsive, and so on, and this appears to be particularly so for those young people who sexually offend against children (Whittle et al, 2006). Young people are raised within social systems, so it also follows that the family, the peer group and wider societal factors (such as the widespread sexualisation of children) may significantly contribute to the risk of sexually harmful behaviours.

The methods used for assessment and prediction of further sexually harmful or abusive acts for young people are more clinical than those used with adult sex offenders, and tend to adopt a holistic approach; there is less research evidence that can be used to create robust actuarial assessment tools (Whittle et al, 2006), and in any case these tools rely on historical data about the subject of the assessment and previous pattern of offending whereas a young person, by virtue of youth, does not necessarily have that prior recorded history (Beckett, 2007). What he or she does have, of course, is a history within the family and within schools and other social settings that may be a rich source of insights into his or her behaviours, relationships, attitudes and social, cognitive and other skills. The young person and family are crucial sources of information about the risk of further harm through sexual and non-sexual offences, and also about vulnerabilities and child protection risks for the young person. Building a collaborative alliance is therefore important and, in doing so, it may be helpful to move away from the customary language of risk and deficits and instead to adopt the terms used by the AIM project, which frames the issues as *strengths* and *concerns* (Morrison and Henniker, 2007).

Risk assessment is complex and 'the factors that may predict the onset of sexual violence may not necessarily be the same factors as those that predict the continuation of future risk of sexual violence' (Grant, 2007, p 73). Assessment and prediction should therefore look broadly at the personal and family characteristics as well as the social and environmental circumstances that may affect the:

- predisposition or motivation for sexually harmful behaviours;
- immediate situations, triggers or opportunities that might precipitate such behaviours;
- incentives to continue (or disincentives to stop) these behaviours;
- strengths and positives that may protect against harmful behaviours and encourage pro-social interactions and relationships. (Adapted from Grant, 2007, p 74)

Interventions should be carefully integrated and should seek an appropriate balance between criminal justice concerns and welfare and social need. It may be necessary to take action to protect actual or potential victims and this may mean that the young person is removed from the family home or living environment, and even placed in a residential setting (Bankes, 2007). Where possible, the family and other significant adults may form part of a protective and supportive network working with professionals.

Hackett argues for an optimistic resilience-based orientation to intervention, but stresses that this,

> Is not about pretending that everything is OK in a young person's life, nor is it about simply focusing on strengths and ignoring difficulties or failing to address the risks that young people present. That would be unethical and dangerous. (2007a, p 113)

However, there may be tensions between pursuing intervention with young people and criminal justice concerns about prosecution and public protection. Where possible, monitoring requirements and restrictions should be carefully negotiated so that they provide necessary protections but do not impede therapeutic goals or impinge unduly on the rights of the young person to privacy, family life and a degree of self-determination. However, such negotiations may be difficult and Calder (2002) feels that New Labour's criminal justice reforms did not build on the progress in interagency working made during the 1990s, but in fact created new challenges by promoting the criminalisation of young people's sexually harmful behaviours, rather than diverting them from prosecution The periods that under-18s spend on the sex offender register are half those for adults, but the value of registration for young people is questionable when considered alongside the risk that stigma and labelling prevent a young person from moving on. That said, MAPPA meetings (see Chapter Eleven, this volume) may provide a useful forum for sharing information and understanding between agencies and agreeing actions. Certainly a recent inspection (Criminal Justice Joint Inspection, 2013) was overall critical of communication and planning between agencies except where they came within structured frameworks such as MAPPA or child protection arrangements. In addition, developments such as the AIM project in Greater Manchester (Morrison and Henniker, 2007) were initially funded by the YJB and worked to promote capacity in local authorities to respond to the risks, needs and vulnerabilities of young people and to build the evidence base for work with this challenging group of young people. This is an exception, however, and overall, provision tends to be piecemeal, with little by way of effective strategic coordination, nationally or regionally (Whittle et al, 2006).

Work with young people who engage in sexually harmful behaviours is also challenging for practitioners. This is an area where self-knowledge and reflection is more than ever valuable:

> Every individual working with cases of sexual abuse among young people will bring to that work their own sexual development, sexual knowledge learned in the context of family rules, their own

understanding and interpretations of cultural rules and their own emotional reactions. (Bankes, 2007, p 85)

Hackett (2007b, p 241) also notes that 'work with young people who have sexually abused forces us to connect issues of sex, violence and children (as abusers) in a way that can be distressing and which can bring aspects of our sexuality sharply into focus'. It is not possible to deliver an intervention and avoid becoming emotionally engaged. In fact, emotional engagement and the therapeutic relationship is more significant in change than the content of the programme (Hackett, 2007b). This means that practitioners need robust support systems and opportunities to discuss young people, their individual needs and their behaviours as well as the professional role and task, whether this is assessment for court, intervention or aspects of case management. This may be more readily available for those working in specialist settings than for those carrying a generic workload which includes only a small number of young people with sexually harmful behaviours. Nevertheless, practitioners should be conscious of the need for appropriate support and safeguards for themselves and to protect against potentially damaging or oppressive practice.

Implications for practice

In recent decades family structures have diversified, yet for most young people families still represent 'home' and security. Relationships within the family are the starting point for learning about the social world and developing understanding and empathy towards others. The concept of attachment is critical to appreciating young people's abilities (or difficulties) in relating to other people and the avoidance or aggressive behaviours, for example, that they might display.

In childhood, the primary orientation is to the family, but in adolescence young people typically begin to see peer relationships as increasingly important, not least as a means of exploring identities and of providing opportunities for new experiences and skills. 'Peer pressure' is often framed negatively, but peer groups can provide many positives, including affirmation of self, role models to emulate and sources of support, guidance and advice. How young people build and maintain peer relationships may well depend on the pattern of attachments they have already established as well as their individual personality traits.

Moving towards adulthood, young people begin to show interest in one-to-one relationships, although exactly when this might happen and the degree of commitment involved may vary considerably. The trend is for marriage and parenthood to be delayed, although for some young people early entry into committed partnerships and/or parenthood may be seen as a positive step, particularly in the face of the many insecurities they might face in the risk society.

Adolescence is a period where young people may experiment with intimate relationships and sexual behaviours. Most do so quite happily or without lasting damage even where the experience has been less positive. However, some young people may be more vulnerable to abuse, exploitation or to developing sexually harmful behaviours themselves. These are sensitive areas for professionals to engage with and, without thought and care, they risk compounding hurt and damage rather than helping. Working collaboratively with the young person as well as with any other professionals involved is beneficial and more likely to provide a safe and supportive framework that enables the young person to make changes.

Practice with young people who are sexually exploited or who display sexually abusive behaviours is not easy professionally or personally. This demands a high degree of practitioner reflexivity and practitioners should be sensitive to how young people are reacting and experiencing their involvement and, conversely, the impact that the work has on them as individuals. Line management supervision, peer support groups or consultancy arrangements each provide essential opportunities for reflecting and exploring anxieties and dilemmas, as well as identifying good practice, and can be used to good effect.

Further reading

Erooga, M. and Masson, H. (eds) (2007) *Children and young people who sexually abuse others* (2nd edn), Abingdon: Routledge.

Kehily, M.J. (ed) (2007) *Understanding youth: Perspectives, identities and practices*, London: Sage Publications/The Open University.

Sanders, T., O'Neill, M. and Pitcher, J. (2009) *Prostitution: Sex work, policy and politics*, London: Sage Publications.

SEVEN

Mental health and well-being

Earlier chapters have argued that young people are seen as embodying risk and, at the same time, as being at risk of exclusion from the labour market and from the norms and expectations of society. Adolescence and developing adulthood involve changes and adjustments that are stressful in themselves. However, if we accept the view that young people are now held more responsible for their life choices – and take on the burden of that responsibility – how does this affect the stress associated with transitions in today's risk society?

This chapter explores aspects of what might be characterised as 'healthy' development and what might threaten a young person's emotional state and sense of well-being. To some extent experiences of stress and of problems are important for young people, providing opportunities to build resilience and coping skills. But sadly, some find their resources are not able to withstand the external pressures they face, or life events such as bereavement or chronic illness. For others, poor functioning or distress is linked to individual or internal (psychological or perhaps genetically influenced) factors. Although many young people are able to resolve problems over time, some disorders are sufficiently severe or long-standing to warrant structured support in the form of medical or psychosocial intervention.

Young people who experience problems with emotional or mental health – referred to in Inventing Adulthoods as 'ill-being' (Henderson et al, 2007, p 88) – are over-represented in the YJS, as well as in the care and educational settings that so often feed young people into the system. So it is important that youth justice practitioners have an understanding of mental health and ill health as well as the confidence and ability to offer support and to access more specialist services where needed. Child and Adolescent Mental Health Services (CAMHS) have developed over the past 15 years, creating links with YOTs and secure establishments, facilitating simpler referral routes which no longer require general practitioner (GP) assessment, and providing potential for consultation and knowledge exchange with YOT case managers and other front-line professionals. So there are opportunities for creativity in offering help and intervention at different levels of need but at the same time it is necessary to recognise that there are situations where 'watchful waiting' is more appropriate.

But what is 'healthy'?

'Normal' and 'healthy' development is not easy to define. Expectations and ideas of what constitutes 'normality' and 'health' are socially constructed. The most readily available definitions are perhaps simplified and are certainly framed from a Western societal perspective (Dogra et al, 2009), yet they are helpful nonetheless as a starting point for discussion. The Health Advisory Service report, *Together we stand* (1995, cited in Walker, 2011, p 50), described mental health in children and adolescents as demonstrated through:

- a capacity to enter into and sustain mutually satisfying personal relationships;
- a continuing progression of psychological development;
- an ability to play and to learn so that attainments are appropriate for age and intellectual level;
- a developing moral sense of right and wrong;
- the degree of psychological distress and maladaptive behaviours being within normal limits for the child's age and context.

The Mental Health Foundation (1999) expanded this, suggesting that children and young people who are mentally healthy will have the ability to:

- develop psychologically, emotionally, creatively, intellectually and physically;
- initiate, develop and sustain mutually satisfying personal relationships;
- use and enjoy solitude;
- become aware of others and empathise with them;
- play and learn;
- develop a sense of right and wrong;
- resolve (face) problems and setbacks and learn from them.

So often young people are framed in terms of risks, problems and deficits, and it is helpful to look sometimes from the other side at the strengths, capabilities and social supports that may enable them to overcome adversities. A resilience approach works from this stance and seeks to build what the Mental Health Foundation describes as:

> The emotional and spiritual resilience which allows us to enjoy life
> and to survive pain, disappointment and sadness. It is a positive sense
> of well-being and an underlying belief in our own and others' dignity
> and worth. (2005, p 8)

This shifts the focus from the young person as the problem to the circumstances or the factors that may be putting strain on the young person's coping strategies and resources (Hamilton, 2011). A Scottish study (Armstrong et al, 1998) explored what young people (12-14 years) felt was important in keeping them healthy. Family and friends were felt to play the biggest part, but young people also talked about having people to talk to, personal achievements and feeling good about themselves. Interventions should aim to enhance positives in these and other areas of a young person's life, as well as addressing environmental or other sources of stress.

A certain level of stress can be quite positive and may even promote adjustment and adaptation to change – in the case of young people, perhaps changed roles, relationships with others or new work-type responsibilities (Hagell et al, 2012a). Managing to cope with such changes can provide a sense of power and growing competence, particularly where the change is acknowledged and recognised. However, stress that is acute or chronic (prolonged) may lead to feelings of incompetence and inadequacy, rather than development and mastery of new skills. Research has shown that negative stress of this kind has clear links with mental ill health, particularly in the aftermath of traumatic events or long-standing exposure to adversity. But overall it does not clearly suggest that life is more stressful for young people now than for previous generations (Hagell et al, 2012a).

Trends in the prevalence and severity of emotional and behavioural problems do not entirely equate to trends in the levels of stress (Hagell et al, 2012a), but they do provide food for thought. Difficulties in defining the problem being investigated, gaining robust sample sizes and collecting data, all affect comparability; nevertheless, Collishaw (2012), looking across a range of studies and information sources, found a general agreement among researchers that emotional problems, such as anxiety and depression, rose over a 30-year period in the late 1900s. Although the rises have recently flattened out, emotional problems are still presenting at a historically high level. Two specific studies suggested that there were particular increases in the number of young people at the more serious end of the problem scale, so it is not just a case of finding more young people with low-level difficulties. Conduct problems – often demonstrated as anti-social behaviour or aggression – seem to have followed a similar course, but other behavioural problems, such as attention deficit hyperactivity disorder (ADHD), have not significantly risen. This suggests that the change cannot simply be put down to wider recognition of particular conditions and willingness to report; there has been a real and sustained increase in emotional and conduct problems (Collishaw, 2012) that may be connected to change in social and family structures.

The sense of having control and power is important in mental health, as illustrated by a small Canadian study involving 41 young people receiving therapeutic services. For instance, one former in-patient, Mark, described mental health as:

> 'Being able to cope with life and my problems and able to control my emotions. And not being so severe in cases when I get angry, not going into a rage. When I get depressed not sinking so low, you know? Just able to control how I feel.' (quoted in Ungar and Teram, 2000, p 235)

And control and empowerment are crucially related to self-identity and to the labels applied to these young people. They were particularly critical of the way they were perceived by the institutions – health, social care, education – that they were in contact with. They were also unhappy about the way that they were constructed as being, for instance, pathological or problematic. Attaining mental health meant rejecting such labels and adopting a more powerful alternative. Critically, however, the young people could only choose from the range of identities and roles available to them, so in this sense their options are socially circumscribed. The significance for mental health seemed to be having choice and control over their identity, rather than the particular identity itself and the extent to which it is socially acceptable. The authors explain that:

> Because this sense of power, experienced through control of one's identity, is so important to the well-being of participants, powerful identities are sometime chosen in contradiction to social norms, particularly where mental health resources are scarce. Counter-intuitively, a youth may choose to act in the role of the very good "delinquent" and be known and accepted for his or her capacity as a criminal rather than accept an "average" or "normal" identity that carries less status but is more widely accepted by society at large. (Ungar and Teram, 2000, p 246)

Thinking about identity and social capital, this raises questions about whether in some instances the choice of identity linked to offending might actually be psychologically quite healthy, at least in the short term, where it brings a sense of competence and social acceptance (even if only within a particular peer group).

Facing degrees of difficulty

In the Inventing Adulthoods study (Henderson et al, 2007), the authors use the term 'ill-being' as a counterpoint to healthy development. But the extent of ill-being may vary considerably, and responses aimed at help, support and ultimately treatment will differ accordingly. Being specific about degrees of difficulty it is necessary to distinguish between:

- *Mental health problems:* a broad range of common emotional or behavioural difficulties affecting the young person. These are typically either low level or of short duration and, although they may cause concern for parents or others, they may not require professional help.
- *Mental health disorders:* a clinically recognisable set of symptoms or behaviour associated in most cases with considerable distress or substantial interference with the young person's functioning. The condition is judged against an internationally agreed system of classification and diagnostic criteria.
- *Mental illnesses:* sometimes used interchangeably with *disorder* but generally refers to more serious conditions. (Adapted from Walker, 2011; Stephenson et al, 2011)

The distinction between these categories is not necessarily clear-cut, and depends on judgement about the severity and duration of the difficulty and the impact on the young person (Stephenson et al, 2011). This again raises questions about who makes that judgement and the standards used for deciding what is abnormal, for instance, and what length of time a young person might experience a difficulty before it is considered a *disorder* rather than a *problem* (Walker, 2011). Mental illness moves into the realm of more specific medical diagnosis and intervention, but even this is hardly neutral and unproblematic given the predominance of white middle-class men in psychiatry and the privileging of medical knowledge over, for instance, young people's accounts of themselves (Walker, 2011).

Case managers within YOTs and many other practitioners in youth justice work at Tier 1 of this framework, as do GPs and other primary healthcare workers (see Table 7.1). Specialist mental health workers with YOTs are normally located at Tier 2 (Callaghan et al, 2003) but may also work at Tier 3, depending on the nature of the task and particular involvement with the case (Dogra et al, 2009).

Intervention at the higher tiers is typically more medicalised, and indeed the medical discourses framing mental health are pervasive (Walker, 2011) and can be deeply pathologising. As a counterpoint, it is necessary to stress the significance of social context and its bearing on mental health. The lower level psychosocial interventions offered at Tier 1 are very important, seeking to address problems and to help young people resolve conflict between their inner emotional states and the pressures they face in the outside world (Walker, 2011). Social interventions are equally important for many of those experiencing more severe difficulties, and should not be neglected because of medical intervention, but should work sympathetically alongside.

Table 7.1: Tiers of intervention (following the Health Advisory Service report, 1995)

	Type	Examples of activities
Tier 1	Primary	– Identification of mental health problems at an early stage – General advice – Treatment for less serious problems – Prevention and promotion of positive mental health
Tier 2	Specialist – often located within multi-disciplinary teams	– Assessment and treatment of mental health disorders – Assessment for referrals to Tier 4 – Training and consultation for staff at Tier 1 – Participation in research and development projects
Tier 3	Specialised – mainly working as a single discipline but networked to other agencies	– Training and consultation to staff at Tiers 1 and 2 – Consultation to families – Outreach in relation to severe or complex needs – Assessment that may trigger treatment at another tier
Tier 4	Intensive	– In-patient and residential treatment – Daycare – Secure forensic units for adolescents – Specialist teams, for example, eating disorders, neuropsychiatric problems

Source: Adapted from Walker (2011, pp 186-7)

What sorts of difficulties or disorders?

As already noted, the prevalence of mental health problems and disorders is hard to gauge. The most widely quoted statistics derive from a survey by the Office for National Statistics (ONS) (Green et al, 2005) which estimates that 1 in 10 young people between the ages of 5 and 16 have a clinically diagnosed mental disorder. This survey focused on three main categories of disorder: emotional problems including depression, anxiety and phobias; conduct disorders, such as oppositional defiant disorders; and hyperkinetic disorders, mainly hyperactivity (ADHD). It also looked at less common conditions including autism and eating disorders (see Figure 7.1).

The ONS data show that mental disorders generally rise with age and are also more prevalent in boys than in girls. This is particularly so for hyperkinetic disorders, where boys outnumber girls by six to one. The pattern is unevenly spread with a greater incidence of mental disorder in families with lower incomes and living in 'hard-pressed' areas, suggesting a strong link with social and environmental factors (Walker, 2011). The nature of the family and support systems also has an impact, with more disorders found in lone-parent and 'reconstituted' families (containing stepchildren). However, young people of Black African, Indian or Pakistani ethnic origin had markedly lower rates of mental disorder (Green et al, 2005) than white young people.

Figure 7.1: Prevalence of mental disorders (%)

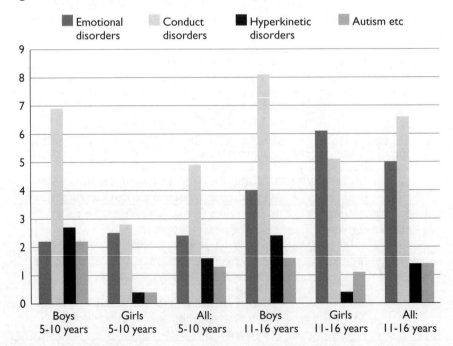

Source: Green et al (2005)

One in five of the children and young people in this survey were diagnosed with more than one disorder, the most common combinations being conduct and emotional disorders or conduct and hyperkinetic disorders. These were overwhelmingly boys (72 per cent), and 76 per cent had a physical or developmental problem alongside their disorders. A larger proportion of this group were behind with schooling than the group of children and young people with only one disorder (49 per cent compared to 27 per cent) (see Figure 7.2).

Although the numbers are still small (estimated at 6-9 individuals in 10,000), autism appears to have increased since the 1980s (Dogra et al, 2009). The condition often becomes apparent during infancy when the child misses normal developmental milestones. Key features include impaired social interactions and communication, including understanding of social behaviours and interpretation of, for example, non-verbal communication. The young person may retreat into a restricted and repetitive repertoire of activities and interests, and may become stressed when faced with unfamiliar situations or change (Dogra et al, 2009). Young people with Asperger's Syndrome, which is related, may have better thinking and communication skills, but may still experience problems in interactions with others and similar repetitive behavioural patterns. This tends to present in adolescence rather than early childhood and, at that age, is often accompanied by anxiety, depression and low self-esteem (Walker, 2011).

Most disorders are more prevalent in boys than girls, particularly those that are externalised and so apparent in behaviours and interactions (for example,

Figure 7.2: Prevalence of mental disorders by ethnicity, 11- to 16-year-olds (%)

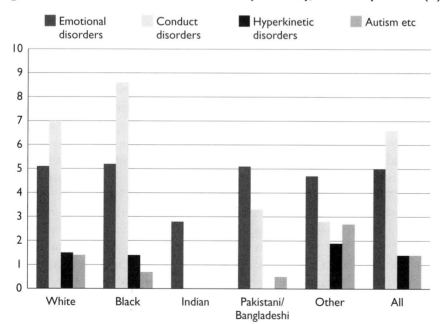

Source: Green et al (2005)

aggression, bullying or opposition to authority). Depression is one area where girls feature more, but the gender differences are even more stark in relation to eating disorders, which may affect as many as 10 girls to every one boy (Dogra et al, 2009). Anorexia nervosa is the most common eating disorder, characterised by significant weight loss, excessive anxiety about becoming fat and distorted body image (Coleman, 2011). Naturally restricting food dramatically or for long periods will have physical effects, including delaying or stopping menstruation, and in extreme cases this can become life-threatening.

Suicide and self-harm

Suicide and self-harm are often seen as on the same continuum of behaviours, but in fact they are very different (Coleman, 2011). Self-harm may involve incidents of poisoning, overdose, mutilation or otherwise causing injury, perhaps through cutting up or scalding. Self-harming behaviours can be hugely distressing for parents and others closely involved, particularly where the young person has not been able to talk about his or her emotional state. They are often expressions of pain and feeling unable to cope, and in that sense self-harm may be a symptom rather the problem in itself. So it is helpful when practitioners avoid focusing on the self-harm, recognising instead the young person's distress and seeking to address what is causing it (Walker, 2011). Furthermore:

> The reaction a young person receives when they disclose their self-harm can have a critical influence on whether they go on to access supportive services. Young people who have self-harmed want responses that are non-judgemental and which are caring and respectful. (Walker, 2011, p 98)

Many acts of self-harm go unreported, and so it is hard to estimate how common it is. One self-report study across schools found that 6.9 per cent of 15- to 16-year-olds had deliberately self-harmed in the last year, but only 12.6 per cent of these incidents had led to a hospital visit (Hawton et al, 2002, cited in Dogra et al, 2009). Where self-harm is repeated, the risk increases and, for some young people, it can become a habitual response to difficult situations or emotions, especially worrying where the young person hides the self-harm over a period of time (Walker, 2011).

Two young people involved in a study by the Mental Health Foundation talked powerfully about their relationship with self-harm:

> 'My emotions can vary rapidly and be very intense. If in an emotionally charged situation, I will either during or shortly after harm myself. I am not good at dealing with emotions or communicating mine to others.' (2006, p 22)

'Cutting for me releases all the built up anger and frustration and pain I feel inside. There are many things that happen to me in my life that cause the pain I feel and how I release it. Mostly the feeling of isolation like being outcast pretty much from relationships altogether. I don't feel like I am a very stable person and I hate myself a lot of the time. I think body image also has a lot to do with my cutting. School is stressful, home life I can't handle sometimes.' (2006, p 18)

Self-harming behaviours are more often found in young people experiencing problems such as depression, low self-esteem and stresses within the family and/or at school (Dogra et al, 2009); young people feeling negative about themselves, hopeless and overwhelmed, whether by their emotions or by external events, are most at risk. A higher rate of self-harm is found among certain groups of young people – for instance, those who are gay, lesbian or bi-sexual and those with learning disabilities (Mental Health Foundation, 2006) – which may be linked to issues about identity and social acceptance. Research also indicates a strong connection between self-harm and childhood sexual abuse and also associations with attempted suicide or self-harm by other family members (Mental Health Foundation, 2006). Self-harm – particularly repeated self-harm – is itself a risk factor for suicide.

Whereas self-harm is more common in young women, young men feature predominantly in cases of attempted or actual suicide (Coleman, 2011). Rates of 'completed' suicide peaked in the UK in 1999, with 18.1 deaths of young men in every 100,000 (ONS, 2008), but have since reduced. Depression is a primary risk factor for suicide (Fitzpatrick et al, 2011), and alcohol and drug use are strongly associated. In terms of youth justice, concerns focus on the risk of both suicide and self-harm for young people in custody. Since 1990 a total of 33 young people below the age of 18 have died in custody, all but two at their own hands (Bateman, 2012a). At the time of writing, the most recent deaths are those of Jake Hardy (17) in HM Young Offender Institution (YOI) Hindley and Alex Kelly (15) in HM YOI Cookham Wood, both in January 2012.

Putting aside the pressing questions about the appropriateness or otherwise of holding young people in prison rather than childcare establishments, a young person may feel extremely frightened and vulnerable on entering custody and this calls for good quality communication between those who know the young person in the community and staff working in the secure establishment, to try to ensure his or her safety and well-being. It must also be recognised that a young person may enter custody with extensive prior experiences of abuse. On occasions these will come to light during the sentence or period of remand, and this may require sensitive handling to ensure that he or she is appropriately supported and safe within the establishment. In other instances, practitioners may already know aspects of a young person's history that may cause him or her to be vulnerable while in custody, and information should be shared with key workers, personal officers or other designated personnel, bearing in mind the sensitivity of this information and the young person's rights to privacy as well as to protection.

Responses to acute conditions

On occasions the levels of distress experienced by a young person may become acute, or he or she will act in ways that are dangerous, even life-threatening. Powers are available under mental health legislation and also the Children Act 1989 to enable medical and social care professionals to intervene, but this is necessarily a complex area because these powers can override the wishes of the young person and, in certain instances, parents, and their use is tightly circumscribed.

The disorders already described are those most commonly seen, but in rare cases a young person may develop psychotic symptoms. Psychosis is not a diagnosis in itself, but a critical state that may indicate illnesses such as schizophrenia or bi-polar affective disorder (manic depression). According to the mental health charity, Mind:

> The word "psychotic" relates to "psychosis" which is a psychiatric term and describes experiences, such as hearing or seeing things or holding unusual beliefs, which other people do not experience or share. For many people, these experiences can be highly distressing and disruptive, interfering with everyday life, conversations, relationships and finding or keeping a job. (2011, p 4)

Essentially, when psychotic, the sense of reality becomes confused and the young person may experience:

- *Hallucinations:* sensing something where there is no real stimulus for that sensation. These may involve any of the senses, including visual or auditory hallucinations (hearing voices).
- *Delusions:* firmly fixed, false beliefs that are not based in any cultural context. They may be persecutory or religious, for instance, and include delusions of grandiosity.
- *Thought disorder:* this includes various forms of distorted thinking, including feelings of being controlled by others or by outside forces. (Adapted from Dogra et al, 2009, p 185)

Mind (2011) also refers to a *flight of ideas*, or making unusual connections between words and ideas.

Schizophrenia in itself is rare in adolescence, but becomes more common, particularly in young men, in the later teenage years. Bi-polar affective disorder is also found infrequently, but can be very difficult to manage when it does present (Dogra et al, 2009). Both can have profound impacts on a young person's development; a psychotic episode or a period of detention for inpatient treatment could be a critical moment associated negatively with disruption and stigma, or positively in terms of help, support and a sense of 'being held'.

In general, voluntary participation in treatment will be sought and legal powers only used as a last resort. The powers under the Children Act 1989 to enable assessment and provision of care and treatment tend to be used in preference to the powers under the mental health legislation, because they are less stigmatising and more age-appropriate (Walker, 2011). The principle should be to use the least restrictive appropriate intervention. However, Part II of the Mental Health Act 1983 has a role in providing for compulsory assessment and/or treatment where needed:

Section 2 permits admission to hospital for up to 28 days for the purposes of assessment.

Section 4 provides for an emergency admission for assessment lasting up to 72 hours.

Section 5 also allows for short-term emergency detention in the absence of doctors or where only one doctor is available to give authorisation.

Section 3 allows an individual to be detained in hospital for the purposes of treatment for up to six months, renewable on application. This is conditional on two medical practitioners confirming that the individual has a mental disorder and that it is necessary for her or his own health and safety or for the protection of others that she or he receives hospital treatment that cannot be provided unless she or he is detained under this section.

The original definition of *mental disorder* in the Mental Health Act 1983 was amended by the Mental Health Act 2007 so that Section 1(2) now states:

... "mental disorder" means any disorder or disability of the mind and "mentally disordered" shall be construed accordingly.

This specifically excludes learning disabilities and drug and alcohol dependence, but is otherwise a broad definition. Significantly, the amendments to the 1983 Act also abolished the need to prove that the disorder must be susceptible to treatment before an individual can be detained, and replaced this with a more flexible criterion that stipulates only that 'appropriate medical treatment' should be available. The treatment can now be in the community as well as in hospital, through a new provision for supervised community treatment after a period as an in-patient.

Post-in-patient care may also be available on a voluntary basis as part of the Care Programme Approach under Section 117 of the Mental Health Act 1983. This places a duty on health and social care agencies to provide aftercare services beyond the period defined for out-patient support, and involves assessment of need, development of a care plan, implementation and review coordinated by a designated key worker (Farrow et al, 2007).

Sensitive issues

Mental health and 'ill-being' is a sensitive area in general, but there are extra specific concerns for young people. One of these relates to consent and the point at which young people are able to consent to or to refuse treatment, even where this is against the parents' wishes. Under the age of 16, parental consent rather than the young person's is needed before voluntary admission to hospital. If the local authority accommodates a child by voluntary agreement, parental responsibility still remains with the parent or carer, and consent should therefore be sought. Where a care order is in place, parental responsibility is shared between the parent or carer and the local authority, so consent should be negotiated and the agreement reached recorded in the young person's care plan (Walker, 2011).

Normally, at 16 or 17, the young person is treated as an adult and must give his or her own consent. The situation becomes more complicated where perhaps a young person has a learning disability or is otherwise unable to give consent, in which case the compulsory powers of the Mental Health Act 1983 come into play (or in more unusual cases, the Mental Capacity Act 2005).

Under 16 a young person may be able to consent to or refuse other forms of treatment, if it is considered that he or she has the capacity to understand the nature of the treatment and the consequences of consent or refusal. This is a complex area and in legal terms refers back to the concept of 'Gillick competence' following a ruling in the House of Lords in 1985 that a 'competent' young person under the age of 16 is capable of giving informed consent. In his judgment Lord Scarman ruled that 'the parents' right yields to the child's right to make his own decision as he reaches sufficient understanding and intelligence' (cited in Dogra et al, 2009). This is legally a difficult area and courts have overruled 'Gillick-competent' young people in extreme situations, particularly where life is threatened, to enable, for instance, force-feeding in cases of anorexia or a blood transfusion where refused by a Jehovah's Witness (Walker, 2011).

Trust and confidentiality are also important concerns for young people (Armstrong et al, 1998). It may be difficult for a young person to disclose to an adult what he or she is experiencing or feeling, perhaps fearing stigma, negative judgements or lack of understanding. For instance, one small study within a YOT found that:

> Young people were generally concerned about confidentiality, regardless of the source of support, and were concerned about how others saw them (eg being "looked down on" by professionals, "looking stupid" for asking questions). (Walsh et al, 2011, p 425)

Telephone helplines were particularly distrusted, and one young person commented that:

> 'Telling a stranger your personal business … when they put the phone down they could have a right ol' laugh … they say it's confidential, but you're not there, so you don't know.' (quoted in Walsh et al, 2011, p 425)

Young people may have unrealistic expectations, being unsure about the limits of confidentiality where child protection issues or potential risk of harm are involved. It is therefore important to be clear where possible about the boundaries and about what may need to be passed on to other agencies and the circumstances that would warrant this. As with other aspects of care, relationships of trust are critical and young people value consistency and continuity (Buston, 2002), appreciating a safe environment in which they can receive help. Transparency about work with other agencies and the exchange of information promotes that feeling of safety.

Mental health intervention within youth justice settings

In the Inventing Adulthoods study (Henderson et al, 2007) reports of mental ill-health – or in their terms, 'ill-being' – were found across the five research sites, but the distribution was unequal and the ability to respond and to resolve difficulties was also influenced by the personal and social resources available to young people. The authors comment that:

> A wide range of acute or on-going situations and experiences may contribute to young people's psychological well-being at any time, and can have critical effects on both their mental health, and their life trajectories. The ways in which young people cope with negative events depends to some extent on the resources they have available to them … it is significant that there was a greater incidence of ill health, bereavement, depression and mental illness in the disadvantaged areas (North of England and in Northern Ireland), where there is also less access to the social capital that can transform young people's trajectories than in the other sites. (2007, pp 97–8)

Given what is known about young people in the YJS and their social circumstances, it would be expected that mental health problems and disorders would be found disproportionately among young people involved with YOTs and in custody. Indeed, research commissioned by the Mental Health Foundation (2002) looked across a range of studies, mainly from the US and the UK, and found that:

- mental health problems were more prevalent for young people in contact with the YJS, estimates varying from 25 to 81 per cent in different studies, being highest among the population in custody;
- the most common disorders are the same as those found in the general population (emotional, conduct and hyperkinetic disorders);

- the detection of mental health problems and disorders is imprecise. In particular, internalising disorders, such as depression, may be under-identified.

The links between mental ill health and offending are complex. The general risk factors for mental ill health and anti-social behaviour and criminality are similar – poor or inconsistent parenting, economic and environmental disadvantage and so on. The nature and strength of attachments are also important. Certain aspects of offending and risk-taking behaviours may also have an impact on well-being by creating stress or by placing a young person in vulnerable situations. Added to which, involvement with the YJS itself and its institutions may cause anxiety and depression (Mental Health Foundation, 2002), and certainly young people may feel very frightened and disempowered when subject to processing through the criminal justice system.

A further UK study by Harrington and Bailey (2005) surveyed 151 young people in custody and 150 in contact with YOTs, finding that almost a third had one or more mental health problems and associated risky behaviours. The young women (22 per cent of the sample) had significantly higher levels of depression, self-harming behaviour and post-traumatic stress. Post-traumatic stress was also found in higher rates among BME young people, but other problems were comparable. Counter-intuitively, the levels of need across the 17 domains surveyed were increased for the community sample, which the authors attribute to better access to education and structured activity in custody, the absence of drugs and alcohol and a contained environment where immediate pressures of family or peer relationships were relieved.

The research base argues for robust systems for intervention within the YJS, but also proactive strategies to divert young people from court proceedings and sentencing where appropriate, in line with the recommendations of the Bradley report (Bradley, 2009). Mental health intervention can be facilitated within the YJS and certainly reviews have shown that provision is improving and becoming more responsive to need (Healthcare Commission, 2009; CQC, 2011). Nevertheless, the systems for mental health and youth justice are both highly controlling, and those controls should be used with care and sensitivity so that they do not exacerbate problems.

It is helpful to think about what might be appropriate approaches to mental health support in the YJS, particularly at the preventative end. Early and accurate identification and assessment is the keystone, but even where a young person is experiencing difficulties, intervention may not be the best course; sometimes it is more helpful to keep a watchful eye on the situation and give the young person space to resolve his or her problems, choosing when and what type of support he or she wants. Also practitioners should recognise where young people will benefit more from positive and self-enhancing activities than a focus on problems. However, where the young person is very distressed and active support is needed, Harris suggests that:

The way through is by creating situations in which the young person can:

- feel safe in terms of a *good enough holding environment*. A good holding environment has the qualities of consistency and reliability
- feel that the *attempt* is being made to understand them in terms of empathic attunement. This eventually enables the containment of strong feelings. (2011, pp 47–8)

The holding environment and who is involved in creating that may vary according to the type or severity of the mental health problem or disorder. In extreme cases, a residential placement may be appropriate, but in most instances, the emphasis will be on the network of care that health, social care and other agencies can provide working with the young person and family.

Feelings of power and disempowerment have been mentioned at several points in this chapter. Medical discourses around mental health tend to place young people in passive roles. This is also strikingly true of the YJS which subjects young people to its processes rather than actively engaging them. Resilience approaches present a different, more participatory model for work with young people experiencing acute difficulties or in crisis. Hart and colleagues (2007, 2008) have designed what they call *resilient therapy*, which denotes both its aim of promoting resilience and of providing forms of therapy and intervention which are fit for purpose and sufficiently robust to offer stability and continuity to children and young people in complex and deeply problematic circumstances. They borrow the notion of *noble truths* from Buddhism and outline four *noble truths* for resilient therapy:

- *Accepting* refers to the need for resilient therapists to engage precisely where the clients are and to take time and care to understand the detail of present circumstances and the implications of histories and legacies;
- *Conserving* incorporates the psychoanalytical idea of containment and the therapeutic benefit of providing safety and boundaries for a client, but has more positive connotations and also refers to the idea of keeping hold of or preserving the good things that exist;
- *Commitment* emphasizes qualities such as reliability and predictability. Ideally a resilient practitioner will aim to stay with the clients throughout their difficulties or at the very least to be open and transparent about the commitment that he or she is able to make;
- *Enlisting* involves harnessing resources to help tackle difficulties, most obviously in terms of drawing in the family and other professionals to work in partnership, but also bringing relevant knowledge and understanding to bear. (Adapted from Hart et al, 2007, 2008)

Resilient therapy (or resilient practice) is future-orientated and focused on outcomes (Hart et al, 2007), challenging both the detail of practice and the strategic aspects of its delivery, in particular:

> The professional defences that often operate in organisations working with the most disadvantaged children and young people, where there may be a tendency for the young person to be pathologised and moved on, or an over-reliance on diagnosis for explanations rather than a "dramatic response to adversity" (Hart et al, 2007). (Hamilton, 2011, p 101)

In responding to more severe mental health disorders, the lead agency may well be CAMHS and social care services often play a significant role. As resilience models are being adopted more widely within CAMHS, youth justice practitioners need to adapt and to open themselves up to the possibilities presented by working across agency boundaries and drawing on expertise and understanding from other professionals to better support and protect young people.

Implications for practice

Young people inevitably face challenges as they grow up. Overcoming difficulties and so gaining confidence and a sense of mastery is part and parcel of moving towards adulthood. It is natural for parents and for professionals to react when a young person is struggling or showing signs of distress, but sometimes it is helpful to check the impulse to 'rescue' and to allow the young person to seek his or her own solutions.

At the same time, it is important to recognise where a young person may need active support and intervention, even medical help, and to offer this where possible in ways that encourage participation and avoid the tendency to pathologise. Medical and criminal justice professionals are powerful relative to the young people they work with, and certainly both systems have means of controlling their subjects – whether through medication or the authority of court orders. Both can also apply potent and potentially stigmatising labels, and youth-centred practice should be sensitive to what that means for young people trying to establish positive identities and a standing in their social world. Resilience approaches offer an empowering model, creating a safe environment and relationships of trust capable of holding a young person while he or she builds strength and finds ways to resolve difficulties.

The majority of young people experiencing mental health problems or more serious mental disorders will receive intervention or treatment in the community on a voluntary basis. Powers under the Children Act 1989 and the Mental Health Act 1983 are used for only a small number of young people, but the latter importantly provides for compulsory admission to hospital for assessment or treatment in acute cases where needed. Compulsory treatment raises significant questions about rights, particularly in relation to consent, to freedom and to bodily integrity (for example, force-feeding), and safeguards are in place intended to ensure its proper and proportionate use.

Gauging what is healthy and what might be outside the expected range of reactions and behaviours is not easy, because we are each so much influenced by our own and by society's norms. Nor is it clear how mental ill health might impact on anti-social behaviour or offending, or how being involved in the YJS might affect a young person's state of mind.

Our understandings tend to be subjective, often relying on our own perceptions and experiences, largely because the existing knowledge and diagnoses focus on symptoms and presenting behaviours, and that does not necessarily shed a great deal of light on what a young person is feeling or why he or she is acting in a particular way. Drawing on ourselves may be helpful in terms of insight and empathy, but it also requires the practitioner to show sufficient self-awareness and reflexivity to avoid making assumptions, to listen with attention and to be mindful of how the young person is experiencing their interaction.

Further reading

Bradley, K. (2009) *The Bradley Report: Lord Bradley's review of people with mental health problems or learning disabilities in the criminal justice system*, London: Department of Health.

Dogra, N., Parkin, A., Gale, F. and Frake, C. (2009) *A multi-disciplinary handbook of child and adolescent mental health for frontline professionals* (2nd edn), London: Jessica Kingsley Publishers.

Hart, A., Blincow, D. with Thomas, H. (2007) *Resilient therapy: working with children and families*, Abingdon: Routledge.

Walker, S. (2011) *The social worker's guide to child and adolescent mental health*, London: Jessica Kingsley Publishers.

EIGHT

Growing up in public care

It is widely recognised that young people with experience of the care system are over-represented in the YJS, particularly within the population of the youth secure estate. Many adult offenders also report histories of being in care, whether for short or for extended periods. What is less clear is the relationship between 'looked-after' status and offending behaviour. The majority of looked-after young people do not offend, but a significant minority do, sometimes continuing already established patterns, sometimes as a response to the experiences or influences within their care placements.

This chapter sets out to provide basic background information about the care system, before exploring young people's experiences of care and caring relationships. It examines again the question of rights and, in this context, questions whether the care system has found an appropriate balance between the rights that young people have to be protected and other rights and needs, such as stability and consistency in relationships. The chapter ends by looking at leaving care and transitions to adulthood, which can be particularly accelerated for a group of young people who, if anything, are likely to need more support than many of their peers.

The care system

Experiences of the care system and pathways through it are extremely diverse, so it is important not to view looked-after children (LAC) as a homogeneous group, and to avoid making assumptions about their lives before entering care and while in care. The main legal provisions are contained in the Children Act 1989 which provides for a child to be 'looked-after' in one of the following ways:

- as subject of a full care order (Section 31) or interim care order (Section 38);
- being 'accommodated' by voluntary agreement with parents or carers under Section 20;
- as subject of an emergency protection order under Section 44.

Looked-after status is also given to young people who are:

- subject of a youth rehabilitation order with an intensive fostering requirement or local authority residence requirement; or
- on remand to local authority accommodation or to custody.

In most cases, looked-after status means that the local authority assumes parental responsibility for the child or young person for all practical purposes. However, where the child or young person is voluntarily accommodated, the sharing of parental responsibility is negotiated with the parent.

The proportion of young people looked-after within each of these legal categories is illustrated in Figure 8.1. On that same day there were also 40 children and young people detained under police powers and a further 160 who were looked-after by virtue of their remand status.

Periods of being looked-after may vary considerably, with significant numbers of young people moving in and out of care quite rapidly (although sometimes returning for a subsequent care episode). Bilson and Thorpe (1988, cited in Taylor, 2006) characterised three distinct care careers:

- 'early leavers': care episode less than six weeks
- 'late leavers': those who leave care between weeks 7 and 52
- 'stayers': those still in care at the end of the year.

Concerns for the YJS are primarily around those young people who have extensive periods in care (the 'stayers') or who may be received into care at critical points during adolescence. Type of placement is important in terms of experience in care, and often young people have been moved through different types of placement.

Table 8.1 shows that the majority of care placements are with foster families, a significant number of these being outside the home local authority. Children's homes and residential schools may be outside of the young person's home local authority. A placement 'out of borough' may result in youth justice services delegating a young person's supervision to another YOT or, conversely, being asked to supervise a young person subject to a criminal court order from another area placed within their locality. Liaison with social care (social services in Wales)

Figure 8.1: 'Looked-after' children, 31 March 2011

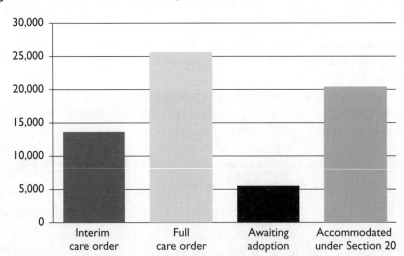

Source: DfE (2011a)

Table 8.1: The pattern of placement for 'looked-after' young people, 31 March 2011

Foster placements	
Within local authority boundary	31,180
Outside local authority boundary	17,350
Placed for adoption	2,450
Placement with parents	3,970
Living independently	2,460
Secure remand	160
Young offender institution or prison	130
Children's homes	
Within local authority boundary	2,610
Outside local authority boundary	2,230
Hostels	880
Other residential care (eg NHS)	920
Residential schools	970
Missing or other placement	200
Total	65,520[1]

Note: [1] After rounding up
Source: DfE (2011a)

is obviously, then, a more complex task, and it is less straightforward for youth justice practitioners to contribute to care planning and review meetings to ensure that work is integrated.

Children's rights within the looked-after child system

A variety of influences acted on the development of the Children Act 1989, one of the most important being the UNCRC 1989. The Act refers to children in the care of the local authority as 'looked-after' or 'accommodated', attempting to remove the previous stigma associated with care. The LAC system also establishes procedural rights in line with Article 12 of the UNCRC.

> Article 12: State parties shall assure to the child who is capable of forming his or her own views the right to express those views freely in all matters affecting the child, the views of the child being given due weight in accordance with the age and maturity of the child.
>
> For this purpose, the child shall in particular be provided the opportunity to be heard in any judicial or administrative proceedings affecting the child, either directly or through a representative or an appropriate body, in a manner consistent with the procedural rules of national law.

Children and young people are therefore involved in planning processes and have the right to contact with family and friends as well as access to complaints procedures and to independent visitors. These arrangements were further consolidated within the Quality Protects initiative running from 1998-2004, monitoring the performance of local authorities against a range of process targets.

These developments are positive in seeking to ensure that young people can voice their wishes and concerns, and also that they have a means of redress if there are problems. However, a rights agenda has other implications for those who are looked-after, particularly in the context of neoliberal politics and a more consumerist orientation to public services. Smith, for example, notes that:

> Statements of rights are often more about protecting agencies from liability than they are meaningful affirmations of their hopes for children. Such interpretations of children's rights can actually get in the way of healthy and just ways of negotiating differences and resolving conflicts, which should happen within the context of daily living and caring relationships. They act to build barriers between children and those who care for them. (M. Smith, 2009, p 11)

The version of rights that has been promoted has tended to prioritise rights of protection – against further abuse from adults, and so on – rather than the right to care. The resulting climate is one that is likely to constrain carers in showing physical affection, for instance, especially within residential settings, and this may have consequences for developing warmth and attachment in relationships. Holland (2010) refers to an 'ethic of justice' taking precedence over an 'ethic of care', and suggests that policy based on the former may be at the expense of attention to the complex emotional and practical caring (and sometimes uncaring) relationships in young people's lives.

Qualitative research sheds an interesting light on young people's experiences. A small study by Holland using a multi-media design found that as young people explored their day-to-day lives, their main interests and concerns were about the relationships they have while in care rather than formal systems and the business of care plans and reviews intended to promote their rights (2010, p 1671). She also found that the young people were involved in more complicated networks of care than the system formally recognises, including relationships with members of extended family (birth family or foster family), but also friends, partners and care staff. And the young people were not passive recipients of care – giving care was also important and perhaps explains why so many of these young people identified pets within their network of care relationships. Social workers did not feature significantly, and Holland attributes this to the focus on the processes of assessment, monitoring and review, which means that less emphasis is given to the relational aspects of the corporate parenting role as personified in the social worker.

This concern was also explored by Munro (2001), who interviewed 15 young people aged 10-17 who had been looked-after for at least two years. They complained about changes of social worker, and Munro tellingly reveals that they had all kept an exact tally of how many social workers had been assigned to them. High staff turnover created difficulties in building relationships, even where the young people got on well with their social worker. In terms of practitioner qualities, reliability in keeping appointments and holding reviews on time was valued, and the young people interpreted lack of attention to these details as evidence that they were low in the social worker's priorities.

Munro's (2001) central focus is on empowerment within care processes. Certainly this is not helped by discontinuity in relationships with social workers as it affects the level of knowledge and trust that exists. The 10- to 12-year-olds in her study were relatively satisfied to have a low degree of empowerment but the older participants had greater expectations of autonomy and choice. Developmentally, young people need to take increasing responsibility for themselves as they progress through adolescence. Munro comments that allowing space for this within the care system is both an ethical requirement and an important developmental task. Yet decision-making processes can frustrate this, giving more weight to protecting the young person than the desirability of allowing a young person to take a risk. Learning from mistakes is a normal part of maturation and looked-after young people should not be prevented from having such opportunities. However, Munro does not underestimate the complexity of the task for social workers, which 'requires a close understanding of the child's level of development, and involves a series of micro-decisions and small shifts of boundaries so that children gradually test out their skills and increase their power' (2001, p 134). It takes courage to allow risk-taking and it seems axiomatic that a social worker who does not have an established relationship with a young person will be more cautious about doing so. The question is how much that might impinge on the young person's need to explore and to take responsibility, and what impact that might then have when he or she leaves the protective framework of the LAC system.

Support and relationships

The previous section alludes to the salience of relationships for young people and this is worth looking at in more depth. It is helpful here to go back to the concept of attachment discussed earlier in Chapter Six. Bowlby's (1953) original ideas focused on the bond between mother and child (or caregiver) and how it affects emotional development and later ability to form relationships of warmth, trust and reciprocity. In the absence of a secure bond with a mother figure, the child was said to experience either partial or complete *maternal deprivation*. More recent thinking suggests that, while attachments to a primary caregiver are the most important, children and young people are capable of forming other attachments even well beyond early childhood. Ideas about attachment should therefore be flexible enough to recognise different forms and levels of attachment, which may not be as intimate as the primary maternal bond, but may nevertheless be meaningful for young people (Taylor, 2006).

Of course, the quality of their attachments is critical for all young people, but especially for those who are looked-after. Secure attachments, established from a basis of trusting early relationships, can allow a child to grow and explore the world with a degree of confidence. Insecure attachments tend to develop where early caregiving has been inconsistent or less available, affecting the quality and strength of bonds and resulting in either avoidance or ambivalence towards later relationships, sometimes even aggression (M. Smith, 2009). Some young people will have poor experiences of caregiving before coming into care, and may therefore have great difficulty in building new relationships. For others, prior experiences may be less significant than experiences while in care, particularly where they are moving between placements and possibly having to change school, with all the loss of stability and continuity that involves. Related to this, Smith outlines how attachment theory can be a useful analytical tool for practitioners, particularly within residential settings, enabling them to understand some of the difficult behaviours they are faced with:

> If, for instance, a child's aggressive behaviours provokes a negative response from their caregivers, this is likely, on the basis of past experience, to replicate past responses confirming in the child a belief that they are bad and unlovable and that caregivers are rejecting ... working from an attachment perspective, therefore, requires workers to be concerned with the causes and meanings of behaviours, not just their manifestations. (M. Smith, 2009, p 77)

Conventional wisdom suggests that positive attachments are more likely to form within fostering placements than in children's homes, and this possibly explains the current preference for fostering over residential settings. However, young people with insecure attachments may find difficulties even within the context of fostering as their baseline for starting to build relationships is so far below that of their peers (Taylor, 2006). This is not to suggest that looked-after young people do not form attachments, and Mark Smith (2009) is keen to advocate the potential for developing attachment within residential settings. He employs the concept of *lifespace*, pointing to the way that residential workers co-exist with young people in their physical space and share small domestic tasks and other day-to-day activities. They are therefore in a position to show consistent interest and care and, over time, to allow a degree of dependency to develop through which young people can be encouraged to move on to independence. This challenges the assumption that residential care should exclusively concentrate on promoting independence and autonomy; as discussed in Chapter One, becoming independent is a gradual process for most young people and a step-by-step approach should also be possible for looked-after young people.

Attachment theory is primarily associated with developmental psychology, but it also features within developmental criminology in the work of Hirschi (1969) and other control theorists (introduced in Chapter Two). In this strain of thinking, attachment is perhaps less fundamental and more concerned with the individual's sensitivity to the wishes and beliefs of those to whom he or she has strong social bonds. In this way, individuals who are strongly bonded can be influenced in the direction of pro-social norms and deterred from 'undesirable' behaviours through fear of disapproval from those whom he or she cares about. Within this framework, Hirschi highlights the role of commitment or attachment to conventional behaviours or institutions, such as education, in providing incentives to conform. Such attachments, whether to individuals or perhaps to employment or a career pathway, may be strong protective factors against offending. Smith et al (2013) suggest that attachment to place may also be important, helping to foster positive feelings of security and belonging.

There are important points to draw for youth-centred practice:

- not all looked-after young people experience difficulties with attachment but, where they do, this may manifest itself within supervisory relationships;
- an attachment perspective may help shed light on, for instance, resistance, challenge or withdrawal from the supervisory relationship, and may assist practitioners in determining how to work with these;
- issues around trust and confidentiality may need careful negotiation;
- the time-bounded nature of certain court orders may be a concern for some looked-after young people and it may be helpful to allow space to discuss this;
- supervision should extend beyond a narrow focus on offending behaviour and should recognise the complexity of the young person's relationships and circumstances while in care (and especially on leaving care);
- where possible, youth justice plans should work alongside care plans, which should cover health, education and recreation, elements which may otherwise be included in a YOT supervision plan.

The links between crime and care

The vast majority of young people who are looked-after have no contact with the YJS. However, the proportion of looked-after young people at each stage of the youth justice process – arrest, pre-court intervention, charge and sentence – is notably higher than the proportion of young people in the general population. In England on 31 March 2011, 8.9 per cent of boys and 5.2 per cent of girls looked-after for more than 12 months had received a conviction or reprimand/final warning compared to 3.7 per cent of boys and 1.1 per cent of girls aged 10-17 as a whole (DfE, 2011a). Furthermore, there appear to be concentrations of offending behaviours associated with particular children's homes (Blades et al, 2011), which are highlighted in the media and thus contribute to a strong public perception that 'being in care equals being in trouble'.

The reasons for this over-representation in the YJS are complex. One key factor has been the tendency for staff in children's homes to call the police following relatively minor incidents. Although this may be an understandable response from an occupational group that is often poorly trained and supported (M. Smith, 2009), the consequence has been a regrettable criminalisation of young people for behaviours, most of which would have been dealt with informally if they had still been in the family home. Precipitating entry in this way may be a primary reason that looked-after young people feature so disproportionately at later stages of the YJS process, and may have contributed to the recent increase in young women in the YJS (Sharpe, 2012).

Thinking more broadly about young people's lives and their critical moments, entry into care or a move between placements may be highly significant, leaving a young person feeling extremely vulnerable and lacking resources to draw on to allow him or her to cope. Interestingly, young people entering and staying in care for over 12 months in adolescence seem to fare worse than those entering much earlier and staying for longer (Blades et al, 2011), who perhaps benefit from greater stability and attachments in care relationships.

Moreover, there is pressure on a young person to establish him or herself quickly after any move, as explained by one young man placed in a children's home:

> 'You know you might not want to do something, but if everyone's there you've got two choices, get in trouble with the people you live with or get in trouble with staff. And if you're living with people you've got to get on with them, so it's an easier life going out and getting arrested, because then you are alright in their eyes, you know, they trust you....' (quoted in Taylor, 2006, p 86)

This demonstrates an element of peer pressure, but what comes over more distinctly is a survival instinct, which in this case overrides personal morality. It is a fairly peremptory calculation of costs and benefits, but the decision to offend is clearly based on pragmatic assessment of the risks involved in two different possible choices. In this instance, the critical moment has provided an impetus towards rather than away from offending, and perhaps there was also an attraction in gaining quick and easy *social capital* to create bonds with others in the resident group.

Abandonment and disruption of relationships were apparent elsewhere in Taylor's research. For instance, another young man in a children's home said:

> 'You've got to get on with the people who live there 'cos you're living there 24 hours a day. I mean staff, you get staff that help, you get staff that don't help, but staff that help are only there certain days a week. There's no one there constant....' (2006, p 87)

Similarly, one young person remarked of his entry into care and into a children's home:

> 'When I was at home I was worried about what me dad might say if I got into trouble with the police and that. But when I got placed into care, I had no one to worry about then ... we ended up getting into cars, shoplifting, stuff like that ... as soon as I was placed into care

I thought that "Well, no one cares" so I just went out and done me own thing then.' (2006, p 83)

It appears that young people may find themselves outwith the informal social controls that operate within families and, to some extent, in communities, once taken into care. Over time, young people may establish new relationships and routines, but sadly, for a minority, this does not happen and their period in care is characterised by disruption and instability.

The behaviour of young people themselves may cause difficulties and placement breakdown. This is not necessarily due to the care experience, as young people may already be engaged in aggressive, self-harming or drink/drug-using behaviours before being taken into care. But for some young people with histories of trauma or abuse, there may be a period after entering care of acting out or expressing – perhaps in destructive ways – feelings that are hard to contain. In Taylor's research, one young woman explained that:

'When I was with me dad, I had never been in trouble with the police in me whole life. I goes into care and this happens, I just went off the rails.... My temper went out of control, I just lost it.' (2006, p 91)

Having a number of young people together in residential units, all of whom are experiencing problems, may exacerbate their individual emotional states, and this can be compounded by feelings associated with being in care itself:

'Obviously when you go into care, I don't know about other kids but me, I was quite angry at the world, because you'd see lots of other kids with their mums and their dads ... you feel quite alienated and you get quite angry and stuff. So you're more likely to lash out at people, fighting and stuff, or have breakdowns.' (quoted in Blades et al, 2011, p 39)

While this gives insights into criminalisation and offending which may be expressive or peer-related, the evidence falls short of proving that the experience of being in care itself is intrinsically linked to offending. A quantitative study conducted across six local authorities (Darker et al, 2008) found that being in care was not the sole cause of offending among its sample, and that offending was more connected to social and individual factors such as non-attendance at school, drug use and conduct disorders. However, these factors were notably more prevalent among the 'looked-after' group than in the population as a whole, and may be further exacerbated by the disruption of being taken into care or moves within care. The authors conclude that services for young people to help them deal with difficulties at an early stage before they become entrenched may have more impact than services later when 'looked-after'.

Care and custody

The worst outcome for looked-after young people is arguably to go into custody, and here inevitably any help they are given will be remedial, making up for previous deficits in educational and other experiences. Paradoxically, for a minority of young people institutionalised through care, being in custody represents safety and is a relatively comfortable experience that they can possibly cope with more easily than their living circumstances in the community. This is a sad indictment of the support and services that have been available to young people in care and as they leave care.

Under the LASPO Act 2012 all young people on remand in custody, whatever the type of secure establishment, are now treated as LAC, regardless of their status on entering custody. For young people subject to care orders, looked-after status continues after receiving a custodial sentence. Care planning processes should be aligned with remand or sentence plans, in particular concerning preparation for release. If a period of remand or sentence is short, a care placement may be held open, but often the young person will find themselves in a new situation on release and the social worker and YOT practitioners should work together to ensure the young person is appropriately supported.

If a young person is accommodated under Section 20 or remanded to local authority care, looked-after status will cease on sentence. However, the local authority must visit the young person and still has a duty to arrange appropriate advice, support and assistance (DfE, 2010a).

Leaving care

If entering care or moving within care can represent critical moments in a young person's life, so can the process of leaving care. When longer periods of extended familial support – practical, financial and emotional – are becoming the norm for the majority of young people, the expectations of autonomy and self-reliance for those who have been looked-after stand in sharp contrast (Jones, 2009). Ironically, it seems that the very young people in most need of continued care and support experience the most abrupt transitions to adult independence and responsibility. Yet, for all its efforts to do otherwise, practice within the care system remains ambivalent about empowering young people. Even the language used emphasises how young people are subject to what is happening to them:

> For many young people entering care, their self-efficacy is very low, their lives seemingly controlled by others: *abandoned* by family, *excluded* from school, *put* into care, *sent* to a children's home, *assessed* by social workers, *placed* with foster carers. (Stein, 2005, p 12)

Historically, young people have typically left care between the ages of 16 and 18, often moving into independence units or other supported accommodation for the last period. Taylor's (2006) research involving 39 young people showed that some had been supported quite well, especially by foster carers. However, others – particularly those who had lived in children's homes – cited problems with inappropriate accommodation, lack of emotional support and drink and drugs. Data on young care leavers at age 19 are currently collected annually; on 31 March 2011 (DfE, 2011a) over 40 per cent were living independently, while 13 per cent were with family/relatives and 20 per cent were in lodgings (supported and unsupported). Two hundred young people (3 per cent) were in custody, a strikingly higher proportion than for the general population of 19-year-olds. It is also notable that only 6 per cent of these young care leavers were in full-time higher education (and 6 per cent part time) while 29 per cent were classed as NEET, again hugely disproportionate to the general population at that age.

Whereas Taylor's research took place before the provisions of the Children (Leaving Care) Act 2000 came into force, the statistics quoted above cover a period after the Act has been in operation for several years, bringing some improvement in experiences of leaving care (Stein, 2006). Essentially the Act recognises the need for coordinated planning in preparation for leaving care, and makes provision for ongoing guidance and support. The most recent set of guidance and regulations states aspirationally that:

> Care leavers should expect the same level of care and support that others would expect from a reasonable parent. The local authority responsible for their care should make sure that they are provided with the opportunities they need, which will include offering them more than one chance as they grapple with taking on the responsibilities of adulthood. (DfE, 2010b, p 3)

Achieving this in practice is a huge challenge, but the original legislation has been bolstered by measures in the C&YPA 2008 that reinforce the requirement for a statutory review of the care plan before a young person can leave a care home. The intention is to create a more graduated move out of care, and to make 18 the normal leaving age rather than 16.

The Children (Leaving Care) Act introduced the role of PA who is responsible for creating a pathway plan. Plans should be in place for all 16- and 17-year-olds who have been looked-after for at least 13 weeks after they have reached the age of 14. If they are still looked-after, they are *eligible children*, and if the period of being looked-after has ceased, they are termed *relevant children*. The local authority also has duties towards former relevant children, that is, any young person of 18 years or older who would previously have been a relevant child or was an eligible child immediately before LAC status ended on becoming 18.

In addition, the Act stipulates that any young person of 16 or 17 who is detained in hospital or custody (remand or sentenced) on his or her 16th birthday will also be considered *a relevant child* if he or she had been looked-after immediately before being detained. The 13-week minimum requirement still applies.

For young people with LAC status, the pathway plan will incorporate the care plan, identifying the advice, assistance and support that will be provided during and after the period of care. For *relevant children*, the pathway plan should spell out how the local authority will safeguard and promote the young person's welfare by providing or offering assistance with finances, accommodation and needs relating to education, training or employment. Once the young person has reached the age of 18, the requirements are less stringent, but the PA should remain involved and offer guidance and support for the young person, particularly in relation to training or education. Ordinarily the practical and financial support ends at age 21 but will continue beyond that if the young person is pursuing a programme of education or training.

Both the Children (Leaving Care) Act 2000 and the more recent *Care matters* Green Paper (DfES, 2006) stressed the critical need for support at a key time of transition. Stein (2006) outlines the suggestion from research that care leavers fall into three categories:

- *Moving on:* making relatively successful transitions and displaying resilience and welcoming the challenge of independent living. These young people were more likely to have experienced stability and continuity in their lives, including secure attachments. They were also more likely to be participating in further or higher education, to have a job they enjoyed or to be a parent themselves.
- *Survivors:* these young people had tended to experience more instability and disruption than the first group, and were also more likely to leave care earlier and in a less planned way. While experiencing further problems after leaving care, they were able to draw on their own resources to cope and saw themselves as independent (despite typically having high levels of agency dependency for practical and financial assistance).
- *Victims:* these young people were the most disadvantaged, with the most damaging pre-care experiences and typically more moves and disruption in care. These are the least likely to have formed a redeeming relationship with a key adult and most likely to have left care younger, following a placement breakdown. Difficulties tended to continue after care and support available was unlikely to be able to help them with their complex needs.

In terms of PAs and pathway plans, it is significant that research points to a key role for agencies offering assistance, which can make a real difference to the lives of those in the survivor group (Stein, 2006). Professional help and support can prevent a young person slipping down into the victim category. Youth justice services can play a useful part in a young person's network, working along PAs, mentors and others giving personal and practical support at a time of transition. And those young people who regrettably find themselves within the victim group must not be forgotten: their needs may be longer term and more deep-rooted but, if care is a moral endeavour, we should continue to reach out to them.

Implications for practice

Looked-after young people may have complicated networks of professionals and carers around them. Youth justice services, relatively speaking a latecomer on the scene, should engage with these networks, communicating and collaborating to ensure that interventions and support are integrated.

There may be issues for looked-after young people about the number of professionals and carers involved in their lives, particularly where there have been negative experiences or inconsistencies. Youth-centred practice should be sensitive to potential concerns about trust and confidentiality. It may be helpful to outline the nature of communication with social care and its purpose, so there is as much transparency as possible.

Attachment theory gives helpful insights into young people's capacity for building relationships and feelings of security or insecurity; it may have particular relevance for those looked-after young people who have experienced abuse or disruptions in their caring relationships. Young people's ability or inability to trust will be evident in their supervisory relationships, and attachment theory may assist practitioners to appreciate why young people may be resistant to authority or to the presence of yet another professional in their lives.

Consistency and reliability is an important ingredient of relationships with all young people, but particularly so for looked-after young people. Maintaining contact, keeping appointments, being on time, following up on actions identified are all significant in fostering feelings of safety and trust.

Some looked-after young people have stable foster placements or other caring arrangements, but this may not hold true for many involved in the YJS. While youth justice practitioners cannot ignore offending or anti-social behaviour, maintaining a narrow focus may mean that the complex social and welfare issues are neglected – as are the links that these may have with vulnerability to offending.

Leaving care may be a difficult transition for looked-after young people and youth justice services can provide valuable support and continuity at a period of change, assisting with practical and emotional issues. However, it is helpful to be clear about the respective roles of social workers, PAs and youth justice practitioners to avoid unnecessary confusion and duplication of efforts, but also to ensure that no significant needs are neglected. Close working with social care and leaving care services is critical: youth justice interventions and plans should be coordinated with care and/or pathway plans, as working together will provide a more secure safety net of support than agencies working in isolation.

Further reading

Smith, M. (2009) *Rethinking residential childcare: Positive perspectives*, Bristol: The Policy Press.

Smith, M., Fulcher, L. and Doran, P. (2013) *Residential childcare in practice: Making a difference*, Bristol: The Policy Press.

Taylor, C. (2006) *Young people in care and criminal behaviour*, London: Jessica Kingsley Publishers.

NINE

Telling tales of alcohol and drugs

Adults have long expressed concerns about young people's leisure activities, their risk-taking and their relationships with alcohol. These have heightened in recent decades as young people have typically gained more free time, enjoy more disposable income and experience longer periods before taking on adult responsibilities. The political response to increased use of a growing range of substances is contradictory: on the one hand, politicians have promoted a culture of consumerism in which the youth market is a key element, while on the other, they show intolerance towards excessive drinking in public and talk tough about maintaining the illegal status of cannabis and increasing disciplinary measures against Class A drug use.

Substance use for under-18s is tightly regulated, mainly by the Misuse of Drugs Act 1971 or by the laws governing sales of alcohol and consumption, whether on licensed premises or in public space. These attempts to circumscribe young people's use are at odds with what is known about their actual use and the notion of 'normalisation' of drinking and drug use in youth culture. Nevertheless, intergenerational differences are not clear-cut: despite discrepancies between official views of drugs and certain substances as seen by young people – cannabis in particular – it is apparent that young people's tolerance and acceptance does not extend equally to all illicit drugs (see, for example, MacDonald and Marsh, 2002).

This chapter first explores the nature of young people's substance use as revealed by large quantitative studies, and looks at indications of change over time, linking these to aspects of culture and policy. While broad patterns and trends are significant, drink and drug use is influenced by social context and individual biographies, so examining life histories and qualitative studies is also valuable. This provides a basis for understanding why some young people progress from recreational to problematic use, seen within the framework of life transitions. Finally, the chapter outlines the development of drug and alcohol policy and the different levels or tiers of services available from prevention through to intensive intervention.

Consuming culture

As youth transitions have extended and become more complex, young people's consumption of material goods and leisure opportunities have assumed growing significance. Choice of clothes, music, communication technologies and even favoured leisure time venues all open new possibilities for developing identities and cultural identification. The commercial sector has sought to exploit this by aiming products and marketing campaigns specifically at young people (France, 2007; Furlong and Cartmel, 2007). Yet society displays deep ambivalence around their leisure activities with 'moral panics' arising, for instance, around binge-drinking while at the same time promoting the development of the night-time economy and allowing the alcohol industry to target products such as alcopops and spirit mixers ostensibly at young adults, but in practice to younger people as well (Norris and Williams, 2008).

Anxieties about young people's hedonistic behaviours are certainly not new, but the emergence of the dance and rave scene in the 1990s associated with stimulant and other drugs brought fresh levels of concerns. The authors of the Inventing Adulthoods study comment that young people's pleasures have been consistently viewed as transgressive and consequently criminalised. The heady mix of music, dancing and various forms of intoxication (often illicit or illegal) has become a particular focus for adult attention:

> The notion of young pleasures as problems was well established long before the post-war consumer boom heralded the birth of the "teenager" but it was the ever-increasing expansion in the leisure-pleasure landscape that has set this perception in stone. (Henderson et al, 2007, p 72)

Interestingly, as a longitudinal study, the researchers were able to note shifts in attitudes and incorporation of substances into lifestyles over time among their cohort of young people:

> In their early teens, a majority were far more accepting of drinking alcohol and smoking than the supply and consumption of illegal drugs (McGrellis et al, 2000); by the time they started work or further education in 1998, drinking and experimentation with cannabis was largely viewed as a "normal" part of growing up and a period of youthful fun that would end with adult responsibility; four years later, clubbing and pubbing, drink and drugs were central to discussions of social life. (2007, p 76)

Despite some variation across the five research sites, this summary illustrates how a range of substances have become embedded in youth cultures and feature in many young people's social activities, which stands in stark contrast to the illegal status of substances such as cannabis, and warrants further analysis.

The proposition that drug use has become 'normalised' among young people was first put forward by researchers on the North West England Longitudinal Study based on a cohort sample followed through their adolescence in the 1990s (Measham et al, 1994; Parker et al, 1998). More recently, Parker et al (2002) returned to their study sample when they were in their early twenties to gather additional data and to refine their concept. They had not suggested in any event a simple and homogeneous acceptance of all illicit substances, but their follow-up work allowed them to explore 'normalisation' in more depth. They propose that there are five key dimensions:

- ease of availability or access
- rates of trying drugs
- rates of drug usage
- accommodating attitudes to 'sensible' recreational drug use especially by non-users, and
- the degree of cultural accommodation to illegal drug use.

From a review of the existing research literature and their own new data, they found clear evidence of increases in the first four of these for cannabis but more equivocal indicators of normalisation in relation to stimulant drugs and ecstasy. Their interviewees were combining alcohol, tobacco and other drugs in ways that were consistent with other research, suggesting a rational consumerist approach that distinguishes between different substances, their effects and associated risks. They noted that using and small-scale supply of drugs – activities previously associated with outsider status – are being adopted by middle-class young people who are otherwise socially conforming and in education or employment (Parker et al, 2002).

This widespread acceptance of cannabis in particular challenges current drug policy based on prohibition. However, the questions surrounding drink and drugs are complex and, as noted by Hammersley et al (2003), normalisation of relatively high levels of consumption is not necessarily problem-free because of potential social and health-related issues. Such consumption is likely to stretch further into young adulthood as transitions are extended (Parker et al, 2002). Moreover, drug use takes place within specific social and economic contexts, and maintaining a strict demarcation between what is perceived as acceptable drug use and 'crossing the Rubicon' (MacDonald and Marsh, 2002) into more problematic use of heroin and crack does seem to be connected with exclusion and difficult transitions. MacDonald and Marsh's research on Teesside, devastated by the collapse of industry in the 1980s, found that recreational drug users referred to leisure and pleasure, but heroin users:

> Talked variously about "not having a care in the world" after using heroin, about it "taking all [their] worries away" and it "wiping away all the bad things that have happened" ... it is not too difficult to understand heroin's appeal in this context as a poverty drug, a drug that they find compelling because its pharmacological effects "blank out" the day to day realities of their social exclusion. (2002, p 36)

Later sections explore the problems that young people may experience with substance use and how these interact with their transitions, but the next section first looks at use across the whole population and trends apparent over time.

Young people and substance use

It is difficult to gather good quality data about the levels at which young people use alcohol and drugs. It is mostly dependent on self-report methodologies that might be unreliable due to under-reporting or exaggeration. In relation to drink and drugs, these tendencies may be affected by health promotion campaigns or local factors (for example, the messages conveyed by school or youth club policies) (Hagell et al, 2012b). Moreover, large-scale samples, especially where based on school populations, may miss specific groups of interest – young people who are homeless, excluded from school or have runaway from home – and may be more suited to establishing typical rather than extreme or unusual behaviours. Nevertheless, there is interesting data available that begins to build a picture of young people's engagement with substances in adolescence.

In terms of alcohol, it is clear there was a general upward trend in young people's drinking from the Second World War to the 2000s in line with the pattern of adult drinking, but detailed information for young people is only available from the mid-1990s (Hagell et al, 2012b). International surveys such as the European School Survey Project on Alcohol and Other Drugs (ESPAD) and Health Behaviours in School-Age Children (HBSC, covering 35 countries in Europe and North America) suggest that the prevalence of drinking in the UK is comparatively high as are indicators of problematic drinking among young people – early onset, reported drunkenness and frequency of drinking (cited in Hagell et al, 2012b).

According to Hagell et al (2012b), the estimates for experimentation with alcohol may not have risen in the past 20 years, which is encouraging. For instance, the School Health Education Unit surveys revealed that the proportions of 12- to 13-year-olds in their sample reporting drinking in the last week had dropped from 41 per cent in 1990 to 24 per cent in 2000 and to 21 per cent in 2008. The equivalent proportions of 14- to 15-year-olds were 50 per cent, 32.5 per cent and finally 31.5 per cent in 2008. However, ESPAD reports in the 1990s and early 2000s indicated that 35-40 per cent of their sample said they had started drinking at age 13 or younger (cited in Hagell et al, 2012b). There are also signs that those who drink are consuming more (Smith and Foxcroft, 2009), and that there has been a significant increase in girls who are binge-drinking (five or more drinks at one time on three or more occasions in the past month) (Plant and Plant, 2006). In the Offending, Crime and Justice Survey (Matthews et al, 2006) involving more than 3,000 10- to 17-year-olds, a third of those who reported drinking at least once a month also reported feeling 'very drunk' once a month (the proportions of girls being slightly higher than boys). This is by no means a definitive picture, but it is not a wholly reassuring one.

The pattern in relation to illicit drugs is even more complex. Again, ESPAD and HBSC surveys confirm that young people in the UK have high levels of use at age 15 compared to their peers in many other countries (cited in Hagell et al, 2012b). The rise has taken place over several decades, although later than the steep rise in alcohol use in the 1960s and 1970s. Hagell et al (2012b), looking across the range of survey data, estimate that in 1987 one young person in 20 had used illicit drugs by age 14-15, rising to one in three by the mid-1990s. However, the trend in the 2000s is not clearly upwards, leading some commentators (for instance, Parker et al, 2002) to suggest that drug use for the next generations of young people may plateau earlier despite early onset of drug use. This seems to be borne out by data from the British Crime Survey 2009/10 (Hoare, 2010) for 16- to 24-year-olds in their sample. This indicates that reported drug use in the 12 months prior to survey for most substances, except cocaine, has either stayed the same or decreased since 1996.

Turning to cannabis specifically, in a Department of Health survey (2005) of almost 10,000 school pupils in England, 11 per cent reported using cannabis at least once in the last year, compared to 13 per cent in previous surveys, but this proportion increased with age to 26 per cent of 15-year-olds. The data for Scotland and Wales suggests similar rates of usage by age 15 (Jenkins, 2006). Rodham et al (2005) looked at the variation in use among different ethnic groups, accessing a sample of over 6,000 15- and 16-year-olds from schools in the Midlands in England. The pupils self-identified their ethnicity as white, Asian, black or 'other', with Asian young people both male (21.5 per cent) and female (5.5 per cent) reporting the lowest past-year cannabis use. This compares to 49.3 per cent of those males describing themselves as black reporting use, 44.3 per cent of 'other' and 33.5 per cent of white (which contrasts with the greater proportions of white males reporting alcohol use). In other research, attempts have been made to sample non-school groups. The 1998/99 Youth Lifestyles Survey involved 4,848 young people aged 12-16, including those truanting or excluded from school. It found that past-year use of cannabis was enhanced for both these groups – in particular for young women – compared to regular school attendees (Goulden and Sondhi, 2001).

Use of heroin and cocaine/crack cocaine is now relatively rare among the under-18s, although the widespread availability of heroin most evident in Scotland and the North of England during the 1980s and 1990s drew in a significant – and worrying – minority of young people. The next section explores early adolescent introductions to alcohol and drugs before dealing with dependent and more problematic relationships with substances.

Drink and drug-using careers

The ESYTC as a large cohort study provides an opportunity to consider the developing patterns of use or abstention from alcohol, tobacco and drugs through the adolescent years, in this case through four successive data collection points (sweeps) when the young people were aged 12 to 15 (McVie and Bradshaw, 2005).

Two characteristics are most striking from this research, both of which are consistent with research from elsewhere. The first is that females are much closer to males in their substance use than in their offending behaviours, where there is a sharp disparity, particularly in the later teenage years (see Chapter Two). The second is that there are relationships between alcohol, tobacco and other substances, which a significant minority of young people use in combination.

Forty-six per cent of the cohort were non-smokers at all four sweeps when data was collected. There was strong evidence of continuity in behaviours as 79 per cent of those who reported smoking at age 12 were still smoking at 14-15. Most of those who said they were smoking daily at age 12 said they were still daily smokers at age 14 (78 per cent) and 15 (70 per cent). Although starting out with similar proportions of smokers, over time a gender gap emerged with significantly more female than male smokers by the age of 15 (McVie and Bradshaw, 2005).

Questions on alcohol use explored both prevalence (how many young people were drinking) and frequency (how often they were drinking). Already by the age of 12, almost half the cohort admitted having drunk a whole alcoholic drink, mostly at Christmas or other occasions. However, one in 20 described him or herself as regular drinkers (at least once a month) and 1 per cent of the cohort reported drinking weekly. The most dramatic rise came before the age of 14 by which time 17 per cent were drinking weekly and 20 per cent monthly, rising to 24 per cent and 25 per cent respectively by age 15. At this stage, only a small proportion (9 per cent) of the cohort had not consumed an alcoholic drink and, in contrast, 10 per cent reported having been drunk five times or more. Again behavioural continuity was evident as over half the young people who said they were weekly drinkers at age 12 were still weekly drinkers at age 15. At the last sweep, around a quarter of drinkers had been involved in fights or trouble-making as a result of drinking, and more than a third felt they spent too much money on alcohol. Other negative effects, such as being sick and missing school, were also reported.

Prevalence of drug use was lower for illegal drugs than for tobacco and alcohol, but similarly rose with age, particularly between the ages of 13 and 14. Over the four sweeps, 37 per cent of the cohort said they had used a drug, most commonly cannabis, and volatile substances such as glue, gas and solvents (although the latter had declined by the age of 15 as the repertoire of other substances had grown). However, the peak age of starting to smoke and to drink seems to be 13-14, whereas experimentation in drug use is likely to continue beyond the age of 15.

There is no inevitable progression from use of one substance to another, but this research indicates interesting relationships. There was a strong association between smoking and drinking which increased with frequency of use. Young people reporting occasional drinking at an early age had an increased likelihood of smoking and drinking regularly later. It was also found that moving to regular use of one substance often happened simultaneously with regular use of another, for instance 47 per cent of drug users reported starting to smoke regularly at the same time that they started to use drugs regularly. This leads the authors to suggest that whatever characteristic or factor causes young people to increase their substance use is common to all three types of substances.

Looking at the characteristics of those young people involved with substances, they could be grouped as: non-users (even at age 15, this comprised almost half the cohort), single substance users, double substance users and triple substance users. Briefly, the patterns that emerged showed that:

- the multiple (double and triple) substance users reported more involvement in delinquency, both in terms of volume and variety of delinquent acts;
- multiple substance users also showed a heightened risk of victimisation;
- at age 13 no differences were apparent, but by age 15, non–users and single substance users had significantly higher levels of self-esteem;
- multiple substance users tended to rate higher on impulsivity measures;
- an increased variety of substance use was associated with less time spent at home, an increased tendency to hang out on the streets and more time spent with other substance users.

The authors (2005, p 37) conclude that their data 'support the notion that multiple substance users represent a fairly vulnerable and risk-prone sector of the population'.

Moving beyond recreational use

Regular recreational drinking and drug use cannot be assumed to be entirely problem-free, as they may have an impact on health, relationships and engagement with education. However, many of these impacts are minor or short term. Most young people will move on from substance use or develop relatively stable patterns of social use. A small minority, however, will experience more serious problems associated with their use of substances and may have greater difficulty in stopping or reducing their use in the absence of adequate support systems and viable alternatives. A disproportionate number of these will present in the YJS, given the associations between drugs, social exclusion and offending (or at least the risk of criminalisation).

It is helpful to look at drug use in the same framework used in relation to offending behaviour in Chapter Two – that is, onset, maintenance and desistance. A small-scale qualitative study by Melrose (2004) sheds interesting light on how her sample of 44 interviewees aged 13-18 became involved with drugs. The sample was identified not because of their known drug use but because they came from groups considered at high risk of drug use as offenders, through being excluded from school or through experience of the care system (or combinations of these). All the young people used alcohol and tobacco. Compared to young people in the general population, a higher proportion of this cohort used other substances and they reported a typically earlier age of initiation. Exploring their reasons for starting to use drugs, Melrose (2004) was able to place the young people into five rough groupings according to whether they sought:

- oblivion, attempting to 'block out' or forget problems or previous traumas;
- acceptance, wanting to 'fit in' with friends and gain peer group approval, for instance: "I was hanging around in a big group, you watch them do it and then you want to. Like, peer pressure and like trying to be like them. You just try it and then you think 'yeah'. You want to be one of them really, don't you? So you think, 'Yeah, I'll try some'" (2004, p 335);
- thrills, curiosity and looking for a 'buzz';
- thrills and acceptance;
- oblivion and acceptance, a combination of escape and presence of drugs in the social environment. For instance, "It was the only way I knew. My mum and all her friends were using and they encouraged me and, at 11, I thought it was cool. It was also a way out of all the grief" (2004, p 336).

Young women represented about a third of the cohort, but approximately half of these were 'oblivion-seekers' or 'oblivion and acceptance seekers' (which is consistent with Barry's 2006 research discussed in Chapter Two). Their drug use tended to precede experiences such as school exclusion, suggesting that they might arise from more deep-seated traumas and family history.

Heroin use was more prevalent among the young women, who were also more likely to administer it intravenously. It is also worth noting that the other sub-group in this sample with marked problematic levels and patterns of use was young people with mixed ethnic backgrounds. Although it is difficult to draw conclusions from such a small sample, it is known that people of mixed ethnicities experience greater social exclusion, are disproportionately represented in the care system and face additional barriers in education (Lewis and Olumide, 2006), all of which are associated with increased risks around drug use.

Maintaining drug-using behaviours and regular drinking may be motivated by seeking social or cultural capital in the same way as offending behaviour, linked to membership of social groups and shared experiences. Involvement in dealing might also represent a form of quasi-employment where legitimate options are closed down. Poor job prospects and economic circumstances may explain in part why some young people continue high levels of drug use into early adulthood, seeking occupation and social networks, although it is important to acknowledge that young people in more advantaged circumstances may also keep using 'socially acceptable' drugs at high levels into young adulthood. Periods of adolescent delinquency tend to be relatively short-lived, but drug-using careers follow a different trajectory and may extend much further into young adulthood (Hammersley et al, 2003).

Higher risks are associated with drink and drug use in communities and economic circumstances which are less secure. This is not to say that poverty itself causes problematic patterns of substance use, but it may create a context in which there is markedly less room to make rational choices about consumption. Drug markets will move in to fill the vacuum left by disappearing industries, as we saw in areas of Scotland and the North of England in the 1980s and 1990s. Moreover, young people who experience difficult and disrupted transitions into adulthood are more likely to use substances in ways that compound their difficulties. They may respond to chronic lack of opportunity by using drink and drugs as a release or by exploiting the alternative opportunities open to them through dealing. Negative life events may also create vulnerabilities to increased or changed patterns of use.

Critical moments may, of course, be positive and may motivate desistance from drugs, but often they place further stress on young people whose coping abilities are already stretched. In one of a series of studies of young people growing up in post-industrial Teesside, MacDonald and Marsh (2002) present the biography of one young heroin user whom they call Richard. He had already progressed from heavy cannabis use to heroin, along with his friends, but was making progress with his addiction through a methadone programme when his mother accused him of stealing from her and threw him out of the family home. This critical moment left him homeless and precipitated a relapse from which he found it difficult to recover, estranged from his mother and with no job or education prospects to provide an alternative purpose. MacDonald and Marsh (2002) refer to the attraction of 'poverty drugs' like heroin for young people experiencing extreme levels of social exclusion, who become caught in what they term 'cork screw heroin careers' (MacDonald et al, 2011, p 142). This is a real danger where social structures and job markets do not provide the means to help young people into more adult-like roles and enable accumulation of social capital. They comment in a later piece on the relatively conventional aspirations of the young people in their research, including the most entrenched offenders and drug users, but:

> Compared with the transitions of non-offenders in our studies, those with the most serious criminal and drug-using careers were at the same time the most chaotic and socially excluded and had the clearest shape and most predictable direction.... (2011, p 151)

Their immediate futures at least were circumscribed by both the physical demands of their dependency and the alternative demands of criminal justice and substance misuse agencies. These young adults on Teesside had already developed deeply problematic patterns of use, whereas the younger cohort in Melrose's (2004) study were at an earlier stage in their trajectories. However, they were at risk of facing the same future difficulties in their transitions. She notes that they were indulging in activities normalised among their less vulnerable peers, but:

> The consequences of this activity, however, are much more risky for those disadvantaged young people than for their peers because this group is already disadvantaged and excluded from key social institutions such as school, the labour market and/or their families. (2004, p 337)

This clearly points to the need for broad social policy rather than narrow interventions focused only on the pharmacological effects of drugs and their links with offending behaviour.

Choices and behaviours

It is evident that that there is a relationship – or a series of relationships – between adolescent substance use and involvement in anti-social and offending behaviours. Broadly speaking, the main hypotheses are (Bean, 2008):

- *Drug use causes crime:* this is the assumption underlying most UK drug policy (discussed later).
- *Crime leads to drug use:* perhaps because criminal subcultures are supportive of drug use, or where environmental conditions provide access and opportunities.
- *Drug use and crime have a common aetiology or origin:* this suggests that the links between drugs and crime may be more indirect, although they may arise from common causes, such as poverty, social isolation and individual psychological factors.

But which of these is the most convincing explanation? Bennett and Holloway's (2005) summary of the research on the links between drugs and crime found clear evidence to suggest that drug use and crime are associated (which is consistent with the ESYTC and other data presented earlier). However, the evidence does not prove that one necessarily causes the other. Studies also point to the strongest associations between crime and heroin, crack and cocaine, whereas they are much weaker for amphetamine and cannabis (Bennett et al, 2008). Rather less is known about the nature of the relationship, particularly where drugs are combined (Bennett and Holloway, 2005).

Bennett and Holloway's (2005) review also looked at the research on young people, which revealed that first drug use typically preceded their first offence. In contrast, the start of Class A drug use tended to occur after the onset of criminal activity.

The picture is therefore complex, and key interfaces between substance use and offending are outlined below:

- *Drug offences:* these include possession, supply, manufacture and cultivation of substances controlled by the Misuse of Drugs Act 1971. For some young people using drugs, their only offence is related to the drug itself, and this raises questions about enforcement and the risk of unnecessary criminalisation.
- *Alcohol-defined offences:* these include driving while under the influence of alcohol and being drunk and disorderly. Under-age drinking is a 'status offence', which means it may be prohibited for young people in situations where it would be acceptable for other social groups to drink. As a consequence, adults

may be charged with selling alcohol to under-18s, allowing consumption of alcohol on licensed premises and so forth.

- *Offences or anti-social behaviour* may occur under the influence of substances, typically because of disinhibiting effects that affect behaviour or impair judgements.
- *Violence:* most commonly associated with alcohol and stimulant drugs.
- *Offending to fund drug use:* thefts and acquisitive crime are most associated with maintaining patterns of heroin, crack or cocaine use.
- *Drinking or drug use before an offence:* this may occur to find 'Dutch courage', for instance, or simply because alcohol or drugs may be present as young people meet to plan or prepare for an offence.
- *Drinking or drug use after an offence:* perhaps in celebration or relief.

Adults frequently express concerns about the risks associated with adolescent drinking and drug use, which may be over-stated in relation to experimental or recreational use (although regular drinking may have a long-term health impact, for instance). In contrast to the rational consumer, some young people are more impulsive in their behaviours or are positively attracted to taking risks, perhaps for the excitement or to gain kudos with peers. Risks cannot be eliminated from life, but practitioners need to be aware of specific risks associated with drinking and drug use, in addition to the obvious risks of accidents while intoxicated. Some young people drink at levels that are dangerous or use drugs in chaotic ways that put them at risk of over-dose. If using intravenously, there are additional risks of contracting infections such as HIV or blood-borne viruses (Hepatitis C, for example). While they are not expected to have expert medical knowledge, practitioners should have a basic level of understanding and be able to work with health professionals to ensure young people have access to appropriate information.

There are also social risks associated with drink and drug use, such as increased vulnerability to victimisation (McVie and Bradshaw, 2005) and exclusion from important social institutions. One of the major risks, however, is that of criminalisation, and the following sections explore drug and alcohol policy and its incorporation into criminal justice.

Drug and alcohol policy

The legal status and regulation of drugs (and to a lesser extent alcohol) has varied over time, reflecting the politics and cultural mores of the day. At the beginning of Queen Victoria's reign, drug use was not considered a social problem, and opium and other drugs were freely available from a range of outlets, primarily for medical purposes. By the turn of the century, with growing concerns about public health and morality, drug use had been decisively framed as a disease (Bennett and Holloway, 2005). The first regulation came with the Arsenic Act 1851 and the Pharmacy Act 1868 and, with increased interest from doctors, the medicalisation of drug use developed into the 1900s. Alongside this, however, from quite an early stage, the Home Office took responsibility for dangerous drugs, and during the First World War issued a series of regulations introducing drug controls as well as restricting the opening times of public houses and alcohol sales. These were followed in the post-war period by the Dangerous Drugs Acts of 1920 and 1923.

So two separate strands in UK policy have co-existed from these early days – legal regulation and law enforcement alongside medical and treatment approaches (Shiner, 2006). Until the 1960s, the medical approach was dominant, and prescribing heroin to what was then a small number of dependent users was permitted under what became known as the 'British system'. However, the drug scene was changing with a greater variety of substances on the market and a bigger, younger and more working-class population of users, which called into question this relatively liberal regime. Since the mid-1980s a more combative and deeply moral attitude to drugs (and drug users) has been uppermost, with a 'war on drugs' often spilling over into a 'war on drug users' (Buchanan, 2008). This coincided with the heroin epidemics of the 1980s and the emergence of HIV and AIDS, both viewed as a threat to public health. It was at this point that young people first attracted attention in the drug policy arena and they have remained an object of concern ever since (Melrose, 2006).

The Conservative government's *Tackling drugs together: A strategy for England and Wales 1995-8* (Home Office, 1995) focused on supply and demand elements of the drug market (Bennett and Holloway, 2005). The strategy also proposed the creation of Drug Action Teams, which was subsequently implemented by New Labour when they took office (Heath, 2010). These partnerships – now Drug and Alcohol Action Teams – continue to oversee the commissioning of substance misuse services for adults and are involved in commissioning for young people.

New Labour's own strategy, *Tackling drugs to build a better Britain* (Home Office, 1998), contained four elements, to:

- help young people resist drug use in order to achieve their full potential in society;
- protect communities from drug-related anti-social and criminal behaviour;
- enable people with drug problems to overcome them and to live crime-free lives;
- stifle the availability of illegal drugs on the streets.

This highlights two strands apparent in New Labour policy in relation to young people over its term in office – prevention and intervention for those already involved with drugs. The focus for adults was explicitly through enforcement and court-ordered interventions, initially the drug treatment and testing order and later the drug rehabilitation requirement as part of the generic community order. Coerced treatment has been less evident for young people, although initiatives at police stations and attached to bail schemes have been developed. The current coalition policy (HM Government, 2010) re-emphasises these two themes, talking about prevention in more holistic terms within the context of children's services, and intervention still largely through criminal justice routes.

Policy in relation to alcohol has developed along a different trajectory because of its legal status. Although in many respects adult drinking is regarded as a public health rather than a crime and disorder concern, public intoxication is definitely on the agenda of Community Safety Partnerships, and this often involves young people and young adults. Control is through a variety of policing and anti-social behaviour strategies in conjunction with measures such as:

- trading standards to limit sales of alcohol to under-18s;
- police powers of group dispersal and confiscation of alcohol;
- fixed penalty notices;
- local by-laws and introduction of 'alcohol-free zones';
- neighbourhood policing and actions to tackle public drinking;
- 'Alcohol Disorder Zones' introduced by the Violent Crime Reduction Act 2006.

Ironically these measures to control have been developed at the same time as licensing laws were liberalised through the Licensing Act 2003. The strategic agenda, set rather later than the agenda around drugs, was first spelt out in the cross-departmental paper, *Alcohol harm reduction strategy* (HM Government, 2004) and updated three years later in *Safe, sensible, social: Next steps in the national alcohol strategy* (HM Government, 2007). This brought alcohol within the same strategic and commissioning arrangements as drugs at a local level, under the auspices of Drug and Alcohol Action Teams. The coalition's *Alcohol strategy* (HM Government, 2012) signals further developments in cross-departmental actions in relation to public health and problematic drinking, highlighting advice and information for under-18s as a priority.

Substance misuse intervention

With many young people, even within the YJS, intervention is a delicate matter. Their substance misuse may be relatively harmless and over-reaction may be ineffective and indeed potentially criminalising. Intervention for young people works therefore across all four levels or tiers of the Models of Care framework established by the National Treatment Agency (NTA), unlike adult services which are very much geared towards dependent opiate use (see Table 9.1).

Services at Tier 4 of this framework are a thorny issue and remain difficult to access (Melrose, 2006). In comparison, DrugScope (2010) report that 24,053 young people were treated for substance misuse at Tiers 2 and 3 in England during 2008/09, the majority in relation to cannabis and/or alcohol. Three per cent of those in treatment identified powder cocaine as the main substance of concern, whereas only 2 per cent (547 young people) presented for help with heroin and 1 per cent (110 young people) with crack. The contrast with adult

Table 9.1: Tiers of intervention

	Type	Examples of activities
Tier 1	Universal	– Provision of drug-related information and advice, screening, referral by universal provision (eg health, schools) or generic services (eg social care, YOTs)
Tier 2	Targeted	– Provision of drug-related information and advice, triage assessment, referral to structured treatment, brief psychosocial interventions, harm reduction – Most YOT drug workers and Drug Intervention Programmes operate at this tier
Tier 3	Specialised	– Provision of community-based specialised drug assessment and care-planned treatment and drug specialist liaison – This will normally be delivered in drug treatment service premises or a hospital setting
Tier 4	Intensive	– This may include in-patient and residential treatment

Source: Adapted from Paylor et al (2012)

services is stark and raises questions about how young people at the age of 18 experience the transition to adult services which are differently orientated and see problem drug use as primarily one of dependent Class A drug use. Young people's substance misuse services take a rather broader view and tend to respond to a range of social rather than medical needs.

Nevertheless, specific powers have been introduced enabling tough criminal justice responses, particularly in relation to Class A drug use. These include:

- drug testing at police stations following a charge for a specified (trigger) offence extended to young people aged 14–17;
- requirements on the youth rehabilitation order for drug treatment, drug testing and intoxicating substance treatment (alcohol, gas, glue, solvents);
- drug testing as a condition of post-release licence.

These powers are not necessarily used to any great extent – in 2010/11, for instance, only 76 drug treatment, 25 drug testing and 48 intoxicating substance treatment requirements were made (Ministry of Justice, 2012a). Nevertheless, the presence of these powers is significant because they encroach on sensitive areas around young people's rights and bodily integrity. Furthermore, the questions around coercion and voluntarism in treatment are complex (Bean, 2008), and particularly so for young people, where indirect pressures might come from family, social workers or other sources. The extent to which this is positive or detrimental may differ for each individual young person.

Generic youth justice practitioners will inevitably find themselves supporting young people involved with substance misuse services, whether mandated or negotiated as an element of supervision. They may also be engaged in more low key work with young people at Tier 1, primarily consisting of advice and psychosocial interventions. Interestingly, Paylor et al (2012) feel that it is important to distinguish between motivation to change behaviour and motivation to talk about problems and potential solutions. Practitioners may feel that a young person is unwilling to address the difficulties that he or she is experiencing because of substance use, but this may be more to do with his or her maturity and emotional development than lack of motivation. Helping a young person to deal with practical issues and to develop useful strategies in many cases is more effective than trying to encourage insights and reflection.

Implications for practice

Youth-centred practice should be sensitive to the social and cultural aspects of young people's drinking and drug use, and the gains that young people perceive from their use. In many respects, most adopt a rational consumerist orientation and are relatively knowledgeable about the range of substances available in their social milieu. However, that cannot be taken for granted, and access to accurate advice and guidance is critical in ensuring that young people are able to make informed choices and to negotiate risks.

As with offending behaviour, drinking and drug use increases over adolescence, both in terms of the numbers of young people involved (prevalence) and how much/how often alcohol and drugs are consumed (volume/frequency). Clearly, under-age drinking and cannabis use is no longer confined to a deviant minority and to that extent is 'normalised', although the acceptance and tolerance of other illicit drugs varies among young people.

There are parallels between the development of offending behaviour and drink/drug use, but also differences. For instance, the gender gap that develops in relation to offending behaviour over the teenage years is much less apparent with drink and drug-using behaviours. Also desistance from drink and drugs as young people enter young adulthood is less marked, suggesting substance use and offending 'careers' may develop independently of each other.

Research indicates a clear association between substance use and delinquent behaviour (offending, anti-social behaviour and other acts), but no proven causal link. The relationships are varied and complex, some dependent on the (il)legal status of drugs rather than the behaviours themselves (for instance, offences relating to possession or supply). It is therefore necessary to look closely at each young person's particular pattern of use and the meanings that it has for him or her, avoiding assumptions about the connections between drink or drugs and his or her offending.

While much substance use is experimental or recreational, a minority of young people develop problematic patterns of use. In adverse socioeconomic circumstances, the pathways out of problematic use may be difficult, and young people may face the same sort of barriers as in their attempts to desist from crime. In addition, Class A drug users are a deeply stigmatised group, and young people may need significant support in their attempts to shed the dual label of drug user and offender.

Substance-related interventions may involve medical treatment but must also address social, psychological and other needs, including helping young people to find new sources of social capital and identities not associated with problematic drinking or drug use. Indeed interventions may entirely consist of actions to address social and welfare issues, enabling young people to exercise choices and to use in ways that are less harmful (to themselves and to others). It takes skill to engage young people and to collaborate with other agencies to offer appropriate support yet, despite the demands, this is a hugely rewarding area of work.

Further reading

Bennett, T. and Holloway, K. (2005) *Understanding drugs, alcohol and crime*, Maidenhead: Open University Press.

Hagell, A. (ed) (2012) *Changing adolescence: Social trends and mental health*, Bristol: The Policy Press.

Hughes, R., Lart, R. and Higate, P. (eds) (2006) *Drugs: Policy and politics*, Maidenhead: Open University Press.

Jenkins, R. (2006) *Cannabis and young people: Reviewing the evidence*, London: Jessica Kingsley Publishers.

TEN

The anti-social behaviour agenda

Earlier chapters have outlined the interventionist nature of the YJS under New Labour and its net-widening tendency to draw increasing numbers of young people into its ambit. This was most evident in the ancillary parts of the YJS dealing with 'pre-criminals' through prevention projects and through the vast machinery now devoted to tackling anti-social behaviour. The legal powers available to respond to anti-social behaviour proliferated under New Labour, in part due to demands from the public and from social landlords. However, through the language associated with anti-social behaviour, politicians were also able to give voice to more generalised concerns about fear of crime, insecurity and lack of community cohesion and, through this, to gain legitimacy for a further raft of control measures. While the detail of these measures is changing under the coalition government, the broad intention is still to have an arsenal of powers available to use against those who offend, but also crucially those who are 'offensive', young people being a key 'suspect population' to be targeted.

In the present *risk society*, young people have become a convenient focal point for adult concerns, particularly marginalised young people unconnected to the labour market and so representing a threat to a fragile social order. The threat is most specifically seen as coming from groups or gangs, primarily (but not exclusively) male. The impact on young people's use of public space is considerable: the effects of dispersal powers, use of mosquito devices emitting high pitched sounds, CCTV and ASBOs have reduced mobility and opportunity for young people to congregate and socialise. Of course, young people can behave in problematic ways, individually and in groups, but it is questionable whether the predominance of criminal justice over social policy responses has been appropriate, and whether it has frustrated its own purposes in further alienating and excluding already disadvantaged young people.

This chapter grapples with this question, looking at how anti-social behaviour has risen up the political agenda and why it has been so decisively problematised, especially in relation to young people. It analyses the policy initiatives and the legal powers that in place under New Labour, particularly focusing on the practical and the symbolic aspects of the ASBO, before outlining the new measures introduced by the coalition government.

The rise of anti-social behaviour

Crime first became highly politicised in the run-up to the 1979 election and has been a constant element of the political agenda ever since. Until the mid-1990s, crime rates and fear of crime were both rising. However, the newspaper coverage and the discourse around crime rarely included anti-social behaviour which tended to be viewed as a separate social rather than a criminal justice concern.

This changed as New Labour, then in opposition, took over the law and order mantle and sought to shape it in its own fashion.

Tony Blair, as Shadow Home Secretary, and other key figures such as Frank Field, MP responded to the charge that the traditional criminal justice focus on specific crimes and specific incidents was inadequate to address the collective and cumulative impact of harm and distress across communities caused by anti-social behaviour – a perceived 'enforcement deficit' (Squires and Stephen, 2005). In part, this reflected societal change and recognition of the problems faced by particular 'hard-pressed' communities lacking in networks and social capital, a major concern of criminologists from the left realist school who had gathered a solid body of evidence testifying to the uneven impact of crime and disorder on neighbourhoods (Burney, 2005).

However, it is also a product of a social period when the certainties and sense of security apparent in earlier decades has diminished in the face of multiple and unquantifiable global risks – environmental, economic, criminal and others. New Labour was seeking a new vocabulary and a new way of articulating the generalised anxieties about the late modern period in talking of anti-social behaviour. Yet anti-social behaviour itself is not new – in one sense it was re-discovered rather than being stumbled on for the first time in the mid-1990s. Drawing on the work of Garland (2000) around cultures of control, Squires and Stephen comment on the attention that anti-social behaviour suddenly attracted and its use as 'a legitimating rationale for new forms of enforcement action in high-crime societies deeply pre-occupied with the reassertion of certain forms of culture and social order thought to be in jeopardy as a result of globalising social change' (2005, p 45).

Yet the attention on anti-social behaviour is not entirely about the attitudes and over-reactions of the 'moral majority', nor the expression of their anxieties and attempts to regain control; while many anti-social acts are relatively minor, there are instances where anti-social behaviour is deeply pernicious and damaging. It is worth considering why such behaviours have manifested and the social conditions surrounding them. Rodger (2008) uses a framework from Elias (1978, 1982) to challenge the prevailing assumptions that individuals engaged in anti-social behaviour are under-socialised and need to be re-educated and re-moralised. Elias talks about the civilising process in complex organised societies and the network of interrelationships and interdependencies that help maintain order, alongside the development of self-control and empathy for others. In this analysis, within a 'civilised' society controls on behaviour at an individual level are internalised rather than being externally applied through force or threat, and at a social level are characterised by greater tolerance and permissiveness. However, Rodger notes the marginalised sectors of present-day society that are increasingly and noticeably outwith the interrelationships and interdependencies that foster mutual understandings and emotional connection. He finds that:

> Perhaps inadvertently, but often deliberately, policy-makers have encouraged the view that those unable to participate fully in the post-

industrial economy and the consumer society do so through their own indolence and unwillingness ... what effectively has happened is that, cumulatively, the "emotion rules" governing the way that the disadvantaged and welfare-dependent are perceived by those in employment has been changing. (2008, p 41)

The result is isolated groups with little incentive to conform to the norms and values of mainstream consumerist society, and harsher attitudes among those in more powerful positions receptive to the use of formalised and authoritarian measures to deal with perceived threat from these groups. What is noticeable is how behaviours are portrayed as individual moral choice, completely divorced from the social circumstances in which they arise or the life histories of the individuals involved (McIntosh, 2008).

Interestingly, in view of the later agenda around young people, the early pressure for action was generated by the growing moral panics around nuisance neighbours. Local authorities and social landlords were lobbying for enhanced powers to deal with problems on their estates, sadly often the legacy of the social policies of the 1980s and the residualisation of social housing (Burney, 2005). This was picked up by Jack Straw as Shadow Home Secretary and in the Labour Party paper, *A quiet life: Tough action on criminal neighbours* (1995). Although the separate notion of 'anti-social behaviour' was not articulated (Burney, 2005), this acknowledged the cumulative impact of successive acts too small individually to warrant criminal action, and explored the potential of civil remedies, in the first instance enhanced forms of the injunctions already available.

So in the mid–1990s, thinking was already turning to the impacts of anti-social behaviour in neighbourhoods, and New Labour were looking to the US for examples of new and different responses. However, the timing of this interest is significant in explaining why and how the resulting policy measures have been used so much against younger people. The murder of James Bulger in 1993 acted as a catalyst to shifting attitudes towards childhood and children and a markedly less sympathetic response to young people. This arose just as searching questions were being asked about the workings of the YJS and its effectiveness – another perceived 'enforcement deficit' (Squires and Stephen, 2005). Coupled with concerns about poor parenting and insights from developmental criminology suggesting that anti-social behaviour is a precursor to later delinquency, the scene was set for a highly active strategy towards tackling the behaviour of young people.

Developing anti-social behaviour policy

On coming into power, New Labour looked in two main directions for ideas about how to pursue its vision for healthier and more secure communities. It declared its intention to develop rational evidence-based policy and in doing so, drew initially on the work of influential left realist criminologists. But thinking from the US was also apparent in the notion of 'broken windows', first proposed by Wilson and Kelling in 1982. This suggested that areas that were run down and neglected by the authorities developed a spiral of decay and criminality:

> At the community level, disorder and crime are usually inextricably linked, in a kind of developmental sequence. Social psychologists and police officers tend to agree that if a window in a building is broken *and is left un-repaired*, all the rest of the windows will soon be broken. This is as true in nice neighbourhoods as in run down ones ... one unrepaired window is a signal that no-one cares. (1982, p 31)

Part of the solution to the 'broken windows' scenario lies in regeneration and promoting community cohesion. However, it also guides the actions of local authorities and other statutory agencies in terms of attention to the environment – for example, promptly removing abandoned cars and drugs paraphernalia – and dealing with low-level nuisance and crime. Anti-social behaviour, vandalism, kerb-crawling and so on can be seen as 'signal crimes' (Innes and Fielding, 2002) which, if not addressed, send a message to local communities about the breakdown of social order just as much as 'broken windows'. The model for dealing with this is the Zero Tolerance approach to policing adopted by Will Bratton, Police Chief in New York under Mayor Rudolph Giuliani. It was claimed that a crackdown on aggressive begging, public drunkenness, graffiti writing and so on had led directly to dramatic falls in homicides, robberies and burglaries over a four-year period. In fact similar reductions in crime were happening elsewhere and it is not clear that the policing approach had much bearing. Nevertheless it is interesting to note the optimistic tone and the publicity about crime going down, allowing the police to turn their attention to anti-social behaviour and minor incivilities. In contrast, although the same trend was experienced in the UK, the tone was markedly more negative, full of moral panic about anti-social behaviour rather than celebrating the reduction in crime (Mooney and Young, 2006).

Zero tolerance approaches made some appearances in the UK, but in general, early developments were more influenced by the work of left realists. These criminologists also recognised the impact of the environment and of persistent low-level crime and nuisance on communities, but were focused on:

> Its origins, its nature and its impact ... most importantly it is realism which informs our notion of practice: in answering what can be done about the problems of crime and social control. (Young, 1986, p 21, cited in Muncie, 2009, p 147)

In aligning with the Labour Party, Young and colleagues wanted to provide an alternative vision for criminal justice, built on evidence of how crime is manifested rather than myths and fears, and on awareness of the social conditions conducive to crime and victimisation (Muncie, 2009). This chimed with the New Labour mantra, 'tough on crime, tough on the causes of crime', and sat neatly alongside the work of the SEU and other initiatives, such as the New Deal for Communities.

Sadly, the influence of left realists was quickly superceded by further realist thinking from right-wing perspectives. Even in its first term of office, but most decidedly in its second and going into its third term, New Labour's criminal justice policy was clearly predicated on assumptions about offenders making rational choices about their offending, and ideas about disrupting lifestyles and 'routine activities' – neither of which takes much account of social circumstances and how these have an impact on individuals and communities. This heralded in a 'phase of expressive, symbolic politics of local crime control' (Hughes, 2007, p 124), deeply exclusionary and divisive in its effects.

That move from a fuller, more holistic view of responding to anti-social behaviour towards greater regulation of behaviour was indicative of developments in New Labour thinking about the role of the state and the obligations of individual citizens. This saw a more consumerist orientation to public services but also a sense of having to contribute to society in order to receive its benefits (anticipating the Big Society rhetoric of the coalition!). And it represents a different sort of contract between the citizen and the state in a post-welfare society, with greater use of criminal and disciplinary sanctions where individuals cannot or will not conform (Rodger, 2008).

This approach has inevitable consequences for disadvantaged communities and individuals with social problems, such as mental ill health, who are less able to participate in this way and to respond to the expectations that they take responsibility. They therefore risk becoming disproportionately subject to disciplinary sanctions, such as withdrawal of benefits, parenting orders or exclusion from social housing. This philosophy is evident in the White Paper, *Respect and responsibility*, which preceded the Anti-social Behaviour Act 2003:

> Our aim is for a "something for something" society where we treat one another with respect and where we all share responsibility for taking a stand against what is unacceptable. But some people and some families undermine this. The anti-social behaviour of a few damages the lives of the many. (Home Office, 2003, Ministerial Foreword)

The notion of the 'something for something' society has a pleasing sound, referring to mutual benefits and obligations, but it is a responsibilising agenda that speaks to the constituency of the 'moral majority'. In contrast, for many who are marginalised or in need, it is an exclusionary rhetoric and has been used to justify increasing control and surveillance of 'suspect populations' – effectively those, such as young people on social housing estates and street sex workers, who challenge cosy ideas about community and acceptable morality.

Community – and what constitutes a community – is a contested concept, but within New Labour discourse the idea of community was frequently presented as unproblematic and as an unalloyed good. Their version of communitarianism was borrowed from the US academic, Etzioni (1993), and aspirations for reinvigorating community ties and relationships of trust are threaded throughout New Labour's policy documents. The reality is, of course, that tightly bonded communities have the potential to be extremely exclusive and to protect the interests of their members. Collective social capital can be employed to negative as well as to positive ends, although this received little recognition from New Labour promoting an agenda about mutual responsibilities and earned rights that emphasised the obligations and responsibilities of individuals towards communities but not the reciprocating responsibilities of communities towards individuals – an expressly one-way flow (Jamieson, 2005). The difficulty, particularly in relation to young people in disadvantaged circumstances, is that:

> Respect and responsibility is a two-way street – it cannot be demanded of children (or of adults too for that matter) who have not the wherewithal or the opportunities to demonstrate responsibility. (Squires and Stephen, 2005, p 82)

But what is anti-social behaviour?

Illegal acts are defined in statute law and further refined through case law. Although there may be controversy about whether particular behaviours should be classed as criminal or not, it is relatively clear what is within the law and what is outside the law. There is no such clarity about anti-social behaviour, which is an 'elastic term' (Burney, 2005) that can be applied to a vast range of behaviours. The CDA 1998 interestingly borrows language from previous criminal law (Public Order Act 1986) in establishing the ASBO:

Section 1 of the Crime and Disorder Act 1998
An application for an order under this section may be made by a relevant authority if it appears to the authority that the following conditions are fulfilled with respect to any person aged 10 or over, namely:

(a) that the person has acted, since the commencement date, in an anti-social manner, that is to say, *in a manner that caused or was likely to cause harassment, alarm or distress* to one or more persons not of the same household as himself; and

(b) that such an order is necessary to protect relevant persons from further anti-social acts by him.

This could be applied to a wide spectrum of behaviours, because effectively – other than domestic violence – very little is unequivocally counted in or out. The legislation is, perhaps deliberately imprecise, but equally worrying is the lack of precision in thinking about the extent and seriousness of anti-social behaviour. The Home Office did attempt to measure anti-social behaviour during a one-day count of incidents on 10 September 2003, which seemed to suggest a significant number of reports to relevant agencies (over 66,000 in total). However, the methodology took no account of possible double reporting, that is, where a single incident was reported by more than one person or to more than one agency, so these dramatic figures may well be vastly inflated.

Although the draft Anti-social Behaviour, Crime and Policing Bill still refers back to the CDA 1998 definition, the Home Office are now tending to use a broader description:

> Anti-social behaviour is any aggressive, intimidating or destructive activity that damages or destroys another person's quality of life.

What is worrying is that certain behaviours encompassed within anti-social behaviour, such as criminal damage, are arguably criminal acts, whereas others are dependent on interpretation and subjective experience. At what point does rowdy behaviour or noise become anti-social, for example? In general, the effect is to blur the distinctions between crime, disorder and anti-social behaviour, so these terms are now frequently used interchangeably and to refer to a widening variety of social and behavioural problems (Matthews and Briggs, 2008). For instance, in one qualitative study (Goldsmith, 2008), a police community support officer described reports of anti-social behaviour involving:

> 'Spitting, swearing, making too much noise, intimidating neighbours or other people on the estate ... playing games ... um ... it could be anything really. It depends on whose reporting it.' (2008, p 227)

The potentially arbitrary nature of complaints is underlined by a 14-year-old interviewed for the same research, who said:

> 'This woman who lives across the road ... she reported me 'cos she said I was being loud in the street but I don't think I was. I was just mucking around with my mates. Like we were making noise, but it was just normal noise.' (2008, p 227)

The history of the Anti-social Behaviour Order

The main tool in New Labour's anti-social behaviour toolbox was the ASBO, which, from the outset, attracted both praise and criticism (Millie, 2009). It was a new kind of order that belonged to civil law but carried a criminal sanction if its conditions were breached. Although a civil order, following a House of Lords judgment in 2002, the standard of proof became virtually indistinguishable from the 'beyond all reasonable doubt' applied in criminal cases (Millie, 2009). Nevertheless, critics voiced fears that ASBOs allowed, on the one hand, for criminal matters to be dealt with through ASBO proceedings, so limiting rights to a full court process to establish guilt and, on the other, for behaviour that was not itself against the law to be criminalised through breach action (Hopkins-Burke, 2008).

The conditions contained in an ASBO were purely prohibitive and in theory were intended to prevent further instances of anti-social behaviour, although in practice it was often unclear whether the conditions imposed were punitive or preventative (Millie, 2009). Certainly in many instances they were experienced as punitive (YJB, 2006a), particularly where they placed wide restrictions on individuals visiting specific localities or making contact with named individuals.

The New Labour government was enthusiastic about ASBOs. In practice, local authorities and the police were notably less so and most needed prompting by the government to use their new powers. The initial take-up was uneven across the country, with some authorities such as Manchester City imposing a large number of orders and others markedly less keen (Burney, 2005; Hughes, 2007). In fact, over time it became evident that the use of powers and behaviours targeted varied considerably from area to area. Matthews and Briggs (2008) researched in three local authorities: in one borough action was taken against street sex workers, whereas this was felt to be inappropriate in the other boroughs; aggressive and persistent beggars were dealt with informally in one borough but were subject to a combination of ASBOs and dispersal orders in the other two; and similarly, the number of informal agreements with young people, known as acceptable behavioural contracts, totalled 188 in one borough, 96 in the second and only 36 in the third over the 12-month period studied.

In a bid to encourage greater use of anti-social behaviour powers, New Labour increased the range of agencies that could apply for ASBOs to include housing associations and the British Transport Police. The Police Reform Act 2002 enabled prohibitions that could cover the whole country – for instance, banning an individual from going within a certain distance of any football ground in England on the day a match is due to be played. That same Act also introduced interim ASBOs, pending a court hearing for a full ASBO, and allowed criminal courts acting in a civil capacity to make an ASBO following a criminal conviction, known as a CRASBO. As a result of these changes and funding mechanisms providing further incentives, local authorities and others were coerced to engage more with the anti-social behaviour agenda, with numbers of ASBOs imposed peaking in 2005 (see Figure 10.1).

These figures show that ASBOs have been used extensively against under-18s and young adults. However, the decision to bring anti-social behaviour policy within the ambit of the newly created Department for Children, Schools and Families in 2007 signalled a greater interest in social prevention rather than enforcement. The later decline in numbers of ASBOs may also be due to more diverse and sophisticated strategies being developed by Community Safety Partnerships in local areas as the limitations of ASBOs used on their own and lack of a long-term impact on behaviours became apparent.

The faltering credibility of ASBOs and the confusing array of powers that accumulated over successive pieces of legislation has resulted in a raft of new

Figure 10.1: Numbers subject to ASBOs by age, 2001-09

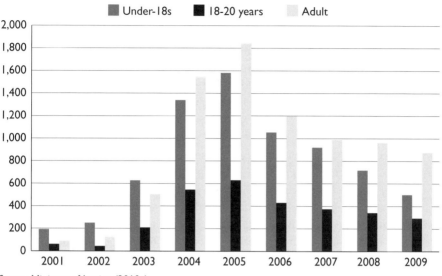

Source: Ministry of Justice (2010a)

measures proposed by the coalition government. Reflecting on the way ASBOs were employed while in force, there is evidence that the original emphasis on behaviours affecting residential neighbourhoods shifted so that the focus became equally on public spaces (Burney, 2005). The role of the police was significant in the mid-2000s in slanting interventions towards enforcement and using ASBOs as an addition to criminal conviction, rather than a benign civil alternative diverting young people and other vulnerable individuals from prosecution. Burney further cites instances where ASBOs have been levered in for explicit crime control objectives in relation to gang activity, commercial companies engaged in fly-posting and drug dealing, commenting that 'it is apparent that the orders have become all purpose instruments, adaptable to any type of crime or disorder, far beyond the neighbourhood problems originally envisaged' (2005, p 102).

Occupying public space

Thinking back to Chapter One, mobility and space to socialise were prioritised by the young people in Inventing Adulthoods (Henderson et al, 2007). Being with other young people, trying out new roles and behaviours, talking through dilemmas and making sense of experiences, all help young people as they move through adolescence and towards adulthood. The street has always been an important place for young people to congregate, particularly working-class young people, as they shift their orientation from the family to their wider friendship groups and social networks. Yet in recent times, the availability of public space has reduced as high streets, shopping centres and other areas have become more privatised and are increasingly monitored by CCTV and security services. One young man involved in a Scottish study tellingly commented that:

> 'There's two CCTV cameras on the main road, one at the top and one at the bottom ... there's one just at the top of that grass, there's one across fae it, there's one just at the lane and then there's one further doon a bit, then there's one just at the park, then there's one at the corner. It's just everywhere ... everywhere you're gettin' watched by a camera.' (quoted in Deucher, 2010, p 266)

As indicated earlier, anti-social behaviour strategies are not applied evenly and consistently. And within local authorities, particular areas may be targeted for activity because they are seen as 'hotspots'. Qualitative research gives insights into how young people experience proactive anti-social behaviour strategies and the resentments these may cause when they are seen as exclusively about the needs and wishes of the adult community and fail to recognise young people's perspectives. Crawford (2009) refers to the symbolic and communicative aspects of anti-social behaviour strategies being more important than their instrumental effects: to adults they might communicate reassurance and a sense of 'something being done', but they may communicate much more negative messages to young people. In his two case study sites where dispersal zones were in operation, young people commented that:

> 'Some of the powers make out that we are all doing something wrong.... It puts across the message that every young person is delinquent. We're always portrayed for the bad things some of us do, it's never the good things.' (2009, p 13)

> 'If they had respect for us and didn't give us names and just think because we are a kid we are going to cause trouble, if they didn't do that I think we would have a lot more respect for them, but as soon as they start giving you a name, then obviously you are not going to respect them.' (2009, p 15)

Where requests to moderate behaviour were explained, the young people said they were happy to oblige, but were more likely to react with resentment and anger if the approach from the authorities was felt to be unreasonable.

This issue was particularly apparent in research involving 23 young men in Glasgow where the author notes a form of 'competitive machismo' developing between the young men who use public space and the police officers who control it:

> 'You're always gettin' pulled for nothin' – it's shite ... it's just pure harassment, as if it's a crime to walk in the street.'

'They're bastards. There's only one polis that's alright ... the others just pull you up and tell you to move along, or that night you're gettin' the jail.' (quoted in Deucher, 2010, p 266)

Feelings of distrust about the use of stop and search powers was also apparent in research on the Hillside estate in the South of England (Goldsmith, 2008) where they again had a negative impact on the relations between the police and young people. In contrast, the young people felt safe within the local youth club, where they believed the youth workers had a deeper understanding of them and the environment in which they were living. Comparing the experiences of young adults who had grown up on the same estate 10 years earlier, Goldsmith (2008, p 235) highlights the more compromised and circumscribed relationship that the study cohort appeared to have with public space.

These three pieces of research illustrate the reactions to young people in groups and the suspicion with which they are viewed. Paradoxically, using the powers of dispersal in the Anti-social Behaviour Act 2003 in the name of public safety may result in young people themselves feeling less safe. In Crawford's (2009) study, young people recognised that being in groups could appear intimidating to others but did not feel that being in a group was anti-social in itself; they saw the problem as a failure to distinguish between just 'hanging around' and being engaged in anti-social acts. Where adults fail to make this distinction, powers to break up groups of young people within a dispersal zone, for instance, can be used indiscriminately and so are experienced as unfair and unjust.

Groups and gangs

The past decade has seen growing concern about young people's involvement in gangs. In the media, this is often connected to minority ethnic communities although research suggests that many gangs also exist in predominantly white urban areas (Bennett and Holloway, 2004; Aldridge and Medina, 2008). The Police and Crime Act 2009 created a gang injunction, an ASBO-type order that can be used in conjunction with other measures to tackle gangs. It is an individual order intended to prevent gang-related violence and, while it is available for 14- to 17-year-olds, applications for this age group must take into account the safety of the young person and any risk of serious harm (Home Office, 2011).

The debate about gangs and gang injunctions tends to obscure the complexities around the understanding of what a gang might be. The size of the problem depends on the definition used, but evidence suggests that youth peer groups are being 'over-defined' as gangs (Squires and Silvestri, 2008, p 25).

Each group or gang is unique, so any attempt to categorise them has limitations. Nevertheless, a model suggested by Gordon (2000, cited in Pitts, 2008) is useful in thinking through different dynamics and affiliations found in groups that he suggests may be loosely differentiated as:

- *youth movements:* social movements marked out by mode of dress or other bodily adornments, a leisure-time preference or other distinguishing features (for example, punk rockers);
- *youth groups:* small clusters of young people who hang out together in public places such as shopping centres;
- *criminal groups:* small clusters of friends who band together, usually for a short period of time, to commit crime primarily for financial gain. These may include small numbers of young and not so young adults;
- *wannabe groups:* including young people who band together in a loosely structured group primarily to engage in spontaneous social activity and exciting, impulsive criminal activity including collective violence against other groups of young people. Wannabes will often claim 'gang territory' and adopt 'gang-style' identifying markers of some kind;
- *street gangs:* groups of young people and young adults who band together to form a semi-structured organisation, the primary purpose being to engage in planned and profitable criminal behaviour or organised violence against rival street gangs. They tend to be less visible but more permanent than other groups;
- *criminal business organisations:* groups that exhibit a formal structure and a high degree of sophistication. They are composed mainly of adults and engage in criminal activity primarily for economic reasons and almost invariably maintain a low profile. (Adapted from Pitts, 2008, p 19)

Although more young people are now involved in highly criminal gangs engaged in the drugs trade (see, for instance, Pitts, 2008), for most, involvement with groups or gangs will fall into one or other of the first five categories.

Much of the research on gangs originates from the US but in the UK, participants in the ESYTC were questioned at ages 13, 16 and 17 about gang membership (Smith and Bradshaw, 2005). More young women than young men identified themselves as members of gangs at age 13, but this reduced significantly in the later teenage years. At age 17, only 3.5 per cent of young women and 8 per cent of young men said they had been part of a gang in the previous 12 months. The sharper decrease for young women parallels their typically earlier desistance from crime and, significantly, the incidence of gang membership was more influenced by the nature of the local neighbourhood than the socioeconomic status of individual families, with more gangs in poorer areas.

The ESYTC research also distinguished between more organised gangs which had a name and an identifying sign, gangs with only one or the other, and gangs with no name or sign. More males than females were members of gangs with both a name and a sign at all ages and, by age 17, the volume of delinquency was eight times greater for members of these gangs compared to young people with no gang involvement. There was also a raised volume of delinquency for young people in more loosely organised gangs (Smith and Bradshaw, 2005).

The link between gangs and delinquency has been hotly debated and, broadly speaking, three perspectives or explanations emerge:

- a selection effect: gangs attract individuals who are already delinquent or violent before joining;
- social facilitation: there is no difference between gang members and non-gang members at the point at which young people join the gang, and it is the gang itself that encourages delinquency through socialisation into its norms and values; or
- enhancement: new gang members are recruited from a pool of individuals who show a propensity to engage in crime and violence, but this intensifies once in the gang (Thornberry et al, 1993, cited in Stretesky and Pogrebin, 2007).

The third explanation may be the most plausible, and issues about friendship, bonding, protection and potentially enjoyable involvement in expressive offending or anti-social behaviour all contribute to the attraction of gang membership. This is illustrated in Deucher's (2010) study in Glasgow, where gang membership provided a means of social support and of gaining compensatory forms of masculine status in the absence of jobs and other conventional routes to male adulthood. While Deucher sees positives for young men he interviewed through their in-group identity and engagement in recreational conflict over territory, he also points to the negative impact on their physical mobility as expressed by one of his participants:

> 'If you walked into [a rival housing scheme], you wouldnae get back oot.' (2010, p 265)

Social mobility for these young men was also affected by being part of a gang as well as their sense of citizenship and engagement in their community. Paradoxically, anti-social behaviour powers and criminal justice sanctions used against such groups may further entrench their isolation and exclusion and make the natural processes of moving away from a primary orientation to the peer group (and therefore towards desistance from crime and anti-social behaviour) more difficult.

Changing behaviours

Anti-social behaviour may be dealt with at a community level through the use of dispersal powers, alcohol banning orders and other measures. The powers also aim to change behaviour at an individual level through acceptable behaviour contracts, ASBOs and the orders that will replace them, as well as the parenting order, making the family a key site for intervention. Sadly, the focus was – and still is – on parenting skills and parental responsibility, neglecting the complex and diverse needs that may contribute to poor parenting (Jamieson, 2005). Millie (2009) refers to this as a 'blame the parent' strategy that diverts attention from social circumstances and the adequacy or otherwise of support systems for families under stress. The intention of both New Labour's Family Intervention Projects and the larger Troubled Families Fund initiated by the coalition government is to offer flexible support at an enhanced level. Worryingly, however, the language used by politicians constructs these families as failing to engage with agencies, not the agencies failing to engage with families in a relevant way, and this is reflected in deeply stigmatising media coverage (Parr and Nixon, 2008).

The parenting order, created by Sections 8-10 of the CDA 1998, imposes requirements on parents or carers to help them support their child in addressing his or her anti-social/offending behaviour. It was originally available when a court made an ASBO or a sex offender order on a child or young person or following conviction for an offence. It is also available where a parent or guardian is found guilty of an offence under the Education Act 1996 relating to non-attendance at school. The Anti-social Behaviour Act 2003 allowed for parenting orders to be made in independent proceedings on the application of the YOT, that is, without the need for an order on a child or young person to be in place. The same Act also introduced the parenting contract as a precursor to a full court order.

The parenting order must contain one or both of two elements: (a) requirements that can last up to 12 months encouraging the parent or carer to exercise a measure of control over the child or young person, by, for example, ensuring he or she attends school regularly or avoids certain places and people; and (b) a requirement on the parent or carer to attend counselling or guidance sessions for up to three months. Subject to certain conditions, this could include a residential course.

One controversy around this focus on parenting and parental responsibility is its gendered impact. Hunter and Nixon (2001) show how single female-headed households have been targeted as a problem and treated punitively in eviction and other legal proceedings. The Home Office does not collect data on the demographic characteristics of those made subject to parenting orders but research in the first three months that parenting orders were available suggested that 79 per cent were made on mothers (Lindfield, 2001, cited in Holt, 2008). Parenting orders can offer valuable support and guidance (Holt, 2008), but such help could be available to families in a less coercive and stigmatising way. There is evidence that in some cases the labelling associated with orders or with intervention from anti-social behaviour officers is acutely felt as punitive. For instance, one parent involved in a small qualitative study commented that:

> 'You can't treat a whole family as responsible for the behaviour of a 12 year old – especially when he's got ADHD. It just isn't right ... they are punishing these children ... they are punishing them for an illness they can't control.' (quoted in Squires and Stephen, 2005, p 139)

Turning to ASBOs, it would appear that they have had a potential deterrent effect and so could influence behaviour. However, they have been most effective with young people when the processes were clear and conditions set were understandable and seemed relevant to the young person, bearing in mind that young people may have a fairly instrumental interpretation of what they are allowed to do and what is forbidden. McIntosh (2008), for instance, discusses research that involved in-depth case studies with two young men subject to both intensive supervision and surveillance programmes and ASBOs, following on from acceptable behaviour orders. In one case, 'Donald' expressed confusion about warning letters from the anti-social behaviour unit for behaviour that he felt was a criminal offence as he could not understand why it was treated as anti-social behaviour and not a crime. Later on, he was made subject to an acceptable behaviour contract and fulfilled the conditions of the contract, so was puzzled why he was then made subject to an ASBO having committed an unrelated offence. Later again, his ASBO prevented him from associating with named individuals, but within a close-knit community he was finding it difficult to avoid these friends, particularly when he was in the presence of other friends with whom he was permitted to spend time. Enforcement of ASBOs did not allow for a distinction between intentional and unintentional breaches resulting, in this instance, in a sense of injustice. It is easy to see how anti-social behaviour interventions could become counter-productive and frustrate any motivation that the young person may have to comply, although, as McIntosh notes, young people's experiences of anti-social behaviour processes and their unintended consequences have not been given a great deal of attention (2008).

A new framework for addressing anti-social behaviour?

It should already be apparent that a complex apparatus was put in place to respond to the real and perceived threat of anti-social behaviour. This included individual measures such as the ASBO and parenting order as well as social responses such as Youth Inclusion Projects and Positive Activities for Young People (see Chapter Fourteen). At a community level, a further range of powers was developed over successive pieces of legislation, creating a complex array of provisions.

Coming into power, the coalition government initially promoted a different rhetoric, less keen on regulating behaviour and more focused on empowering local communities, but this transformed in the aftermath of the riots in 2011 (Heap and Smithson, 2012). The new, smaller range of orders to replace and extend the previous powers (Home Office, 2012) were intended to provide swifter and more flexible remedies for anti-social behaviour linked to the localism agenda and the role of the Police and Crime Commissioners. But in practice the coalition government has turned back to the type of centrally driven conduct regulation that they criticised under New Labour (Heap and Smithson, 2012).

The new powers are:

- community protection notice, dealing with litter, defacement, noise and other environmental issues;
- community protection order (public space), allows restrictions to be applied to prevent anti-social behaviour in local areas, and is more flexible than the powers it replaces;
- community protection order (closure), replaces a range of powers to close down premises (for example, crack houses) into one power;

- direction power, replaces the dispersal order and does not require the designation of a specific dispersal zone so removes bureaucracy and enables swifter action;
- criminal behaviour order, replaces the CRASBO and the drinking banning order. Will be available in criminal courts on conviction but will itself be a civil order that can include positive requirements as well as prohibitions. A breach would constitute a criminal offence punishable by up to five years in prison;
- crime prevention injunction, replaces the ASBO and four other orders. It will be a civil injunction requiring a civil standard of proof (basis of probability). The test will be that the individual has engaged in conduct capable of causing nuisance or annoyance to any person and that it is just and convenient to grant the injunction. There would be no minimum or maximum terms set out in law, similar to other injunctions.

In addition to these, the White Paper, *Putting victims first: More effective responses to anti-social behaviour* (Home Office, 2012), announced the introduction of a *community trigger* whereby community members have the right to demand that agencies take action against anti-social behaviour. Local areas will decide the thresholds to be applied and how this will operate, and pilots are currently in place in three authorities. New systems of police call handling and more effective identification of high risk victims are also being piloted. An extra – and potentially controversial – feature appeared in the draft Anti-social Behaviour, Crime and Policing Bill for the first time – *the community remedy*. This places an obligation on each local policing body to produce a list of potential actions that individuals engaged in anti-social behaviour or crime could be required to undertake as an alternative to formal court proceedings.

Altogether, these new measures do allow more flexibility and discretion to tailor responses to the needs of local areas, but they are still significant formal powers for the control of behaviours. They may create opportunities for improved practice, but there are real risks as well, certainly in terms of the potential to impose rapid punitive restrictions if local politics and networks of relationships demand. Although wrapped up in a rhetoric of empowering beleaguered communities, it is far from clear that the measures will assist to any real extent in creating appropriate and inclusive resolution of problems.

Implications for practice

It is important that practitioners understand the context in which anti-social behaviour has been highlighted as a major social problem. It represents a channel for more general adult concerns at a time of great insecurity and an attempt to control and regulate behaviours. But it is also the case that experience of persistent anti-social behaviour is deeply troubling, particularly for those who feel least empowered to deal with it and to make sure it stops. Consequently, criminal justice agencies are under great pressure to be seen to 'do something about' anti-social behaviour.

Clearly anti-social behaviour has become firmly associated with young people. In certain situations this is justified, in others less so, and there are instances where simply 'hanging around' is viewed as problematic, without reference to what the group of young people is actually doing. Restrictions on where young people can meet and their social space have implications – being together in groups is an important part of growing up and developing a social identity. Anti-social behaviour policies focused on enforcement rather than negotiation with young people can result in a sense of injustice and exclusion, and there is a necessary role as advocate and broker for them.

The question is how to develop appropriate and proportionate responses to anti-social behaviour that do not result in all young people in a particular area being treated with suspicion. Using a youth-centred approach, YOTs are able to influence practice in localities, working through strategic groups at local authority and neighbourhood levels to ensure that legal powers and relevant support services are used flexibly and to maximum effect, without undue negative impacts. This sounds logical and straightforward but may be less easy in practice if multi-agency groups are overly focused on enforcement. Success relies on building alliances with other agencies and formulating credible proposals for action, involving young people and local communities in seeking solutions wherever possible.

YOTs may also have influence in individual cases, particularly where there is multi-agency discussion before a court order is imposed. It may be that suitable restrictions could be placed on bail or post-custody licence conditions, so a separate order for anti-social behaviour is not needed. YOT practitioners may also advise on the wording of prohibitions and positive requirements so these are appropriate and do not unduly impinge on rights or prevent a young person engaging in constructive developmental activities.

In terms of work with individual young people, practitioners also have a role in ensuring that young people understand the expectations of them and are supported to comply with any prohibitions or requirements. Advocacy may also be important if orders need to be amended or in instances of minor infringements.

Finally, practitioners may feel antipathy towards elements of the anti-social behaviour agenda, especially where media hype seeks to blame young people. Nevertheless, it is important to engage with the other agencies involved to help develop a balanced approach, both in individual cases and at a more strategic level. This means appreciating the imperatives for police and community safety departments to relieve anti-social behaviour pressure points and to achieve measurable reductions in reports of anti-social behaviour, and working with them in constructive ways towards those goals.

Further reading

Burney, E. (2005) *Making people behave: ASB, politics and policy*, Cullompton: Willan.

Millie, A. (2009) *Anti-social behaviour*, Maidenhead: Open University Press.

Squires, P. (ed) (2008) *ASBO nation: The criminalisation of nuisance*, Bristol: The Policy Press.

Squires, P. and Stephen, D. (2005) *Rougher justice: ASB and young people*, Cullompton: Willan.

Section 3

ISSUES FOR YOUTH JUSTICE PRACTICE

ELEVEN

Aspects of risk

This book has already established that concerns about risk lie at the heart of current youth justice practice, shifting its focus somewhat away from welfare (although the two remain inextricably linked). Present-day society is markedly *risk-averse* and, in relation to young people, adults are highly sensitised to a variety of risks, including risks that result from neglect, abuse and illness, for example, and the various risks that might arise from young people's offending or anti-social behaviour. Other behaviours are also seen as 'risky': drink and drug use, sexual practices and offences such as driving stolen cars. But these tend to be conflated into a general notion of young people and 'riskiness', whereas keeping the distinctions is helpful in determining specific and appropriate responses.

Research, such as the Inventing Adulthoods (Henderson et al, 2007) and Disconnected Youth? studies (MacDonald and Marsh, 2005), show that young people are also highly attuned to risk and many are skilful in negotiating the risks that they face. The starting point for discussions in this chapter is young people's perceptions of risks and risk-taking. Their views of what is acceptable risk and what is not may differ from adults, but are also affected by the context in which the risk decision takes place.

Risk assessment is a core requirement of youth justice practice and is now framed by the use of structured assessment tools. These are more helpful in assessing risk of re-offending than harm or serious harm, and the chapter goes on to consider the challenges of complex risk assessment and the use of professional judgement. Attention then turns to intensive interventions with young people in community settings such as ISS schemes, questioning their purpose and the impacts they might have.

The chapter then goes on to look at the research on young people and violence, outlining links with early development and attachment, which indicate that violent young people represent a worrying and typically highly damaged group among offenders. Contrary to popular belief, they are a minority within the YJS and the system, on the whole, is not well prepared to respond to their multiple needs. The chapter concludes by examining risk management across agencies, focused on public protection or safeguarding.

Young people navigating risks

The notion of risk is pervasive, present in public discourse, in the way that problems are framed, and in policy responses. In relation to young people, 'risk' encompasses concerns about vulnerability, exclusion and marginalisation, often unhelpfully confused with concerns about risk of harm (Kemshall, 2007). In a *risk society* individuals are responsiblised in relation to their life choices, but only too often this is assumed to be a relatively straightforward and rational process and that individuals can develop a high degree of reflexivity and ability to assess and reassess their options. Failure to do so may then be characterised as poor decision-making or imprudence on behalf of the individual (Boeck et al, 2006). This means that certain policy areas such as public health work on the presumption that better and more accessible information will influence sexual or drug-using behaviours – for example, if young people are given information and options, most will rationally choose not to take risks (Spencer, 2013). But to what extent does this reflect the reality of decision-making for young people? And are risks that young people recognise the same that adults see?

From psychological perspectives, young people's risk-taking may be explained by neurological changes (Coleman, 2011) and by impulsivity and increased tendencies to seek rewards or sensations towards mid-adolescence (Steinberg, 2010). Sociological studies give other insights into young people's relationship to risk and how it is influenced by wider social and cultural norms, the specific social context and the power relations in that context, and habituation – activities, such as injecting heroin, viewed at first as risky, seem less so as they become routine and 'normalised' (France, 2000). Interestingly,

> How young people cope with, and manage social exclusion may well have an impact on the types of risks they are willing to take. Managing "differences" and being outside of dominant street and peer groupings may well require certain young people to take risks as a method of being accepted or being seen to "fit in".... Risk taking therefore arises because of a hierarchy of power in which groups who control social space and culture influence the behaviour of others. In this context risk-taking becomes a strategy of avoidance and a method of gaining social acceptance and safety. (France, 2000, p 328)

The Action Risk project (Green et al, 2000; Mitchell et al, 2001) explored young people's daily negotiations around risk. The study took place in one small geographical area, Townville, which has suffered the effects of industrial and urban decline, and so presented unusually high risks for young people related to economic marginality, environment and health. The study undertook qualitative interviews with two groups, young men and young women who were mothers, who were recruited through networks and were therefore self-selecting.

Risks were very much in the forefront of these young people's considerations. The young women took fewer active risks than the young men, but they were more conscious of physical danger, violence and personal safety, whereas the young men were more likely to associate risk-taking with positive qualities such as excitement (Mitchell et al, 2001). What is interesting is that in their accounts, 'young people frequently depicted themselves as risk managers and survivors rather than as "problematic" or "deviant" risk-takers' (2001, p 223). Official discourse has particularly focused on young parenthood as a risky and irresponsible life choice but this is not how these young mothers viewed themselves. Indeed, despite the initial 'risky' act of unprotected sex, they spoke positively of motherhood as a means of moving towards adulthood and adult status, bringing with it a sense of growing personal maturity and responsibility (2001).

For young men, risk-taking was sometimes a positive search for a 'heroic' identity, through driving stolen cars and other activities. In fact there was an underlying theme in the way that both genders talked about risk in terms of putting themselves in physical danger (Green et al, 2000). However, on other occasions the young men described taking risks as defensive or reactive, so for them it was about rather more than simple pleasure seeking. Their accounts show that:

> To be a "normal" young man in Townville is to engage with risk but to survive with one's masculine identity intact requires the development of appropriate risk management strategies. Indeed survival on the streets of Townville requires skilful risk management, especially with the ever present risk of physical violence. (Mitchell et al, 2001, p 227)

Managing risk and 'risk reputations' (Green et al, 2000, p 113) was thus seen as important for identity and connected with status and social recognition, but was also a pragmatic response to a specific environment holding many physical, social and environmental risks. In some respects, these young people conformed to gendered stereotypes of young men fighting and chasing thrills and young women more passively 'at risk' through early parenthood. Yet they rejected such stereotypes and often interpreted or experienced the risks they faced, the risks they took and their risky identities quite differently (Mitchell et al, 2001). Many risks related to the environment, crime, use of cannabis and so on were 'normalised', accepted as part and parcel of everyday life, whereas others were seen as worrying. Critically, these different perceptions were based on the experience of living in Townville and its culture:

> Young people are constantly engaged in risk assessment, actively creating and defining hierarchies premised upon different discourses of risk as "normal" and acceptable or "dangerous" and out of control. Beneath these hierarchies, we must recognise the importance of the context of specific lived experiences. This was demonstrated in relation to older young people's distinction between recreational users of drugs and addicts ie "smack heads" on the streets of Townville. (Green et al, 2000, p 124)

This research illustrates that young people view risks and assess them in socially and culturally specific ways, which is the subject of further research by Boeck et al (2006) analysing young people's risk decisions in relation to social capital. This started with two key questions concerning:

* the resources that the individual has, that is, the competence and capacity to act, choosing alternatives and implementing choices; and

- the structural and contextual constraints affecting use of those resources.

The sample surveyed for this research included 131 young people accessed through YOTs and Youth Inclusion and Support Projects (YISPs) and 458 young people recruited through local schools and youth groups (whose offending/non-offending status was unknown). Debates about social capital frequently assume that it is necessarily positive and that possession of social capital will tend to enhance pro-social norms, which is not inevitably the case. This research found two groups of young people, those with tightly bonded networks, and those with more diverse networks built around school or college. While there may be fluidity and movement between these groups over time, it is interesting that the majority of the YOT/YISP cohort tended to fall into the first group, with limited social contacts and activities based around their immediate home environment and peer groups. At interview, they also tended to express a sense of fatalism about their future. Boeck et al (2006) describe many of these young people in a state of *risk stagnation* – while their lifestyles and offending may in themselves be risky, leaving that lifestyle also carries risks that they may not be prepared or equipped to take. Referring back to the work of MacDonald and Marsh (2005) in East Kelby (see Chapter Five), the authors comment that, rather than being devoid of social capital, these young people had forms of bonding capital which help them cope with everyday life and the risk of exclusion, but may be extremely restricting when it comes to taking positive risks and grasping opportunities. In contrast, young people with more open and flexible forms of social capital are better able to engage with *risk navigation*, capitalising on contacts and resources in order to move towards a markedly more ambitious vision of the future.

Risk in youth justice

In line with other public services – health, social care and probation – New Labour's reformed YJS adopted structured methods of assessment, in this case the framework around Asset and Onset (for those at an early stage of offending), based on research indicating personal characteristics and circumstances that may be associated with offending, although not necessarily directly causing it (Case, 2007). It is important to identify such risk factors and to use this knowledge to inform interventions or actions to manage risk. However, it is equally important to recognise that risk assessments based on structured tools are designed for practitioners and for the various needs of the YJS, which includes ensuring that work is purposeful and to assist in targeting resources. They are not primarily designed with a broad view of multiple risks or with the engagement of young people in mind, but neither do they prevent practitioners actively seeking to understand young people's personal narratives about their lives and their perceptions of risk. Baker and Kelly (2011, p 70) discuss the need for sensitivity in the assessment process around any potential conflicts between the adult and the young person's perspectives, and suggest that practitioners should be:

- taking a collaborative approach within a prescriptive context;
- seeing young people's responses to risk as rational within their lived experiences; and
- allowing young people to describe and give meaning to their own lives rather than simply asking them to for information to be analysed from an adult perspective.

In this way the view of the individual young person can be integrated into the risk assessment, and this should ensure that both the risk assessment and any plan of action arising from it is meaningful and relevant (Baker and Kelly, 2011). With this in mind, the new assessment system, Assetplus, may be helpful in allowing more scope for young people to contribute to assessment and to consider strengths and motivations (YJB, 2011).

Making the young person central to the assessment requires the practitioner to be confident in the assessment process and to be able to work creatively with any required assessment format. The current core Asset form covers static or fixed characteristics such as offending history and care status, then goes on to gather information over 12 separate areas or domains, including living arrangements, lifestyle, education/employment and substance use, which may be more amenable to change. Issues or problems within any domain are termed *dynamic risk factors*, and the practitioner is asked to score these areas according to their potential impact on offending.

This approach, built on the risk factor prevention paradigm (see Farrington, 2007), works on the premise that identifying and addressing indicators of risk and strengthening positive or *protective factors* as early as possible in the development of a young person, will be most successful at preventing later offending and other negative life outcomes. Moreover, that focusing on risks and those areas of need that might create risks if left unaddressed is likely to have the most impact on further offending. The compelling logic of this idea rather belies the difficulties in accurate risk prediction in individual cases, rather than across large populations, and the uncertainties that exist about exactly how risk factors influence behaviours and the complex relationships between risk factors (Kemshall, 2007). These concerns are explored further in Chapter Fourteen; for the present, the significant point is that the risk factor prevention paradigm dominated risk assessment practice in the YJS under New Labour, and that it is questionable as the sole basis for looking at risk, particularly risk of harm rather than risk of re-offending. As Case (2007, p 97) notes, 'the RFPP does not allow a complete understanding of *how* and *why* risk/protective factors work and don't work'. He argues that the existing knowledge of risk factors developed within a narrow research framework could be enhanced by a more open approach and the inclusion of more qualitative and other research findings. It does seem that the coalition government are adopting this approach in developing Assetplus (YJB, 2011), incorporating new knowledge about desistance and also consideration of speech, language and communication needs (YJB, 2013a).

In youth justice as in probation, risk assessment based on knowledge derived from large-scale studies of offenders can be helpful as guidance in indicating the probability of particular behaviours occurring. However, even where statistical methods looking at static risk factors are combined with practitioner assessment of dynamic risk factors in tools such as Asset (or even Assetplus), the accuracy of predicting reconviction for a specific individual is greater than prediction of harmful behaviour. This is even more so for young people than for adults, because typically they have less offending history on which to base an assessment. Essentially, it is easier to recognise patterns and to anticipate common behaviours than unusual ones, which means that assessing the likelihood of serious violence – which is relatively rare among young people – and how imminent it might be requires the practitioner to draw extensively on his or her body of knowledge and judgement. Areas such as age, maturity, impulsivity, cognitive development and social relationships need to be considered, as well as the positive characteristics, attitudes and supports that the young person may possess.

Furthermore, assessment tools assist in the gathering of information but the task of analysis still rests with the practitioner, who is expected to assess the salience of different risk factors and to interpret what they then might mean in order to respond appropriately (Baker, 2007). In cases of violent behaviour, this means being specific about the nature of the violence, the level of harm that might ensue, the specific circumstances where it is most likely to occur and possible triggers. It is also necessary to distinguish between harm and *serious harm* defined in Section 224(3) of the CJA 2003 as *death or serious personal injury, whether physical or psychological.*

A variety of sources should be used to gather information, which allows for cross-referencing and checking of validity. Views or accounts from different parties may differ, and essentially it is the assessor's role to 'produce a new narrative that takes account of conflicting perspectives' (Baker and Kelly, 2011, p 76). Within the Asset framework, the 'Risk of serious harm' form is used to record this information and the practitioner's judgement about the likelihood and potential impacts of violence. Specialist tools may also be used to assess specific concerns such as mental health or violence.

It is helpful to view assessment as anticipatory, the best guess about what might happen or a hypothesis that should be testable against the evidence available (Baker et al, 2011). Research suggests that, in practice, practitioners often tend to gather evidence to support and reinforce existing beliefs or explanations. More open practice involves a process of constantly reviewing hypotheses in the light of change and as new information or a change in circumstances appears (Baker, 2007). A robust approach to analysis and decision-making is needed, one that considers a range of possibilities and demonstrably chooses the one that fits the available evidence most closely, thus promoting *defensibility* rather than cautious and defensive practice. Risk assessment is a 'highly fallible undertaking' (Whyte, 2009, p 82), and perhaps what practitioners should aim for is not complete accuracy but that the methods and judgements involved in their assessment will stand up to scrutiny.

It cannot be assumed that the techniques of assessment and risk management used with adult offenders will transfer across to work with young people (Kemshall, 2007). Risks, needs and vulnerabilities may be intertwined in complex ways, and it is important not just to look at those risks that are most immediately related to crime (*criminogenic needs*), but to seek a more holistic view that that takes account of early childhood experiences and development (Boswell, 2007). In determining how to respond to the concerns highlighted in assessment, Kemshall (2007, p 14) proposes the following principles to inform risk management:

- risk management should be just, proportionate and fair and targeted at well-assessed risk factors;
- interventions should have regard to level of maturity, learning capacity and the social skill level of children and young people;
- cognitive behavioural programmes should be age-appropriate, sensitive to the learning style of the young person and supported by appropriate motivational work and reinforcement;
- a traditional learning style is likely to be inappropriate for many young people, as many of them will have had unsatisfactory experiences in school.

Because young people's circumstances may be chaotic and may change rapidly (Blyth, 2007), risk management also needs to be capable of responding quickly. A number of agencies may be involved with young people with complex difficulties, so quality, accuracy and timeliness of communication is essential. And communication with the young person should be clear and effective as well, particularly in situations of crisis or when needs become acute.

What about persistent offenders?

Risk of harm, of course, is not the only concern for the YJS: persistent offending has also received attention, specifically through the development of fast-track processes through the court and the introduction of what was initially known as the Intensive Supervision and Surveillance Programme (ISSP, now termed ISS). This intensive programme has certainly been used for young people subject to MAPPAs (Sutherland, 2009), but more individualised and flexible packages of intervention are often appropriate for those who are highly damaged and/or in need of therapeutic intervention. Evaluation also suggests that in many ways the structure of the ISS is more suited to young people with chaotic lifestyles and persistent patterns of offending, than for those with serious offences but fewer social and criminogenic needs (Moore et al, 2006).

ISSPs were introduced in YOTs progressively from 2001, drawn from examples from the US and earlier UK models, including those scattered projects working with prolific offenders that ultimately became the Prolific and Other Priority Offender scheme and then IOM. Until the youth rehabilitation order became available with a new range of requirements, an ISSP had no separate legal status, but could be delivered as part of a community order, a bail support programme or a notice of supervision or licence on release from custody.

There are criteria relating to either persistence or seriousness of offending, and young people can only be subject to an ISS requirement on a youth rehabilitation order where the *so serious* criterion for custody is met, reflecting its intended use as an alternative to custody. However, increasing numbers of young offenders are finding themselves on these highly restrictive programmes, going straight from referral orders and almost bypassing the other potential steps in the sentencing ladder. Although specifically designed as a diversion from custody at a point where there was extreme pressure on over-stretched prison accommodation (Moore et al, 2006), ISS has actually been credited with widening the youth justice net, bringing more young people into intensive forms of supervision and creating risk of custody for some through breach of their demanding orders (Graham, 2010).

ISS can be very flexible, with different programme lengths and intensities according to where the young person is allocated within the YJB's risk classification framework, the Scaled Approach. The baseline requirement for the original ISSP started with a minimum of 25 hours per week intervention, although over time variations have been introduced to accommodate the younger age group, those young people in employment and 'extended' programmes over 12 months. The YJB stipulates that each individual programme should contain elements of:

- education, training or employment
- offending behaviour
- interpersonal skills
- family support
- restorative justice.

Arrangements are in place for both face-to-face contact and monitoring of young people outside normal office hours by means of an electronic curfew. In theory, the majority of the hours should be provided through training schemes or school/alternative education placements for under-16s, but this can be a difficult group of young people to engage or maintain in structured activities and, in some instances, practitioners face a real challenge in creating coherent packages with sufficient elements of relevant intervention.

Such high levels of contact allow all sorts of possibilities for creative and highly supportive responses to young people's needs, but the national evaluation of the then ISSPs suggested that their popularity with sentencers was due to the ability to place restrictions on young people and to incapacitate (Moore et al, 2006). Interestingly, the evaluators note that 'these interventions, while potentially rehabilitative are used because they are punitive. More specifically, the programmes can help ensure that the offender receives his or her "just deserts" by enabling courts to tailor the punishment to the current offence' (2006, p 25).

In an even more stinging tome, Smith identifies the purposes and impacts of the ISS:

> It exerts a direct and explicit control of behaviour through its use of surveillance, compulsory attendance and mandatory activities; it provides a framework for supposedly individualised and calibrated intervention programmes; it develops a rationale grounded in notions of normal and socially useful attributes and activities. (2011, p 87)

Tightly structured and backed up by stringent enforcement, the stakes are high for young people on these programmes:

> A failure to comply and a refusal to take up the opportunities offered by ISSP can only be taken, in these terms, as confirmation of the initial pre-programme prognosis; these are "persistent" and ultimately incorrigible individuals for whom coercion and containment are the only realistic options in the interest of community safety. (2011, p 87)

Herein lie some of the real difficulties with ISS: it is about control not engagement, and allows limited flexibility to individualise programmes. The emphasis on sustaining a high number of hours of contact works counter to the professional obligation to develop quality relationships and interventions that are meaningful and appropriate, although, ironically, quality of relationships is a critical element in encouraging young people to comply with demanding requirements.

The funding mechanism for ISSP was initially centralised from the YJB and was ring-fenced for ISSP purposes, so restricting the ability of YOTs to 'grow' a selection of potential interventions of different intensities that could be put together to form individually tailored programmes for young people. This has been a real lost opportunity to develop responses to young people with persistent patterns of offending, and critics have argued that there have been deleterious impacts in terms of drawing young people unnecessarily into intensive forms of supervision (Smith, 2007) and often, hastening their path to custody. It has also encapsulated many of the worst aspects of youth justice under New Labour: a highly managerialist framework; emphasis on processing and containing young people, not intervention; a stretching of the boundaries of acceptable levels of control and surveillance; explicitly 'normalising' impulses that tend to direct young people to a restricted range of conventional sporting and other activities; and a moralising and correctional tone. This is not to deny that good work has often taken place within ISSP/ISS, but that such good work is not encouraged by the structure in place and has developed despite, rather than because of, it. Similar to young people who may pose a risk of serious harm, persistent or prolific young offenders often have complex needs and difficult personal histories. Sadly, the YJS has not been enabled to rise to the challenge that they present, although new possibilities such as intensive fostering, in the areas where that exists, may be promising.

Young people who commit violence

Whereas minor assaults are relatively common among young people, serious violence is a much less common event, particularly violence that is deliberate and instrumental rather than expressive. Serious sexual offences are also relatively rare. As an indicator, during 2010/11, of 72,011 sentences passed on 10- to 17-year-olds, 418 were imposed under Sections 90/91 of the Powers of the Criminal Court (Sentencing) Act, which provide for sentences of over two years for young people up to and including the juvenile equivalent of a life sentence. A further 36 young people were sentenced to detention for public protection, which is an indeterminate sentence equating to the imprisonment for public protection sentence for adults under the CJA 2003 (see Chapter Eighteen for a full explanation of these sentences). A subset of these sentenced young people were sentenced for offences of serious violence (such as grievous bodily harm, malicious wounding and, most seriously, attempted or actual homicide).

The risk factors for violence, as opposed to offending behaviour in general, are reasonably well known: the most obvious one is being male. Tracing the histories of violent young people it is apparent that many have displayed challenging behaviours from a young age. They may also experience problems such as biological vulnerabilities, neuropsychological deficits, difficulties within the family, social environment and school, and deviant peer groups and attitudes (Losel and Bender, 2006, cited in Boswell, 2007). These may be mitigated by positive interventions and supportive relationships, but in the absence of these, the combinations and interplay of these factors will increase the likelihood of violence. Boswell comments that, 'young people with these kinds of profiles are very familiar to researchers and criminal justice professionals. They frequently embody the child victim ... and the adolescent perpetrator in one person' (2007, p 45).

Boswell conducted research in the 1990s on children and young people imprisoned under Section 53 of the C&YPA 1933 for what were then called 'grave offences' (the legislation that preceded the current rather wider legal provisions for long-term sentences). She examined 200 case files and found that among these young people, 72 per cent had experienced abuse: in 28.5 per cent of these cases the abuse was emotional, in 29 per cent it was sexual, in 40 per cent it was physical and 1.5 per cent involved organised or ritual abuse. Twenty-seven per cent of the young people abused had experienced more than one type of abuse (Boswell, 1996). This replicates other research by Bailey (1996) with a small sample of young people convicted of murder, who found high levels of both physical and sexual abuse. Boswell sadly concluded that:

> There seems little doubt that child abuse and childhood experience of loss, when no effective opportunity is provided for the child to make sense of these experiences, constitutes unresolved trauma that is likely to manifest itself in some way at a later date. Many children become

depressed, disturbed, violent or all three, girls tending to internalise and boys to externalise their responses. (2007, p 46)

Bailey's (1996) study only involved 21 young people, 19 of whom were male. Nevertheless her analysis and discussion provides food for thought. As well as abuse, she found heightened levels of neuropsychological problems in her sample, which seems to resonate with Moffitt's (1993) characterisation of life course persistent offenders (discussed in Chapter Two). She also highlights the significance of attachment patterns, specifically for these young people, insecure attachments arising from parenting which is chronically inconsistent or rejecting:

> Over time the child learns a model of relationship in which anger and insecurity become core features. Unchanged, these hostile, angry models of relationships place the child in at heightened risk of problem behaviour including aggression. Additionally, as they enter adolescence the young person may view him/herself as incompetent and less in control. In contrast, competent adolescents are able to seek autonomy in ways that both meet their needs and respect the needs of others. (1996, p 21)

Writing as an adolescent forensic psychiatrist, Bailey is interested in pursuing work with young people within a 'therapeutic alliance' (Bailey et al, 2007), but she also notes the role of other aspects of support and services, including education, vocational training and family contact, to help them achieve the 'developmental tasks' of adolescence (Bailey, 1996). A coherent package of intervention delivered in the context of warm and consistent relationships is most likely to be achieved within closed institutions such as residential units or Local Authority Secure Children's Homes (LASCHs) (although research has indicated that the 'secure' element of secure care may be more prominent than the 'care' aspect; see Barry, 2009). For young people held in prison-type establishments or hospital settings, it may be more difficult for the YOT case manager to be part of the supportive network and to be actively involved in preparing a young person for eventual release. Options for holding a young person safely in the community with 'wraparound' support and services are still under-developed (Whyte, 2009), although intensive fostering is now available in some areas, and simple considerations of cost may inspire efforts to think in the direction of community provision.

Managing risk through multi-agency groups

YOTs themselves are comprised of different agencies and several practitioners may be working with any one person. As well as managing those complexities, the YOT case manager may have to engage with other organisations outside of the YOT and, in cases where higher levels of risk are involved – whether risks posed by or to the young person – with formal structures that bring agencies together to share information and to assess and manage risk. The principal risk management structure in the CJS is the MAPPA established by Sections 67 and 68 of the Criminal Justice and Court Services Act 2000. MAPPAs primarily oversee intervention with adult offenders (Kemshall and Wood, 2009) but their remit also covers young people who meet the eligibility criteria. This becomes complex where a young person who poses a risk is at the same time extremely vulnerable and subject to child protection procedures under the aegis of the Local Safeguarding Children's Board (LSCB). Both sets of risk management meetings should run in parallel with the offending and the safeguarding concerns being dealt with by separate groups, who should nevertheless be in communication and able to coordinate their actions; in such instances, the YOT case manager may be an important common element and a link between the two. If a young person in the MAPPA system is in local authority care, children's social care should be involved and represented at any meetings (Jones and Baker, 2009).

The main agencies involved with MAPPA are the police, probation and prisons, who are designated as 'responsible authorities'. YOTs are classified by the CJA 2003 as bodies with a 'duty to cooperate', although that position is anomalous as they are the only 'duty to cooperate' agency with direct supervisory responsibility for individuals (Jones and Baker, 2009). Arguably they should have been more centrally involved in the structure of MAPPA from the outset, whereas in fact research has suggested considerable uncertainty and ambivalence about MAPPA within YOTs and resistance in some instances to considering young people as 'risky' from MAPPA coordinators (Sutherland, 2009). This has been partially addressed over time, and certainly the influence of the YJB in sharpening up risk-related practice within YOTs, not least through the introduction of the Scaled Approach and a dedicated MAPPA referral system, has ensured that they now have stronger connections (Monk, 2009).

It is crucial in the context of a risk-focused penality that YOTs engage with MAPPA and that they contribute their particular expertise and knowledge of work with young people (Sutherland, 2009). The principal agencies involved are adult-centred, and key participants and decision-makers in meetings such as the MAPPA coordinator and chair may have varying degrees of confidence and understanding of the issues faced by young people and associated risks, needs and vulnerabilities. MAPPA participants may also be unsure about the nature of YOT involvement with young people and their responsibilities. It is not appropriate to treat young people as 'mini-adults' (Kemshall and Wood, 2009), and this places an onus on YOTs to explain the special needs and characteristics of young people coming within the MAPPA framework, and also to be clear about the specific duties of the YJS where public protection sits alongside other concerns about safeguarding and protection. Relatedly, Sutherland comments that:

> If YOTs participate in MAPP meetings without clearly stating their obligations (for example, reducing re-offending, public protection, child welfare, child protection) then they might be viewed as

> "youth probation" with the same emphasis on public protection and
> compliance, whereas there is a distinction between what YOTs and
> the probation service deliver. (2009, p 49)

The implications of this are twofold: first, a young person whose behaviours
indicate a risk of serious harm should not be excluded from full and rigorous
consideration within MAPPA simply because of youth and, second, MAPPA
decisions should be informed and sensitive to the young person's age and stage
of development. As Sutherland observes, 'young people as a distinct but far from
homogenous group, may require handling with kid gloves (that is, with care and
sensitivity), but this may be hard to realise when they commit acts that seem un-
child-like' (2009, p 55).

Examining the criteria for referral to MAPPA and its three-tiered structure
does give some indication of why YOTs may be marginal to its working just on
the basis of numbers (although accurate statistics are not available; see Kemshall
and Wood, 2009). There are three categories of offenders eligible for MAPPA:

1. Registered sex offenders, that is, offenders required to comply with the
   notification requirements of the Sexual Offences Act 2003 (the 'sex offender
   register').
2. Violent and other sexual offenders sentenced to 12 months or more in custody.
3. Other offenders, not falling into Category 1 or 2, who are considered by the
   'responsible authority' to pose a risk of serious harm to the public. The offender
   must have a conviction that indicates that he or she is capable of causing serious
   harm and should be identified as falling within this category by the 'responsible
   authority' initially dealing with him or her.

In the case of Category 3 offenders, the YOT may be the agency initially in
contact with the young person but, not being a 'responsible authority', the YOT
cannot ultimately make the judgement about eligibility for Category 3. The YOT,
however, does have responsibility for notifying the MAPPA system of any young
people who receive a custodial sentence of over 12 months for violent and sexual
offences (this includes detention and training orders as well as Sections 90/91
and indeterminate sentences).

Notification to MAPPA does not necessarily mean that the individual case will
be managed in a multi-agency way, as there are three levels of case management
in MAPPA:

- *Level 1:* 'ordinary' risk management involving only one agency. For young
  people the single agency concerned will be the YOT, and most young people
  notified to the MAPPA system will be dealt with at this level.
- *Level 2:* active involvement of more than one agency and coordination of
  interventions to manage the presenting risk of harm.

- *Level 3:* Multi-agency Public Protection Panels to manage the *critical few*, drawing together key active partners who take joint responsibility at a senior level for the management of these offenders in the community. Cases managed at Level 3 will typically be the most complex and/or requiring unusual resource commitments. This level may also be used for cases that are not assessed as high or very high risk, but may attract considerable media or public attention. Given the media hype that can blow up around cases of violence involving young people, it is not inconceivable that management of young people at Level 3 is warranted on that basis.

Interestingly, for all the emphasis on structured decision-making using evidence-based tools in the CJS, research has shown that practitioners and managers at MAPPA meetings are drawing on a mixture of clinical and actuarial knowledge to inform their judgements on risk (Kemshall et al, 2005), reflecting the complex and contingent nature of the behaviours, situations and risks being considered. MAPPA meetings are a forum for information exchange between agencies and also a means of exploring possible analyses and understandings of risk. This can be an open and challenging process, but it is also possible for decision-making to become subject to collective distortions or 'group-think' (Beckett, 2010), resulting in the risk of harm being grossly under- or over-estimated. Kemshall (2002, p 107) talks of the potential for a 'closed professional system' allowing little challenge to established views, with a great deal of subjectivity involved. Clearly MAPPA meetings – and other multi-agency meetings around child protection, anti-social behaviour and so on – can operate in that way, but at their best they can provide a robust and coherent means of enabling the principal agency involved to manage risk and to marshal resources from other agencies in this endeavour. In that sense, there are opportunities for YOTs to exploit at managerial and practitioner level through constructive, rather than reluctant, engagement with MAPPAs.

Implications for practice

The YJS is charged with the task of reducing a variety of risks and must engage with the complexity of the multiple demands on its resources, particularly where young people are vulnerable as well as 'risky'. Youth-centred practice requires a sophisticated understanding of risk that can appreciate and respond to the way that the individual young person might view 'risk choices'. This suggests that restrictions and constraints should be used conservatively and with careful consideration so that risk is managed in an effective and targeted way, but without undue impact on the young person's rights and developmental needs. Better prospects lie in working collaboratively with young people, exploring incentives for change and helping them in the task of self-managing risk.

The YJS, in common with other public services, has adopted structured forms of assessment. These have been useful in establishing greater consistency and reliability in conducting and recording assessments, but are more accurate in assessing the risk of re-offending than risk of serious harm, where practitioner judgement is still essential.

Assessment involves collecting information from a variety of sources, checking its validity and, crucially, interpreting and analysing information. A structured format may help with the first two of these, but the third is a skilled professional task that requires practitioners to apply their understanding and knowledge of human development, behaviours and social circumstances. Assetplus may be more helpful in this regard than the original Asset framework. Assessment can be more or less systematic and more or less informed: aiming to be as systematic and as informed as time and resources allow does not take away the element of uncertainty but can ensure that assessment, and decisions and actions based on assessment, can stand up to scrutiny and are defensible.

It is not necessarily the case that all children who experience significant trauma, loss or abuse in early years will later display harmful behaviours, but research suggests that these elements are disproportionately present in the early lives of young people who commit serious violent offences. Work with these young people is sensitive and may involve CAMHS or other specialist services to help resolve the long-term impact of such experiences. Youth-centred practitioners should be conscious of their role and contribution within a network of support and intervention, particularly in relation to key points in sentencing or in parole decisions where risk assessment is critical.

Practitioners should be aware of the potential for bias in their assessments. In theory, sharing the task of risk assessment and management, as in MAPPA meetings and child protection case conferences, should challenge the assumptions and the limitations that might be present in any single agency approach, producing a more robust and well-informed assessment. However, this is dependent on the dynamic of the meeting and how open the process is – groups can be collectively cautious and may close down rather than explore new understandings or approaches.

Good assessment practice means being able to develop explanations or hypotheses based on a sufficient amount of available evidence, and being open to changing ideas and hypotheses when new evidence arrives or where the validity of existing evidence is questioned. Whether the risk assessment is a group or an individual process, the outcome is tentative rather than definitive, and should always be open to review. This is hard to hold on to – although necessary at the same time – in practice cultures that demand that judgements be definite, not provisional, and in the face of tasks such as reports for court or for the parole board requiring specific guidance about risk and the most appropriate actions in the light of risk assessment.

Further reading

Blyth, M., Solomon, E. and Baker, K. (eds) (2007) *Young people and 'risk'*, Bristol: The Policy Press.

Kemshall, H. (2003) *Understanding risk in criminal justice*, Maidenhead: Open University Press.

Moore, R., Gray, E., Roberts, C., Taylor, E. and Merrington, S. (2006) *Managing persistent and serious offenders in the community: Intensive community programmes in theory and practice*, Cullompton: Willan.

TWELVE

Safeguarding young people

Safeguarding is of paramount concern for youth justice because of its interest in the safety and well-being of the young people within its ambit. More specifically, some young people within the YJS pose risks to other children or young people. Some young people may experience abuse or neglect, and practitioners need to be confident about responding where indicators arise. Other young people may be subject to ongoing child protection procedures, requiring practitioners to work and to share information within multi-agency settings. These situations make complex demands of professionals and, of course, individual young people may at the same time behave in ways that create risks for others and be at risk themselves, which adds further dimensions of complexity. So it is vital to have clear and effective links between youth justice and children's social care (in England) or social services (in Wales), and mutual understanding of roles and accountabilities.

This chapter lays out the responsibilities and procedures in relation to child protection. However, over and above that it explores the wider concerns about safeguarding and how they have been encompassed within recent social policy, focusing on early intervention to address problems and circumstances that might have an impact on well-being and healthy development. Policy is in the midst of change following Professor Eileen Munro's review of the child protection system (Munro, 2011b). This chapter outlines the nature of change, and attempts to create a more child-centred system, looking at the implications for social work and for youth justice.

So what is safeguarding?

The term 'safeguarding' has come into use relatively recently in official documentation relating to children and young people (Frost and Parton, 2009). Before New Labour came into office, the emphasis had been very much on child protection, but the incoming government took a broader view, seeing safeguarding as a means of reframing the issues and problems evident in the child protection system. *Working together to safeguard children: A guide to inter-agency working to safeguard and promote the welfare of children* (DH et al, 1999) was the first guidance explicitly to refer to safeguarding, although the concept had been fundamental to the earlier Children Act 1989 and its 'child in need' provisions (Frost and Parton, 2009).

The current version of *Working together* defines safeguarding as: protecting children from maltreatment; preventing impairment of children's health or development; ensuring that children are growing up in circumstances consistent with the provision of safe and effective care; and taking action to ensure that all children have the best outcomes (DfE, 2013, p 7). The guidance describes child protection as 'a part of safeguarding and promoting welfare. This refers to the activity that is undertaken to protect specific children who are suffering, or are likely to suffer, significant harm' (DfE, 2013, p 85).

Under the Children Act 2004, responsibilities for safeguarding lie primarily with local authorities that have children's services responsibilities (county or unitary authorities) working in collaboration with other agencies. With this in mind, the Act,

- created the posts of children's commissioners for England, Scotland and Wales;
- required leadership at local authority level through a director of children's services and an elected member with lead responsibility for children;
- replaced Area Child Protection Committees with Local Safeguarding Children's Boards;
- in Section 10 placed a duty on local authorities with children's services responsibilities to promote the cooperation of 'relevant partners' (such as YOTs) with a view to improving the well-being of children; and
- in Section 11 introduced statutory requirements for 'relevant partners' to discharge their functions having regard for the need to safeguard and promote the welfare of children.

This framework was intended to encourage early identification and resolution of problems, with all agencies involved with young people contributing to the overall aim of safeguarding. At a strategic level, each agency is expected to ensure that its workforce is skilled and confident in recognising potential abuse or neglect and in picking up early indicators of risk factors. This was expected to reduce the numbers of young people experiencing difficult circumstances and situations of abuse, which would then be reflected in fewer referrals to social care of children in need/in need of protection. In reality, this has not happened: Munro cites information from the Children in Need Census 2010 suggesting that referrals to children's social care in England rose by 1 per cent from 2008/09 to 2009/10, and that the number of children and young people receiving support as a 'child in need' increased by 25 per cent (2010, p 6). More children are being made subject to child protection plans, 42,300 in 2010/11 compared to 25,900 in 2004/05 (Green, 2012). And similar increases in referrals and requests for services are also evident in Scotland, Wales and Northern Ireland (Stafford et al, 2012).

This is a dramatic rise in numbers that could be explained as practitioners being cautious in their decisions after the inquiry into the death of Peter Connolly and their vilification in the press (Stafford et al, 2012). The increase could also be attributed to a more positive awareness of safeguarding concerns among practitioners in universal services (Green, 2012). However, the most credible analysis is that the child protection system is in crisis, and that the worthy attempt to take a more holistic approach through safeguarding has compounded rather than resolved essential conflicts. The Munro review, initiated by the incoming coalition government in 2010, is viewed as a critical moment by many (Blyth and Solomon, 2012), particularly as the government accepted the majority of its recommendations (DfE, 2011b) and has acted on them. However, a sense of history is needed in order to understand why the Munro review was so necessary and the prospects for constructive change.

A brief history of child protection

Concerns for child welfare and upbringing were clearly evident in the Victorian era and provided the impetus for introducing early powers of protection through legislation such as the Prevention of Cruelty to Children Act 1889 (Beckett, 2007).

Subsequently, the juvenile court was created in 1908 with jurisdiction over young people who were deprived and neglected, as well as those involved in offending. These concerns also underpinned the influential C&YPA 1933 and the development of the welfare state after 1945 as it began to take more responsibility for ensuring that social and economic conditions supported families and parenting. The Children Act 1948 required each local authority to set up a children's department employing child welfare officers, so providing a more secure base for the emerging profession of social work.

These changes were indicative of a broad concern with the welfare and development of children and prevention of delinquency. It was not until the 1960s and the 'discovery' of the 'battered baby syndrome' by C. Henry Kempe and colleagues that the abuse of children specifically came to the fore. The anxieties that this raised were amplified by the public outcry over a series of child deaths and the resulting inquiries, the most influential being the 1974 inquiry into the death of Maria Colwell. This was especially significant because it exposed what had previously been a private activity between social worker and client to intense public scrutiny (Frost and Parton, 2009). Other landmark inquiries concerned Jasmine Beckford (1985), and Tyra Henry and Kimberley Carlile (both 1987). The particularly critical reports from these inquiries received widespread publicity, while other, more favourable, reports were systematically overlooked (Munro, 2008). Collectively these reports highlighted inadequacies and blamed the social work professionals involved for their failures to predict risk, to communicate effectively and to take decisive action (Beckett, 2007). Selective media attention of this type has been – and continues to be – highly significant in shaping a narrow and defensive response to protecting children in England and Wales, in contrast to 'family service' models, for instance, in Belgium, Germany and Scandinavian countries (Stafford et al, 2012).

In the 1980s, attention moved from physical to child sexual abuse, in part because of feminist campaigns highlighting exploitation and abuse in domestic situations. The publicity surrounding the unfolding events in Cleveland in 1987 raised a different type of outcry about the powers of professionals to override the 'rights' of parents (Beckett, 2007). This time it was doctors as well as social workers in the spotlight (Frost and Parton, 2009), as over 100 children were removed from their families to an emergency place of safety in Middlesbrough General Hospital.

So this provided the context for the Children Act 1989 that remains the critical child protection legislation in England and Wales. Responding to the Cleveland case, as well as key reports and expert opinion, it set out an approach based on the principle of partnership with parents wherever possible. It tried to shift the balance towards prevention and family support through the 'child in need' provisions of Section 17. These imposed a duty on each local authority to safeguard and promote the welfare of children in need within their area, representing:

> Perhaps the first attempt in the Anglophone world to carry out a serious appraisal of the impact of the child protection system(s) which had developed since the 1960s. It attempted to keep to a minimum situations where social workers would rely upon a policing and investigatory approach dominated by a narrowly defined forensic concern, and aimed to put in its place an emphasis, wherever possible, on providing help and support with the agreement of parents and children. (Stafford et al, 2012, p 37)

However, the progressive aspects of the Act and the attempt to incorporate the expectations of the UNCRC 1989 by promoting prevention and early intervention were introduced in the strikingly unsympathetic political context of the 1990s and were out of step with the dominant social and political philosophy of the Conservative government (Frost and Parton, 2009). Few extra resources were made available for extended family support, and almost inevitably the result was a further concentration of social work effort on child protection cases.

On taking power in 1997, New Labour took a broader and more proactive approach, investing in initiatives to tackle social exclusion such as Sure Start (Frost and Parton, 2009) and improvements to the care system through Quality Protects. It was ambitious in its ideas for reforming and integrating children's services, and was further prompted to act by Lord Laming's inquiry into the death of Victoria Climbié (Laming, 2003). Consistent with earlier inquiries, his report highlighted poor communication and cooperation between agencies which meant that crucial information was not shared, resulting in the child's tragic – and sadly preventable – death. The *Every Child Matters* Green Paper (DfES, 2003) responded by setting out a vision for integrating children's services and for establishing safeguarding as a priority across a wide range of agencies, which later became the Children Act 2004.

Throughout the public sector New Labour adopted a managerial and process-driven approach; safeguarding and child protection were not excepted from these broad trends in social policy. The interagency guidance updated in 1999 was further revised in 2006 for England and again in 2010 (DCSF, 2010), eventually comprising 390 pages in the main document and a further 424 in supplementary guidance (Munro, 2010). The Inspection framework was tightened, and similar to youth justice, timescales for activities were imposed as well as structured forms of assessment, both specialised assessments for social workers and a more generic assessment for other professionals working with children in the form of the CAF or Common Assessment Framework.

While acknowledging that these initiatives were individually well designed and well intentioned, the Munro review (2010) found that the cumulative effect was over-regulation of practice and too great an emphasis on processes and procedures instead of relationships and the quality of service to children, young people and families. The first part of the review, a systems analysis, suggested that:

> Earlier reforms have also contributed to the growing imbalances in that they have tended to focus on technical solutions – increasing rules, more detailed procedures, more use of ICT – while giving less attention to the skills to engage with families, the expertise to bring about enduring improvements in parenting behaviour, and the organisational support that enables social workers and others to manage the emotional dimensions of the work without it harming their judgement or their own well-being. (Munro, 2010, p 7)

Munro also identified the child protection system as being shaped by:

- the importance of the safety and welfare of children and young people and the understandable strong reaction when a child is killed or seriously harmed;
- a commonly held belief that the complexity and associated uncertainty of child protection work can be eradicated;
- a readiness, in high profile public enquiries into the death of a child, to focus on professional error without looking deeply enough into its causes; and
- the undue importance given to performance indicators and targets which provide only part of the picture of practice, and which have skewed attention to process over the quality and effectiveness of help given. (2011b, p 6)

Youth justice must work constructively with the uncertainty and unpredictability of offending behaviour. Uncertainty is also at the heart of child protection work, but social workers and others are under pressure to deliver certainties and safety, too often resulting in defensive practice and compliance with procedures instead of prioritising time with children and parents (Munro, 2011b). Munro's recommendations are intended to address the professional and organisational constraints on practice, setting out a far-reaching vision for the future, which is discussed later in the chapter.

Overseeing safeguarding and child protection

Section 13 of the Children Act 2004 created LSCBs; they are established by local authorities with children's service responsibilities, and health, education and criminal justice agencies are statutory partners.

LSCB functions:
- to develop, audit and challenge policies and procedures for safeguarding and promoting the welfare of children;
- to raise awareness of how individuals and organisations can safeguard and promote the welfare of children;
- to monitor and evaluate effectiveness of how the authority and partners individually and collectively safeguard and promote children's welfare and advise on improvements;
- to participate in service planning;
- to listen to children, young people and their families and to draw on their insights when engaged in their other functions;
- to review serious cases (where abuse or neglect is known or suspected and where a child has died or been seriously harmed and there is cause for concern about how agencies have worked together) and advise on lessons to be learnt;
- to collect and analyse information about child deaths, putting in place procedures for ensuring a coordinated public health and safety response.

Source: Preston-Shoot (2012, p 27)

This is a large strategic agenda complicated by the fact that LSCBs are also expected to look at the detail of practice on the ground (Preston-Shoot, 2012). In England, LSCB activity should link in to the work of the Children Trust Board that has a more operational role in service planning and delivery in each local area. In Wales the LSCBs link into statutory children's partnerships and again, while maintaining independence, they should be informing and influencing the development of services. This is challenging and, almost inevitably, LSCBs have made progress but have not brought about the transformational change and renewed emphasis on safeguarding that New Labour hoped for. The priorities of future policy – refocusing schools on educational attainment, health service reform and the involvement of Police and Crime Commissioners – may also deflect attention away from partnership work and the broader landscape of safeguarding (Solomon and Blyth, 2012). More positively, the present government has accepted Munro's recommendations to strengthen the role and impact of LSCBs by ensuring that they report annually to the chief executive and leader of the local authority and other senior strategic leaders on the effectiveness of early help and protective services (DfE, 2011b).

The 'child in need'

The primary legislation governing child protection is still the Children Act 1989, the more recent Children Act 2004 emphasising structural change in services and governance, rather than child protection per se. The main responsibilities for local authorities relate to the 'child in need' and the 'child in need of protection' provisions.

Section 17(10)

A child shall be taken to be in need if:

a. He is unlikely to achieve or maintain, or to have the opportunity of achieving or maintaining, a reasonable standard of health or development without the provision for him of services by a local authority under this Part

b. His health or development is likely to be significantly impaired, or further impaired, without the provision for him of such services, or

c. He is disabled.

On 31 March 2011, 382,410 children and young people were classified as falling within Section 17, the majority through abuse or neglect, although there were also significant numbers assessed as children in need because of disability or family stress. A total of 63,680 were males and 53,790 were females aged between 10-15, and there were also 38,990 males and 31,290 females over the age of 16 (DfE, 2011a). Needs and vulnerabilities are demonstrably not restricted to younger children, but these statistics may reflect a tendency to treat these older age groups as children in need rather than invoking the heavier and more specific powers to take actions to protect (Rees and Stein, 2012).

Considering 'children in need of protection', Section 47 places a duty on children's social care (or social services in Wales) to investigate within a period of 48 hours where a child:

i. has been made subject to an emergency protection order under Section 44;
ii. is in police protection;
iii. has contravened a ban imposed by a curfew notice (Crime and Disorder Act, 1998); or
iv. where they have reasonable cause to suspect that a child who lives, or is found, in their area is *suffering, or is likely to suffer significant harm*.

In Section 31, *harm* is defined as ill-treatment or the impairment of health or development, but it is a matter of judgement where this becomes *significant*:

Section 31(10)

Where the question of whether harm suffered by a child is significant turns on the child's health or development, his health or development shall be compared with that which could reasonably be expected of a similar child.

Not every referral to children's social care results in a Section 47 enquiry, depending on the circumstances, level of risk involved and degree of parental cooperation. Nevertheless, Section 47 places an important duty on local authorities to act promptly and under this section, 111,700 enquiries were started during 2010/11 (DfE, 2011a).

In emergency situations, Section 46 empowers a police officer to remove a child and retain him or her in police protection for up to 72 hours. However, where possible, the local authority should apply to the court for an emergency protection order under Section 44 of the Act, which gives authority to remove a child and places the child under the protection of the applicant. The court must be satisfied that there is reasonable cause to believe a child is likely to suffer *significant harm* if:

- he or she is not removed to different accommodation; or
- he or she does not remain in the place in which he or she is then being accommodated.

The alleged perpetrator may be removed rather than the child by using exclusion requirements in interim care orders or emergency protection orders, subject to the legal requirements being met. Finally, an emergency protection order can also be made if Section 47 enquiries are being frustrated because the authorised person is being refused access and the applicant has reason to believe that access is needed as a matter of urgency.

Making a child protection referral

Before making a referral, it is good practice to discuss concerns with the family and to try to secure their agreement unless this is likely to place the child at increased risk of significant harm. Procedures are detailed in *Working together to safeguard children* (DfE, 2013) which now requires local areas to develop and publish clear arrangements for how cases will be managed post-referral.

It is initially the responsibility of the social worker to clarify with the referrer:

- the nature of the concerns;
- how and why they have arisen; and
- what the needs of the child and family appear to be.

Both the referrer and children's social care should record discussions and agreed actions. A telephone referral should be followed up in writing and the written referral should be acknowledged within one working day of receipt. Children's social care should decide and record the next steps of action within one working day, having discussed the case with the referrer and sought additional information from agency records or other professionals, as necessary. Next steps could be:

- no further action – this should communicated to the person making the referral with reasons;
- an emergency strategy meeting involving the police, children's social care and any other agencies appropriate to the case if urgent action is felt necessary to protect a child from significant harm;
- an initial assessment by children's social care undertaken within seven days. This should identify whether a more comprehensive core assessment is needed.

An initial assessment should involve seeing and speaking to the child and family members, as appropriate, drawing together existing information from a range of sources and involving and obtaining information from other professionals in contact with the child and family. Children's social care should then decide on the next course of action, involving the parents in discussion unless this increases the risk for the child. It may be that the child is not considered to be at risk but is a 'child in need' under Section 17, in which case services may be offered either immediately or after a more in-depth assessment.

Normally if the initial assessment indicates that risk of significant harm is suspected, a strategy discussion is held to determine whether to proceed with a full Section 47 enquiry and what measures are needed in the interim to protect the child. Youth justice practitioners will be involved in these strategy discussions where they have initiated the referral to children's social care or where they have significant involvement with the child or key figures around the child. The discussions should give direction about how to progress with the enquiry – access issues, whether interpreters are required, and so on. Strategy discussions may also address whether to press ahead with a criminal investigation and the timing of investigations, and will determine whether the situation is such that parental consent for communication with relevant agencies should be waived.

If enquiries are conducted under Section 47, this will usually result in one of three outcomes:

- Concerns are not substantiated, so child protection measures are not necessary, although other support or onward referral may be offered.
- Concerns are substantiated, but the child is not considered to be at continuing risk of significant harm – a plan may then be agreed between key agencies and child/parents without the need for a full case conference.
- Concerns are substantiated, and the child is judged to be at continuing risk of significant harm – in this instance, a full case conference will be convened by children's social care within 15 days of the strategy discussion.

The child protection case conference

The initial case conference is intended to 'bring together and analyse, in an interagency setting, all relevant information and plan how best to safeguard and promote the welfare of the child' (DfE, 2013, p 40). The conference usually involves:

- the family or carers
- the child (if appropriate)
- a legal adviser from the local authority
- a manager from social care who does not have line management responsibility for the case to act as chair.

A written report should be available from the social worker who conducted the Section 47 enquiry. Other professionals attending should bring with them details of their involvement with the child or family members, and it is helpful if written reports are submitted in advance. Providing good quality information is critical and it is important to be clear about the basis of what is presented and 'whether statements are of fact, observation, allegation or opinion' (Williams, 2008, p 163).

The conference focuses on whether the child is at continuing risk of significant harm or not. The child and parents/carers may take part in the meeting but cannot be involved in any decision on that key question. If the conference decides that the child is at continuing risk, a formal child protection plan is formulated, and the conference must then put together the outline child protection plan in as much detail as possible. The chair determines what category of abuse the plan falls under (physical, emotional, sexual abuse, neglect or a combination of these).

The conference then:

- appoints the lead statutory body (children's social care or the NSPCC) and a lead social worker;
- identifies membership of the core group of professionals and family members who will develop and implement the child protection plan;
- establishes timescales for meetings of the core group, production of a child protection plan and for child protection review meetings; and
- agrees an outline child protection plan with clear actions and timescales, including a clear sense of how much improvement is needed, by when, so that success can be judged clearly. (Adapted from DfE, 2013, p 40)

The outline child protection plan should strike a balance between securing the child's safety and well-being and respecting the principle of family unity (Williams, 2008). The plan should specify the responsibilities of each professional in the conference and what tasks have been allocated at the meeting, with timescales. Part of the professional role is to seek clarity about what is expected if the meeting has not made this sufficiently clear.

The first meeting of the core group should take place within 10 working days to flesh out the outline child protection plan and progress the core assessment. This group will meet with the frequency necessary to conduct its monitoring role between case conferences. The first review case conference should take place within three months of the initial conference, and then at least once every six months.

The child protection plan continues until:

- a review conference judges that the child is no longer at continuing risk of significant harm;
- the child and family have moved to another local authority area, in which instance the case is transferred; or
- the child has reached 18 years of age, has died or has permanently left the UK.

Being a 'protected child'

The UNCRC underlines key participatory rights for children and young people in Article 12. In relation to child protection procedures, the professional dilemma is, first, how to enable participation in ways that are age-appropriate and, then, how much influence the information or views expressed should have, alongside other considerations. As young people get older, their views about their own situation and what might happen should carry more weight, in line with their greater levels of understanding and maturity. However, it is still a challenge for the child protection system to respond appropriately, despite the requirements of the UNCRC and the good intentions expressed in guidance to listen to the wishes of the child. Essentially, the tension is that:

> The child protection system now is attempting to empower children by giving them a voice, but the system is structured historically on the basis of the need to maximise communication between adults. (Sanders and Mace, 2006)

Research in Wales found that there were notable discrepancies between what social services departments claimed in their policy documents and the evidence of children and young people's participation from other documents such as minutes and reports from case conferences (Sanders and Mace, 2006).

Participation, then, is not easily achieved. This was recognised by Munro, partly in her consideration of children's experiences in the second report of her review (2011a) and partly through a study conducted through the Office of the Children's Commissioner for England that interviewed children and young people with experience of child protection proceedings (Cossar et al, 2011). The children felt that it was important not just to be heard, but also to know how their views would be taken into account in the confusing process of professional decision-making (Clifton, 2012). It is for the adults to judge the degree to which the child's views influence or more strongly determine what happens, and how this is balanced with what is in the child's best interests.

The power imbalance between the adult social worker and the child is probably most acute at the stage of the initial child protection conference because the primary duty of the practitioner is to protect the child from significant harm. Bell (2011) stresses how the context of the investigation affects the child's involvement throughout the process. Her study of 27 children and young people (aged 8-16) subject to child protection procedures showed that initial reactions to social workers fell into three groups (mixed feelings, threat, or welcoming the protection offered) depending on how safe they had felt in their home. However, they all experienced an initial sense of bewilderment and fear. Despite having the processes explained to them, most said that they understood relatively little of what was happening and had been unable to absorb information they were given at the time. Only a minority attended the initial case conference, and for these it was a difficult experience; they talked about a sense of exposure, feeling out of control and disempowered, disliking the invasion of their private family lives and the number of professionals present at discussions. Young people may be conflicted when asked to disclose information that they are conscious may have consequences for others, such as parents. More positively, young people were more comfortable in review case conferences, perhaps because procedures were more familiar, and felt empowered when offered choices, for instance, about the gender or ethnicity of their social worker and where they were seen (Bell, 2011).

Further studies specifically relating to 11- to 17-year-olds (Rees and Stein, 2012) reveal that practitioners tend to view young people as more resilient and less vulnerable to risk than younger children (although the research evidence on resilience does not necessarily bear this out). They found that practitioners often felt that child protection processes were not the most appropriate because the system did not recognise young people's need to exercise choice and control so their needs were often being addressed through Section 17 provisions instead. Young people who had been through formal child protection procedures said that concerns about trust and confidentiality were most important. However, they also talked about other issues in building relationships with helping professionals, such as being allowed areas of choice and control, clarity about roles, being able to access their workers and continuity of relationships.

Young people and sexual exploitation

One significant area of safeguarding for youth justice is the risk of sexual exploitation, including young people involved in commercial sex. It is difficult to quantify how many young people might be involved at any one time, but the *Paying the price* consultation (Home Office, 2004) quoted an estimate of 5,000 across the UK, roughly four females to every one male. It is apparent that many adults in prostitution were initiated before they were 18 (see, for instance, O'Neill and Campbell, 2001).

In the UK, young people under 18 involved in prostitution have been encompassed within the child protection framework since 2000, and are therefore officially described as young people subject to sexual exploitation or abused through prostitution. Outside official sources, however, in the press and elsewhere they are still often referred to as 'child prostitutes', which minimises their exploitation and implicitly gives them partial responsibility for their own abuse (Goddard et al, 2005).

These two opposing views seem to embody the inherent conflicts and ambiguities at the heart of policy. The first concern is that criminal law can still be used against young people who are deemed to be persistently and voluntarily returning to prostitution, so questions of motivation and status as victim are paramount (Phoenix, 2002, 2006). In practice there are few prosecutions for soliciting or other offences but the fact that criminal sanctions remain available for young people is hugely symbolic. Second, many adult services for sex workers have withdrawn from work with young people. Third, for multi-agency services the boundaries between care and control, welfare and punishment, are being blurred (Phoenix, 2003). Finally, the nexus of control and regulation for these young people is growing. Phoenix comments that:

> Young people in prostitution are thereby caught in three interlocking systems of regulation: (i) social welfare based services for abused children which frequently offer the young people more of the same social services intervention that they have already experienced and often rejected; (ii) harm minimisation, re-educative programmes of sexual health outreach (where such programmes continue to work with young people); and (iii) criminal justice sanctions where nothing else works. (2006, pp 88-9)

In contrast, Pearce (2006) notes that understanding and responses to young people subject to sexual exploitation have improved. She also points to what may be helpful developments in integrated joint agency work and new offences in the Sexual Offences Act 2003, for instance, relating to grooming and adults abusing positions of trust. However, there are still challenges in moving towards a child-centred way of working, particularly with young people who are increasing in autonomy and seeking to find their own solutions to problems, and for whom a child protection intervention may not be the most appropriate. Selling sex or trading it for shelter, food and companionship may seem like a viable short-term survival strategy to the young person, and may well be preferred to the children's homes or supported housing projects that might be offered as an alternative.

The future of children's social care

Ensuring that the child protection system becomes more child-centred is very much at the heart of the Munro review (2011b). The 15 recommendations fall into four themes:

1. Valuing professional expertise
2. Sharing responsibility for the provision of 'early help' (this is the term Munro uses in preference to 'early intervention')
3. Developing social work expertise and supporting effective social work practice
4. Strengthening accountabilities and creating a learning system.

The coalition government have accepted most of Munro's recommendations (DfE, 2011b). In relation to 'early help' the government have accepted outright the recommendation for a process of reviewing and redesigning the way social work is delivered. Two further recommendations are accepted in principle. The government wish to widen the scope of the first to ensure that safeguarding and promoting the welfare of children is a central collective consideration for all bodies involved in the current health service reforms. They have not made a commitment to Recommendation 10, which advocates a new statutory duty on local authorities and partners to secure the sufficient provision of early help for children, young people and families. While they have said they would consider the recommendation further (DfE, 2011b), as Green (2012) points out, the current economic circumstances are unpromising for a new duty of this kind.

The other significant areas involve changes for the social work profession, including a Principal Child and Family Social Worker for each local authority, matched with a national post of Chief Social Worker, to advise the government. These changes, in conjunction with a framework for improvements in training and development, are intended to improve the status of social work.

What Munro (2011b) wants to create is a child protection system that is open and capable of learning, in a way that was stifled by bureaucracy, targets and audits. The changes under way should be positive for social work, seeing a return to the use of professional discretion and judgement, although it remains to be seen whether this enhances their standing in the eyes of the public and of the media. However, Munro's concerns are chiefly with child protection, with little reference to safeguarding throughout her three reports. The role of what she terms 'early help' will be critical in maintaining support at lower levels of need and ensuring that the welfare of children and young people stays firmly on the agenda of all agencies, including youth justice services.

The practitioner perspective

Safeguarding and child protection are not straightforward. If they were, the guidance in *Working together to safeguard children* (DfE, 2013) and its pervious versions would have eradicated child abuse altogether. Rights and wrongs are not clear-cut and practice inevitably treads on sensitive areas – the respective rights of parents and the child, the belief in the privacy and integrity of the family unit, and the level of intrusion by the state that is warranted in any given situation.

When thinking about good practice, it is helpful to recognise that:

- what is considered abusive behaviour varies according to social and cultural norms and expectations;
- ideas about what is appropriate or 'good enough' parenting are similarly influenced by social attitudes but, for each individual practitioner, they are also shaped by his or her unique experiences of growing up and of parenting;
- protecting children is a complex process, involving subtle choices about when and how much to intervene in family lives.

This is an area of practice where self-knowledge and the qualities of critical reflection are more important than ever, influencing work with young people at risk or already involved in the child protection system, as well as relationships with other agencies and the exchange of sensitive information.

Implications for practice

Reflective practitioners should be conscious of how the child protection systems in the different jurisdictions of the UK have been shaped by history and events, notably highly publicised child deaths, and to varying degrees have focused on protection, rather than wider welfare and preventative concerns. As with other areas of risk, these systems have been chasing an unattainable goal. Consequently, social workers have been too readily and publicly blamed and other professionals are hyper-sensitised to the risk of 'getting it wrong'.

Attempting to address concerns about social work and professional standards, New Labour created a broader safeguarding agenda that responsibilised all agencies working with children and young people, including YOTs, prevention projects and the youth secure estate. This has implications both for the delivery of services *having regard to the need to safeguard and promote the welfare of children* and the underlining of responsibilities to pass on appropriate concerns about 'children in need' or 'children in need of protection' to children's social care/social services.

There is often anxiety about taking action because practitioners are worried that they will be criticised for failing to act or to notify others. However, the central concern should be the welfare of the young person, not the practitioner's anxieties, which need to be managed sufficiently to enable a proper assessment of what action to take. Sometimes it is appropriate to wait until more information becomes available and allows a more complete appraisal of the situation. The principles of youth-centred practice also suggest that concerns should be shared with the young person, wherever appropriate, and the practitioner should be clear about what may be disclosed to children's social care and the implications.

It follows that practitioners should be confident in their knowledge about child protection procedures, enabling them to work within the procedures and structures without feeling too constrained by them. Understanding the nature and purpose of the various processes involved makes it easier to judge what level of information and what action is needed at what points.

Although social workers are the lead professional group in child protection, youth justice practitioners can take a key part in supporting young people through the system, demystifying processes, acting as advocates at appropriate points and encouraging active participation.

Child protection concerns, even where they do not result in a formal referral, inevitably have an emotional impact. It can be damaging to ignore the feelings that surface. Practitioners should seek safe opportunities to explore any issues raised for them both immediately, depending on who is available at the time, and more strategically, through line management supervision, peer support or any mentoring arrangements in place.

Further reading

Beckett, C. (2007) *Child protection: An introduction* (2nd edn), London: Sage Publications.

Blyth, M. and Solomon, E. (eds) (2012) *Effective safeguarding for children and young people: What next after Munro?*, Bristol: The Policy Press.

Munro, E. (2008) *Effective child protection*, London: Sage Publications.

Williams, J. (2008) *Child law for social work*, London: Sage Publications.

THIRTEEN

Collaborative and multi-agency working

Partnership arrangements are fundamental to the YJS: they are built into its present structure through the range of agencies represented in strategic management groups and within YOTs themselves, and are also needed to provide a network of other agencies to call on for specialist services and support for young people. This means the context for youth justice is complex, requiring YOT managers and practitioners to engage with partnerships and collaborative working both in the criminal justice arena and with children's services. Doing so successfully is no mean feat, yet, despite requiring considerable investment of time and energy, the effort can pay huge dividends in resources, improved access to services and increased influence within partnership groups.

Multi-agency work inevitably makes demands of practitioners who must be able to adapt to different types of teams and workgroups, some stable and others time-limited with a specific purpose in mind. This chapter explores the nature of teamwork across agencies and the skills needed to work purposefully and successfully with others towards an agreed end. It considers potential barriers, such as agency cultures, different assumptions and ways of framing problems, and difficulties in communication, examining these first in the context of the creation and development of YOTs, before considering how these might affect attempts to reach out to external agencies.

The most sensitive issues for partner agencies concern exchange of information, and it is important that practitioners understand the key ethical dilemmas involved. Young people and their families have rights to privacy and confidentiality that should be balanced against statutory duties to protect and to prevent harm through offending. This chapter lays out the legal framework and professional obligations, considering the proportionate and proper exchange of information.

Finally, discussion turns to young people and parents, exploring their views and experiences of multi-agency work and how different professionals work together, identifying the effects of poor coordination and the benefits when professionals work in synergy.

Defining partnership and collaboration

When talking about different agencies working together, a confusing array of terms are used, sometimes interchangeably but frequently marking important distinctions or different levels of 'joined-up' enterprise. Partnership featured centrally in New Labour thinking across social and criminal justice policy, and was vaunted as being inherently beneficial to those receiving services. Of course, where agencies work well together, so that communication and provision is coherent, it adds up to more than the individual efforts of single organisations. But research suggests that, for young people, interventions from more than one agency are most appreciated when they are relevant to their needs, have a clear, shared sense of purpose, and are streamlined (Harris and Allen, 2011). This is not necessarily easy to achieve and, in starting to identify the challenges and how to overcome the barriers to 'joined-up' working, it helps to start with definitions of the terms that are used in the literature and their specific meanings within this chapter.

White and Graham (2010, p 249) refer to *partnerships* as structural arrangements ('who we are') in contrast to *collaborations* that are about action ('what we do'). Collaboration then involves a set of skills and approaches, and 'is at the heart of contemporary models of working with offenders. It is an essential part of this work. As such, learning to work collaboratively is not a luxury or something we should do reluctantly' (2010, p 245). Collaborations may be *vertical*, in the sense that they work across different levels in one organisation, or *horizontal,* involving managers or practitioners at the same level in different organisations (2010). Collaborations seek to coordinate planning and actions in a sustained way (Payne, 2000), but may have a fixed life span.

Within the current policy context, partnerships provide the means for collaborative enterprise to take place. They can take various forms such as:

- statutory partnerships – examples include Community Safety Partnerships and LSCBs where the member agencies are mandated and the purpose is framed in law;
- contractual partnerships – such as arrangements between YOTs and voluntary agencies paid to deliver prevention work or specialist interventions;
- service-level partnerships – these might exist where there are overlapping areas of work and possibly targets that have been aligned across agencies. Arrangements, including respective roles and responsibilities, may be formalised in service-level agreements;
- problem-solving partnerships – where agencies come together because they have a common interest or goal. The partners may agree a written policy or protocol, laying out the detail of arrangements and actions.

This list refers to partnerships at various levels, from the highly strategic to the operational, where practitioners come together to coordinate work with individual young people. The power relationships in the forms of partnerships may differ, and it is certainly not the case that all agencies meet in partnerships on an equal footing. Agencies have varying levels of influence (including political influence) and resources to bring with them, so the dynamics within partnerships – and multi-agency groups that meet under partnership arrangements – may be complex.

The term *multi-agency* refers to different organisations coming together to pursue shared strategic goals, but with each engaged in its own activity and with its own responsibilities within the overall plan. *Multi-disciplinary* and *multi-professional* are occasionally used instead, differing only in that they give emphasis not just to the agencies involved but to the contribution of different professions with their values and unique areas of expertise. Multi-agency groups may meet on an ad hoc basis, around a particular family, for instance, or as a formal arrangement, as in MAPPA. For the sake of clarity, within this book, mixed groups of professionals whose work is integrated and who are co-located – such as YOTs – are referred to as *interagency* teams.

Youth offending teams in context

YOTs in themselves are unusual organisations and represent perhaps the most systematic example of New Labour's push for 'joined-up' working across agencies (Souhami, 2008). They are not a legal entity in themselves (Thomas, 2009): the Crime and Disorder Act 1998 requires the local authority ultimately to take responsibility and other statutory partners must contribute to the strategic management and the operational resources of the team. Initially the resources were often given in the form of seconded staff members, but over the years it has become more common to see agencies making a direct financial payment (Morgan and Newburn, 2012).

The law allows a great deal of flexibility at a local level so that partners have been able to determine the initial shape of the YOT and its subsequent development. The location of a YOT within local authority structures and the configuration of the strategic groups to which it relates are critical in the way that it works and how far its influence is able to reach. Furthermore, the landscape of both criminal justice and children's services shifted considerably during New Labour's period in office as community safety, tackling anti-social behaviour and crime prevention assumed priority on the one side and the integration of children's services under the Every Child Matters agenda on the other. So maintaining complicated networks of relationships has been a considerable task for YOT managers, made more complex by the moves that many YOTs have made between departments. One recent study (Hopkins et al, 2010) found that, of 98 YOTs responding to a survey, more than half had changed location and therefore line management arrangements within the previous five years. Most moves were towards children's social care or wider children's services. However, seven YOTs responding were managed within community safety departments at the time of the survey, six were within the chief executive's department and four were free-standing.

YOTs each have a multi-agency management board or steering group comprising senior managers from the statutory partner agencies and other agencies by local agreement. YOTs are also accountable to strategic groups such as Community Safety Partnerships and children's services partnerships, but the ability for the local authority and partners to determine priorities and actions has been considerably tempered by the role of the YJB. Although it had no direct line management function, in the early days of YOTs it exerted considerable influence through its performance framework, the development of detailed National Standards and provision of funds (often ring-fenced for specific activities such as prevention work) (Morgan and Newburn, 2012). This effectively meant that steering groups and the local strategic bodies were monitoring YOTs according to the YJB agenda (and ultimately the government agenda) (Smith, 2007). Although this centralised control relaxed somewhat during the latter stages of the New Labour administration (Graham, 2010), and has loosened even more under the coalition government, the governance of YOTs and their accountabilities are still multifaceted.

Of course, one facet of accountability around YOTs is the accountability that partner agencies have to each other for their strategic input and resourcing of the YOT. The workforce has changed over the time that YOTs have been in place, reflecting new ways of making partner contributions and the tendency for local authorities to employ staff directly for YOTs (Morgan and Newburn, 2012). In particular, just looking at New Labour's third term in office, secondments from social services/children's social care fell from 2012 in 2005/06 (YJB, 2006b) to 406 in June 2010 (YJB, 2010) and education from 272 to 159 (see Figure 13.1).

The implications for YOTs relate less perhaps to sustainability (because partnership funding is still available) than to the extent to which they remain a vibrant interagency enterprise (Thomas, 2009). Souhami (2008, p 222) highlights the risk of 'eroding the diversity at its core. An increasing proportion of permanent staff in multi-agency teams obstructs the refreshing of specialist skills and services that secondment provides.'

Elsewhere she expresses concern that, rather than being a mix of professional disciplines, YOTs are starting to create a profession of their own:

> It appears that the relocation of youth justice services beyond agency boundaries may paradoxically have led to the development of a new, multi-agency profession. The expansion in their size, funds and status

Figure 13.1: Trends in the YOT workforce, 2005/06 and 2009/10

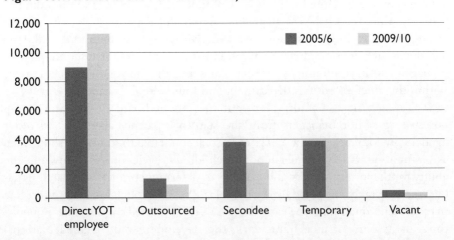

Source: YJB (2006b, 2010)

appears to have led working in a YOT to become seen by practitioners across a range of agencies as a long-term career choice rather than a short-term secondment. An increasing proportion of staff are now permanently employed as YOT workers or in "technical" secondments whereby staff are unlikely to return to their home agency. Rather than operating beyond boundaries, it appears that new boundaries are now being drawn around YOTs. (Souhami, 2009, p 189)

The learning from interagency teams

As YOTs have become an established entity in each local area, the extent to which they are still a lively mix of agencies and disciplines is debatable. Interestingly, Walker (2011) raises the same question about CAMHS as they have become more institutionalised within the network of children's services. The cultures within a newly created agency develop and mature over time, as a 'community of practice' (Wenger, 1998) forms through interactions and exchange of knowledge within the team. For YOTs, the tendency to form a more homogeneous ethos may also be driven by the fact that:

> Organisational culture is apparently unifying, and this strongly appeals to management's concern with projecting an image of the organisation as a community of interests ... culture penetrates to the essence of an organisation – it is almost analogous with personality in relation to the individual. (Fincham and Rhodes, 1999, p 430)

Of course, there is not now a monolithic culture within YOTs any more than there is in its partner agencies, but something more recognisable as a collection of youth justice identities and approaches has emerged. This has served YOTs well in terms of establishing status within the networks of other agencies, although the initial energy and enterprise that characterised them have long gone (Robinson, 2013). It is useful to look back at the early experiences of YOTs coming together and what learning can be drawn about the nature of professional identities and cultures that may be applicable more generally across multi-agency settings. At that point managers and practitioners were joining YOTs imbued with their own agency and professional values and culture, as well as the practices that express such values and cultures.

Souhami's (2007) ethnographic study of the first year in the life of one YOT describes the development of the team and analyses changes and threats to the occupational identities of team members. Her understanding of occupational identity and culture is that they are not fixed but are constantly negotiated and re-negotiated within workplace relationships. In this sense, participation in new work activities and routines is important in establishing new identities (Frost and Robinson, 2007). But Souhami's study, in common with others (for instance, Anning et al, 2010, looking at integrated teams in children's services within the

ESRC-funded Multi-agency Teams in Children's Services [MATCh] project), shows what an uncomfortable process this might be at the outset as previous work identities are 'de-stabilised'; the way of seeing the world and of conceptualising problems, the values and assumptions shared within one professional group may not be challenged to any great extent, but are open to question when interagency teams come together (Frost et al, 2005). Typically there may be a period of insecurity and even conflict until new joint understandings and new norms are established – at least to an extent that is comfortable on a day-to-day basis.

Language is highly significant in communicating and reinforcing the values and concepts central to a profession. One of the tasks within a new interagency (or multi-agency) team is to find a common language through which shared understandings can be developed. Research within CAMHS (Salmon and Rapport, 2005) and Sure Start (Morrow et al, 2005) suggests this is not an easy process, and depends on the willingness of participants to ask questions and to seek clarifications. It is important that agencies have sufficient awareness of each other's analytical frameworks and the explanatory models used to make sense of presenting behaviours or situations. To give an example leaning somewhat on stereotypes, a young person's aggression may be viewed as a reaction to social circumstances (social work), frustration at lack of progress in the learning environment (education), learned responses to stress (psychology) or anti-social behaviour encouraged by peers (youth justice). It is necessary to give a little and to appreciate other perspectives:

> The differences that individual practitioners bring must be included in the inter-agency process rather than ignored, bull-dozed over or pushed into a corner. Some strong element of compromise is suggested here rather than seeking a "right" or "superior" answer. (Walker, 2011, p 149)

In Souhami's (2007) study, the YOT was created from the basis of the previous social work youth justice team, with practitioners from other agencies joining this established team. She recounts how new staff felt initially marginalised by the use of jargon and technical terms used by the social workers: knowledge and familiarity with these terms served to delineate the boundaries of the team and who was included or excluded. In one sense, it also reinforced the in-group and out-group dynamics at a point where the social workers felt their position in the team and the nature of their particular – but rather ambiguous – expertise was under threat. It clearly took time for staff to feel sufficiently safe for the acceptance and compromise that Walker (2011) describes to take place.

Although this period of anxiety and conflict within the YOT might be seen as a classic example of Tuckman's (1965) 'storming' phase in group development, the situation was in fact more complex as the team did not have a fixed membership and, in fact, grew, relocated and built a wider network of partnerships and collaborations over the first year of its existence. Along the way, questions arose for those joining the team about the extent to which they were specialist workers and their involvement in generic tasks. Both here and within the MATCh project looking at a more diverse range of interagency teams (Frost and Robinson, 2007; Anning et al, 2010), shared tasks and routines emerged as important. Although this raised issues about status and professional identity, it also provided a means of establishing common ground and a sense of allegiance to the new team. Resolving the tension between specialism and genericism is critical to successful interagency work and the reworking of new professional identities. Souhami (2007, p 24) outlines a key dilemma within YOTs about the extent to which specialist practitioners retained their separate professional identities because 'without some degree of generic YOT identity, the absorption of staff into different agencies into a single team creates scope for inter-agency conflict.' Walker puts this in a different light talking about CAMHS when he says that, 'this change moves from the position of "I" and "you" or "they" to "we" and "us". "How can my agency sort out this child and adolescent mental health problem?" to "How can we help the inter-agency team begin to address this problem?"' (2011, p 150).

On the one hand, in asking professionals to engage in interagency work, they are expected to 'confront, articulate and lay to one side the distinctiveness of their long-established "tribal" beliefs and behaviours' (Anning et al, 2010, p 71), but on the other, they are required to contribute their particular professional expertise within a new context, not to erase what is special and distinct. There may be a blurring of boundaries between different professions, but they should not merge entirely. Helpfully, Abbott et al (2005) refer to the concept of *role release* (transfer of skills and sharing of expertise) and *role expansion* (understanding the concepts and language of another discipline) as essential ingredients in multi- (or inter)agency working. Frost and Robinson further identify the benefits of professionals maintaining a 'balanced view ', finding that 'professionals could live with difference. They could maintain core values under pressure, but still contribute to overall shared aims within teams with diverse membership, participating in a re-distribution of knowledge and greater co-ordination of provision' (2007, p 192).

This is not necessarily easy as Robinson and Cottrell, again referring to the MATCh project, observe:

> It appeared that professionals in multi-agency teams were often challenged to contain and embrace diversity, often within a dominant team model, while not sacrificing those personal beliefs which underpin their own commitment. They were challenged to reflect on which of their own beliefs about practice are imbued with core values, and which can be modified through the development of new, shared knowledge within the team. (2005, p 531)

This requires that professionals are secure in their own professional identities and are able to hold on to their core values in the face of competing pressures and in situations where views from one or more other professional groups are most prominent (Robinson, 2011).

The YOT context has shifted and there is now a more unified and settled YOT identity. Yet some of the messages coming from research on their early days – reinforced by research in integrated children's services – are still instructive about the nature of collaborative work and the characteristics of successful partnership working.

So what helps and what hinders good collaboration within partnerships?

It is axiomatic that successful collaboration requires a shared sense of purpose and a vision for how to progress jointly agreed aims and objectives. This presupposes commitment to the joint enterprise even where the joint approach taken is not the most advantageous for the individual agency. Within mandated partnerships, this may be present to greater or lesser degrees and certainly, as partnerships develop, the 'early adopters' keen for collaborative working may be replaced by 'conscripts' who are less willing and able to adapt (Anning et al, 2010).

The key to collaboration lies in the quality of relationships of trust between individuals and between organisations, but, as Gilling (2005) notes, both may bring substantial 'baggage' to the partnership table. And organisations may come together on very unequal terms. This may create difficulties from the outset, particularly in collaborations that are less close and interdependent, meaning that there is less pressure for dominant partners to concede influence and power to others in order to progress.

A review of the literature around collaborative working (Williams, 2009) found that the identified barriers fell into four main areas:

- structural
- procedural
- financial
- professional.

Using the example of YOTS, structural barriers might include their location and line management arrangements, so determining the relative influence of partner agencies as well as the influence that the YOT itself may be able to exert on partners. They may also include differences in pay and conditions for practitioners with broadly similar levels of responsibility, reflecting differentials in the status and power of their parent agencies. Procedural difficulties might present in the transfer of information between agencies. There may be disagreement about the financial or other resources given by agencies to a YOT, or an imbalance in contributions that effectively marginalise one or another agency. Professional issues were clearly evident in the early establishment of YOTs, not just in the Souhami study (2007), but elsewhere, for example, Burnett and Appleton's (2004) research in one rural YOT. Williams (2009) found that professional concerns were the most commonly raised in the broad partnership literature, and that these were most apparent between the criminal justice and health and social care agencies. Such agencies, of course, are key elements within youth justice at both management and operational levels.

Clear communication and good management systems can help overcome some of these barriers between agencies. These may include written procedures outlining expectations and individual agency roles, as well as explicit terms of reference for partnership groups. They may also assist in negotiating the complex network of accountabilities around YOTs and *who* exactly is accountable *to whom* and *for what*. Accountabilities may be: *upwards* towards strategic partnership structures and to the YJB; *sideways* in terms of peers (partner organisations and managers at the same level); or *outwards* in terms of the wider community, victims and the young people and families involved in the YJS. White and Grove (2003, cited in Walker, 2011, p 256) suggest that there are four key elements involved in successful partnerships: respect, reciprocity, risk-taking and realism. Certainly the first three of these are dependent on relationships characterised by trust and mutuality. Without this, the partnership is unlikely to move into previously uncharted territory and to explore new ways of responding to complex problems. Realism is an interesting quality – partnerships need to be aware of their capacities and limitations, establishing stretching but achievable aims and timescales, so that there is a possibility of success that then generates confidence and motivation to move further.

At a practice level, collaborations work best where practitioners:

- are not fixed on rigid role demarcations and are able to 'blur' their professional boundaries without allowing them to become 'fuzzy' and therefore risky in terms of neglecting key roles or responsibilities (Kemshall, 2008);
- deal with other professionals in an open and transparent way;
- communicate clearly and establish common understandings;
- use shared language to explore beliefs and attitudes and to resolve differences;
- are motivated and willing to share with others and to access professional knowledge outside their own sphere;
- are confident in being able to express and work in line with their own values;
- are clear about which areas of norms and values are open for negotiation and adaptation and what is essential for the practitioner to hold to.

Core values have already been mentioned as critical in keeping a sense of professional identity, and they are also important in helping the practitioner maintain an individual stance, even where the pressure of group decision-making is going in another direction:

> A strong sense of core values can act as a bulwark against the pressures to conform to the priorities and world view of dominant partners or even personalities. Values are the critical determinant for practitioners

as to what is acceptable and what is, effectively, a line that cannot be crossed. (Robinson, 2011, p 48)

Reflections on sharing information

The appropriate exchange of information is one of the more tricky areas around collaborative and partnership working. Souhami (2008) identifies the potential for unacceptable practices to develop within the informal exchanges that take place in interagency teams, which is ironic when the ease of communication was seen as one of their primary benefits. In other settings the concerns may be about barriers to exchange – perhaps technical, but perhaps reflecting conflicts about values and beliefs between organisations or professional groups (Williams, 2009). Confidentiality often presents as a concern around health and drug services. Within the MATCh project, one social worker highlighted different agency expectations and the frustrations these raised:

> 'There's issues around confidentiality, health records ... the health worker and the drugs worker have confidential files which don't go on the system so you can't access that information.

> '... I'm used to working in an arena where we do share things all the time and so to have somebody come in with a very strict confidentiality policy makes it very difficult.' (quoted in Robinson and Cottrell, 2005, p 555)

There is a responsibility on agencies, and professionals within agencies, to ensure that personal information is treated in a fair and ethical manner, with due regard to the rights of individuals under Article 8(i) of the European Convention on Human Rights (ECHR) (respect for private and family life, home and correspondence), and the common law duty of confidence. In general, informed consent should be sought from young people and/or parents before information is shared, but this may be obtained in a generic way at the start of a multi-agency intervention rather than separately sought for each individual exchange. As a starting point it is helpful to look at the government's *Information sharing: Guidance for practitioners and managers* (DCSF, 2009, p 11):

Seven golden rules for information sharing

1. Remember that the Data Protection Act is not a barrier to sharing information, but it provides a framework to ensure that personal information about living persons is shared appropriately.
2. Be open and honest with the person (and/or their family where appropriate) from the outset about why, what, how and with whom information will, or could be shared, and seek their agreement, unless it is unsafe or inappropriate to do so.

3. Seek advice if you are in any doubt, without disclosing the identity of the person where possible.

4. Share with consent where appropriate and, where possible, respect the wishes of those who do not consent to share confidential information. You may still share information without consent if, in your judgement, that lack of consent can be overridden in the public interest. You may need to base your judgements on the facts of the case.

5. Consider safety and well-being: base your information-sharing decisions on considerations of the safety and well-being of the person and others who may be affected by their actions.

6. Necessary, proportionate, relevant, accurate, timely and secure: ensure that the information you share is necessary for the purpose for which you are sharing it, is shared only with those people who need to have it, is accurate and up-to-date, is shared in a timely fashion and is shared securely.

7. Keep a record of your decision and the reasons for it – whether it is to share information or not. If you decide to share, then record what you have shared, with whom and for what purpose.

When intervention takes place in an interagency or multi-agency setting it is good practice to be open and transparent with young people and/or their parents about how and when the information that they give will be recorded and passed between the different agencies working with them. The presumption should be that consent to share information is sought, but there are instances where *public interest* will override the duty of confidentiality and/or where consent is not required. Where possible the young person or parents should be informed where information has been or will be exchanged on this basis, but on occasions the urgency of the situation or risk of harm is such that this is not appropriate. Similarly, judgements may be needed if seeking consent or disclosing that information will be shared would prejudice the prevention, detection or prosecution of a serious crime.

Public interest may arise where professionals have a statutory duty to:

• protect children or young people from *significant harm*
• protect vulnerable adults from *serious harm*
• promote the welfare of children
• prevent crime and disorder.

Information can be shared for the purposes of these statutory duties under the provisions of the Children Acts of 1989 and 2004 and, in the latter case, Section 115 of the CDA 1998 and/or within the guidelines set for MAPPA. The key factor is what is necessary and proportionate in the circumstances (DCSF, 2009).

One area specific to the YJS is the provision of information about victims with a view to offering restorative processes, involvement in YOPs on referral orders or contribution to court reports. Information exchanged for specific purposes such as these will, in most instances, be governed by information exchange protocols or agreements, offering useful guidance for practitioners about what is or is not permissible.

Sharing other sorts of information – such as aggregated data about academic performance, school attendance and (re)conviction rates – is less sensitive where the data are anonymised. However, this is still significant within partnerships because information can be used to inform decisions and to prioritise resources, as well as to monitor performance and the impact of projects or interventions. Again, this needs to be used and interpreted in ways that are ethical and constructive. In particular, practitioners and managers should be aware of the limitation of data and, where taken out of context, that they may give a skewed picture of reality. To some extent this may be balanced by qualitative data, perhaps gained from interviews, focus groups or questionnaires, exploring the experiences of young people, victims or others with a stake in youth justice. In a partnership context, this is about examining what information is available to evaluate youth justice or connected services honestly and rigorously, not just looking at headline figures.

On the receiving end ... young people's experiences

So what does the qualitative research suggest about young people's experiences of working with groups of professionals? Small studies within education and CAMHS (Harris and Allen, 2011; O'Reilly et al, 2012) seem to suggest that joint working is appreciated, but that quality of communication is essential in inspiring confidence and showing that agencies are working together. For instance, one parent said:

> 'I'd liked to have had some documentation from CAMHS and school to say they'd both met and they agree on issues and that they're going to work together.' (quoted in O'Reilly et al, 2012, p 5)

The involvement of other professionals within the school environment seems to be helpful for engagement in education. In Harris and Allen's (2011) study, young people were positive about relationships with family workers, youth workers and others who provided support and activities, allowing them to address some of the problems they had been experiencing at school. One Year 10 pupil commented that:

> 'Time with the youth worker is my time, like no one else has it. That's important because it allows me to think out loud and be myself, which is good. I'm not someone I'm supposed to be.' (2011, p 409)

Although this small study only involved 10 schools in one area, it highlighted four important issues that seem to resonate more widely. First, complex and multifaceted problems could only be addressed where services were sufficiently 'joined-up'. Second, the local authority has a critical role in ensuring services are coordinated. Third, partnership actions must have a clear purpose that is understandable to young people. As an illustration, one young person in Year 6 described an example where this was not the case, saying, "'The police woman came into our maths lesson; don't know what that was for'" (2011, p 412). Finally, within this study, it was apparent that, although young people were engaged by different agencies, they had little influence over the decisions made about the services that were offered or the way they were organised (Harris and Allen, 2011).

Literature on young people's view of integrated working within YOTs is sparse, although it does appear that YOT practitioners seem to be viewed favourably compared to other professionals (Hart and Thompson, 2009). Fielder et al (2008) examined the relationships between YOTs and developing children's trusts, and as part of that study explored the perceptions that young people and parents held about integrated working. At that stage, various forms of interagency and multi-agency structures were being planned or created, and there was considerable diversity in local arrangements in the six areas where case study YOTs were located.

None of the case study YOTs were involved in integrated children's services teams, although crime prevention projects such as YISPs probably came closest. The young people and parents had little direct experience of integrated working, but were asked about the concept of joint work between agencies. Information sharing was a key concern for young people in the focus groups because of privacy and for some, fear of being judged or labelled due to their offending behaviour. While they recognised that sharing information could be helpful, young people and parents agreed that this should be done with care and on a 'need to know' basis. Although they felt that joint working could mean better help and support, young people did not like the idea of practitioners coming together to discuss them. Yet at the same time, they said that they did not like having to repeat information to different practitioners. The role of lead professional could be one way round these issues, but parents were more enthusiastic about that idea than the young people. One parent in fact commented that:

> 'A lot of the time they don't have the same people, so that the child, or that individual is constantly telling his story over and over again ... you've got to remember that child is sitting there and having to see different people all the time, that is very difficult for the child ... if that child were to see the same person all the time, I think it would be a lot easier.' (quoted in Fielder et al, 2008, p 69)

Certainly the participants in this study reported gaps in provision and lack of understanding of wider needs in schools and other settings, so indicating that more integrated working may be helpful, despite the apprehensions they expressed.

Implications for practice

Working across agencies can be productive, if challenging. The impetus under New Labour for 'joined-up' services did not fully take account of the demands that greater integration makes on organisations and individual practitioners. Done well, services are more coordinated and usefully complement each other to provide a robust network of support and intervention; however, poor integration creates a tangle, not a network (Walker, 2011), and can be extremely frustrating for those giving and for those receiving services. Youth-centred practice appreciates how receiving complex packages of services might be experienced, and enables young people to make best use of services by communicating well and being clear and open about working relationships and the capacities and roles of the agencies involved.

Sharing information is one of the more sensitive areas to be tackled as agencies come together, raising real dilemmas about the power of agencies and respect for individuals. There are legal requirements and obligations in relation to rights to consider but also duties to protect and to prevent crime. Careful thought is needed before sharing information – whether or not consent has been granted – to ensure that what is passed over is appropriate, proportionate, timely and accurate.

The early experience of YOTs and of children's services coming together in integrated teams produced interesting research probing the nature of professional identities and how these need to adapt in the context of multi-agency and interagency teams. Flexibility about role boundaries and expectations is helpful, but too much blurring around the edges means that the special expertise and responsibilities of individual agencies can be lost. This was clearly a live issue in the development of YOTs where practitioners had to seek a balance between a generic YOT identity and involvement in common tasks, and maintaining their specialist role.

This is an important context for critical reflection; practitioners who are successful in multi-agency and interagency settings must be secure in their own professional identity, knowledge base and occupational values. This requires a high level of self-awareness and confidence, because of the give and take involved in these stretching, but deeply rewarding, areas of practice.

Further reading

Anning, A., Cottrell, J., Frost, N., Green J. and Robinson, M. (2010) *Developing multi-professional teamwork for integrated children's services* (2nd edn), Maidenhead: Open University Press.

Payne, M. (2000) *Teamwork in multi-professional care*, Basingstoke: Palgrave Macmillan.

Souhami, A. (2007) *Transforming youth justice: Occupational identity and cultural change*, Cullompton: Willan.

FOURTEEN

Prevention and pre-court intervention

Under the 'just deserts' framework of the 1980s, diversion from prosecution and cautioning flourished. By the time New Labour came into office, the political mood had changed and a markedly more active and interventionist approach was favoured. Although not the only influence, emerging understandings from research about developmental pathways and criminal careers helped shape New Labour thinking. The suggestion that the precursors of risky or offending behaviours could be spotted early and interventions put in place to 'nip youth offending in the bud' (Home Office, 1997, p 2) seemed rational, in line with their attempts to create evidence-based policy and an attractive approach to sell to the public – neither too punitive, nor too lenient.

New Labour quickly put in place a strategy for early intervention through measures for dealing with anti-social behaviour and a more structured framework of pre-court intervention. Other interventions focusing on particular groups of young people or neighbourhoods quickly followed. It was hoped that the time and resources devoted to early intervention – whether angled towards social need or enforcement – would prevent later anti-social behaviour and criminality. But for most of New Labour's period in office, it failed to do so. This chapter explores the problems with an approach that is over-reliant on the predictive potential of the risk factor prevention paradigm and its underpinnings in developmental criminology. It looks at the nature of interventions, the extent to which they met the social, welfare and other needs of children and young people and the implications of drawing young people into the YJS – even the increasingly permeable margins of the YJS – at an early age.

The coalition government is more wary than New Labour about the potential to criminalise young people unnecessarily and wastefully process them through the YJS. So what openings might be found as prescriptive early intervention is abandoned, and what risks might this create? The chapter ends by exploring what the potential for early intervention or 'early help' might be, advocating an approach that responds to social contexts and opportunities, that recognises the potential to develop social capital and avoids locating problems in the individual young person or family.

Diversion as prevention

The YJS under New Labour was so bent on intervention that until recently the notion of diversion had been effectively forgotten. However, diversion occupied a significant place in the relatively recent history of youth justice, and it is worth revisiting the beliefs and assumptions that informed the practice of cautioning in order to look at its rediscovery in the present period.

The 1970s, with the partial implementation of the C&YPA 1969, saw an increase in the use of both custody and interventions such as intermediate treatment in the community. In the 1980s the YJS returned to what seemed to be a more expressly punitive stance, particularly in relation to the minority of young people with serious or persistent patterns of offending. However, a different and contrasting approach to the majority coming to the attention of youth justice was informed by notions of 'just deserts', proportionality and systems management focused on key decision-making points. The loss of faith in welfare intervention and lack of evidence of its efficacy contributed to an unusual degree of consensus between politicians, policy-makers and practitioners around the belief that, if intervention was ineffective and even potentially damaging, the best principle to act on was 'do no harm' (Smith, 2011). This meant that diversion should be used wherever possible and that, where punishment was appropriate, it should be the minimum necessary to reflect the nature and seriousness of the offences. This principle of proportionality thus guided decision-making rather than assessment of welfare or social need, as had previously been the case. The 'doctrine of diversion' (Graham, 2010) included diversion from custody through a range of 'alternative to custody' schemes, but also an expansion of cautioning to divert young people from prosecution (R. Smith, 2007).

In 1970, 35 per cent of young people (under-17s) who were arrested received a caution (Muncie, 2009), which is a warning administered by the police following an admission of guilt. Cautions could be formal and so recorded, or informal, based on the discretion of the police concerned. Muncie feels that 'there is little doubt that police discretion to *informally* caution made a significant impact on reducing court appearances and protecting young people from the stigma of a criminal record (as well as reducing police paperwork)' (2009, p 256). The number of young people diverted from court rose throughout the 1970s, and in 1985 formal cautioning was promoted by Home Office Circular 14/1985 to the extent that, by 1990, two thirds of 14- to 16-year-old boys and almost 90 per cent of all girls 16 years and under were receiving formal cautions for indictable offences (Graham, 2010). In the late 1980s and into the 1990s, as the proportions of young people who were cautioned continued to rise, fewer young people were prosecuted and, of those who were, a higher proportion received community disposals (R. Smith, 2007). Meanwhile the number of young people placed on care orders or sent to custody declined (Smith, 2011), in the latter case by a dramatic 82 per cent within a decade (R. Smith, 2007). The impact of cautioning was therefore felt throughout the YJS, in the number of young people being processed, but also in the first appearance in some areas of reparative options as part of cautioning and diversion (R. Smith, 2007).

It is difficult to assess the effectiveness of cautioning because the extent of offending prevented is unknown. The lower numbers of young people in the court system is one powerful indicator, but some commentators have pointed to the potential for net widening in the expansion of formal cautioning rather than informal means of dealing with minor offending (Bateman, 2002). More positively, Home Office Statistical Bulletin 8/94 (cited in Evans, 2008) found that 85 per cent of those cautioned in 1985 and 1988 were not convicted of a 'standard list' offence within two years of their caution (although reconviction may not equate to re-offending). Similarly, Nacro (2006) cite later research suggesting that 81 per cent of children and young people receiving a caution in 1994 were not reconvicted over a two-year follow-up period.

The 1980s were a relatively optimistic period for youth justice, with a growing sense of a specialist professional area of work (Smith, 2011). However, the social climate as a whole in the Thatcher era was not benign, and the espousal of a 'just deserts' framework in youth justice moved it explicitly away from welfare and towards a more punishment-orientated approach, albeit bounded by concerns for proportionality. This was more evident in relation to the probation service that was recast as a deliverer of 'community penalties', but the CJA 1991 also created youth courts to deal exclusively with criminal matters for young people. The jurisdiction of these new courts covered 17-year-olds, so extending the remit of the previous juvenile courts, and powers to transfer matters to the family court were removed, thus forging a greater separation between criminal and care proceedings (Morgan and Newburn, 2012). This had significant implications for youth justice as the 1990s progressed and the attitudes towards young people committing offences became harsher.

By the time that New Labour took office the use of cautioning had already declined from 73.6 per cent of young people dealt with formally by the police in 1992 to 61.4 per cent in 1997 (Bateman, 2002). In a distinct change of tone from earlier pronouncements, Home Office Circular 18/94 warned against repeat cautioning (R. Smith, 2007), and this was also picked up by the first of two critical – and highly influential – reports by the Audit Commission, *Misspent youth* (1996). The Audit Commission was broadly in favour of intervention in the form of 'caution plus' and examples of projects in other European countries. Although the validity of their data and the conclusions drawn from them has been questioned (Jones, 2001), New Labour were receptive to their views and used them as a basis of a new and more structured system of pre-court intervention. Alongside this, they also drew on the findings of the Cambridge Study in Delinquent Development (see, for example, Farrington, 1994; Loeber and Farrington, 2000) and a more recent study by Graham and Bowling (1995) to develop their approach to interventions based on risk factors and, specifically, early intervention.

Systems of pre-court intervention

New Labour responded promptly to the criticisms that the Audit Commission (1996) made about repeat cautioning and the lack of intervention with young people at an early stage of their offending. Section 65 of the CDA 1998 created a new system for pre-court intervention that limited police discretion and was intended to provide an effective two-step process before young people were taken to court. The flexibility that existed under the previous arrangements was thus greatly – and controversially – reduced.

Under this system, a first offence was met with a reprimand, a final warning or criminal charges, depending on its seriousness. The lowest level of response was a reprimand, effectively a verbal warning delivered by the police on one occasion only. A second offence or a first offence judged to be sufficiently serious could result in a final warning, which involved a police warning and then referral to a YOT that would assess the young person for a programme of intervention. Any further offending following a final warning would automatically result in a charge being brought as second final warnings were allowed in very limited circumstances. Reprimand and warnings were citable in court in the same way as previous convictions. Although the intervention offered under a final warning was voluntary, Bateman (2002, p 137) comments that due to age and immaturity and the nature of the final warning itself, 'there is little doubt that the young person will experience the process as one of implied coercion.' In fact, if a young person who had received a final warning subsequently went to court, the YOT would report on his or her compliance, so a decision whether or not to participate in a 'change programme' could have later consequences.

Reprimands and final warnings could only be given where a young person admitted the offence and where there was sufficient evidence to secure a realistic prospect of conviction if the matter was taken to court. If a young person denied the offence or where the offence was considered sufficiently serious, charges would be brought. For indictable offences (those dealt with in the Crown Court) the Crown Prosecution Service was involved, but otherwise the assessment of seriousness and decisions about reprimand, final warning or charge rested with the police using gravity scales. Effectively, they were – and still are in the coalition's new pre-court arrangements – the gatekeepers to the YJS. Interestingly, looking at that role, research on the early implementation of final warnings (Holdaway, 2003) raised questions about police officers' determinations of guilt (that is, the extent to which they tested and clarified what young people said about their offences and their admissions) and their judgement of seriousness, as opposed to the adequacy of available evidence.

Hine (2007) also explored issues around guilt and the circumstances in which young people admitted offences, critical in terms of accepting the fairness and legitimacy of the final warning process and any intervention offered by the YOT. In Hine's study many of the final warnings had been given for violence and, in some young people's accounts, the question of who initiated the incident and the roles of victim and perpetrator was unclear. Young people also tended to admit to offences in order to escape the stressful situation they found themselves in at the police station, so foregoing their due process rights to a detailed examination of their alleged behaviour and proper consideration of the extent of guilt or culpability. Hine comments that:

> The boundary between "naughtiness and serious wrongdoing" is certainly not clear cut in the eyes of young people, nor for that matter to the police. We see from the examples given here that young

people do not generally deny the act, but that they do question the interpretation of events and frequently deny criminal intent behind their actions. The system no longer allows them to be children with childish intent, but rather views them as potential serial offenders who must be stopped at the earliest opportunity. (2007, p 7)

There were a number of concerns associated with the final warning scheme which was credited with speeding young people's entry into the formal court system, with only two possible stages before a young person had to appear in court (Graham, 2010). It is questionable whether the net widening associated with final warnings inevitably resulted in the criminalisation claimed by some critics, given the evidence of variation in practice between YOTs as final warnings were implemented (Holdaway, 2003). However, it was notable that the number of young people given penalty notices for disorder, reprimands and final warnings rose significantly to a combined peak of 146,500 in 2006, when pressure was being brought to bear on criminal justice agencies to meet targets for offences brought to justice; pre-court disposals counted towards these targets and young people committing minor offences were easy pickings, as it were (Morgan and Newburn, 2012). It is no coincidence that custody rates for young people were also peaking during and shortly after this period.

This is not the end of the concerns about New Labour's approach to pre-court interventions; studies also suggest doubts about the quality of interventions associated with final warnings, and whether they were effective and suited for their purpose (Smith, 2003). Certainly, the YJB target of delivering 'change programmes' on 80 per cent of all final warnings did not represent an efficient use of resources, leading to overuse of the same standardised groupwork and other activities used for young people across the YOT caseload. It is also the case that some young people on final warnings had complex needs that could not be met with the level of resources available and expectations of time-limited 'change programmes' (Holdaway, 2003), so effectively they were not receiving the forms of early intervention that might have benefited them.

Despite the doubts and criticisms levelled at final warnings, the YJB seemed keen to expand pre-court initiatives, and in 2010 established pilots for the youth conditional caution. The coalition government is less enthusiastic about formal processes, more cautious about the possibility of criminalising young people and, in a time of austerity, does not have money available for extensive early interventions. Their new framework for out-of-court disposals, effective from April 2013, bears some similarities to the previous interventions, but is not based on an automatic 'two strikes and you are out' principle. Essentially, the options available to the police are:

- no further action
- community resolution (which is informal and may involve restorative justice)

- youth caution – the YOT is notified and for a second or subsequent caution must offer assessment and an intervention programme
- youth conditional caution – this involves a YOT assessment and joint decision-making about appropriate conditions (YJB, 2013b).

The flexibility in this system is welcome, but the fact that conditions given to young people may be punitive as well as rehabilitative or restorative does not suggest that this framework is entirely benign. It is also early in its implementation, and only time will show how many young people are dealt with at each of these stages, how effectively it prevents entry into the formal parts of the YJS and whether it eases the unnecessary criminalising of young people associated with the final warning scheme.

What might 'early intervention' mean?

Another important strand in New Labour policy was crime prevention, largely based on the growing evidence of factors associated with problematic behaviours. The Cambridge Study, highly influential in its thinking, does not lie entirely within the realms of developmental psychology, but has close links to it. One of the most important areas of discovery from the Study, which is in line with other long-term cohort studies, is the significance of early experiences, and particularly childrearing. Farrington (2007) discusses the risk factors which may appear in childhood at an individual or a family level. Individual risk factors associated with anti-social behaviour and offending might include: low intelligence and attainment; poor development of empathy; impulsivity; and limited social and cognitive skills. Family-related factors could be: parents or other family members involved in crime; large family size (although there are a number of explanations for why this might this might be a risk); quality of supervision and monitoring of children; harsh or inconsistent discipline; child abuse and neglect; and families who are disrupted or in conflict. Both Loeber and Farrington (2000) and Moffitt (1993) also describe young people with more serious and entrenched patterns of offending having displayed disruptive behaviours from an early age.

It is all too easy to regard findings of this kind as a helpful checklist for prediction, although in fact it is rather easier to recognise these factors looking back over a young offender's life than it is to identify prospectively which young people will offend on the basis of these risk factors (Farrington, 2007). Even Loeber and Farrington are more tentative about the developmental model they suggest, in which:

> Specifically, we hypothesise that the *initial* risk factors for child delinquency lie, first, within the individual child (such as impulsive behaviour) and, second, within the family (such as parents' child-rearing practices). (2000, p 749)

They then describe the range of risk factors expanding as the child grows and is exposed progressively to a greater number of influences and experiences outside the home. However, there are complications in trying to separate out the nature of the link between risk factors and later behaviours, as Farrington explains:

> A major problem of the risk factor prevention paradigm is to determine which risk factors are causes and which are merely markers or correlated with causes. It is also important to establish processes or developmental pathways that intervene between risk factors and outcomes.... Risk factors tend to co-occur, making them difficult to disentangle. Independent, additive, interactive and sequential effects of risk factors need to be studied. (2000, p 7)

Sadly, these nuances tended to be lost when translated into New Labour policy (O'Mahoney, 2009). Nevertheless, the development of Sure Start announced in 1998 held promise. Based on evidence from the Perry Pre-school Project (see Farrington, 2006) and the Headstart initiative in the US, Sure Start was intended to tackle social exclusion and disadvantage in a broad social programme (R. Smith, 2009). With substantial investment, the programme had expanded by 2006 to be accessible to 800,000 pre-school children and families (Doyle, 2008).

Over time, however, the rhetoric around family intervention changed, and Sure Start centres were absorbed into local authority services as children's centres, with a clear emphasis on inclusion through work and provision of childcare (Clarke, 2009). In this sense, a SID policy has been adopted, while at the same time a focus on 'problem' families through Family Nurse Partnerships and Family Intervention Projects has taken on dimensions of a MUD approach (Clarke, 2009; Nixon and Parr, 2009). This was also reflected in a change of tone and shifting goalposts for other early intervention projects such as On Track and the Children's Fund, aimed at 8- to 13-year-olds. Their original wide brief thus became more focused on explicit crime prevention targets which, certainly for Smith (2011), undermined their capacity to improve young people's lives and to promote inclusion.

The risks in focusing on risk

The early intervention initiatives promoted by the YJB took two forms. First, social programmes such as Summer Splash and Youth Inclusion Projects (YIPs) were targeted at specific neighbourhoods. Alongside these, initiatives aimed at individual young people were developed including YISPs and Positive Activities for Young People (PAYP). The YJB devoted a considerable amount of resources to prevention programmes (Graham, 2010), quickly overcoming initial agency reluctance to intervene with the younger age group and ensuring that they were embedded in the reformed youth justice landscape. In a survey of YOTs (Carol Goldstone Associates, 2010), the majority had devoted more than 10 per cent of resources to work with young people who had not yet offended. The targeted age group became lower over time, with junior versions of YIPs being developed to cover the same 8- to 13-year-old age group as YISPs, which concerned critics in view of the processes of identification and targeting for these interventions (Smith, 2006). McCarthy (2011), for example, discusses the high level of discretion allowed to social workers and other professionals and the class assumptions influencing judgements about *potential* as well as *actual* offending behaviour.

Second, the anti-social behaviour agenda was less directly controlled by the YJB, but, as actions to tackle anti-social behaviour became more firmly associated with young people, the YJB also pushed a strategic agenda around surveillance and enforcement. Anti-social behaviour was seen as a precursor of crime and thus a target for intervention, although many of the measures available (ASBOs, child curfews, dispersal orders) were about prevention and prohibition, not positive support and guidance.

Both wider social interventions and those relating to anti-social behaviour are allied with risks and, in the former case, actuarial methods of assessing risk, primarily through the structured format of Onset, which is part of the Asset suite of assessment tools. They were thus subject to the managerialism that pervaded the whole of the YJS, and have been viewed as being about risk control rather than help and support. Although young people have undoubtedly benefited from help and support through various prevention projects, success is judged in terms of prevention or reduction of offending and behavioural change rather than personal development or welfare needs – a narrow rather than a holistic focus, at least as far as managerial goals are concerned (Smith, 2006). And it is also difficult to isolate the impact of, for instance, YISP intervention when other agencies are involved at the same time, or where the family or school situation changes (Walker et al, 2007).

Other concerns are voiced about the coercive nature of involvement in prevention activities and the language of 'non-negotiable support and challenge' used in official documents such as the YCAP (HM Government, 2008). Solomon and Blyth, for instance, observe that:

> There is a danger that any carrot and stick approach to current early intervention strategies will tip some young people and their families further over the edge and away from participating in effective neighbourhood and local services. Any engagement with services that is contingent on good, responsible behaviour with sanctions applied to enforce compliance may not be sufficient in encouraging young people to lead law-abiding lives. (2009, p 6)

Of course, the amount of 'carrots and sticks' employed may differ significantly between different projects and types of intervention, but it is concerning that help and support is no longer given unconditionally. Relationships and responsiveness are critical in encouraging participation, not coercion, and in this regard, it is interesting to note the words of one academic with a long history in youthwork who comments that 'my experience, through practice, is that young people remain pretty adept at circumventing unwanted intervention and fairly responsive to engagement that seems credible and relevant' (Williamson, 2009, p 16). This is a particular challenge in relation to the young people who face the most difficult or chaotic circumstances and who may have already had negative experiences of professionals. The danger is that the response to resistance or ambivalence is further disciplinary or control measures, which may only serve to compound difficulties.

An evaluation of YISPs (Walker et al, 2007) highlighted the importance of engagement, with some young people motivated to participate in what was offered but others unwilling despite the efforts of keyworkers. Parents and children interviewed for the qualitative elements of the research were overall positive about YISP involvement, and reported improvements, for instance, in family relationships and general behaviour. Progress in other areas such as education seemed more fragile. On the whole, 'success' very much depended on the quality of key worker relationships, consistency being a key element, and also access to mainstream services and facilities to ensure that positive changes could be sustained. In this regard, it is important that prevention projects are not used as a substitute for welfare services that are the responsibility of other agencies, and that they are networked with other agencies so that they can effectively facilitate access rather than themselves acting as stop-gap provision.

One of the main concerns highlighted by this evaluation (Walker et al, 2007) and reflected elsewhere was that many of the parents had been asking for help for some time before referral to YISP. It is deeply regrettable that in so many cases support and guidance is not offered at an earlier stage and outside of the YJS before a young person comes to the attention of the police or presents as a problem at school. Clearly much good work has taken place in YISPs, YIPs, PAYP and similar projects, but they are available to a selected group of children and/or young people designated as 'risky' or 'at risk', being targeted rather than universally available. This raises the questions of how effective targeting might be and also the potential for stigmatising or for labelling young people within projects. Indeed the very funding mechanisms for prevention work, which is often delivered by voluntary agencies or dedicated parts of the YOT, encouraged the tendency to emphasise the 'riskiness' of the young people engaged in the project (Kelly, 2012). Furthermore the lack of stability in grant funding was a real threat to consistency and sustainability of provision (Carol Goldstone Associates, 2010) and prevention activity, which is non-statutory, has hugely reduced in the current climate of austerity. YOTs are clearly not first in line for monies available under the Early Intervention Grant (House of Commons Justice Committee, 2013).

A fundamental criticism of prevention based on the risk factor prevention paradigm is that it individualises risk and does not challenge the wider social and political contexts that create risks for young people. O'Mahoney, for example, notes that:

> The RFPP [risk factor prevention paradigm] is a one size fits all framework which ... tends to support the legal and political status quo and to marginalize radical discourses that question fundamental definitions and mainstream values and practices in all cultures ... a related problem is the RFPPs focus on the individual as the unit of analysis. (2009, p 107)

In this regard, the paradigm seemed to present a rational but ultimately safe basis for New Labour policy, which favoured targeted rather than universal social provision, and avoided confronting the challenge of social and structural inequalities. Yet social contexts are important, and so are individual choice and agency: pathways are not so clearly pre-determined as the RFPP tends to suggest, and research is beginning to explore young people's perspectives and their ability to use social capital to shape their own lives (Kemshall et al, 2007). Such research and alternative approaches are explored in a later section, while the next section outlines the structure of pre-court interventions.

Prevention: moving beyond the risk factor prevention paradigm

One of the key characteristics of the RFPP is that it tends to individualise risk. Put crudely, it characterises the young person or family as a bearer of risk and the task becomes then to address risk factors, problems and deficits and to strengthen resilience. This sounds relatively straightforward, but 'in short, the RFPP flatters only to deceive. Its indiscriminate embrace of an embarrassing wealth of risk factors creates only the illusion of explanation' (O'Mahoney, 2009, p 113). In other words, identifying indicators of risk does not necessarily tell us how to address them, particularly where there are multiple interlocking aspects of risk. Translating individualised prevention into practice may be more complex and messy than anticipated, even if the 'right' young people and families are targeted (and that is not a given).

It is instructive to consider how initial targeting might take place. First, findings from the large cohort study, the ESYTC, indicate that policing practices are significant in drawing young people into the ambit of the YJS and keeping them there. McAra and McVie argue, on the basis of self-reports from young people, that:

> The police do disproportionately target certain groups of young people who might accurately be described as "the usual suspects". This suspect population comprises (for the most part) young boys from lower class backgrounds and broken families, who live in areas of high social deprivation, who have an active street life (and who consequently form a core component of the population *available* for policing). (2005, p 9)

Although it is the nature or seriousness of offending that first attracts police attention, other processes ensure that, once identified as a problem or as a trouble-maker, that status or label sticks to the young person. Having 'form' is a powerful predictor of ongoing contact – often adversarial – with the police (McAra and McVie, 2005). Second, further findings from the ESYTC expose the role of professional gatekeepers to the YJS in recycling the same young people – again, the 'usual suspects' – around social welfare and youth justice systems, whereas other young people offending in comparable ways escape agency intervention altogether (McAra and McVie, 2007). Elsewhere, McCarthy (2011, p 502) argues on the basis of a study of pre-court case conferences that the judgments are often based on middle-class norms and expectations through which 'professionals actively construct signs of class and non-respectability as requiring forms of correction and sometimes criminalisation.' He describes structures of identification commonly involving such items as untidy homes, classroom horseplay and shouting and screaming in the home, which are not obviously equated with offending.

So the process of identification and targeting is not necessarily objective and may tend, at the same time, to over-concentrate on certain categories of young people, while neglecting others who may benefit from intervention. Furthermore, it is important to recognise that:

> The deeper the usual suspects penetrate the youth justice system, the more this is associated with *inhibited* desistance from offending … our principle message, therefore, is that the key to tackling serious and persistent offending lies in minimum intervention and maximum diversion. (McAra and McVie, 2007, p 319)

But if prevention activities shift their focus from the individual, what other actions might be appropriate? Looking at institutional processes might be productive, including the nature of decision-making around exclusions and behaviour management in schools. Restorative justice interventions could be used more extensively to deal with conflict and minor offending in schools and children's homes. Restorative justice might also be used to respond to anti-social behaviour as an alternative to acceptable behaviour contracts and ASBOs. Detached youthwork and street-based drugs agencies may also work to good effect where there are uneasy relationships between young people and the communities in which they live. The precepts of youthwork have much to offer and are sadly neglected in prevention work – participation, empowerment and social education. It does not preclude targeted work and may have a specific role with anti-social behaviour or crime prevention (Williamson, 2009), but adopts an inclusive and broadly social approach in contrast to the recent preference for individualised and developmental explanations for delinquency in its many forms.

It is worth considering the role of the social in young people's development, moving beyond the individual, family and immediate social context that are the concerns of the more psychologically based RFPP, the linked notion of criminal careers and the deeply normative impulses underlying these approaches. A sociological perspective looks across the life span and acknowledges the social systems and structures that help shape individual pathways. Hayes makes a useful distinction when he says:

> From a pathways perspective, prevention seeks to reduce the overall likelihood of negative pathways and increase the incidence of positive, while early intervention seeks to alter an emergent pathway. (2007, p 205)

Prevention may be promoted by broad social programmes that foster inclusion and are differentiated according to need but that are universally accessible, difficult as this may be in tough economic times. They should seek to assist young people with the 'developmental tasks' appropriate to their age, that is, the skills or knowledge that are then built on in order to progress to the next stage (Lawrence, 2007). So this might include a diversity of training opportunities on leaving school or different types of educational and social support for young people at the point of starting secondary school. Early intervention, in Hayes' view, should recognise and respond to the fact that the onset of different types of problem behaviours may typically occur at different ages as young people encounter new social contexts, so 'early intervention' means at an appropriate time, not always early in life. In this sense, it equates more to Munro's (2011b) notion of 'early help' than early intervention informed by developmental criminology:

> Early in life? Or early in the pathway? When it comes to both indicated and selective prevention, early in life is only a matter of early in the pathways that emerge in the early years. Many other pathways emerge later in childhood, adolescence and even adulthood. From a life-span developmental perspective, early in life is never enough! (Hayes, 2007, p 219)

It is also helpful if early intervention is appreciative of the way that young people view their worlds and the choices available to them. The extent and types of social capital that a young person possesses may influence the way that he or she negotiates pathways and takes decisions in relation to more risky choices (Kemshall et al, 2007). Also, in terms of the options available for young people, 'it is not just a matter of "what is", it is also a question of "what is perceived to be" at any particular time in terms of accessibility of opportunities and their attractiveness' (France and Homel, 2007, p 13). Furthermore, early intervention must respond to the findings of research that show that:

> What young people really value is not so much programmes and content, but a good supportive relationship with an adult who is not judgemental and is able to offer guidance and advocacy when needed.

Trust and respect are important qualities that help young people negotiate their way through difficult decisions and circumstances.... The focus of prevention efforts should be on changing social arrangements to create opportunities and systems that facilitate the formation of such supportive structures. (France and Homel, 2007, p 23)

Implications for practice

Prevention, diversion and early intervention each throw up dilemmas for the YJS at the levels of both policy and practice. If, as Williamson (2009, p 14) argues, what was once viewed as 'benign neglect' might now be 'tantamount to malign indifference' in the context of difficult transitions to adulthood, social exclusion and unequal access to opportunities and resources, what is the appropriate focus for these activities? What exactly are we trying to prevent? Where should we intervene, when and with whom? And even more controversially, when should we leave well alone?

New Labour took a proactive stance, stipulating that prevention of offending should be the principal aim of the YJS and a core purpose for each of its constituent agencies. But how best to achieve this was less clear. Early actions included replacing the previous cautioning system with a new pre-court structure of reprimands and warnings, introducing the ASBO and initiating a range of diversionary and prevention activities which could reach as far as eight-year-olds.

These developments have been controversial because of the net widening and criminalising potential, particularly of ASBOs and the 'two strikes and you are out' nature of the final warning scheme. Indeed, the numbers of young people in the YJS and, most worryingly, those in custody, grew throughout most of New Labour's term in office. This is not to deny that much good work in prevention and early intervention took place, especially in projects with a social rather than an enforcement orientation, but targeting and funding mechanisms explicitly emphasised risks, rather than needs, and the goal of crime reduction over providing help and support as a moral good in itself.

Further concerns arise about the influence of the risk factor prevention paradigm and the way that claims for its predictive potential have been exaggerated as it has been brought into practice. It has contributed to the tendency to individualise risk and to view young people and their families as bearers of risk without reference to their social context and the potential impact of exclusion, poverty and disadvantage. Furthermore, it assumes that young people's pathways are largely determined from a young age, downplaying the way that young people make choices and exercise agency – albeit within the range of possibilities available to them – to create their own routes towards adulthood.

Prevention and early intervention can be delivered in forms that take more account of social structures and systems, and which are more able to work with young people to support them in negotiating risks and making choices. Again, notions of social capital, of enabling young people to build and to deploy resources, and of collaborative rather than adult-directed work may indicate different and more productive ways to offer help and support.

Further reading

Blyth, M. and Solomon, E. (eds) (2009) *Prevention and youth crime: Is early intervention working?*, Bristol: The Policy Press.

France, A. and Homel, R. (eds) (2007) *Pathways and crime prevention: Theory, policy and practice*, Cullompton: Willan.

Wood, J. and Hine, J. (eds) (2009) *Work with young people: Theory and policy for practice*, London: Sage Publications.

FIFTEEN

Challenging practice in the courts

Despite the increase in prevention activities and the re-awakening of interest in diversion, the court remains at the heart of the YJS. Its aim is to dispense justice in a fair and impartial way, yet the youth court is a formal setting, and sadly young people too often find themselves subject to its processes rather than being able to participate in them. Even where procedures are faithfully followed and the law strictly implemented (an aspect of *procedural justice*), there are instances where the outcomes are still inappropriate or where they have a disproportionate impact on the individual young people (an issue of *substantive justice*). Judicial decision-making is not always experienced by young defendants as fair and just; nor is it, in many cases, by victims. Setting aside the fact that the laws themselves may be flawed, the justice system is imperfect because it is run by human beings, so inherently holds the potential for inconsistency and subjectivity in decision-making. Yet the other side of the coin is that it benefits precisely because it is run by human beings capable of showing compassion, empathy and understanding in response to the young people before them.

The key role of the youth justice practitioner in court is to individualise and to humanise its processes by delivering oral and written reports, providing information and advice, and conducting breach proceedings. Through all of these the practitioner can help the court understand the young defendant and his or her unique circumstances, needs, feelings, motivations and areas of risk. But this is challenging practice that requires a confident knowledge of court processes and an ability to work with other agencies, in particular to negotiate the power differentials that can form a barrier between youth justice and legal professionals. This chapter demystifies court processes and highlights the possibilities for proactive practice in court, increasing the credibility of the YOT with sentencers and helping empower young people.

Young people in court

The court system (civil and criminal) in England and Wales is organised in a hierarchical way. This means that decisions made at one level can be challenged or 'appealed' and then be re-considered by a higher court. For criminal cases, there are two levels of court, the magistrates' court and the Crown Court, with the Court of Appeal and the recently established Supreme Court sitting above.

The youth court is a magistrates' court presided over by specially trained magistrates collectively referred to as the Youth Court Panel. It only deals with criminal matters, civil matters such as family proceedings and applications for ASBOs being dealt with elsewhere in the magistrates' court system. Within the legal system offences are classified as:

- *summary:* relatively minor offences, including motoring, soliciting, being drunk and disorderly;
- *indictable:* serious offences such as murder, rape, robbery; and
- *triable either way:* offences such as theft and fraud where the seriousness may vary.

In adult courts the separation of court responsibilities is relatively clear-cut: summary offences can only be dealt with at a magistrates' court, and indictable offences at Crown Court. Offences classed as 'triable either way' could be sentenced at either court depending on the circumstances and, for example, the extent of damage caused or the value of goods stolen. In contrast, the youth court, despite its summary jurisdiction, is empowered to sentence for a wider range of offences. It is able to impose custody for up to two years in the form of a detention and training order, whereas the maximum in an adult magistrates' court would be six months (12 months for multiple offences). As an illustration, 53,642 young people faced proceedings in a youth court for indictable or triable either way offences in 2010/11 compared to 34,719 for summary non-motoring offences (Ministry of Justice, 2012a).

Young people may be dealt with in an adult magistrates' court if they are jointly charged with an adult and in certain other circumstances such as when an adult has aided and abetted a young person in committing offences.

The number of young people sentenced in Crown Court is relatively small but significant, because by definition these are the young people most likely to receive custody or intensive community orders (2,050 in 2010/11, whereas 38,672 were sentenced in a magistrates' court, including a youth court; see Ministry of Justice, 2012a).

The court is primarily concerned with issues of justice, and these are imbued with questions about rights. The Human Rights Act (HRA) 1998 incorporates the ECHR Articles into domestic law. The most immediately relevant is Article 6 which concerns the right to a fair and public hearing within a reasonable time by an independent and impartial tribunal established by law (which would include the youth court). It refers to the principle of innocence until proven guilty and further in Article 6(3) establishes the accompanying rights for each individual to be informed promptly and in detail, in a language which he or she understands, of the nature and cause of the accusation being made, and the means to prepare a defence (access to legal advice, ability to question witnesses and so on). This is reflected in the provisions of Article 40 of the UNCRC 1989. However, ensuring that court proceedings are timely and accessible to young people is more easily achieved within the youth court setting than in the relative formality of the Crown Court.

Article 5 of the ECHR concerns the right to liberty and security, and ensures that individuals should not be deprived of their liberty except where detention is lawful, for instance, following conviction by a 'competent court'. The UNCRC further states that:

Article 37(b)

No child shall be deprived of his or her liberty unlawfully or arbitrarily. The arrest, detention or imprisonment of a child shall be in conformity with the law and shall be used only as a *measure of last resort* and for the shortest appropriate period of time.

The use of custodial sentences for under-18s in the UK has been controversial and it is questionable whether custody was a *measure of last resort* during the New Labour era. Finally, Article 8 of the ECHR concerns the right to respect for individual, private and family life which may be compromised not only by penal measures such as curfews, but also by civil measures such as parenting orders.

Taking account of age and maturity

Article 3 of the UNCRC states that in all actions taken by public bodies, including courts of law, *the best interests of the child shall be a primary consideration*. Furthermore, the UN Standard Minimum Rules for the Administration of Juvenile Justice (the Beijing Rules) requires in Rule 5.1 that *the juvenile justice system shall emphasise the well-being of the juvenile*. Sensitivity to age and maturity are central in ensuring that the well-being and best interests of the child or young person are appropriately taken into consideration.

In England and Wales, the welfare principle was established by the C&YPA 1933 which states that:

Section 44

Every court in dealing with a child or young person who is brought before it, either as an offender or otherwise, shall have regard to the welfare of the child or young person.

This still features in Section 142A of the CJA 2003, but regard to welfare must now be balanced with the principal aim set out for the YJS in Section 37 of the CDA 1998, which is the prevention of offending by children and young people. Although Section 9 of the CJ&IA 2008 specifying the purposes of sentencing has not been brought into force, the court is also likely to consider the aims outlined there, namely, punishment, reform and rehabilitation, public protection and reparation – not an easy accommodation in many cases.

Good practice suggests that the young person (and parents or carers, as appropriate) should be informed of the basis on which court proceedings have been instigated so that that he or she is able to understand why the action is being taken and can make a decision about plea. The Magistrates' Court Rules require that the magistrates explain the nature and grounds for the proceedings to the young person in terms suitable to his or her age and level of understanding. In certain instances, this may be difficult, if the young person has a limited attention span or learning disability, for example, in which case the parents or carers may be informed instead. The court officer may also need to take an active role to ensure that the young person is able to follow the proceedings as far as possible and to make sense of what is taking place, liaising with defence solicitors, parents, carers and other professionals involved as appropriate.

After the youth court has made its decision – whether it concerns bail, requests for further enquiries or sentencing – this should be explained to the young person and parents by the court in simple language. However, it is often helpful for the court officer to talk to the young person and/or family before they leave the court precinct to make sure that he or she fully understands what the court has decided and what the next steps will be. The comments of Plotnikoff and Woolfson in a scoping study they conducted for the YJB are highly relevant in this regard:

> Most of the 65 young people in our sample, nearly all of whom were repeat offenders, initially did not admit that there were things they did not understand about the court process. Many were full of bravado in discussing their court experiences, particularly those seen in groups who were reluctant to acknowledge any difficulties in front of others. Eventually, however, those seen individually and many seen in groups acknowledged a wide range of problems of understanding in the courtroom. They were heavily reliant on their solicitors' interpretation afterwards of what had happened. Some were able to articulate that they wanted more things to be explained to them before court and in the courtroom without having first to ask for an explanation or to admit they did not understand.
>
> *Source:* Plotnikoff and Woolfson (2002, p 28)

In both the youth court and Crown Court, proceedings are governed by a practice direction, *Treatment of vulnerable defendants* (Ministry of Justice, 2012d), which states that:

> (III.30.11) At the beginning of the proceedings the court should ensure that what is to take place has been explained to a vulnerable defendant in terms he can understand, and at trial in the Crown Court it should ensure in particular that the role of the jury has been explained. It should remind those representing the vulnerable defendant and the supporting adult of their responsibility to explain each step as it takes place, and at trial to explain the possible consequences of a guilty verdict. Throughout the trial the court should continue to ensure, by any appropriate means, that the defendant understands what is happening and what has been said by those on the bench, the advocates and witnesses.

Appearing in the Crown Court may be a confusing and intimidating experience for a young person, in spite of any efforts that the court itself may make, for instance, taking frequent breaks and removing wigs and other formal dress. Youth justice practitioners may also find the environment unfamiliar and be unconfident about liaising with, and on occasions instructing, barristers. Nevertheless, all the professionals involved should try to help the young person participate in proceedings and to have his or her side of the case presented.

The conduct of court proceedings clearly has welfare implications not least because young people could become distressed or alienated by the way they have been treated or simply afraid at what might happen to them. As an illustration, two of the young people in the Plotnikoff and Woolfson research said:

> 'I thought I had no right to speak in court except to the solicitor. The solicitor told me to say if there was anything I didn't understand. There were things, but I was too scared to say so in court.

> 'No one said you could ask a question. Because I was told to say "No comment" at the police station, I thought I couldn't say anything at court.' (2002, p 29)

Nevertheless the decisions made in court have more of an impact on welfare than the court processes themselves. The most obvious is where a young person is remanded or sentenced to custody, but other decisions also have impacts: decisions such as bailing a young person to stay at a relative's address rather than the parental home, imposing a curfew, prohibiting a young person from contact with a named individual, for instance, may positively or negatively affect his or her welfare. Accuracy of information and assessment assists decision-making and in this sense striving for the best is almost a moral imperative for practitioners.

Parents and the court

Parenting and reinforcing parental responsibility were major preoccupations for New Labour, and this seems unchanged under the current coalition government. Of course parents and other carers are important in terms of supporting young people through the court process, encouraging compliance and reinforcing the learning from subsequent interventions. The critical question is whether, and to what degree, compulsion assists this. Powers in relation to parents are not new but were significantly increased in the New Labour reforms to the YJS.

First, under Section 33A of the C&YPA 1933 the court *must* require a parent to attend if the young defendant is under the age of 16, and *may* require a parent to attend if the defendant is 16 or 17 years old. 'Parent' is taken to mean any individual who holds parental responsibility for the young person. Where this is the local authority, a representative of children's social care should act as supporter and be in attendance.

Second, if a young person is convicted of an offence, the court may make a parental bind-over for a period of up to three years or until the young person becomes 18, with a recognisance not exceeding £1,000. Under the terms of a bind-over, the parent must take proper control of and exercise control over the young person and, where a youth rehabilitation order has been imposed, ensure that he or she complies with its requirements.

Third, where the young person is under the age of 16, the parent can be made to pay any fine imposed if the court feels this is appropriate. In certain circumstances, parents can also be made to take over payments of a fine where a young person has defaulted.

Fourth, Section 8 of the CDA 1998 introduced parenting orders that have now been extended so they are available to the court in a number of criminal and civil proceedings (see Chapter Ten). Altogether this represents a considerable range of powers in addition to the 'voluntary' parenting interventions that YOTs provide.

Persistent young offenders

Another focus for New Labour concerns was persistent patterns of offending. While all court proceedings involving young people should be conducted so as to reduce unnecessary delays, New Labour's campaign in 1997 particularly emphasised the need for swift administration of justice for persistent young offenders (PYOs), reflecting concerns expressed by the Audit Commission in *Misspent youth* (1996) about the average length of time from arrest to sentence. One of their five key election pledges was to halve the 142 days it was then taking to conclude court proceedings, and targets were set accordingly across the YJS as they came into office under the 'Reducing delays' initiative. Although there is no legal definition of a PYO, for the purposes of the 'PYO pledge', those who came into scope were identified as:

> A child or young person sentenced in any court on three or more separate occasions for one or more recordable offence, and within three years of the last sentencing occasion is subsequently arrested or has an information laid against him or her for a further recordable offence.

Young people falling into the PYO group are still highlighted within the system and are 'fast-tracked' to sentencing, with particular attention to 'not guilty' pleas and the prompt listing of trials.

Persistence of offending features elsewhere in New Labour legislation. Certain sentences are only available for young people who are identified as *persistent offenders*. These include a youth rehabilitation order with intensive supervision and surveillance or fostering requirements for 10- to 14-year-olds, and also the detention and training order for young people aged 12-14. Although *persistent* is not defined in legislation, the Sentencing Guidelines Council (2009, p 11) suggests that the court might apply the following test:

> i. In most circumstances, the normal expectation is that the offender
> will have had some contact with authority in which the offending
> conduct was challenged before being classed as "persistent"; a

finding of persistence in offending may be derived from information about previous convictions but may also arise from orders which require an admission or finding of guilt – these include reprimands, final warnings, restorative justice disposals and conditional cautions; since they do not require such an admission, penalty notices for disorder are unlikely to be sufficiently reliable;

ii. A young offender is certainly likely to be found to be persistent (and, in relation to a custodial sentence, the test of being a measure of last resort is most likely to be satisfied) where the offender has been convicted of, or made subject to a pre-court disposal that involves an admission or finding of guilt in relation to, imprisonable offences on at least 3 occasions in the past 12 months.

Bail and remand decisions

Decisions about whether to release a defendant on bail involve a delicate balancing of interests, especially as the defendant is innocent until proven guilty (Slapper and Kelly, 2009). Public protection must be weighed against individual rights and, for young people, considerations of welfare. The main legislation in relation to bail is the Bail Act 1976, which applies to young people as well as to adults. Section 4 creates a presumption in favour of bail but provides for exceptions to this right where the court believes there are grounds for believing that the defendant, if released on bail, would: fail to surrender to custody; interfere with witnesses or otherwise obstruct the course of justice, whether in relation to himself or some other person; or commit a further offence.

A young person may also be denied bail if:

- the court is satisfied that he or she should be kept in custody for reasons of protection or welfare;
- he or she is already serving a custodial sentence;
- he or she, having previously been released on bail, has been arrested for absconding or breaking the conditions of bail;
- the offence is indictable or triable either way and he or she was on bail in criminal proceedings on the date of the offence;
- the case is adjourned for further enquiries or for a report and it appears it would be impracticable to complete the enquiries or report without keeping him or her in custody. (Adapted from Moore, 2009, p 125)

Section 4 of the Bail Act establishes that sentencers should have regard to the following when considering bail:

- the nature and seriousness of the offence;
- the defendant's character, previous convictions, employment record, associations and community ties;

- the defendant's previous record as regards past grants of bail;
- the strength of the case against the defendant;
- any other factor that appears to be relevant. (White, 1999, p 142)

Although the penal climate has become harsher and less tolerant of risk since the Bail Act first came into force, unconditional bail is still widely used for young people. Effectively all this requires is that the defendant presents at the police station or at court at the stipulated date and time. In contrast, there is much more restricted access to bail for those who have committed more serious offences or for those who have more entrenched patterns of offending.

Conditional bail under Section 6 of the Bail Act was introduced with the intention of reducing the need for custodial remands. The court may impose any conditions it considers necessary where bail would otherwise be refused or to make defendants available for enquiries or reports. Commonly used conditions include: residence, curfew, reporting to the police station and not contacting the complainant or witnesses in the case. Many YOTs provide bail supervision and support packages that may be a specified condition, as may attendance at YOT interviews for the preparation of reports. In October 2005, electronic monitoring became available to help enforce curfew conditions. This may be used for 12- to 17-year-olds but only in situations where the young person meets specified criteria in relation to the nature of the current offence or history of offending while on bail or remand to local authority accommodation. An assessment of suitability from the YOT is also required.

The increase in the use of conditions has raised concerns about whether the restrictions imposed are proportionate to the risks they pose. The CJS has moved a long way from the due process concerns with defendants' rights that motivated the original Bail Act 1976 and, on occasions, heavy restrictions are now considered acceptable on even very young people, ostensibly in the interests of crime control (see Figure 15.1).

Of course, not all young defendants are granted bail. Thankfully what was a complex array of remand provisions has now been simplified by the LASPO Act 2012, bringing 17-year-olds into the same framework and requiring local authorities to pay for remands into custody. Under the new arrangements, the court can remand a young person to local authority accommodation, with or without additional conditions, or to youth detention accommodation. The latter – effectively a remand in custody – is only available for a 12- to 17-year-old who meets a specified criterion in relation to the nature of the current offence or history of offending while on bail or remand. The court must also consider that a remand to youth detention accommodation is necessary either to:

- protect the public from death or serious personal injury (serious or psychological) occasioned by further offences committed by the child; or

Figure 15.1: Remand decisions, 2010/11

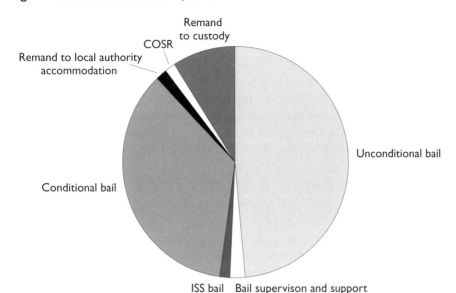

Source: Ministry of Justice (2012a)

- prevent the commission by the child of further imprisonable offences. (Ministry of Justice, 2012c, para 30)

More on young defendants in Crown Court

While there is a statutory presumption that young people will be sentenced in the youth court, there are instances where the sentencing powers of that court might be considered inadequate for the offences in question. The youth court cannot deal with homicide cases. In addition, it may commit a young defendant to Crown Court where the charges relate to:

- offences that for an adult carry a maximum term of at least 14 years' imprisonment (for example, aggravated burglary, cultivating cannabis, possession of a firearm with intent to endanger life);
- sexual assault under specific sections of the Sexual Offences Act 2003;
- death by dangerous driving or causing death by dangerous driving while under the influence of drink or drugs (if the defendant is aged 14 or over); or
- offences committed with an adult who is being tried on indictment and where the court considers that both the adult and the young person should be tried on indictment in the interests of justice. (Adapted from Moore, 2009; Slapper and Kelly, 2009)

The first two categories above fall under what is known as the 'grave crimes' provisions. Where a youth court considers that the appropriate custodial sentence is likely to be longer than the two-year maximum it can impose, it may decline jurisdiction and commit to the Crown Court for trial and/or sentencing. Chapter Eighteen outlines the custodial sentences available in more detail. What is significant here is the caution urged by the Sentencing Guidelines Council (2009, p 27), whose guidance states that committal should only take place when the charges are of such gravity that a sentence exceeding two years is 'a realistic possibility'. For persistent offenders aged 12-14 and young people 15 years and over, the guidance suggests that committal is appropriate only where a sentence 'substantially beyond the two year maximum for a detention and training order is a realistic possibility.'

The needs of vulnerable young defendants have been recognised but rather less so than those of vulnerable young witnesses (Jacobson and Talbot, 2009). Pressure groups have asked for the 'special measures' for witnesses under the Youth Justice and Criminal Evidence Act 1999 to be available to vulnerable defendants. As a result they may now give evidence by live television link or the use of an intermediary. These might alleviate some of the anxiety associated with appearing in the Crown Court in particular, although it is still likely to be a daunting experience for young defendants, and there are sensitive questions about how age and maturity might have an impact on fitness to plead (Jacobson and Talbot, 2009). The conduct of a case and the possible use of special facilities may be discussed in a preparatory meeting of the legal and other professionals involved, known as a Plea and Directions Hearing, and this is one forum where the YOT can put forward views about enablers and barriers to participating in proceedings.

Assessments for court

The YOT may be required to provide assessments at various stages in the court process to assist in decisions about bail addresses or conditions, vulnerability of a young person if remanded in custody or adjournments for specialist assessment. However, the most pivotal contribution is the assessment contained in a pre-sentence report, whether oral or written. This is rather different to the dynamic ongoing nature of assessment in the course of supervision or an intervention in that it is a snapshot, a one-time view of what is happening:

> Reports are documents associated with decisions fixed in time and context. They condense information into a digestable form and are organised so as to lend a purposeful narrative to that information. (Baker et al, 2011, p 104)

To that extent reports involve interpretation and judgement, going beyond the simple presentation of information. The author must select what is relevant and appropriate to draw to the attention of the court, and this should include the young person's (and possibly parents') perspective. The court will already have the facts of the case but will not know why the offence occurred, what might have motivated it or how the young person feels about it. A thorough offence analysis addresses each of these and comes to a view about the seriousness of the main offence, which should then lead to a preliminary indication of whether sentencing should fall within the first tier, community order or custodial band.

A pre-sentence report should present the considered judgement of the author about the case and the most appropriate outcome. It should be clear what is factual and what is opinion, although in practice that distinction may not be so straightforward as it sounds (Canton, 2011). Opinion should be evidenced and flow logically from the information provided, which should be gathered from an appropriate range of sources. It is important that the report is understandable to the young person because of its potential for engaging him or her in the court process and at the beginning of YOT involvement. That aside, there are critical questions about the purpose of reports and their intended audience. The primary aim is to inform sentencing, but how far reports should seek to influence or persuade is a matter of debate (Canton, 2011). In fact, magistrates may resist the conclusion of a report that they see as 'constructing a case' or as overly sympathetic.

Related to this latter point, a study by Phoenix (2010b) of decision-making in the youth court suggests that magistrates value the information in reports and the expert opinions of YOT practitioners, but tend to add to these by drawing on their personal experiences and 'common-sense' understandings to make their own assessments of risk. Under the YJB, risk assessment has become highly structured and promoted as a key aspect of the pre-sentence report, based on Asset and linked more recently to the Scaled Approach. Although Phoenix's research took place in one local justice area that may not be representative, it nevertheless poses questions about the components of risk assessment and the extent to which the risk-thinking and actuarial approach underpinning the risk factor prevention paradigm are accepted in reality. It may be that what is most valuable about a court report is what it communicates about and to an individual young person, and that the assessment of risk has been over-emphasised, whereas it is only one of the elements necessary to formulate an appropriate response. Risk, in any event, cannot easily be separated from the considerations of welfare, maturity, motivation, family relationships, emotional state and so on that should also be covered in the assessment.

The report should end with a clear proposal of how the court might proceed to sentencing, with relevant details of activities, programmes or other agencies to be involved, and the objectives for any intervention proposed. It may also be necessary to explain why particular courses of action may not be appropriate – why a specific programme might be unsuitable or the possible negative impacts of custody, for instance. In essence, 'the conclusion brings together the strands of the narrative that began with the offence analysis. There should be no surprise endings' (Baker et al, 2011, p 114).

Breach proceedings

The majority of breach proceedings relating to referral orders, youth rehabilitation orders and detention and training orders are dealt with in the youth court. Youth rehabilitation orders made in the Crown Court must be returned to the Crown Court except where a direction was made when the order was imposed to enable proceedings to be taken in the lower court. The court is notified of the alleged failure to comply in a document known as *an information* which is completed by the responsible officer, usually the YOT case manager. A breach of referral order must be referred back to the court by the Youth Offender Panel rather than the YOT itself.

The youth justice practititioner role in court is complex in relation to breach proceedings in that it combines the functions of prosecutor and expert adviser to the court (Baker et al, 2011). In the first instance, the practitioner outlines the allegation as laid out in the *information*. As with any other allegation, if the defendant admits the breach, the case can proceed quickly to resolution. However, in other cases, a breach trial will be held and the YOT is required to present its case, citing agency records, letters of appointment, work instructions and so on, as appropriate. Witness statements may be used if they are more efficient than calling other YOT practitioners to court. The defendant is able to argue his or her position and, ultimately, the court decides whether the defendant has *failed to comply without reasonable excuse* or not on the basis of the evidence presented.

If the defendant admits or is found to be in breach, the court must then decide what actions to take or sanctions to impose, guided by the breach report from the YOT that should:

- summarise the order and the period during which the author has been the *responsible officer*;
- outline the failure(s) to comply, including details of instructions given and any warnings;
- indicate the extent to which the defendant has complied with the order at the point where breach proceedings were instigated and since;
- provide relevant personal information about the defendant, including any barriers to engagement and compliance and what could be done to encourage compliance in future;
- provide a risk assessment covering harm, likelihood of re-offending and harm to self;
- provide positive information about the young person and future plans;
- give a view about whether the order should continue and any amendments that might be appropriate, or specify what sentence might otherwise be more suitable for the defendant.

As with a pre-sentence report, the conclusion and proposal should be authoritative and address issues relating to motivation, behaviour and management of the order.

Again, a breach report communicates both to the magistrates and to the young person. In fact, Baker et al point out that:

> In this instance, the young person is an important reader of the report; what is said, the tone in which it is said and the proposal itself are part of the wider breach experience which will affect their future engagement with the youth justice system. (2011, p 118)

Implications for practice

The YJS is centred round the adversarial court system. While many young people are diverted from court and the presumption is in favour of prosecution, where it happens, taking place in a youth court, the fact that young defendants may still appear in Crown Court is hugely symbolic. The YJS is struggling to fulfil the competing demands of welfare, rights, retribution and public protection for young people, and these tensions are most apparent in the court arena. Despite recent efforts to ensure that court processes are less alien and intimidating, the central question of whether prosecution in court, particularly Crown Court, is appropriate at all remains untouched.

Court proceedings must be conducted in line with the HRA 1998 and the UNCRC, which underline important rights such as the right to a fair, impartial and timely hearing. The challenge is to ensure that these rights are given due expression and that young defendants are able to contribute to court proceedings rather than finding themselves passively subject to them. In most cases, young people's interests would be better served by a more problem-solving and participatory approach, with an emphasis on decision-making in other, more informal settings. Expansion of restorative justice looks in that direction, but in the meantime the concern for practice is how best to engage with sentencing in courts and the procedures there.

There are three aspects to the YOT role in court. First, the practitioner is able to offer guidance and expert opinion to inform the court's deliberations in terms of bail, remand and sentencing. Written reports are a valuable opportunity for the practitioner to present the young person in context, and to create a narrative that enables the court to better understand the defendant and his or her actions, and then to formulate appropriate responses.

The next key role is that of prosecutor, where a young person is in breach of a court order. On the one hand, this is a use of authority and a demonstration of accountability to the court, but on the other, it may also present an opportunity for re-engaging a young person and talking constructively about compliance and commitment. The attitude that the YOT takes to enforcement before, during and after prosecution communicates powerful messages about the way that it works with young people and listens to them.

Finally, the practitioner is well placed to help and support the young person (and parents) in court, explaining what is happening and interpreting what that might mean for him or her. It is important to stand alongside the young person, figuratively but sometimes also literally – a reassuring presence in the midst of what may be a confusing or intimidating experience.

Court practice is not easy, and it is true to say that some practitioners feel more comfortable in the court environment than others. The courts are far from perfect as a means of dispensing justice, but youth-centred practice can contribute greatly to the quality of decision-making through the oral and written information presented and the working relationships built with other professionals as well as the young people involved in court proceedings and their families.

Further reading

Baker, K., Kelly, G. and Wilkinson, B. (2011) *Assessment in youth justice*, Bristol: The Policy Press.

Johnstone, G. and Ward, T. (2010) *Law and crime*, London: Sage Publications.

Smartt, U. (2009) *Law for criminologists: A practical guide*, London: Sage Publications.

SIXTEEN

Restorative justice and the referral order initiative

Chapter Fifteen outlined the court system, which in the UK casts the defendant and the prosecutor, acting on behalf of victim(s), as adversaries. However, this is not the only way to deal with disputes, whether civil or criminal; during the 1990s proponents of broader restorative justice (RJ) practices started to attract greater attention internationally, presenting challenges to conventional forms of Western justice and promoting more participative, problem-solving approaches. Some claim that the RJ movement (insofar as it is a coherent movement) derives from the ways that indigenous communities, principally in New Zealand and North America, have responded to those who transgress social norms or who commit wrongs against others. Others have been critical of the tendency to romantise 'traditional justice' but, in any case, the RJ concepts and practices being developed in more complex societies look strikingly different by virtue of more fluid and diverse community bonds.

What constitutes RJ is not easy to define, and its key elements have been subject to debate and considerable controversy. One question relates to its relationship with the legal justice system – whether RJ should replace retributive justice, whether the two should be integrated, or whether restorative interventions should be part of the conventional justice system, as a sentencing option, for example. Other questions relate to the type of offences and offenders considered appropriate for an RJ approach. In England and Wales, RJ has been adopted primarily for early stage offending and for use with young people. New Labour sought to institutionalise RJ through the provisions of the CDA 1998 and, more specifically, the Youth Justice and Criminal Evidence Act 1999, which introduced the referral order as an almost automatic disposal for young people pleading guilty on their first sentencing occasion in court. Although intending to be a vehicle for RJ, this chapter questions the extent to which it has achieved this in reality, due in part to the nature of the order itself backed by coercion, and in part to the issues arising in implementation. It examines what has happened to the optimism about RJ in New Labour's early period, the competing pressures and penal philosophies that shaped the particular way it became incorporated into the youth justice landscape and the renewed interest shown by the coalition government.

So what is restorative justice?

One of the concerns around RJ is that there is no clear-cut definition of what it is (Goodey, 2005): in many respects its most marked characteristic is that it seeks to offer ways of resolving problems and conflict that differ from retributive justice, but there are a variety of different approaches, methods and emphases encompassed within the RJ movement. RJ is therefore flexible and not necessarily restricted to criminal matters, being also used in relation to problems such as bullying, anti-social behaviour or neighbourhood disputes (Dignan, 2005). The following attempts at offering definitions capture important differences but also illustrate commonalities:

> [Restorative justice] gives victims the chance to tell offenders the real impact of their crime, to get answers to their questions and to receive an apology. It gives the offenders the chance to understand the real impact of what they've done and to do something to repair the harm. Restorative Justice holds offenders to account for what they have done, personally and directly, and helps victims to get on with their lives. (restorativejustice.org.uk)

Referring more broadly to who might be involved in RJ:

> A process whereby parties with a stake in a particular offence come together to resolve collectively how to deal with the aftermath of the offence and its implications for the future. (Marshall, 1996, p 37)

And focusing on the processes involved:

> Restorative justice is not restricted to a particular approach or programme but is applicable to any that have the following characteristics:
>
> - an emphasis on the offender's personal accountability by key participants; and
> - an inclusive decision-making process that encourages participation by key participants; and
> - the goal of putting right the harm that is caused by an offence. (Dignan and Marsh, 2001, pp 85-9, cited in Bazemore and Schiff, 2005, p 32)

These definitions demonstrate one of RJ's other features, which is the preference for informal rather than formal means of reaching a resolution. Certain RJ advocates note the dichotomy between retributive justice and RJ, unequivocally favouring the latter (see Table 16.1).

Such clear oppositions are not universally accepted, and other RJ proponents are more comfortable with the idea of conventional retributive justice and RJ co-existing (Marshall, 1999; Dignan, 2005), not least because the courts and formal proceedings are still necessary in cases where the perpetrator is not willing to engage with restorative processes. Voluntary participation on some level is needed, nevertheless, and there is considerable debate about the role of coercion and

Table 16.1: A comparison of retributive and restorative justice

Retributive justice	Restorative justice
Crime is a violation of the state, defined in purely legal terms devoid of moral, social, economic or political dimensions	Crime is a violation of one person by another, and is understood in the whole context
Focus on establishing blame, on guilt, on the past (did he or she do it?)	Focus on problem-solving, on liabilities and obligations, on the future (what should be done?)
Adversarial relationships and process normative	Dialogue and negotiation normative
Imposition of pain to punish and deter/prevent	Restitution as a means of restoring *both* parties; reconciliation/restoration as a goal
Justice defined by intent and by process: right rules	Justice defined as right relationships: judged by the outcome
Interpersonal and conflictual nature of the crime obscured, repressed; conflict seen as individual versus the state	Crime is recognised as interpersonal conflict: value of conflict is recognised
Encouragement of competitive, individualistic values	Encouragement of mutuality
Action from state to offender: – victim is ignored – offender is passive	Victim and offender's role is recognised in both the problem and solution: – victim's rights/needs recognised – offender is encouraged to take responsibility
The community is on the sideline, represented in the abstract by the state	Community as facilitator in restorative processes
Stigma of crime cannot be removed	Stigma of crime can be removed by restorative actions
No encouragement for repentance and forgiveness	Possibilities for repentance and forgiveness

Source: Adapted from Zehr (2013, pp 33-4)

whether it is helpful in some circumstances to overcome initial unwillingness. Again, a variety of positions are evident in relation to this question.

Briefly, structured RJ interventions or programmes tend to fall into four categories:

- reparation activities
- victim–offender mediation/restorative conferencing, which usually involves a meeting between the victim and offender, but can be conducted through a proxy
- community circles, which can be either focused on community integration and support or, more firmly within the criminal justice system, sentencing
- family group conferences, modelled on practices from New Zealand.

McCold and Wachtel (2003, cited in Bazemore and Schiff, 2005) identify three stakeholders as essential within RJ – victims, offenders and community – and have developed a hierarchy of restorative programmes based on their intentions and ability to engage all three. Programmes can therefore be assessed as fully, mostly or partly restorative or, conversely, non-restorative. The structures to deliver RJ in the UK and its implementation discussed later in this chapter are evaluated according to this hierarchy and also a set of principles specified by van Ness and Strong (1997, cited in Bazemore and Schiff, 2005, pp 32-3):

1. the principle of repair;
2. the principle of stakeholder participation – this refers to the active engagement of victims, offenders and communities as early and as fully as possible; and
3. the principle of transformation in community and government roles and relationships.

Rather than identifying interventions and practices as restorative or not, these principles can be used to gauge where they might sit on a spectrum of restorativeness. The third principle is the most difficult to achieve in practice; taken to its full extent it would mean not only transforming attitudes and ways of dealing with crime, but fundamental change in the structures of society and inequalities in relationships. At a more local level, it may involve strengthening communities or whole-school approaches to problematic behaviours, for example, but in a US review of restorative programmes, even these impacts were shown to be inconsistent (Bazemore and Schiff, 2005). Resources and political will are significant in achieving this sort of transformative change and these do not always accompany attempts to introduce restorative practices.

The question of community

Restorative interventions involving only the immediate stakeholders – offenders and victims – tend to individualise crime and the responsibilities for dealing with the after-effects of crime. This severely limits the power of the restorative approach and such interventions are necessarily restricted to situations where an offence has an identifiable victim or victims who are willing to participate. Furthermore, the possibilities for reintegrating the offender back into the community – or integrating for the first time for many disaffected young people (Gray, 2005) – are limited if the community is not involved.

The notion of community and communitarianism is an important underpinning for RJ, particularly in relation to the concept of *reintegrative shaming* (Braithwaite, 1989). The community may be involved as a direct stakeholder if affected by the offences or behaviours concerned; otherwise community members may participate in restorative interventions as a proxy or representative of community interests. The 'community' as stakeholder may be significant in helping the offender understand the impacts of his or her actions and in inducing a sense of shame (explored in the next section), but also, critically, in demonstrating forgiveness, providing opportunities for repairing harm and for redemption. In this sense, 'community' within a communitarian framework sits somewhere between the extremities represented by collectivism and individualism, holding the offender accountable to a tangible local grouping, whether brought together through physical proximity or shared interests.

There is a deeply moral element to this view of community and the assumed consensual views of community. Braithwaite famously commented that:

> Low crime societies are societies where people do not mind their own business, where tolerance of deviance has definite limits, where communities prefer to handle their own crime problems rather than hand them over to professionals. In this, I am not suggesting the replacement of the "rule of law" with the "rule of man". However, I am saying that the rule of law will amount to a meaningless set of formal sanctioning proceedings which will be perceived as arbitrary unless there is community involvement in moralising about and helping with the crime problem. (1989, p 8)

Dignan (2005, p 101) notes, however, that the RJ literature tends to presume that communities are 'reasonably benign, tolerant, likely to espouse broadly progressive values and that communitarianism is therefore "a good thing".' The reality may be very different, and it is questionable whether community as evoked by RJ proponents is symbolic rather than being a substantive and practical site for delivering justice (Goodey, 2005). In many instances in complex modern societies communities are hard to identify, and community bonds may be more or less secure. Communities may be self-protective and exclusive; the ways in which they promote and reinforce their social norms and expectations may be experienced as oppressive. Furthermore, they may feature gross inequalities in power and influence (Johnstone, 2002). Despite all of this, restorative practitioners may still be able to identify and find creative ways of tapping into new communities, connected perhaps to clubs or leisure pursuits, professional associations, faith groups or colleges, reflecting the more diverse nature of present-day social networks and investments. In this regard, Goodey (2005, p 210) stresses the importance of working 'for' not just 'with' the community in order to achieve long-term impacts, including a reduction in offending.

The role and the power of 'shaming'

As restorative practices are diverse, a variety of intellectual, political and social drivers have helped shape their development in different contexts. RJ has been criticised for its lack of rigorous theoretical foundation (Matthews, 2006), a gap at least partially filled by Braithwaite and his writing on *reintegrative shaming* (1989). Although this notion and its underpinning moralising framework has not influenced all forms of restorative practices, it has particular links with the kinds of

RJ interventions adopted in the UK and the nature of restorative policy transfer from other countries, in particular Braithwaite's native Australia.

Superficially Braithwaite's proposition is relatively straightforward: shame is a powerful emotion, particularly where the shaming is carried out by individuals (or by extension, a community or organisation) of significance to the offender, and coupled with the opportunity to make amends and therefore to be 'redeemed'. Retributive justice also uses shaming, explicitly in the past through the use of ducking stools, stocks and public whippings, and in the present in the way that court appearances and criminal records affect reputation. However, Braithwaite makes a distinction between:

> Shaming that leads to stigmatisation – to outcasting, to confirmation of a deviant master-status – versus shaming that is reintegrative, that shames whilst maintaining bonds of respect or love, that sharply terminates disapproval with forgiveness, instead of amplifying deviance by progressively casting the deviant out. (1989, p 12)

Braithwaite argues that shame is an important element of socialisation and the acquisition of internal social controls on behaviour. Interestingly, and in contrast to other advocates of RJ, he does not see RJ as an alternative to punishment as he feels that punishment can be delivered where it is agreed by all parties and therefore legitimated, followed by acceptance back into the community. In this case the punishment, whatever it might consist of, has a communicative value and underlines disapproval of the offence.

Shame is not normally viewed in a positive light, associated both with a loss of dignity for offenders and the potential to promote an oppressive conformity (Johnstone, 2002). Moreover, it is not inevitable that shaming will be followed by forgiveness and acceptance by the community and, where this fails, the results can be extremely destructive and disintegrative (Matthews, 2006). Matthews also questions whether shame is the most important motivating factor, and highlights the significant part that loss of trust may play. In particular, he suggests that establishing or reinstating trust may be a more appropriate objective of restorative practices than inflicting shame on offenders.

Despite these misgivings, Braithwaite has hugely influenced restorative practices, specifically being involved with the development of an RJ conferencing model in the town of Wagga Wagga in New South Wales. This scripted format was subsequently adopted in the UK by Thames Valley Police in 1998 and has been disseminated from that base. In many respects, New Labour was receptive to the emphasis on shaming and moral re-education as it came into office in 1997 looking for new approaches to criminal justice that moved beyond the previous punishment and welfare orientations. It also seemed to meet the need for rational and evidence-based policy (although trying to assess the impact of RJ practices on recidivism data and other criteria used for standard penal interventions rather misses the point when RJ practices are aimed at different outcomes; see Whyte, 2009).

Restorative justice in the UK

Restitution as an aspect of restoration was first introduced to England, Wales and Scotland in 1964 through the Criminal Injuries Compensation scheme. Unlike other restorative measures, this does not depend on an offender being convicted (Dignan, 2005). Other measures delivered through the CJS include court-ordered compensation and community service; the latter was re-branded as community punishment and then community payback or unpaid work, but when first introduced in 1973, its aims were explicitly reparative (although relating to the community rather than individual victims; see Dignan, 2005). In terms of the evaluation criteria outlined earlier, these initiatives are limited in their restorative potential, although they were landmark developments in their time.

During the 1980s there were ad hoc attempts, often led by the probation service, to develop reparation and mediation schemes with a fuller restorative vision. In 1985, the Home Office funded mediation projects in Cumbria, Coventry, Wolverhampton and Leeds, working with young offenders referred by the police or courts (Goodey, 2005). Yet despite promising early findings, official support proved ambivalent and was ultimately undermined by the growing victims lobby that was gaining publicity and following a different trajectory with the rise of Victim Support (Crawford and Newburn, 2003).

It was not until New Labour came into office in 1997 that RJ was given prominence in criminal justice policy, with an explicitly communitarian tone. The *No more excuses* White Paper (Home Office, 1997, para 9.21) characterised their version of RJ as involving:

- *Restoration:* young offenders apologising to their victims and making amends for the harm they have done;
- *Reintegration:* young offenders paying their debt to society, putting their crime behind them, and rejoining the law-abiding community;
- *Responsibility:* young offenders – and their parents – facing the consequences of their offending behaviour and taking responsibility for preventing further offending.

Within youth justice, the CDA 1998 quickly established RJ as an element of new provisions such as final warnings and action plan orders, as well as creating a new RJ requirement that could be attached to a supervision order. Sections 73 and 74 introduced the reparation order under which a young person could be required to make reparation either to the community or to a specified person or persons. The order is expressed in terms of hours up to a maximum of 24 hours to be completed within three months.

There has been little official interest in mandating RJ with adult offenders, although developments such as Circles of Support and Accountability for sex offenders are growing in significance (Hanvey et al, 2011). The contrast with young people is stark, reflecting the political pressures to find new ideas and approaches to the 'problem' of youth. In England and Wales, RJ was put forward as a constructive response within a reformed system designed to intervene in young people's lives more decisively and to underline the responsibilities of young people and their parents. Given that they are offender-focused rather than victim-focused, reparation and referral orders have at least promoted RJ in some form into a central place within the YJS (Goodey, 2005), but RJ remains 'an ambitious and ambiguous project' (Crawford and Newburn, 2003) in youth justice. Certainly as time has progressed, research indicates that the YJS has been more successful in responsibilising young people than it has in restoring victims or (re)integrating young people into their communities (Gray, 2005). It is telling, for instance, that in the pilots of the referral orders brought in by the Youth Justice and Criminal Evidence Act 1999, victims were present at only 13 per cent of the initial panels convened for young offenders (Crawford and Newburn, 2003). The following section outlines the provisions for referral orders and explores the achievements and challenges in implementation, which has not been easy within a penal system dominated by concerns about punishment and managerial efficiencies (Earle and Newburn, 2001).

Referral orders – the basics

The referral order is now firmly established as the main sentencing provision for young people appearing for the first time in a youth or magistrates' court (but not Crown Court). Provisions have now been extended so it is also available on subsequent sentencing occasions. However – and critically – it cannot be used where the young person has pleaded 'not guilty' to all the offences before the court and in these cases, if he or she is convicted, the magistrates have all other sentencing options available.

The court can only make a referral order where the sentence for the offence(s) is not fixed by law *and* the court is not proposing to impose a discharge (absolute or conditional) *or* a custodial sentence *or* a hospital order under the Mental Health Act 1983. If these circumstances are met, the referral order is mandatory for young people appearing in court for the first time for imprisonable offences, but discretionary in subsequent court appearances, in relation to summary (non-imorisonable) offences or where the young person has entered mixed pleas to the charges. The court may make a parenting order, a compensation order or an order for costs alongside the referral order.

The referral order permits the court to delegate its decision-making powers to a youth offender panel (YOP) involving volunteers from the community. The court establishes the legal basis of the order and non-compliance with the order must be brought back to the court to be dealt with, as the YOP itself has no legal status.

The basic requirement of the referral order is for the young person to attend meetings of a YOP and to agree a contract with the panel which will last for a period set by the court, between 3 and 12 months, starting from the date that the contract is signed (this is known as the *compliance period*). The intention is to divert young people from formal court proceedings and to provide a more deliberative forum with greater opportunity to engage the young offender in reparation and in problem-solving. The referral order is therefore a strange hybrid, attempting to work on restorative principles but with a strong coercive element because it is still an order of the court and therefore enforceable. The development of the referral order drew from practices in Australasia and North America, as well as the Scottish Hearings system closer to home (Newburn and Crawford, 2002). However, it is not a direct replica of any of these models and combines disparate elements in a unique way, in certain respects successfully but in others less so.

Youth Offender Panel meetings

The YOP, comprising two community volunteers and a YOT practitioner, meets to set the initial contract with the young person, to periodically review progress and to deal with problems such as non-compliance or inability to fulfil elements of the contract. The young person is not entitled to have legal representation at the YOP, and concerns about lack of such due process safeguards were one of the more controversial areas when referral orders were first introduced (Haines and O'Mahoney, 2006). However, if the young person is under the age of 16, the parent or carer is required to attend and, for 16- and 17-year-olds, may be ordered by the court to attend. The following may also be present:

- victim, an individual direct victim or representative of a corporate victim, for instance. A victim may bring another person with him or her as support;
- a member of children's social care if the young person is looked-after;
- other individuals important to the young person (for instance, from school or the youth service); and
- other members of the YOT who know the young person or who may inform the setting of the contract.

The YOT practitioner has a variety of tasks before the first meeting of the panel, including preparing the young person and ensuring that he or she (and parents or carers) are aware of the panel process and his or her rights. The YOP also requires a written report with assessment of the young person's offences, circumstances and needs, as well as information about risks and public protection. This should address maturity and development, outlining possible age-appropriate interventions. Depending on the nature of the offence, the YOT should also liaise with the victim or corporate representative so that views can be sought and attendance at the initial YOP facilitated, if appropriate. There are defined timescales for convening the initial panel meeting that may work against securing informed consent and preparing a victim adequately for the meeting (Crawford and Newburn, 2003), so it is now possible for the victim to attend a later panel instead (Ministry of Justice, 2012e).

In the meeting itself, the YOT practitioner should assist but not lead discussion, providing information where needed and offering guidance on issues such as proportionality of contract conditions. The meeting is chaired by a community panel member, but the YOT practitioner participates in the decision-making rather than having a purely advisory role, creating a complex set of responsibilities and accountabilities (Crawford and Newburn, 2003).

The evaluation of the pilot referral order schemes found that the panel meetings had established themselves within a short period of time 'as constructive, deliberative and participatory forums in which to address young people's offending behaviour' (Newburn et al, 2002, p 62). One young person commented that:

> 'It makes you think about what you are doing. Talking to people was good because it made me realise I had a problem. I've been arrested a few times for this so now I realised I had to do something. I had a problem and they helped.' (2002, p 40)

The intention of using members of the community is perhaps because they are potentially closer to the young people attending panels, without the barriers that professional status creates. Nevertheless, important power differentials still exist, and more recent research (Botley et al, 2010), albeit with a small sample group, found that these young people were not playing the participatory role originally envisaged and that they described listening to the adults and taking a rather passive role themselves (although, as in the earlier evaluation, they felt they had been treated fairly and with respect). This research suggested that more information for young people would encourage more active involvement, which would clearly have beneficial effects for the negotiation of appropriate and realistic elements in the contracts agreed at initial panel meetings.

After setting the contract, the YOP should be reconvened at least every three months to review the young person's progress on the referral order, informed by a written report from the YOT case manager. However, the YOP may call a meeting at any stage in order to review the order or to deal with any other matter, such as non-compliance. Review panels are able to change the conditions on contracts to respond to altered circumstances or to better secure future compliance; this is particularly important with more intensive contracts with a number of elements. Conversely, where good progress has been made, the review panel may refer the case back to court for revocation. The young person may also request that a meeting is called to consider variation of the contract or a referral back to court for revocation of the order.

At the end of the compliance period, a final review meeting should be held. If this meeting agrees that the referral order has been satisfactorily completed, the order will be discharged when the compliance period expires. If the panel feels that the contract has not been satisfactorily completed, it may refer the offender back to court for an extension to the compliance period, although this would be unusual. In most instances, this is an opportunity to give positive feedback and to note the young person's progress.

More about contracts

The restorative potential of referral orders rests on young people's participation in agreeing the contracts, but power differentials at panel meetings as well as age, maturity and confidence may affect how and how much they are able to engage. In the evaluation of pilot referral order schemes (Newburn et al, 2002), despite young people's involvement in discussions, almost 90 per cent of elements on contracts were suggested by either the community panel members or YOT practitioner. It is also significant that, where victims were present, they contributed only 14 per cent of the elements considered. Two comments from the young people involved in Botley et al's research illustrate the difficulties, first in a young person recognising that he or she has something to contribute and, second, in being involved in negotiations:

> 'Not just anyone can write a contract, there's people specific for that role, hence the people at the panel meeting.'

> 'I know with me when I go to things, I just want to get it over and done with, I just want to get home and back to what I was doing ... it would be better if they gave you the opportunity [to contribute to what's in your contract], it's up to you whether you take it or not.' (2010, p 11)

In terms of the types of elements that feature on contracts, Crawford and Newburn (2003) noted that in the pilot schemes, the most common compulsory elements on all contracts were some form of reparation activity (40 per cent of the total). This was mainly indirect reparation, perhaps reflecting the low level of victim attendance at panel meetings. Mediation and direct reparation were rare. Letters of apology to victims constituted 38 per cent of reparation elements and community reparation 42 per cent. This is particularly concerning in the light of other research (Gray, 2005) which found that it was common for letters of apology not to be sent to victims, which means they were functioning as a mechanism for responsibilising young people rather than reparation.

  The involvement of members of the community in YOPs creates the potential to draw on a wider network and a greater range of activities than is available to the YOT on its own, and in this sense contracts may be able to go beyond the sorts of interventions encompassed in youth rehabilitation orders and other sentence plans. Sadly, this potential has not been exploited, and contracts rely extensively on YOT-delivered interventions, such as anger management and offending behaviour work, or schemes involving leisure pursuits or mentoring that come within the YOT ambit (Crawford and Newburn, 2003). Crawford later comments that:

> What has struck me most has been the manner in which youth offender panels, under bureaucratic and managerial pressures, have

become routinised, normalised and standardised, losing much of their party-centred creativity and flexibility in the process. Standardised hours of community reparation, packaged activities drawn from a pre-determined list (like coats off a peg) and standard-term contracts, all leave less scope for the deliberative qualities of the panel. (2006, p 133)

Further research (Crawford and Burden, 2005) found that the distinction between work aimed at addressing a young person's offending behaviour and reparation was often unclear: restorative activities should focus on repair, healing and the needs of the victims first and foremost, rather than being conducted because of their instrumental value in preventing re-offending.

The role of the YOT practitioner in the panel meeting can help ensure that the nature and the purpose of compulsory elements – those the young person is obliged to do – are clear and realistic. Some elements may be identified as voluntary where the young person can opt in or out, and this may be appropriate for ongoing contact with a drugs agency or with the youth service, for example. This may offer a young person a welcome degree of choice and reintroduce some of the lost flexibility and creativity that Crawford (2006) laments. Outside the panel meeting, the YOT case manager will focus on engagement and making sure arrangements are in place for the young person to complete the elements of the contract, including a suitable sequencing of activities. Although encouraging compliance is an important part of the role, enforcement is the responsibility of the YOP rather than the case manager.

What happens when the referral order goes wrong?

While the referral order is partly restorative in nature and, in principle, the elements making up the contract are negotiated, the young person's participation is clearly not voluntary. The coercion involved in the referral order can be viewed as a positive feature in that it has ensured a steady flow of young people into the YOPs, but it does limit the restorative potential of the process:

> In the case of referral orders, coercion provides the capacity to move certain restorative values to the very heart of the youth justice system. The loss of voluntariness, it would appear, is the price paid for this. (Crawford, 2006, p 130)

The YOT case manager must keep records of compliance with the order and progress that is reported to the YOP at a review meeting or an extra panel if a more rapid response is required. The YOP may refer a young person back to court in the interests of justice where the young person is unable rather than unwilling to complete the order. Referral back for breach action occurs where the YOP feels there is there is no reasonable explanation for:

- failure to attend a panel meeting
- failure to agree either an initial or a revised contract
- failure to sign either an initial or a revised contract
- failure to comply with one or more conditions of a contract, including attending appointments with the YOT
- unsatisfactory progress towards completing the contract.

The referral back to court is accompanied by a written report from the YOP and the court then determines whether the young person is in breach and what should happen. Future actions include allowing the order to continue, revoking the order and re-sentencing or discharging the order (if the young person is not found to be in breach and the compliance period has ended, or if the court takes the view that the order has been satisfactorily completed).

If a young person commits further offences while subject to a referral order, the court may extend the compliance period to cover the new offences. Otherwise, when the court sentences for the new offence, this has the effect of automatically revoking the referral order and any associated orders. It may also re-sentence for the offences relating to the referral order, taking into account the extent to which the young person has complied with the referral order contract.

Assessing restorative justice in the reformed youth justice system

Crawford (2006) refers to RJ being introduced in a 'cold climate', where the publicity and the rhetoric around ASBOs have rather drowned out the more positive messages about the referral order initiative. RJ and referral orders have been co-opted into the responsibilisation and remoralisation agendas, with relative neglect of their creative and restorative potential. Although some victims have benefited from attending meetings with young people or from contact, whether direct or indirect, the extent to which the needs of victims and communities as a whole have been met is questionable. One issue is clearly the targets and timescales set for referral orders which often militate against victim attendance at panels (Crawford and Burden, 2005). Further issues were uncovered in a recent qualitative study involving 41 young people on referral orders that found that:

> Young people, especially male teenagers find the idea of apologising "on demand" in front of a panel of strangers extremely difficult. These young people had fragile self-esteem and a need to feel respected: they quickly shut down if they felt challenged. (Newbury, 2011, p 261)

This study also questioned 'black and white' assumptions about guilt and responsibility. The case examples here illustrated 'grey' cases such as a young woman assaulting another young woman who had written racist graffiti about her and a friend on school premises (the school had known about the graffiti and had not addressed it). A further case example relates to an instance where the young person was not ready to apologise and the victim left the meeting very upset, leading Newbury to conclude that:

> It is dangerous to assume that because the approach is *intended* to be restorative all parties will automatically benefit from it. It is unethical for victims to be used as a means to make young offenders "face the consequences of their offending behaviour" if there is no intrinsic benefit for the victim in the process or, worse, if there is a risk that the victim may be further victimised by it. (2011, p 263)

One of the main concerns is the low level of victim involvement and the ready resort to community reparation. Gray's (2005) research suggested that young people uniformly view this as punitive, not restorative. She also criticises the lack of reintegrative elements in the restorative and reparation activities on offer, and the general presumption that reintegration is an individual moral endeavour, without any necessity to address structural inequalities and provide resources and opportunities: 'The end result is that restorative justice has become harnessed to the interests of reinforcing "moral discipline" and, as Garland (2001: 199) argues "disconnected from the broader themes of social justice"' (Gray, 2005, p 954).

Significantly Gray's research did not cover referral orders: the findings from studies on referral orders are generally more positive. However, it must be noted that the original evaluation of the pilot referral order schemes commented that the referral orders and YOPs were more successful at delivering *procedural justice* (treating young people fairly, allowing them to have a say) and *substantive justice* (appropriate sanctions/outcomes) than achieving restoration (Newburn et al, 2002). In this sense, the referral order can be viewed as relatively positive, and certainly benign compared to other ways of dealing with young people. However, it has not been transformative, either in terms of rethinking criminal justice processes or meaningful involvement of communities (other than the community panel members themselves).

So where does that leave us? The implementation of RJ seems to have fallen a long way short of its potential. Its popularity with New Labour and now with the coalition government in part rests on the diversity of understandings of RJ and its potential to be both positive and punitive (whether purposefully so or unintentional) (Haines and O'Mahoney, 2006). Nevertheless, there can be some optimism about current attempts to expand RJ within the new range of pre-court measures that could prevent many young people entering the YJS. And on a broader level, restorative principles and values should not be forgotten because:

> Restorative practice can mean different things to different people, but in most of its guises it presents challenges to establishment thinking on justice, particularly for young people, on how to achieve a constructive

shift from sterile punishment to better forms of problem resolution and social integration. (Whyte, 2009, p 117)

Implications for practice

RJ is now firmly embedded in the YJS within the referral order scheme and as an element of other interventions, both pre-court and as part of a sentence. This means that all youth justice practitioners encounter RJ and so need to understand the key underpinning principles – repair, stakeholder involvement and transformation of community and governmental role and relationships – and to take a critical view of how (and how far) these are achievable within the present YJS.

There are ways that practitioners can move practice in a more restorative direction, particularly where they are involved with YOPs. Relationships with community panel members can be developed so as to make best use of what they bring in terms of non-youth justice areas of expertise, their contacts and their knowledge of the community. This necessarily means the practitioner letting go of power and influence, and implies time and effort to build up trust and confidence on both sides. The results, however, may be fruitful, opening fresh and different dimensions to practice as well as greater involvement of a key stakeholder.

The quality and creativity of referral order contracts also deserve attention. It is regrettable when elements are selected from a set menu, when imagination and a little effort may secure interventions, activities and forms of reparation much more responsive to the individual young person's needs – and in some instances, to the victims as well. An outward-facing approach can be much more helpful to a young person looking to the future and thinking beyond what is often a relatively short period on a referral order.

Participation is critical to the success of restorative practices and listening to what young people say is fundamental. YOPs provide a forum for this and are useful on an individual basis. However, there is a further untapped potential for young people to help develop meaningful reparation and to contribute to improved services. This can be approached in creative ways: for instance, for the young people involved in Bortley et al's (2010) research quoted earlier, participation in focus groups which explored their experience of RJ delivered through YOPs was counted as a reparation activity.

RJ remains a contentious area and in many respects its potential has been curtailed in the way that it has been promoted in England and Wales. The referral order and the range of reparation activities have value although perhaps for reasons other than their ability to restore and reintegrate. The power of RJ may rest more in the symbolic way that it offers a counterpoint to conventional retributive justice and suggests that there are different and more inclusive approaches. The reality of implementation may fall short of the restorative vision – whichever particular vision might be subscribed to – but that does not mean that RJ should be neglected nor allowed to become routine and hollowed out. In fact, it means that renewed attempts should be made to involve greater numbers of young people in meaningful reparation and more fully restorative interventions such as mediation, learning how better to engage with RJ as we go.

Further reading

Braithwaite, J. (1989) *Crime, shame and reintegration*, Cambridge: Cambridge University Press.

Crawford, A. and Newburn, T. (2003) *Youth offending and restorative justice: Implementing reform in youth justice*, Cullompton: Willan.

Dignan, J. (2005) *Understanding victims and restorative justice*, Maidenhead: Open University Press.

Johnstone, G. (2002) *Restorative justice: Ideas, values, debates*, Cullompton: Willan.

SEVENTEEN

Working with young people on community sentences

Previous chapters have looked at policy and interventions aimed at young people at an early stage of involvement with the YJS (although not necessarily early in their anti-social or drink/drug-using behaviours). In comparison, fewer young people are made subject to community sentences, effectively at this present time the youth rehabilitation order (YRO). Under community sentences, the YOT has a more explicit mandate to work with individual young people and will typically do so more intensively and for longer periods than with young people subject to pre-court disposals and even referral orders. This inevitably demands more of practitioners in terms of engagement, maintaining purposeful relationships and securing compliance with both the basic requirements and, more importantly, the key objectives of orders.

Before the YRO came into force, a variety of orders were available to the court with differing purposes, including punishment, deterrence, control and constraint, rehabilitation and restoration. The YRO is structured so that it encompasses all of these within one multipurpose order through a menu of requirements that can be used alone or in combination, offering flexibility and the potential to individualise sentencing. However, used without thought, orders can be overloaded with requirements or contain requirements that conflict or counteract each other's effects. Youth-centred practice aims to work confidently and creatively with YRO requirements, including those such as exclusions from geographical areas or prohibitions from specific activities, which may run alongside YOT intervention. This creativity extends to court reports and the proposals put to sentencers, as well as engagement with young people post-sentence and the arrangements for putting the order into practice – the timing and sequencing of requirements, who is involved in delivery and enabling the young person to be an active participant. This chapter looks at the processes and skills demanded of practitioners in addition to the legal framework around sentencing and enforcement.

A short history of community sentences

Probation orders were first introduced over 100 years ago by the Probation of Offenders Act 1907. In 1974 community service orders (now known as unpaid work or community payback) became available for young people 16 years and over, as probation orders already were. For the younger age group, the main disposal was the supervision order under the C&YPA 1969. Although operating in the community rather than closed settings, these were all separate developments: it was not until the CJA 1991 that they were bracketed together as 'community sentences' along with the attendance centre order, curfew order and a new order combining probation supervision and community service.

The CJA 1991 was a watershed in a number of ways:

- it created a new sentencing framework based on retributive notions of justice and proportionality, whereby the amount of 'punishment' or 'restriction of liberty' should reflect the offence and its level of seriousness;
- the nature of the 'punishment' was not specified and could take a number of forms, including rehabilitative punishment in the form of accredited programmes;
- within this framework, the probation order became a sentence of the court, whereas previously it had been used as an alternative to sentencing;
- it promoted 'punishment in the community' which required probation and the then social services departments to shift their practice from the historic injunction to 'advise, assist and befriend' young people towards tighter and more offence-focused supervision (Hopkins-Burke, 2008);
- it attempted to provide greater consistency and uniformity through introducing the first set of national standards circumscribing work with adults and young people (Hedderman and Hough, 2004).

Mike Nellis highlights the implications for the probation service of a new approach to sentencing that was:

> [P]remised on a "just deserts" philosophy, albeit one that left room for rehabilitative objectives within fixed sentencing frameworks. It insisted nonetheless on a language of punishment, whilst offering the probation service a "centre-stage" role in a more integrated criminal justice system. (2001, p 28)

Effectively this enabled the probation service to take a more prominent position in the CJS even as its social work methods fell out of favour, by accepting a more straightforwardly punitive role in both its work with adults and to a lesser, but still significant extent, with young people. The new notion of 'restriction of liberty' referred to the commitment involved in complying with supervision, which was an important reframing of probation intervention that would previously have been seen almost exclusively as positive in terms of help and support. The effect on youth justice work in social services was less dramatic, but interventions were still required to become more structured and more closely linked to the nature and extent of offending behaviour.

Within the 'just deserts' framework there were three categories of offence seriousness and the use of custody and community sentences was limited by thresholds that had to be met before the courts could impose such sentences.

First tier penalties	*'Not serious enough'* to justify a community sentence
Community sentences	*'Serious enough'* to warrant such a sentence
Custody	*'So serious'* that only such a sentence can be justified or to protect the public from serious harm

There was an almost immediate backlash to the strict proportionality framework of the CJA 1991 as a more punitive regime took hold in the Home Office under Michael Howard. Consequently, key parts of the Act were quickly dismantled (Worrall and Hoy, 2005). Nevertheless, proportionality remains a critical consideration in the sentencing of adults and the *so serious* criterion must still be met before the court can pass a custodial sentence of any kind. Similarly, in rationalising what had become a confusing array of community sentences into one, the CJA 2003 stipulates that the offence(s) must be *serious enough* before the perpetrator can be made subject to a generic community order.

It has taken longer to introduce a generic community sentence for young people, but the YRO enacted by the Criminal Justice and Immigration Act (CJ&IA) 2008 has been available since 30 November 2009. The court may only impose a YRO where it considers that the offence(s) is punishable by imprisonment and that it meets the *serious enough* threshold. The court must also consider suitability and proportionality as well as the young person's family circumstances and how they might be affected by the order. In making a new YRO, the court must revoke any previous reparation order or YRO still in force.

More about the youth rehabilitation order

The YRO is intended to be used flexibly, with 16 requirements available from which the court can select to create a package of interventions – at least in theory – responding to a young person's assessed risks and needs (Graham, 2010). The court is also able to impose more than one order on the same sentencing occasion for multiple offences. Where they contain the same requirements, these may run either at the same time (concurrently) or one after the other (consecutively) within the legal limits set for length or number of hours.

In addition to the 16 requirements, there are two further provisions that can be used where a custodial sentence would otherwise be imposed (intensive fostering and ISS). Schedule 1 of the CJ&IA 2008 contains the specific powers relating to all these requirements. Because they are so disparate, it is helpful to look at what must legally be considered in the sentencing of young people. This applies to all sentences but is relevant to the YRO in particular because it is capable of being used in so many different ways to diverse ends.

Section 142A of the CJA 2003 states that the court must have regard to the principal aim of the youth justice system – the prevention of offending by children and young people – and to the welfare of the child or young person in accordance with Section 44 of the C&YPA 1933. Legislation also specifies the purposes of sentencing. Although this particular section of the CJ&IA has not been implemented, the court is likely to consider the following as a rationale for the sentencing decision:

i.   the punishment of offenders
ii. the reform and rehabilitation of offenders
iii. the protection of the public, and
iv. the making of reparation by offenders to persons affected by their offences.

This is complex and tensions may arise between these aims and purposes, most obviously where punishment or actions to protect the public could have implications for welfare. Youth justice practitioners in court or through written reports are well placed to assist in decision-making, aiming to ensure that the court strikes an appropriate balance.

The requirements are presented here in groups and are related to the aims and purposes outlined above, beginning with the particular requirements with which the YOT is most intimately involved (see Table 17.1).

The supervision requirement is the most straightforward requirement and at the same time, in practice, the most sophisticated, precisely because it is so multipurpose. In legal terms it asks the young person to *attend appointments with the responsible officer or another person determined by the responsible officer, at a time and place determined by the responsible officer* (Schedule 1, para 9, CJ&IA 2008).

This sounds deceptively simple; in reality the supervision requirement can be critical in underpinning a package of interventions in a YRO. It should give

Table 17.1: YOT-delivered requirements

Requirement	Duration	Notes
CJ&IA 2008 Schedule 1 Paras 6-8 Activity	For specified number of days up to 90-day maximum	The order must either specify the activity or the place where the activity will take place, as well as specifying the number of days May include specified residential activities
Para 9 Supervision	Up to 36 months	
Para 11 Programme	Specified number of days	Must be a 'systematic set of activities' – effectively a structured intervention, which may be residential if so specified
Para 12 Attendance centre	Up to 36 hours	Up to 12 hours if aged under 14 12-24 hours aged 14-15 12-36 hours aged 16-17 An attendance centre must be available in the relevant local justice area

purpose and coherence to the order, and the relationship between the young person and YOT case manager (the *responsible officer*) developed in supervision is often crucial in motivating and supporting a young person to comply with and complete other requirements. The case manager may also be the one who gives detailed instructions about, for instance, times and venues for activity or programme requirements. Conversely, many YROs comprise only the one supervision requirement yet still deliver by negotiation a range of interventions within that supervision process. In 2010/11, of more than 23,000 YRO requirements imposed, 40 per cent were supervision requirements. In comparison, 15 per cent were activity requirements and a further 6 per cent were programme requirements (Ministry of Justice, 2012a).

In most instances what takes place within a supervision requirement would be seen as rehabilitative or possibly restorative, where the aim is to heal relationships and to help a young person reintegrate into family or community. However, such rehabilitation, perhaps levering in additional intervention through activities or structured programmes, may have explicit objectives around reducing re-offending and public protection. This is particularly so in the case of the YRO with ISS, which is technically a combination of an extended activity requirement (between 90 and 180 days) with supervision and curfew requirements. These provisions in the CJ&IA 2008 give a legal status to ISS for the first time although it previously existed as a requirement of a community order (see Chapter Eleven). The YRO with ISS is available only where the offences reach the custody threshold (the *so serious* criterion) and there are further age-related restrictions on its use.

Treatment requirements

Treatment requirements are almost by definition delivered by specialist agencies or specialist workers placed within the YOT. Although legally a treatment requirement does not need a supervision requirement to be made alongside, in practice treatment and supervision often work in tandem, involving close liaison in certain complex cases (see Table 17.2).

Although primarily rehabilitative, treatment requirements may be perceived by young people as punitive or unduly restrictive depending on the quality of relationships and the different elements of treatment. Drug tests may also be a sticking point if they are felt to be invasive or unpleasant. The court may only impose a drug treatment requirement where the YOT has assessed suitability and where a young person expresses willingness to comply. However, even where a young person consents, that does not necessarily mean that he or she is ready to engage or to change behaviours, in which case careful negotiation around goals may reveal health, social, family or other concerns that the young person feels are important and could form the basis of initial work.

Table 17.2: Treatment requirements

Requirement	Duration	Notes
Paras 20-21 Mental health treatment	Any specified period while the YRO is in force	– Court must be satisfied that the condition requires and is susceptible to treatment, although the original requirement for a registered mental health practitioner to provide an assessment has been relaxed – The order must specify either the institution or the practitioner responsible for delivering or directing treatment, which may be as an in-patient
Para 22 Drug treatment	Any specified period while the YRO is in force	– Court must be satisfied the young person is dependent on or has a propensity to misuse drugs, and that this is susceptible to treatment. The order must specify either the institution or the practitioner responsible for delivering or directing treatment, which may be as an in-patient
Para 23 Drug testing	Any specified period while undergoing treatment	– Can only be made where a drug treatment requirement is imposed at the same time. The minimum frequency of testing must be specified
Para 24 Intoxicating substance treatment	Any specified period while the YRO is in force	– Intoxicating substance means alcohol or other substances capable of causing intoxication (but not drugs) – Court must be satisfied the young person is dependent on or has a propensity to misuse such substances, and that this is susceptible to treatment. The order must specify either the institution or the practitioner responsible for delivering or directing treatment, which may be as an in-patient – Requires assessment of suitability

Requirements that are the responsibility of other services

Unpaid work (UPW) requirements are delivered by the probation service and protocols should be in place between the YOT and the local probation trust (or other probation provider if contracted out) specifying liaison and other arrangements. In legal terms, the young person must *perform for the number of hours specified in the order such work at such times as the responsible officer may specify in instructions* (Schedule 1, para 10(5), CJ&IA, 2008). In 2010/11, 1,696 UPW requirements were imposed, representing 6 per cent of the total requirements for that year (Ministry of Justice, 2012a) and a significant minority of UPW placements. Placements should be carefully considered so that young people are not at risk from older offenders and, because of their age, they are not required to wear high visibility jackets (see Table 17.3).

Table 17.3: Requirements delivered by other services

Requirement	Duration	Notes
Para 10 Unpaid work	40-240 hours	– Only available for young people who are 16 or 17 at the time of conviction. Requires an assessment of suitability – Ordinarily hours must be completed within 12 months, but this can be extended
Para 17 Local authority residence	Up to six months	– Requires the young person to reside in accommodation provided by or on behalf of the local authority specified in the order – Needs consultation with the local authority and with the parent or guardian (unless impractical) – May not extend beyond the young person's 18th birthday
Para 25 Education	Any specified period while the YRO is in force	– Requires young person to comply with educational arrangements made by parents and approved by the local authority in which he or she is resident – Needs consultation with the local authority
Para 18 Fostering	Up to 36 months	– This is effectively an alternative to custody, so the *so serious* criterion must be met. Requires consultation with the local authority and parents (unless impractical) – Supervision requirement must be made alongside – Note that these fostering arrangements may not be available in all areas

In comparison very few local authority residence or education requirements are made (25 and 196 respectively in 2010/11) (Ministry of Justice, 2012a). In either case the responsible officer sits within the YOT, liaising with the relevant departments within the local authority. The intensive fostering requirement more explicitly involves the YOT because it must work in conjunction with a supervision requirement, reflecting the nature of support for young people with complex needs.

Physical restrictions and restraints

Several requirements contain powers to restrict movements or activities. These are not interventions per se and should not be used as punishment although they may form part of risk management arrangements for a young person. The challenge for practitioners is ensuring that these requirements are used proportionately and with regard to the rights and welfare of the young person concerned. It is also important that there is a means of monitoring compliance, otherwise they are effectively unenforceable and therefore become highly questionable. Again, this is another instance where YOT practitioners in court or in written reports can be proactive in offering advice and guidance about appropriate use of, and specific wording for, requirements such as:

- prohibited activity – up to 36 months (para 13)
- residence – up to 36 months (para 16)
- exclusion – up to 3 months (para 15).

Paragraph 14 contains powers relating to curfews which may be electronically monitored (para 26) and may now be made for between 2 and 16 hours a day for a maximum period of 12 months. What is appropriate in terms of the duration of the curfew and daily time periods depends on the young person's maturity and developmental needs, and advice from the YOT may be critical in decision-making. It is also important to note that the YOT is responsible for enforcement action where the curfew is part of a package of interventions on the YRO; otherwise that role falls to the company contracted to provide the monitoring.

The importance of assessment

The YRO is intended to provide a flexible, but essentially flat, sentencing tariff rather than a ladder effect where young people are escalated upwards towards custody. It can be used in different ways on successive sentencing occasions, and so may be helpful and responsive to the needs and problems of individual young people. However, the structure of the YRO could also lend itself to being used in ways that are punitive and controlling (Smith, 2011), depending on how the order is constituted, the elements that are included and how they are framed. This places an obligation on the practitioner to conduct thoughtful and thorough assessment that can best ensure that the order is set up and implemented to positive effect.

Good management of a YRO starts with the pre-sentence assessment, which should encompass the views of young people and their parents on what has happened and any areas they perceive as problems. Beckett (2010, p 25) describes assessment as 'a judgement made about a situation in order to decide how to act'. Pre-sentence the judgement informs the proposal made to the court and the detail that is presented. Post-sentence the judgement determines aspects of implementation and how the young person (and family) is engaged in the order. Thinking more specifically about youth justice:

> Assessment is a dynamic, multi-faceted process of information gathering and analysis that leads to in-depth understanding of a young person's offending behaviour. It provides the basis for the planning of interventions in order to
>
> - help a young person avoid re-offending;
> - assist a young person to achieve their potential
> - help to protect victims and communities. (Baker et al, 2011, p 12)

This clearly makes the link between assessment and action or intervention. Assessment in that sense is not an end in itself and it comprises far more than collecting information; what is significant is how the information is analysed and interpreted and then used. Baker et al (2011) identify the key stages in assessment as being:

1. Preparation
2. Gathering and recording information
3. Developing understanding
4. Making judgements
5. Making decisions

Whether the assessment is for court or sentence planning, there is a task involved, but also an element of process (Trevithick, 2012), particularly where assessment is ongoing throughout the course of an order. Communication is an essential ingredient in building relationships and a shared sense of purpose. The value of using clear, accessible language may sound obvious, but so often professionals fail to do this (Trevithick, 2012).

The tide is now turning against prescription in professional practice, and once again towards the use of judgement. This does not mean that structured forms of assessment and tools will be abandoned, but it puts emphasis on their rigorous use and critical awareness of their strengths and limitations (Whyte, 2009). One concern is that they seem to offer a pseudo-scientific approach that promises certainty in situations that are mostly imbued with uncertainty. The judgements that professionals make are best guesses, hypotheses, if you like, about the situations, motivations and causes in question (Baker et al, 2011). Structured assessment tools, rather than giving answers, may be most valuable in their transparency, enabling the reflective practitioners to test how robust their judgements are and the validity of the information, assumptions and theories on which they have based them (Whyte, 2009).

Engaging young people

A structured approach to planning intervention as well as to assessment has multiple benefits, although practitioners should be careful to ensure that the task does not eclipse the important processes that take place – establishing joint understandings, collaborative decisions where possible, negotiation, setting boundaries and clarifying roles. Certainly at the beginning of an order, the young person may feel uncertain and anxious (Seymour, 2013), and building rapport means being sensitive to such feelings and making efforts to draw in the young person. The completion of a plan is an end product, but other valuable products can be generated on the way to that end, including establishing an open and empathic approach and encouraging the young person's ownership of goals.

Identifying and framing objectives is an essential part of the process. These should be informed by holistic assessment and analysis of available information so that they are timely, appropriate and realistic. The risk factor prevention paradigm tends to focus on problems and to generate negative or *avoidance goals*: strength-based orientations suggest positive or *approach goals* capable of capturing and giving expression to the young person's feelings and priorities. A young person is most likely to be engaged where there is a positive incentive, where he or she is given help in working towards a goal that he or she wants, and may then be more willing to accept other areas of work or constraints relating to risk and public protection alongside. This suggests that it is necessary to seek a balance between the case manager's agenda and the young person's agenda (and sometimes that of parents or carers), so that the needs of both sides are negotiated and, where possible, agreement is reached. Motivation is also dependent on a feeling of achievement, and setting small objectives that effectively represent step-by-step progress often pays dividends.

Assessments should not be completed and then regarded as set in stone and neither should supervision plans, which must respond to changing circumstances, needs and risks within the dynamic contexts of young people's lives. It is worth bearing in mind Canton's advice about being open to reassessment in the course of intervention because:

> Some objectives may emerge as more immediately compelling than had been appreciated; others may become apparent as the offender becomes more aware of or more prepared to disclose them; other objectives again may turn out to be much less relevant than had at first appeared. Yet, not least because of the volatility of motivation, practitioner and client must work determinedly in an agreed direction. (2011, p 94)

This points to the need for a sense of purpose and moving together towards identified goals, with clear ideas of what would count as success (Beckett, 2010). Reviewing and crediting progress may help engagement and participation in deciding on the next actions or targets. And in reality, giving encouraging feedback and exploring what has gone less well must take place within the context of a relationship.

Research on young people's views of helping relationships sheds lights on the characteristics that they value, which Hill (1999, p 141) summarises in relation to social workers as being:

- a genuine willingness to understand the young person's perspective and to convey empathy;
- reliability (keeping promises, being available, punctuality);
- taking action; and
- respecting confidences.

He goes on to say that young people do appreciate professional relationships and will accept advice about their behaviour once a basis of trust has been developed – these qualities would seem to be pre-conditions for developing trust. Hill's observations are reflected in de Winter and Noom's (2003) peer research with homeless young people in the Netherlands, which highlighted the ambivalence often felt about wanting support on the one hand, and independence on the other, and the problems that arise due to poor communication and lack of trust. The young people wanted more than 'professional care' and sought qualities such as personal contact, emotional support and humour. They also asked for a greater say in their personal journeys and for opportunities to be consulted about aspects of the services they were receiving (from negotiation over house rules to the types of emergency shelters and supported accommodation available). Yet if young people's participation within social work or supported environments is difficult to negotiate because of existing cultures, power differentials, resource constraints and so forth, in a youth justice setting, where young people are subject to mandate rather than accessing the service by choice, this is even more so.

It is worth thinking back to Article 12 of the UNCRC that provides for the right of children and young people to have their views heard in all matters concerning them. Bringing this into effect in the current YJS is problematic: the young people who enter the YJS are often disempowered relative to other young people and historically the system has tended to work in ways that further disempower them, individually and as a group. This has been compounded since the youth justice reforms in 2000 by a highly interventionist and risk-focused approach. While good practice can – and does – still take place within that framework, young people's ability to influence the workings of the youth justice machinery has been limited.

The National Youth Agency (NYA) report, *Voice and influence in the youth justice system* (NYA, 2010), explored the question of participation within individual orders and in service design and delivery through interviews with a small sample of young people (33 from 6 YOTs), and data collected via an electronic questionnaire and practitioner interviews (involving 27 YOTs). Young people's views of YOT services were mixed, with some positive feedback and some highly critical comments, particularly where it was felt that YOT workers were inconsistent or applied double standards. One young person, for instance, said:

> 'If we are late we get a warning letter, if the workers are late they tell us to get over it.' (quoted in NYA, 2010, p 6)

Young people felt more able to influence their individual intervention or supervision plans than the development or design of services. However, a further small exploratory piece of research found that:

> Despite the positive relationships that some young people had with their individual workers, they described their experiences in very passive terms – something that happens to them or is done to them rather than something they can actively engage with and help shape and design. It would appear that the idea of contributing to case

planning in this way seemed foreign to the young people we spoke to. (Hart and Thompson, 2009, p 24)

In both pieces of research the YOTs tended to emphasise review processes as a vehicle for participation and some had instituted exit interviews at the end of orders. These processes are significant in their own right as all interventions should have defined beginnings and conclusions – it is important to 'end well', providing closure and minimising the sense of loss when agency contact ceases. However, it is also a useful point at which to explore young people's experiences of YOT involvement and to seek feedback that can be used to inform service development.

The evidence from the NYA report (2010) suggests uncertainty and divergent views exist among the practitioner group about what participation means and how to encourage it. While some practitioners were clearly working in ways that foster engagement and empowerment, the low level of awareness of children's rights and the UNCRC overall is concerning. Moreover, few of the YOTs in this study had a structure for consulting and involving young people in the design and delivery of services. Where this did happen – and there were examples of innovative practice and Voice and Influence workers being in post – this was often located within prevention projects and ISS, rather than core YOT services. This whole area of participation warrants more specific attention and leadership from the YJB (Hart and Thompson, 2009). The NYA (2010) also calls for specific resources and dedicated workers to be allocated in order to push this forward and to capitalise on the interest being shown within YOTs.

But what happens when young people don't engage?

In an ideal world, young people would comply with both the letter and the spirit of their orders, and would also respond to any opportunities offered to help improve services and YOT arrangements. But we live in a far from ideal world and many orders sadly end in breach proceedings. In certain cases, breach can be avoided by careful consideration of the requirements of the order and how it is managed so it is realistic and achievable. Similarly YOT workers can anticipate and try to remove barriers to engagement, being proactive about texting young people with appointment reminders, making sure parents are involved and supportive of plans or perhaps accompanying young people when they have contact with new services or have to visit unfamiliar places. Yet even with these efforts, enforcement is still necessary in some cases.

Familiarity with requirements around enforcement and breach proceedings should assist case managers in using their discretion wisely and ensuring that court action does not result in unduly punitive outcomes. Indeed, the Sentencing Guidelines Council (2009, p 21) state that:

> The primary objective when sentencing for breach of a YRO is to ensure that the young person completes the requirements imposed by the court.

Where the failure arises primarily from non-compliance with reporting or other similar obligations, where a sanction is necessary, the most appropriate is likely to be the inclusion of (or increase in) a primarily punitive requirement.

Legally there are two basic underpinning requirements for a young person subject to a YRO that are enforceable as though they are a requirement imposed by the order:

- *Keep in touch with responsible officer in accordance with such instructions as he may from time to time be given by that officer.* 'Instructions' include dates and times of appointments or work details and also standard sets of rules agreed with the young person at the start of an order, allowing the YOT to specify what would be considered inappropriate and therefore breachable behaviour or language while on their premises or on activities related to the order.
- *Notify the responsible officer of any change of address.*

The powers relating to breach, revocation or amendment of the YRO are contained in Schedule 2 of the CJ&IA 2008. There is an element of judgement as to what might constitute a reasonable excuse for non-compliance with a requirement of a YRO. Where a young person gives an explanation for an absence or other failure to comply, the responsible officer should record clearly whether the failure is judged to be acceptable or not. Because YROs are used for a young age group, the legislation allows more flexibility than is the case with the adult community order, with breach action following the third unacceptable failure to comply rather than the second.

The youth court (or magistrates' court if a young person has reached the age of 18) is notified of an alleged breach in what is known as *an information*. This should be specific about the requirement(s) the young person has failed to comply with and the grounds for breach action. The young person is then brought before the relevant court (depending on age and whether the YRO was made in Crown Court) by virtue of a summons or warrant.

Where the court is satisfied that an offender has failed *without reasonable excuse* to comply with any of the requirements of the order, the court may take no action and leave the YRO to continue, if it feels this is justified. Otherwise, taking into account the extent to which the young person has complied with the order, the court may:

- impose a fine of up to £2,500;
- amend the terms of the order by imposing requirements in addition to or instead of the existing requirements (note that there are restriction on adding ISS and intensive fostering requirements); or
- revoke the order and re-sentence in any way that the court could have done on the original sentencing occasion had the order not been made.

Where new requirements are added to a YRO or substituted for the previous requirements, the court cannot go outside the upper and lower limits set for the requirement in the CJ&IA 2008 except in the case of the UPW requirement (the court is able to impose a 20-hour requirement for breach whereas the usual minimum is 40 hours). In addition, the fostering requirement may be extended beyond its normal 12-month limit up to 18 months from the date it was first imposed. Under the LASPO Act 2012, the court may extend the end date for completion of any requirement on the order even if this takes the order beyond the usual 36 months maximum, but may only do so once.

Rather than amending the YRO, the court may choose to revoke the order and to impose a custodial sentence. The Sentencing Guidelines Council (2009) suggest that before doing so the court should be satisfied that the YOT and other local authority services have taken all the steps necessary to ensure that the young person has been given the appropriate opportunity and support necessary for compliance. This is intended to ensure that custody is used as a *measure of last resort* and is not imposed as a punishment where other ways of responding to the breach might be appropriate and effective. However, additional powers exist where a young person is deemed to have *wilfully and persistently* refused to comply, and these effectively reduce the restrictions on the use of custody.

Commission of a new offence does not constitute a breach of a YRO in itself. However, sentencing is tricky in that a new order cannot be made alongside the existing one. The court may either use a different type of penalty, such as a fine or discharge, or it can revoke the existing order and re-sentence for the original offences as well as for the new offences.

Enforcement is a difficult area; it is not necessarily the case that strict application of rules improves compliance, although consistent and transparent decision-making is necessary to encourage belief in the legitimacy and fairness of enforcement processes. Flexible and creative thinking may be needed and, of course, there are instances where an application to the court to revoke or amend the order in the interests of justice may be more appropriate than breach action. Where a young person is unable rather than unwilling to respond to the order, perhaps due to social circumstances or a learning difficulty, this might be more helpful in securing future compliance. Judgements are complex but the question of maturity is critical in considering and interpreting motivation and young people's behaviours in relation to supervision, particularly thinking back to psychosocial factors such as *responsibility*, *perspective* and *temperance* (Cauffman and Steinberg, 2000; see Chapter One), and distinguishing between 'adolescent defiance and more calculated resistance' (Seymour, 2013, pp 83-4).

In the first instance case managers aim to enable young people to comply with the requirements of their YROs and to break their patterns of offending. This may be termed *formal compliance*, and goes as far as following the rules and meeting the contact and other requirements specified. Over and above that, *substantive compliance* involves a more fundamental acceptance of pro-social norms and values, and is more indicative of change that is long-term and embedded.

In looking at the psychology of compliance, Anthony Bottoms (2001) has proposed a useful model illustrated in Figure 17.1. He suggests there are four basic reasons for complying, and most practitioners will recognise these.

At different times, YOT case managers will work with all four of these types of compliance and will be aware of tools – ranging from physical constraints to interpersonal skills – related to each. Ultimately, compliance is dynamic and changes over time, the desired change being represented in Figure 17.2 (adapted from Robinson and McNeill, 2008).

The fourth type of compliance in Bottoms' (2001) model is normative, which involves adopting and internalising norms and values that are more in line with those of wider society. Relationships are critical in promoting normative compliance, as it is through attachment to individuals who espouse clear values and model pro-social behaviours that the process of accepting their worth and legitimacy takes place. Thinking about this type of compliance, the case manager assumes particular importance, as this is the pivotal practitioner–young person relationship and sets the tone for the young person's experience of supervision. Two aspects of this were apparent in Seymour's interviews with young people under supervision to probation officers in the Republic of Ireland. The young people valued the fact that their supervisors persisted in efforts to help and did not give up on them:

Figure 17.1: Types of compliance

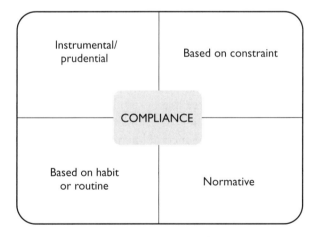

Figure 17.2: Promoting compliance

> The nature and circumstances of their young lives meant that personal and family problems were not uncommon and young people, reluctantly at first, turned to their probation officers for advice and assistance. It was the support extended to them in these circumstances, combined with the trust that was built over time that was most likely to be attributed to changing their opinions about their probation officers and their perceptions of the supervision process. (2013, p 125)

The other aspect relates to trust within the relationship and how young people feel about their supervisors' view of their behaviours, as expressed by 'Dan', thinking about what would happen if he were to re-offend:

> 'It would make me feel, to be honest, ashamed of myself. It would make me feel very sad in a way because I've disappointed her, because she's done so much for me and if that's the way I pay her back, that's not the way, you know?' (quoted in Seymour, 2013, p 127)

Chapter Three introduced discussion about how supervisees perceived the purpose of supervision and the role of supervising officers (Barry, 2000). They were seen as either reactive ('monitors') or pro-active ('mentors'). Monitoring of behaviours and compliance is clearly an element of supervision, and this can be done in ways that set appropriate boundaries and model pro-social attitudes and responses to conflict, to disagreement or to imposing rules, for instance. However, Barry's interviewees emphasised that they were themselves responsible for change and:

> Social workers could not stop people offending as such, but could support them in (a pro-active sense) in the process of desistance ... in general, offending was seen as a by-product of problems of lack of money, boredom, drug/alcohol abuse, unfair discrimination or pressure from friends. It therefore seemed to them to make sense to address any practical or emotional problems, on the assumption that offending would reduce accordingly. (2000, p 589)

This was also apparent in Seymour's research – although small-scale (involving only 20 young people), this showed clearly how advocacy and accessing services and resources assist young people to move on, creating positive social bonds or dealing with barriers. A mentoring and problem-solving approach promises most in terms of encouraging the adoption of normative attitudes and behaviours, finding a balance of attention to rights, risks and opportunities to look to the future and to build positive forms of capital.

Implications for practice

The CJA 1991 first introduced the concept of the 'community sentence' within a justice framework that demands that the sentence passed should reflect the seriousness of the offence(s) before the court. Currently more attention is paid to prevention of offending and persistence, but proportionality still remains a key principle in sentencing and for intervention post-sentencing, placing limits on the extent of punishment and guarding against undue intervention on welfare grounds.

The requirements available on the YRO are varied and may fulfil different aims such as punishment, rehabilitation, public protection and restoration, thus opening opportunities for practitioners to create orders well suited to the needs of individual young people. However, the challenge for youth-centred practice is to maintain coherence and to build packages of interventions that are focused, realistic, effective and, above all, meaningful to young people.

Research suggests that intervention is most likely to be successful where there is a strong relationship of trust at the core. The case manager role is thus critical, drawing in the young person, encouraging engagement and communicating clearly and openly. The case manager is responsible for the key processes of assessment, planning, intervention (although this may be delivered by others) and review. These require considerable skills and also personal qualities such as warmth and honesty that are important and valued by young people.

A young person subject to a YRO is not a voluntary client and certain aspects of the court order are not negotiable. The case manager must be able to use authority consistently and in ways that are open and transparent but also responsive to age, maturity and any other factors that may affect the young person's understanding. Compliance and motivation should be emphasised, rather than enforcement, through attention to careful planning, negotiation and sequencing of interventions so that the young person feels he or she has a say and can chart progress towards achievable goals. An understanding of compliance and different modes of compliance assists the case manager in managing the order appropriately, ensuring that breach action is taken only where appropriate and necessary after barriers to engagement and positive incentives have been explored.

Encouraging young people's participation is a thorny issue for youth justice where it is less developed than in other children's services, perhaps in part due to the directive nature of criminal justice and the power issues underpinning court-ordered interventions. Research suggests that participation is encouraged at the level of input into assessments, planning and review of orders, although not consistently (Hart and Thompson, 2009). Initiatives around participation in service design and delivery are less embedded, despite often good intentions. This is an area crying out for development, and youth-centred practice should push for a change in ethos to allow young people influence and space to be heard.

Further reading

Baker, K., Kelly, G. and Wilkinson, B. (2011) *Assessment in youth justice*, Bristol: The Policy Press.

Beckett, C. (2010) *Assessment and intervention in social work: Preparing for practice*, London: Sage Publications.

Trevithick, P. (2012) *Social work skills and knowledge: A practice handbook*, Maidenhead: Open University Press.

Whyte, B. (2009) *Youth justice in practice: Making a difference*, Bristol: The Policy Press.

EIGHTEEN

Imprisoning young people

It is fitting to end by considering the use of custody for young people, as this debate connects with many of the concerns already outlined: the willingness to imprison young people and to hold the majority in prison rather than childcare establishments speaks volumes about the way society views young people and their rights; those young people held in custody are disproportionately disengaged from education, come from relatively disadvantaged social and economic backgrounds, have experience of the care system, and face the most challenging issues in their transitions to adulthood; and the arrangements for holding young people in custody and supporting them on release have shown limited success in addressing the many difficulties – personal and social – that these young people face.

The crux of the debate concerns the extent to which the CJS should – and the extent to which it does in practice – recognise that children and young people have needs and vulnerabilities different from those of adults that affect how, and how far, they can appropriately be held responsible for their behaviours. It also engages the notion of collective responsibility for ensuring that children and young people are nurtured, and that they are offered support and opportunities to grow and to develop within a positive social learning environment appropriate for age and stage of development. In recent decades, the individual has been emphasised over society, and individual responsibility over collective social responsibility, so creating a climate in which the government has been able to sell high custody rates for under-18s to the public as a virtue, even in the face of empirical evidence that it is often the casualties of imperfect social supports and institutions who end up in prison, and that prison tends to have a negative impact, rather than a positive effect, on their offending post-release.

It is encouraging that the use of custody has steadily reduced since a peak in 2008. This chapter examines these trends and the underlying social, political and other pressures reflected in the way that custody is used at any given time. It also outlines the current custodial sentences available and explores young people's experiences in custody and on release.

Exploring concerns about the use of custody

Taking away the liberty of any individual is a serious matter, and the state's power to do so must be exercised according to the rule of law. It is particularly controversial in relation to a child or young person because of the difficulty in judging responsibility and culpability for actions in the light of age and maturity. Decisions are also complicated by the need to consider the young person's welfare and development, which may be adversely affected, for example, by removal from family and disruption to education. As key human rights instruments have gained purchase (principally the ECHR, through the HRA 1998, and the UNCRC), the UK has found itself criticised for its relatively low age of criminal responsibility, the numbers of young people who are held in custody and the conditions in which they are held (Muncie, 2009: Bateman, 2012b).

Specific articles from the UNCRC relate, principally Article 37 which directly addresses the punishment of children including the loss of liberty:

Article 37

States Parties shall ensure that:

(a) *No child shall be subjected to torture or other cruel, inhuman or degrading treatment or punishment.* Neither capital punishment nor life imprisonment without possibility of release shall be imposed for offences committed by persons below eighteen years of age;

(b) No child shall be deprived of his or her liberty unlawfully or arbitrarily. The arrest, detention or imprisonment of a child shall be in conformity with the law and shall be used only as *a measure of last resort and for the shortest appropriate period of time*;

(c) Every child deprived of liberty shall be treated with humanity and respect for the inherent dignity of the human person, and in a manner that takes into account the needs of persons of his or her age. *In particular, every child deprived of liberty shall be separated from adults* unless it is considered in the child's best interest not to do so and shall have the right to maintain contact with his or her family through correspondence and visits, save in exceptional circumstances....

Serious questions have been asked about whether custody has indeed been used in the UK as a *measure of last resort* (Jacobson et al, 2010). The average length of sentence has also increased, raising doubts about whether terms imposed are, in fact, *the shortest appropriate period of time* (Graham, 2010). Moreover, although conditions have improved since the YJB took over the commissioning of placements, there are still concerns about the numbers of young men being held in prison settings (albeit establishments for under-21s), the ratio of staff to young people and the range of services offered in comparison to more child-centred secure settings.

Specific issues arise in relation to young women in custody as they are fewer in number. Historically, under-18s have been held alongside adult women, a practice challenged by the Howard League for Penal Reform in a test case involving a 16-year-old placed in a prison environment. The judgement did not find the Home Office decision unlawful, but Mr Justice Hooper was openly critical in relation to what might be in the best interests of the young person concerned. Subsequently the YJB made a commitment, not to remove all young women from prisons, but to accommodate 17-year-olds in discreet units currently within four prisons (Howard League for Penal Reform, 2005), and to place 15- and 16-year-old young women in other secure establishments.

Article 3(1) states that, in all actions concerning children including those decisions taken in court and within institutions – and by extension YJB decisions on the type of custodial placement offered to a young person – the best interest of the child should be a primary consideration. There are also requirements for institutions, services and facilities to conform to appropriate standards in terms of safety, health and so on (Article 3[3]), which are important as all forms of custody involve a significant caring element. Tellingly, despite Article 19, which commits state parties to child protection measures, and additional articles relating to social and other aspects of development, the provisions of the Children Act 1989 did not originally apply to all young people in custody. However, in 2002 the Howard League for Penal Reform won a judicial review against the Home Office which established that the Children Act does apply to under-18s held in YOIs as well as those in other secure settings (Howard League for Penal Reform, 2005; Whyte, 2009). The 'Munby judgement', so called because of the judge ruling on the case, underlined the fact that children in custody are children first and foremost (Hollingsworth, 2008). Consequently, the local authority have duties under the Section 17 'child in need' provisions as well as responsibilities for child protection, and each custodial establishment is now represented on the LSCB for the area in which it is sited. This is highly significant: prisons and the other parts of what is known as the juvenile secure estate are closed institutions, and by their very nature there is relatively little scrutiny of their day-to-day workings, so having systems in place for reporting abuses and for outside bodies to investigate is an essential step on the way to providing a safer environment.

As with other aspects of rights, there is a clear gap between the standards set out in the international conventions and what happens in the 'real world'. The rights may exist in law, but challenging breaches or questionable practices is not easy. Among the adult prisoner population there is a constituency that is relatively well informed and litigious, but this is very much less so for the young population in custody. The activities of campaigning organisations and children's charities are therefore critical in raising public consciousness and highlighting concerns such as the over-use of restraint and access to the prison regime. Furthermore, young people may not be able to articulate their complaints or concerns readily, so youth justice practitioners working with young people in custody must be prepared to take time and to listen, so they can judge whether there is a matter that should be challenged and whether they should stand ready to act as advocate.

A brief history of secure establishments for young people

The framing of rights and remedies for infringements or breaches of rights is a relatively recent development. However, many of the detrimental features of penal practices and custodial institutions that the human rights instruments seek to address are not new. Different types of establishments have been instituted at various times, reflecting the beliefs, social mores and political pressures of the day. While there has always tended to be agreement among adults that a troubling number of young people need to be subject to controls, the size of that group and the types of control felt appropriate have varied (Hagell and Hazel, 2001), in essence depending on the extent to which these young people are viewed as 'villains' or 'victims', as children or offenders.

ChapterThree discussed the early penal institutions in the form of a specialised youth prison at Parkhurst and reformatories. Only three years after theYouthful Offenders Act 1854, industrial schools were established under separate legislation. During the Victorian period, the recognition of children and young people as distinct from adults was developing but there was ambiguity about whether the response to delinquency should be correctional or educative.This tension was still apparent when borstals were first introduced in 1908.At the time they were hailed as a liberal initiative in that they separated under-21s from adult prisoners and emphasised training (Muncie, 2009), yet they still operated an essentially punitive regime. This stood in contrast to the trend towards welfare and psychosocial intervention that produced the C&YPA 1933 (Hagell and Hazel, 2001).Although under Section 53 of that Act children and young people could receive long-term or indeterminate sentences for what were termed 'grave crimes', the general thrust was anti-custodial and this was most explicitly seen as reformatories were replaced by approved schools (Goldson, 2006).

The period immediately after the Second World War saw an attempt to re-establish a sense of social order which resulted in the CJA 1948 and the introduction of a new custodial provision, the detention centre, capable of delivering the proverbial 'short, sharp, shock' (Hagell and Hazel, 2001). Despite the predominance of welfare thinking until the *Children in trouble* White Paper (Home Office, 1968) and the C&YPA 1969, punishment also had its advocates. Specifically, in 1961, the minimum age for borstal training was reduced to 15 years, and it became easier to transfer young people from approved schools and borstals to prisons (Muncie, 2009). Indicative of these competing views and attitudes, after the election of a Conservative government in 1970 the measures in the C&YPA 1969 intended to divert the majority of young people from custody were dismissed as unduly permissive and were never enacted.The result was an increase in both social work interventions and the use of custody (Hopkins-Burke, 2008).

Paradoxically, a Conservative administration with an explicitly 'law and order' agenda took office in 1979, yet the number of young people in custody fell throughout the following decade as diversion and cautioning schemes developed, encouraged by the government (Bateman, 2012b). And this was despite tough rhetoric harking back to 'short, sharp shocks' and the introduction of a new custodial sentence, youth custody, to replace borstal training as well as the re-branding of detention centres and youth custody centres in 1988 as young offender institutions (YOIs).

Over the years there have been many different types of establishment, some starting with an explicitly punitive regime, others with a rehabilitative or educational orientation. Interestingly, it is apparent that over time there tends to be a degree of convergence: in particular, tough regimes find they must introduce more varied elements in order to manage and accommodate the complex needs of young people. Conversely, pressure from approved schools struggling to respond to difficult behaviours resulted in measures restricting liberty, including the creation of three secure units in the mid-1960s (Hagell and Hazel, 2001). Significantly, young people could be sent to these secure units for welfare reasons rather than as a sentence of the court (and young people can still be placed in the present-day equivalent, LASCHs, for behaviours that cause concern, but may not be criminal, or at least have not been prosecuted as a criminal offence).

The YJB commissions the current youth secure estate which is made up of YOIs, LASCHs and secure training centres (STCs), an innovation involving private sector providers brought in by the Criminal Justice and Public Order Act 1994. The former head of the YJB feels that these all involve significant shortcomings and is particularly critical of the prison service which provides the majority of placements (see Figure 18.1), describing it as 'an organisational tanker, difficult to turn around, the staff insufficiently child-centred' (Morgan, 2009, p 16). Responding to concerns about the nature of the secure estate for young people, the coalition government's Green Paper, *Transforming youth custody* (Ministry of Justice, 2013b), sets out early thoughts about new 'secure colleges'. The intention to enhance education and training and to improve continuity with community provision is clearly welcome, but it is difficult to have confidence that these plans will be transformative, given the general inertia of a system dominated by prison institutions and the history of previous attempts at change.

Figure 18.1: Type of custodial placement on 30 December, 2005-11

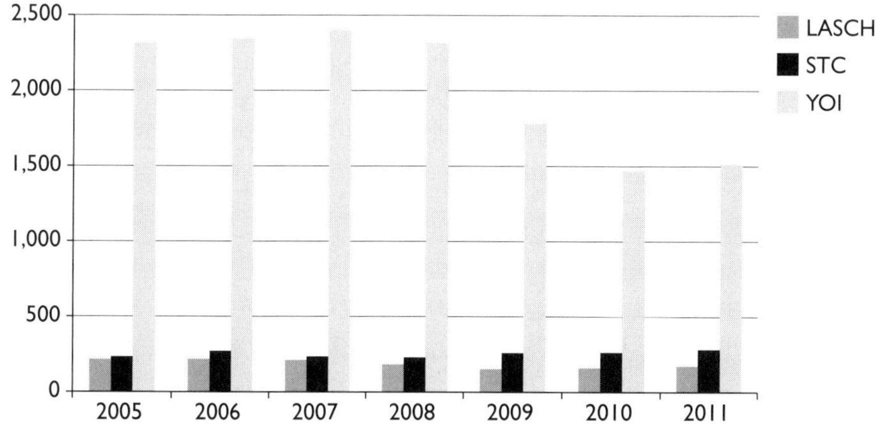

Source: Ministry of Justice (2012a)

Recent trends in the use of custody

As already noted, use of custody for young people in general declined in the 1980s. Whereas in 1970, roughly 3,000 14- to 16-year-old males were held in custody, this had risen to nearly 8,000 in 1982, then reduced sharply to fewer than 2,000 by 1990 (Hagell and Hazell, 2001) under the 'just deserts' approach epitomised in the CJA 1991. However, those with more serious or persistent patterns of offending did not necessarily benefit from such leniency, particularly where they had failed to comply with any of the 'alternative to custody' programmes on offer. This tougher attitude anticipated the move towards a harsher approach as the 1990s progressed, accelerated after the murder of Jamie Bulger and the reaction of the then Home Secretary, Michael Howard.

From this point onwards three distinct influences had an impact on the rate of youth custody, the first of these being the generally more unsympathetic views of young people discussed earlier in Chapters Three and Four in the context of an increasingly fearful and insecure society. The second was the highly interventionist YJS created by the CDA 1998 reforms which eschewed the use of diversionary mechanisms such as cautions and brought greater numbers of young people into the ambit of the penal system. The third was a new custodial sentence, the detention and training order, that could be made for periods of 4-24 months in the youth court. It was sold as a more rehabilitative measure, with planning objectives set for the custodial period and the whole of the second half of the sentence in the community under the supervision of the YOT. This made it attractive to some sentencers, although sadly this rehabilitative promise was not realised in practice (Bateman, 2008). In reality, the four-month order also appealed to those magistrates keen on the purported deterrent effect of the 'short sharp shock', and this further pushed up the numbers of young people sent to custody as the order became available (Graham, 2010).

Accordingly, during 2000/01 the average population of under-18s held in custody rose to 2,807 (Ministry of Justice, 2012a), and this upward trend continued during the 2000s, reaching peaks in 2002 and again in 2007/08 before starting to fall (see Figure 18.2). It may seem that these numbers are relatively small in comparison with early periods of youth justice history, but most of these young men are in prison-type accommodation which was not the case before (Hagell and Hazel, 2001) (see Figure 18.1).

Analysing trends in immediate custodial sentences imposed as well as custodial population, it is clear that the use of the detention and training order has declined, although the use of longer-term sentences has not (see Figure 18.3). However, this has been counteracted by an increase in the length of those sentences that were made, particularly in 2002, coinciding with the Street Crime Initiative that put the spotlight on robberies and other street offences (Graham 2010). Reasons for the increase in the population in custody are complex but, as well as the factors already mentioned, the changed attitude among youth justice practitioners and managerial systems promoting enforcement (Bateman, 2011) have swelled the numbers of young people given custodial sentences after breach of a community sentence. It is telling that in profiling more than 3,000 young people in custody, Jacobson et al (2010) found that 21 per cent were sentenced for a breach of statutory order or of bail as their primary offence.

The YJB itself recognised the concerns associated with the over-use of custody and over the years has sought to monitor and, latterly, to limit, the proportion of

Figure 18.2: Average population in custody 2000/01 to 2010/11

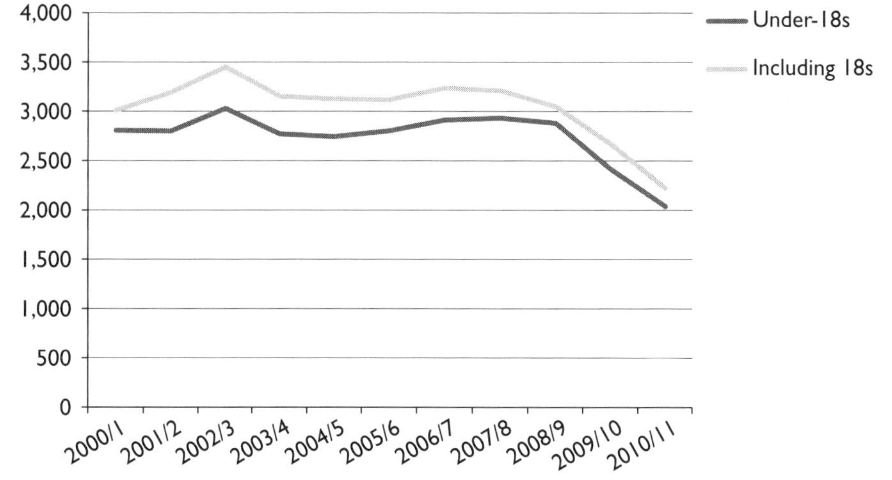

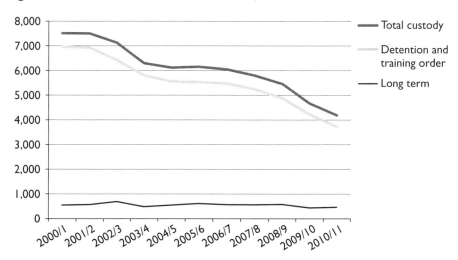

Source: Ministry of Justice (2012a)

Figure 18.3: Immediate custodial sentences, 2000/01 to 2010/11

Source: Ministry of Justice (2012a)

sentences resulting in immediate custody (Graham, 2010). It introduced what was then called ISSP in selected areas in 2002 and later extended the scheme nationally to provide a robust and highly restrictive community sentence. But this failed in the same way that so many previous 'alternatives to custody' have, by drawing in young people who would have received a less intensive community sentence rather than custody and through increased risk of breach action. Identifying effective strategies to reduce the use of custody represents a tough challenge, one that requires change at all levels of the system, not just at the point of the sentencing decision, and awareness of the multitude of pressures that contribute to the impetus towards custody (Bateman, 2005). Part of this impetus is that custody and prisons have a symbolic presence in public consciousness and form a formidable benchmark against which community sentences and all other disposals are measured (Muncie, 2009).

Nevertheless, since 2008 the number of young people in custody has reduced and this reduction has been sustained, even after the riots in 2011. It is not entirely clear why, but it seems to be connected to the smaller number of young people entering the YJS – in YJB terms, 'first-time entrants' (FTEs). A closer examination of the figures from 2005 onwards shows that the decrease is mainly due to detention and training orders, with some reduction in custodial remands, suggesting that the 'softer end' of youth justice business is being diverted either out of the system or towards other court disposals (see Figure 18.4).

Bateman (2005) clearly notes the correlation between the use of diversion and the use of custody – when the former increases, the latter goes down. This happened in the 1980s and the relationship still holds true today, albeit in a context where youth justice is much more highly politicised (Bateman, 2012b). The introduction of the youth conditional caution and restorative justice to divert young people from custody has been important; so too was the change of New Labour tone as it came to the end of its period in office and its determination to avoid young people entering the YJS expressed both in the YCAP (HM

Figure 18.4: Population in custody, 2005-12

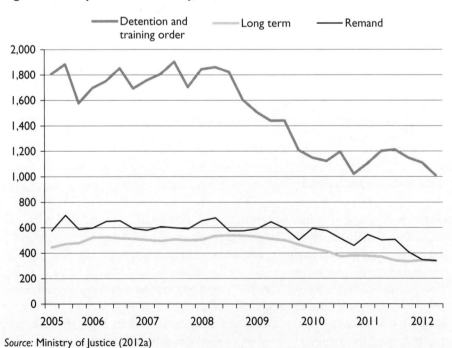

Source: Ministry of Justice (2012a)

Government, 2008) and through the introduction of a target to reduce FTEs to the YJS (Graham, 2010; Bateman, 2012). The target relating to FTEs remains in place under the coalition administration. Other aspects of their approach do not appear so encouraging, as the early push for rehabilitation gives way to a more punitive rhetoric (Bateman, 2012b), but they have considered the merits of passing the full cost of custody on to local authorities and have pressed ahead with this for remand placements, although not custodial sentences.

Optimism about the reduction in the use of custody should be tempered by realisation of the fragile nature of this decrease and how easily it could be reversed. Similarly, although there are lower numbers involved, custody still has a disproportionate impact on particular populations of young people. Recent research among young people in custody has found that:

- 71 per cent had been involved with, or in the care of, the local authority before entering custody;
- one in eight had experienced the death of a parent or sibling;
- 40 per cent had previously been homeless;
- 25 per cent had special educational needs;
- 90 per cent of young men and 75 per cent of young women had been excluded from school;
- 13 per cent of those interviewed in prison reported being regular crack users and 12 per cent regular heroin users;
- in a YJB study, 19 per cent of 13- to 18-year-olds had depression, 11 per cent anxiety, 11 per cent post-traumatic stress disorder and 5 per cent psychotic symptoms. (Research findings collated by the Prison Reform Trust, 2011)

Figure 18.5: The under-18 population in custody by ethnicity, 30 June 2012

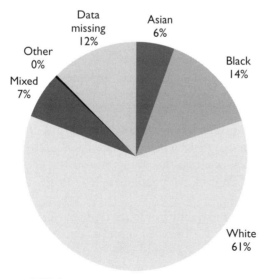

Source: Ministry of Justice (2012a)

Young people from minority ethnic groups or with mixed parentage are also disproportionately represented in custody. According to the UK Census in 2001 (NSPCC, 2012), the under-18 population in England and Wales was comprised of approximately 5 per cent of various Asian backgrounds, 4 per cent black African or Caribbean and 2 per cent of mixed parentage. Compare this to the population in custody illustrated in Figure 18.5.

The detention and training order in detail

There are restrictions on the use of custodial sentences for young people that apply to detention and training orders as well as to long-term sentences. First, with only limited exceptions, the young person must be legally represented. Second, before passing a custodial sentence, the court must consider that the offence or combination of the offence and one or more offences passes the *so serious* threshold originally established by the CJA 1991. There are extremely limited circumstances in which this may be disregarded. Third, the court must obtain and consider either a new pre-sentence report or a recent report if one is available.

Additionally, the Sentencing Guidelines Council (2009, p 23) state that:

> Before deciding to impose a custodial sentence on a young offender, the court must ensure that all the statutory tests are satisfied – namely
>
> i.   That the offender cannot be properly dealt with by a fine alone or by a youth rehabilitation order
> ii. That a youth rehabilitation order with intensive supervision and surveillance or with fostering cannot be justified, and
> iii. That custody is the last resort
>
> And in doing so should take account of the circumstances, age and maturity of the young offender.

Originally introduced by the CDA 1998, the present legislation governing detention and training orders is the Powers of the Criminal Court (Sentencing) Act 2000. In addition to the general restrictions on the use of custody, the detention and training order has age-related restrictions. If the young person is over 12 but under the age of 15 when convicted, the court may only impose an order if it is of the opinion that the young person is a persistent offender. The order is not currently available for young people who are still 10 or 11 years old when convicted.

Under the detention and training order, a young person can be sent to custody for periods of 4, 6, 8, 10, 12, 18 or 24 months, and will serve half that period in custody and half in the community subject to a notice of supervision. The length of the sentence should take account of time spent on remand. Early release arrangements also apply so the actual period spent in custody may be reduced.

Where the young person is sentenced for more than one offence, the court may order detention and training order terms to be served consecutively, but only up to a maximum of 24 months.

Planning meetings are held shortly after the sentence is made and at regular intervals during the sentence. The YOT case manager is expected to attend and actively to pursue plans for release, ensuring where possible, continuity of care and appropriate services, as well as attending to arrangements for accommodation and education.

Requirements on a notice of supervision

- To keep in touch with your supervising officer in accordance with any instructions given
- If required, to receive visits from your supervisor at home
- To reside permanently at an address approved by the supervisor and to notify the supervisor of any stay away
- To undertake only work approved by your supervisor and to notify him/her in advance of any proposed change
- Not to travel outside the UK without prior permission of the supervisor
- To be well behaved and not to commit any offence or do anything that could undermine the purpose of your supervision

---

Additional conditions may be included in the notice of supervision if there are particular circumstances or public protection concerns. These may include:

- an electronically monitored curfew;
- a period on ISS; or
- any of the additional conditions that may be added to licences on adult determinate sentences as laid out in Probation Instruction 7/2011.

Unlike long-term sentences, breach action in relation to a detention and training order is pursued through the court. The YOT case manager lays an information before the court in the same way as for a YRO, in most cases the youth court acting for the local justice area where the young person lives, or the magistrates' court if the young person is aged 18 at the time of the allegation. Following a finding of guilt, the court may:

- impose a fine of up to £1,000 (£250 if the young person is under 14);
- order him or her to be returned to custody for either three months or the remainder of the term of the detention and training order, whichever is shorter; or
- impose a period of supervision for either three months or the remainder of the term of the detention and training order, whichever is shorter.

Powers recently introduced by the LASPO Act 2012 now allow the court to impose these sanctions even where the notice of supervision has expired before the breach action comes to court.

Where a young person is convicted of a new imprisonable offence committed while under supervision, the court may order the young person to be detained in custody for a period not greater than the length of time between the commission of the offence and the end of the detention and training order. The court is also able to sentence separately in respect of the new offence and this may include a custodial sentence, in which case, the two periods in custody may be served either concurrently or consecutively.

Long-term imprisonment

Relatively few young people receive sentences longer than the maximum term of 24 months available for the detention and training order. A small number of these are indeterminate sentences whose very rarity presents challenges to the YOT, both in terms of the typically higher level of risk and the relative unfamiliarity of dealing with the particular sentencing and parole processes involved.

Indeterminate sentences are those without a definite or fixed end date. The young person's equivalent of the life sentence – detention during Her Majesty's Pleasure – may be made under Section 90 of the Powers of the Criminal Court (Sentencing) Act 2000 for murder and under Section 91 for other offences such as rape that would attract a discretionary life sentence for an adult over 21. The CJA 2003 created 'public protection' sentences, specifically in relation to young people the provision for the detention for public protection sentence. The adult version, imprisonment for public protection, was controversial on a number of fronts; consequently both sentences were abolished by the LASPO Act 2012.

At the time of sentence, the judge sets a tariff that is the minimum period to be served – the punitive part of the sentence, if you like. Release from an indeterminate sentence is dependent on the decision of the parole board, who review the sentence as it comes up to the first possible release point – the tariff date – and then periodically until they feel it is safe to release the individual. This additional period in custody is the preventative part of the sentence. The YOT case manager is required to prepare reports for the parole dossier on progress and plans for the young person's release responding to assessed risk and needs. As parole board members may not be specialists in dealing with young people, it is especially important that the YOT case manager's report is well informed and assesses aspects of, for instance, maturity and development as they relate to risk (Kemshall, 2009b).

Determinate sentences going beyond the maximum two-year term for the detention and training order may be imposed under Section 91 of the Powers of the Criminal Court (Sentencing) Act 2000. These are available where the offences would attract a term of 14 years or more for an adult over 21 or for certain sexual and motoring offences. The difference between these and the indeterminate sentences is that they have a fixed release date at the halfway point and a requirement for supervision until the end of the sentence under a licence similar to the notice of supervision already outlined.

An extended sentence under Section 228 of the CJA 2003 was another form of determinate sentence that allowed the court to impose a fixed term of imprisonment and then an additional period of supervision on licence. Release is automatic at the halfway point of the custodial term (disregarding the extended licence supervision). Like the detention for public protection sentence, the original Section 228 extended sentences have been abolished (although there are still young people in the system on detention for public protection and extended sentences).

Rather confusingly, a new extended sentence has been created by the LASPO Act 2012, reflecting the criteria set for the detention for public protection and original extended sentences. They are:

- conviction for a violent or sexual offence specified in Schedule 15 of the CJA 2003;
- the court must consider there is a significant risk to members of the public of serious harm by the young person committing further specified offences.

Serious harm in this context means death or serious personal injury, whether physical or psychological. The court is required to consider whether detention for life under Section 91 of the Powers of the Criminal Court (Sentencing) Act 2000 would be appropriate before it imposes an extended sentence. The court determines the custodial term, which must be four years or over, and then an additional period on licence (up to five years for a violent offence and eight years for a sexual offence). Some prisoners serving these extended sentences are only released with the approval of the parole board, but those falling within the youth justice remit are released on licence two thirds of the way through the custodial term.

Post-custody licences on both determinate and indeterminate sentences can be supplemented by additional conditions detailed in Probation Instruction 07/2011, depending on the level of risk and individual circumstances. Licences are enforced using executive powers of recall through the Public Protection Casework Section (at the National Offender Management Service). Recall may result from non-compliance with conditions, further offending or behaviour that indicates that the individual poses a heightened risk of harm to others. There are emergency as well as standard recall procedures.

Experiences of prison

So far the discussion of statistics about imprisonment, human rights instruments and statutory provisions for sentencing and the management of sentences has been quite technical. But what of young people's perspectives and experiences of custody? It is an overtly physical experience in terms of containment, but also in relation to issues such as bullying, use of restraint, body searches and separation/segregation. As long ago as 1994, The Howard League highlighted how these issues had an impact on young people and reflected their experiences. For instance:

> 'I was getting bullied in here for food and tobacco, but I threw hot water in the face of the bully and now I've been charged with assault. I've been thumped in the mouth to be taxed [made to pay]. It happens at work, in the gym, in the showers ... two or three came into the shower when I was getting ready to leave and got cigarettes off me ... the gate to the showers is sometimes left open....'

> 'It's better here than any other place I've been in, but it still goes on....' (1994, p 43)

The more child-centred LASCHs and STCs tend to provide safer and more responsive environments for young people than YOIs, with lower staff/resident ratios. Nevertheless, the findings of two qualitative studies in residential settings in Scotland (Barry, 2009) suggested that, while the young people did feel safe in secure children's homes, they also indicated that what they experienced was more 'controlling' than 'caring', particularly in relation to sanctions such as restraint and separation. One 14-year-old male commented that:

> 'You are asked to go to your room. If you refuse the staff there will try to get you to your room. If they can't ... you are dragged.... How would you feel with your room emptied and your toilet locked, stuck in a cell basically? You go off your head 'cos you can't get out.' (2009, pp 87–8)

Other recent research by UserVoice found negative feelings about restraint across different types of establishment. Examples of comments from young people in a LASCH, STC and YOI respectively included:

> 'When I first got restrained on the corridor for spitting and fighting with staff I felt anger getting locked in my room.' (2011a, p 20)

> 'I think restraining should only be used in a really difficult situation instead of just when young girls refuse to go to their room or education, it's disgusting.' (2011a, p 15)

> 'In my cell, I felt embarrassed, it was painful and I felt helpless. It made me angry.' (2011a, p 17)

Young people are routinely searched on entering establishments, and this also generates strong feelings. Another study by User Voice found that young people accepted that body searches were part of the regime, but still found the experience awkward and humiliating, especially in establishments were it was handled with less sensitivity. For instance, one young man in a YOI said:

> 'It was not that nice, but it has to be done for safety reasons. It was not that nice because I didn't know them. It was a new strange place and I had been in court all day.' (2011b, p 31)

Young women in this research tended to have a stronger emotional reaction, understandable particularly where they had previously suffered abuse or rape:

> 'When I had my first full search I was 14. It was horrible as I have been sexually abused and I didn't feel comfortable showing my body as this brought back memories. They told me if I didn't take my clothes off they would do it when they got permission.' (2011b, p 21)

What is striking from this research is how far young people are accepting of what would be considered intolerable intrusions in other settings. To some extent surviving within custodial establishments means adjusting to rather different boundaries around personal space and privacy than in family or other community settings (although perhaps the difference would appear less for children who have been 'looked-after'). This is not to suggest that establishments ignore young people's rights, needs and dignity. Good procedures are often in place, and certainly there have been numerous initiatives and attempts by the YJB to establish 'safer custody' arrangements within the youth secure estate, but with limited impact (Goldson and Coles, 2008). Even the smaller establishments are still relatively impersonal and have their own institutional imperatives around security and managing the population they hold (maintaining 'good order and discipline').

It has already been noted that BME young people are over-represented in the youth secure estate. Research also suggests that their experiences are more negative with the exception of specific areas such as respect for religious beliefs. For instance, an HMIP (Her Majesty's Inspectorate of Prisons) survey of 15- to 18-year-olds in prison found that:

- BME young men reported worse experiences of what they were offered on arrival than white young men;
- only 75 per cent of BME young men reported feeling safe on their first night compared to 81 per cent of white young men;
- fewer BME young men felt that staff treated them with respect (58 per cent compared to 66 per cent for white young men);

- BME respondents reported more negative experiences in relation to the rewards schemes, adjudications, applications and complaints procedures than white young men;
- fewer BME young men were involved in work or training or offending behaviour programmes. (Adapted from Summerfield, 2011)

In the foreword to that report, the Chief Inspector of Prisons was concerned that both BME and Muslim young men were less positive about their relationships with staff than white and non-Muslim prisoners. Almost a third of Muslim young men said that they had been victimised by a member of staff, compared to 23 per cent of non-Muslim young men (Summerfield, 2011, p 8).

A small-scale qualitative study, part of The Children's Society Just Justice initiative, sheds further light on the coping strategies developed by black young people in custody (Wilson, 2006). From the 45 interviewees, two main strategies emerged, the first of which is described as 'keeping quiet', not so much a passive response to authority but an awareness that reacting may produce negative consequences. Peer support was seen as important, as illustrated by these comments:

> 'I don't argue back with them. I just turn the other cheek and smile. I try and keep calm because I've got a bad temper and so I am polite and calm. If I think I am going to argue with them and they're making a big commotion or fuss I go back to my pad and just sit there and be mad about it.'

> 'They [the white prisoners] don't talk to each other – they're not like us.' (2006, pp 17-18)

However, there were times when such forbearance reached its limit or where staff had crossed a line and then the young people described themselves as 'going nuts':

> 'I'd flare up eventually and stop being polite. I'd go for an officer even though it would make my sentence longer. At the end of the day I'm not going to take shit from nobody.' (2006, p 18)

The 'keeping quiet' strategy for these black young men was important in the light of their minority status and experiences of direct and indirect racism in custody. To some extent it may be a strategy more widely adopted by young people in order to cope with the pains and stresses of imprisonment. Related to this, for 'Jack', a white young man presented as a case study by Morgan, there was a process of habituation and closing down emotionally. Compare his description of first entering custody at the age of 12 with his later view of imprisonment:

> 'I was very scared. It's intimidating, very intimidating. I was bricking it when I first went in. I mean, for the first, I think, four or five days

I didn't come out my room. Ten to 16 was the age range. There was a lot of bullying that used to go on. I mean, there's bullying everywhere, but it was really bad in them, sort of, young years.'

'If you've got a cold heart and that here, it's easy in here. Yeah, that's about the main thing I have learned in here ... how to bottle feelings. Took me to 21 to learn it properly.' (2012, pp 81–3)

Young people with extensive experience of custody may become institutionalised, missing out on the opportunity to develop emotional and practical resources to cope 'on the out', particularly where custody follows on from experience of the care system. 'Wayne', a young man with mixed parentage, is the centre of a second case study presented by Morgan that shows the extent to which this can happen:

'I feel safer in jail than I do outside. In jail you know what you are doing all the time, there's a schedule, it's like a path, you know you can't fail. Jail is my upbringing and jail has taught me about things.' (2012, p 84)

What happens after custody?

It is a shocking indictment of our childcare system and the level of support available to assist resettlement when young people like 'Wayne' feel more comfortable in custody than they do in the community. He describes his last period of freedom as disorientating and too much for him to handle:

'I was distracted by everything around. Even if someone called me about a job or directed me that way, there were so many things around me to do, I was lost. I would start off the day and say I'm going to hand out a few CVs, and then someone would call me and say meet me wherever and I would completely forget what I was going to do. It's really hard when you get out. There were a few opportunities for me to do good when I got out but it was too much, it's a big world for me and I didn't know where my head was at.' (quoted in Morgan, 2012, p 85)

The experience of custody is difficult for many and, even for those who can cope with the system, it does little that is constructive to prepare them for life post-custody. Both entering and being released from custody may represent critical moments in a young person's life, particularly if his or her circumstances are insecure. Accommodation, provision of education or training and continuity of specialist health and care services are important. Planning processes are set up to ensure that the YOT case manager in the community is working with relevant local authority departments and services to ensure that arrangements are satisfactorily in place, but this is a difficult task, especially so when social care and/or housing have other more immediate problems to address than a young person who is for the present being cared for and housed in custody.

It is interesting to look at the patterns that emerge from a thematic inspection of resettlement by HMIP (2011) focusing specifically on accommodation and education, training and employment. As part of this research, 61 young men approaching their release date were interviewed, and a survey was undertaken involving a further 770 young men in nine different YOIs. Although all establishments in this study had a resettlement policy, there was little evidence of up-to-date profiling of resettlement needs. Training plans were completed in the majority of cases and targets were set, although in both this and Summerfield's (2011) research, the young people suggested they had not been actively involved in the process. The targets also tended to be broad, making it harder to work towards them and to know when steps had been taken to achieve them. It is even more concerning that the targets did not adequately identify and mobilise the resources needed for success. Instead they put the onus on young people so, in effect, responsibilising them and individualising their social and welfare needs rather than dealing with systemic problems and structural inequalities (Gray, 2011).

What is most worrying is the last-minute nature of plans for release arising from these deficits. For instance, 24 of the 61 interviewees in the HMIP report were not returning to live with family and of these, 17 did not know where they would be living (including 13 of the 18 LAC). This partly reflects the pressure on available accommodation within local authorities, and also the change in statutory responsibilities for accommodating young people who reach the age of 18 during sentence: overcoming factors such as these requires a pro-active approach at local authority level. Follow-up data available for 41 young people indicate that one month after release only 23 were still in the same accommodation and six had been returned to custody. Three young people had been placed in a B&B on release and after a month one was still there. Only 13 young people had education, training and employment placements on release, and the picture in terms of maintaining and finding such placements post-release was variable (HMIP, 2011).

While the above is only a snapshot, it powerfully illustrates how far there is to go in terms of responsive and effective resettlement services. New initiatives such as the resettlement consortia being piloted in two regions (HMIP, 2011) may provide a more robust framework and generate services that help young people desist from crime. Certainly a more strategic approach is needed. But this is not all – the government should take a good hard look at the number of custodial sentences imposed (Gray, 2011) and the stress that they create for other services trying to pick up the pieces of young people's lives on release and to help them deal with the disruption, stigma and social exclusion that follows in their wake.

Implications for practice

This book has highlighted throughout the extent to which young people in the YJS are marginalised and lacking in social capital – those resources, networks and contacts that can help a young person to move on and to make important steps in the transition to adulthood. This is most acute for young people in custody, whose prior experiences of exclusion and stigma are compounded while being held in a system that explicitly punishes, controls and disempowers.

Despite improvements with the YJB as commissioner of custody placements, the majority of placements are still in YOIs rather than childcare establishments. This centralised system may have permitted some local authorities to neglect their responsibilities for young people during sentence (Newman and Blyth, 2009), increasing the challenge of reintegration into the community.

In the UK we use custody as a sanction more readily than other comparable jurisdictions, reflecting generally unsympathetic views of young people engaged in anti-social behaviour or offending. From the early 1990s the numbers of young people under 18 in custody grew steadily despite a marked drop in the numbers of offences and prosecutions. This trend has been in decline since 2008. This seems connected to having fewer young people entering the YJS rather than changing public attitudes about the acceptability of using custody for young people, and is an important indicator of the earlier stages where levers for change might effectively be applied.

Taking away any young person's liberty raises serious questions about rights, and here the UK government has been criticised because custody has not been used as a *measure of last resort*, because decisions have often demonstrably ignored *the child's best interests* and because of the conditions in which children and young people are held, particularly within prison service establishments. The use of restraint, searches and segregation are all controversial.

Youth-centred practice recognises the above and does not accept custody as a fact of life. As a society we should be ashamed that we have used custody to the extent that we have done recently in the name of public protection. In fact the high reconviction figures for young people post-custody strongly suggest that it defeats its object in deterring crime and successfully rehabilitating young people – the opposite is true, and particularly so when services are disjointed and do not offer a continuity of care and an acceptable degree of stability when young people are released.

The current reduction in custodial sentences presents an opportunity and, in a time of fiscal constraint, it is timely to press the advantage and call for more – and more diverse – community facilities rather than expensive secure establishments. This is an interesting moment in youth justice and there is surely a moral obligation on those involved in the system to argue for change in a more positive and humane direction that appreciates the strengths and qualities of young people, understanding their predicaments instead of condemning them out of hand for what they do.

Further reading

Bateman, T. (2013) *Incarcerating children: understanding youth imprisonment*, Abingdon: Routledge.

Blyth, M., Newman, R. and Wright, C. (eds) (2009) *Children and young people in custody: Managing the risk*, Bristol: The Policy Press.

References

Abbott, D., Townsley, R. and Watson, D. (2005) 'Multi-agency working in services for disabled children: What impact does it have on professionals?', *Health and Social Care in the Community*, vol 13, no 2, pp 155-63.

Aldridge, J. and Medina, J. (2008) *Youth gangs in an English city: Social exclusion, drugs and violence*, ESRC end of award report, Swindon: Economic and Social Research Council.

Anning, A., Cottrell, J., Frost, N., Green J. and Robinson, M. (2010) *Developing multi-professional teamwork for integrated children's services* (2nd edn), Maidenhead: Open University Press.

Archard, D. (2007) 'Children's rights and juvenile justice', in M. Hill, A. Lockyer and F. Stone (eds) *Youth justice and child protection*, London: Jessica Kingsley Publishers, pp 250-65.

Armstrong, C., Hill, M. and Secker, J. (1998) *Listening to children*, London: Mental Health Foundation.

Arnett, J.J. (2004) *Emerging adulthood: The winding road from the late teens through to the twenties*, New York: Oxford University Press.

Audit Commission (1996) *Misspent youth: Young people and crime*, London: Audit Commission.

Bailey, S. (1996) 'Adolescents who murder', *Journal of Adolescence*, vol 19, no 1, pp 19-39.

Bailey, S., Vermeiren, R. and Mitchell, P. (2007) 'Mental health, risk and anti-social behaviour in young offenders: strategies and opportunities', in M. Blyth, E. Solomon and K. Baker (eds) *Young people and 'risk'*, Bristol: Policy Press, pp 53-72.

Baker, K. (2007) 'Risk in practice: systems and practitioner judgement', in M. Blyth, E. Solomon and K. Baker (eds) *Young people and 'risk'*, Bristol: Policy Press, pp 25-38.

Baker, K. and Kelly, G. (2011) 'Risk assessment and young people', in H. Kemshall and B. Wilkinson (eds) *Good practice in assessing risk*, London: Jessica Kingsley Publishers, pp 66-83.

Baker, K., Kelly, G. and Wilkinson, B. (2011) *Assessment in youth justice*, Bristol: Policy Press.

Bankes, N. (2007) 'Placement provision and placement decisions: resources and processes', in M. Erooga and H. Masson (eds) *Children and young people who sexually abuse others* (2nd edn), Abingdon: Routledge, pp 77-87.

Barratt, D. and Ayre, P. (2000) 'Young people and prostitution: an end to the beginning?', *Children & Society*, vol 14, no 1, pp 48-59.

Barry, M. (2000) 'The mentor/monitor debate in criminal justice: "What works" for offenders', *British Journal of Social Work*, vol 30, pp 575-95.

Barry, M. (2006) *Youth offending in transition: The search for social recognition*, Abingdon: Routledge.

Barry, M. (2007) 'The transitional pathways of young female offenders', in R. Sheehan, G. McIvor and C. Trotter (eds) *What works with women offenders*, Cullompton: Willan, pp 23-39.

Barry, M. (2009) 'Youth justice policy and its influence on desistance from crime', in M. Barry and F. McNeill (eds) *Youth offending and youth justice*, London: Jessica Kingsley Publishers, pp 78-94.

Barry, M. (2012) 'Young women in transition: from offending to desistance', in F. Losel, A. Bottoms and D.P. Farrington (eds) *Young adult offenders: Lost in transition?*, Abingdon: Routledge, pp 113-27.

Batchelor, S. and McNeill, F. (2005) 'The young person-worker relationship', in T. Bateman and J. Pitts (eds) *The RHP companion to youth justice*, Lyme Regis: Russell House Publishing, pp 166-71.

Bateman, T. (2002) 'Living with final warnings: making the best of a bad job?', *Youth Justice*, vol 2, pp 131-40.

Bateman, T. (2005) 'Reducing child imprisonment: a systemic challenge', *Youth Justice*, vol 5, pp 91-105.

Bateman, T. (2008) 'Detention and training orders', in B. Goldson (ed) *Dictionary of youth justice*, Cullompton: Willan, p 135.

Bateman, T. (2011) '"We now breach more kids in a week than we used to in a whole year": The punitive turn, enforcement and custody', *Youth Justice*, vol 11, no 2, pp 115-33.

Bateman, T. (2012a) 'Two more children die in English prisons', *Youth Justice*, vol 12, no 2, pp 146-8.

Bateman, T. (2012b) 'Who pulled the plug? Towards an explanation of the fall in child imprisonment in England and Wales', *Youth Justice*, vol 12, no 1, pp 36-52.

Bateman, T. (2013) *Incarcerating children: understanding youth imprisonment*, Abingdon: Routledge.

Bazemore, G. and Schiff, M. (2005) *Juvenile justice reform and restorative justice: Building theory and policy from practice*, Cullompton: Willan.

Bean, P. (2008) *Drugs and crime* (3rd edn), Cullompton: Willan.

Beck, U. (1992) *Risk society: Towards a new modernity*, London: Sage Publications.

Beckett, C. (2007) *Child protection: An introduction*, London: Sage Publications.

Beckett, C. (2010) *Assessment and intervention in social work: Preparing for practice*, London: Sage Publications.

Beckett, R. (2007) 'Risk prediction, decision-making and evaluation of adolescent sexual abusers', in M. Erooga and H. Masson (eds) *Children and young people who sexually abuse others* (2nd edn), Abingdon: Routledge, pp 233-55.

Bell, M. (2011) *Promoting children's rights in social work and children's care: A guide to participatory practice*, London: Jessica Kingsley Publishers.

Bennett, T. and Holloway, K. (2004) 'Gang membership, drugs and crime in the UK', *British Journal of Criminology*, vol 44, pp 305-23.

Bennett, T. and Holloway, K. (2005) *Understanding drugs, alcohol and crime*, Maidenhead: Open University Press.

Bennett, T., Holloway, K. and Farrington, D. (2008) 'The statistical association between drug misuse and crime: A meta-analysis', *Aggression and Violent Behaviour*, vol 13, pp 107-18.

Bilson, A. and Thorpe, D. (1998) *Childcare careers and their management*, Fife: Research, Development and Information Unit.

Birdwell, J., Grist, M. and Margo, J. (2011) *The forgotten half: A Demos and Private Equity Foundation report*, London: Demos.

Blades, R., Hart, D., Lea, J. and Willmott, N. (2011) *Care: A stepping stone to custody? The views of children in care on the links between care, offending and custody*, London: Prison Reform Trust.

Blyth, M. (2007) 'Serious incidents in the youth justice system: management and accountability', in M. Blyth, E. Solomon and K. Baker (eds) *Young people and risk*, Bristol: Policy Press, pp 73-84.

Blyth, M. and Solomon, E. (eds) (2012) *Effective safeguarding for children and young people: What next after Munro?*, Bristol: Policy Press.

Blyth, M., Newman, R. and Wright, C. (eds) (2009) *Children and young people in custody: Managing the risk*, Bristol: Policy Press.

Boeck, T., Fleming, H.J. and Kemshall, H. (2006) 'The context of risk decisions: does social capital make a difference?', *Forum: Qualitative Social Research: Social Research*, vol 7, no 1, Article 17.

Boswell, G.R. (1996) *Young and dangerous: The backgrounds and careers of Section 53 offenders*, Aldershot: Avebury.

Boswell, G.R. (2007) 'Young people and violence', in M. Blyth, E. Solomon and K. Baker (eds) *Young people and risk*, Bristol: Policy Press, pp 39-51.

Botley, M., Jinks, B. and Metson, C. (2011) *Young people's views and experiences of the youth justice system*, London: Children's Workforce Development Council.

Bottoms, A. (2001) 'Compliance and community penalties', in A. Bottoms, L. Gelsthorpe and S. Rex (eds) *Community penalties: Changes and challenges*, Cullompton: Willan, pp 87-116.

Bottoms, A. and Shapland, J. (2011) 'Steps towards desistance among male young adult recidivists', in S. Farrall, R. Sparks, S. Maruna and M. Hough (eds) *Escape routes: Contemporary perspectives on life after offending*, Abingdon: Routledge, pp 43-80.

Bourdieu, P. (1986) 'The forms of capital', in J. Richardson (ed) *Handbook of theory and research for the sociology of education*, New York: Greenwood, pp 241-58.

Bowlby, J. (1953) *Childcare and the growth of love*, Harmondsworth: Penguin.

Bradley, K. (2009) *The Bradley Report: Lord Bradley's review of people with mental health problems or learning disabilities in the criminal justice system*, London: Department of Health.

Braithwaite, J. (1989) *Crime, shame and reintegration*, Cambridge: Cambridge University Press.

Brooks-Gunn, J. and Warren, M. (1985) 'The effects of delayed menarche in different contexts: dance and non-dance students', *Journal of Youth and Adolescence*, vol 14, pp 285-300.

Brown, B. (1999) 'You're going out with who? Peer group influences on adolescent romantic relationships', in W. Furman, B. Brown and S. Fiering (eds) *Contemporary perspectives on adolescent romantic relationships*, Cambridge: Cambridge University Press.

Brown, S. (2005) *Understanding youth and crime: Listening to youth?* (2nd edn), Maidenhead: Open University Press.

Bryan-Hancock, C. and Casey, S. (2010) 'Psychological maturity of at-risk juveniles, young adults and adults: Implications for the justice system', *Psychiatry, Psychology and Law*, vol 17, no 1, pp 57-69.

Bryan-Hancock, C. and Casey, S. (2011) 'Young people and the justice system: Consideration of maturity in criminal responsibility', *Psychiatry, Psychology and Law*, vol 18, no 1, pp 69-78.

Buchanan, J. (2008) 'Understanding and engaging with problematic substance use', in S. Green, E. Lancaster and S. Feasey (eds) *Addressing offending behaviour: Context, practice and values*, Cullompton: Willan, pp 246-64.

Burman, M. and Batchelor, S. (2009) 'Between two stools? Responding to young women who offend', *Youth Justice*, vol 9, no 3, pp 270-95.

Burnett, R. and Appleton, C. (2004) 'Joined-up services to tackle youth crime', *British Journal of Criminology*, vol 44, no 1, pp 34-54.

Burney, E. (2005) *Making people behave: ASB, politics and policy*, Cullompton: Willan.

Buston, K. (2002) 'Adolescents with mental health problems: what do they say about mental health services', *Journal of Adolescence*, vol 25, pp 231-42.

Butler, L. and Elliott, C. (2007) 'Stop and think: changing sexually aggressive behaviour in young children', in M. Erooga, H. Masson (eds) *Children and young people who sexually abuse others* (2nd edn), pp 185-99.

Calder, M.C. (2002) 'Structural changes in the management of young people who sexually abuse in the UK', in M.C. Calder (ed) *Young people who sexually abuse: Building the evidence base for your practice*, Lyme Regis: Russell House Publishing, pp 265-308.

Callaghan, J., Pace, F., Young, B. and Vostanis, P. (2003) 'Primary mental health workers within youth offending teams: a new service model', *Journal of Adolescence*, vol 26, pp 185-99.

Canton, R. (2011) *Probation: Working with offenders*, Abingdon: Routledge.

Carol Goldstone Associates (2010) *Survey of youth offending teams: The report*, London: National Audit Office.

Case, S. (2007) 'Questioning the "evidence" of risk that underpins evidence-led youth justice interventions', *Youth Justice*, vol 7, no 2, pp 91-105.

Case, S. (2010) 'Preventing and reducing risk', in W. Taylor, R. Earle and R. Hester (eds) *Youth justice handbook: Theory, policy and practice*, Cullompton: Willan, pp 90-100.

Cauffman, E. and Steinberg, L. (2000) '(Im)maturity of judgement in adolescence: Why adolescents may be less culpable than adults', *Behavioural Sciences and the Law*, vol 18, pp 741-60.

Cavadino, M., Dignan, J., Mair, G. (2013) *The penal system: an introduction*, London: Sage.

Cherry, S. (2005) *Transforming behaviour: Pro-social modelling in practice*, Cullompton: Willan.

Chui, W.H. and Nellis, M. (2003) 'Creating the National Probation Service – New wine, old bottles?', in W.H. Chui and M. Nellis (eds) *Moving probation forward: Evidence, arguments and practice*, London: Pearson Longman, pp 1-18.

Clarke, K. (2009) 'Early intervention and prevention: lessons from the Sure Start programme', in M. Blyth and E. Solomon (eds) *Prevention and youth crime: Is early intervention working?*, Bristol: Policy Press, pp 53-68.

Clifton, J. (2012) 'The child's voice in the child protection system', in M. Blyth and E. Solomon (eds) *Effective safeguarding for children and young people: What next after Munro?*, Bristol: Policy Press, pp 51-68.

Coleman, J.C. (2011) *The nature of adolescence* (4th edn), Hove: Routledge.

Collishaw, S. (2012) 'Time trends in young people's emotional and behavioural problems 1975-2005', in A. Hagell (ed) *Changing adolescence: Social trends and mental health*, Bristol: Policy Press, pp 9-26.

Connolly, M. and Ward, T. (2008) *Morals, rights and practice in the human services*, London: Jessica Kingsley Publishers.

Cook, D. (2006) *Criminal and social justice*, London: Sage Publications.

Cossar, J., Brandon, Dr M. and Jordan, P. (2011) *Don't make assumptions: Children and young people's views of the child protection system and messages for change*, London: Office of the Children's Commissioner.

Coy, M. (2007) 'Young women, local authority care and selling sex: findings from research', *British Journal of Social Work*, vol 38, no 7, pp 1408-24.

Coyle, A. (2005) *Understanding prisons: Key issues in policy and practice*, Buckingham: Open University Press.

CQC (Care Quality Commission) (2011) *Re: Actions: A third review of healthcare in the community for young people who offend*, London: CQC.

Crawford, A. (2006) 'Institutionalising restorative youth justice in a cold, punitive climate', in I. Aertsen, T. Daems and J. Robert (eds) *Institutionalising restorative justice*, Cullompton: Willan, pp 120-50.

Crawford, A. (2009) 'Criminalising sociability through anti-social behaviour legislation: Dispersal powers, young people and the police', *Youth Justice*, vol 9, no 1, pp 5-26.

Crawford, A. and Burden, T. (2005) 'Involving victims in referral orders and young offender panels an evaluation of Leeds Youth Offending Service', in *Criminal Justice Review 2004-5*, Leeds: Centre for Criminal Justice Studies, pp 34-8.

Crawford, A. and Newburn, T. (2003) *Youth offending and restorative justice: Implementing reform in youth justice*, Cullompton: Willan.

Criminal Justice Joint Inspection (2013) *Examining multi-agency responses to children and young people who sexually offend: A joint inspection of the effectiveness of multi-agency work with children and young people in England and Wales who have committed sexual offences and were supervised in the community*, London: HM Inspectorate of Prisons.

Darker, I., Ward, H. and Caulfield, L. (2008) 'An analysis of offending by young people looked after by local authorities', *Youth Justice*, vol 8, no 2, pp 134-48.

DCSF (Department for Children, Schools and Families) (2009) *Information sharing: Guidance for practitioners and managers*, London: DCSF.

DCSF (2010) *Working together to safeguard children*, London: TSO.

Deucher, I. (2010) '"It's just pure harassment ... as if it's a crime to walk in the street": Anti-social behaviour, youth justice and citizenship – the reality of young men in the East End of Glasgow', *Youth Justice*, vol 10, no 3, pp 258-74.

de Winter, M. and Noom, M. (2003) 'Someone who treats you as an ordinary human being', *British Journal of Social Work*, vol 33, pp 325-37.

DfE (Department for Education) (2010a) *The Children Act 1989: Guidance and regulations: Local authority responsibilities towards former looked after children in custody*, London: DfE.

DfE (2010b) *The Children Act 1989: Guidance and regulations: Volume 3: Planning transitions to adulthood for care leavers*, London: DfE.

DfE (2011a) *Children looked after by local authorities in England (including adoption and care leavers) – Year ending 31 March 2011*, London: DfE.

DfE (2011b) *A child-centred system: The government's response to the Munro review of child protection*, London: DfE.

DfE (2012) *Building engagement, building futures: Our strategy to maximise the participation of 16-24 year olds in education, training or work*, London: DfE.

DfE (2013) *Working together to safeguard children*, London: DfE.

DfES (Department for Education and Skills) (2003) *Every Child Matters: Change for children*, London: DfES.

DfES (2006) *Care matters: Transforming the lives of children and young people in care*, London: DfES.

DH (Department of Health), Home Office and Department of Education and Employment (1999) *Working together to safeguard children: a guide to inter-agency working to safeguard and promote the welfare of children*, London: TSO.

DH (2005) *Smoking, drinking and drug use among young people in England 2004: Headline figures* (www.dh.gov.uk).

Dignan, J. (2005) *Understanding victims and restorative justice*, Maidenhead: Open University Press.

Dignan, J. and Marsh, P. (2001) 'Restorative justice and family group conferences in England: Current state and future prospects', in A. Morris and G. Maxwell (eds) *Restorative justice for juveniles: Conferencing, mediation and circles*, Oxford: Hart Publishing, pp 85-102.

Dobrowsky, A. (2002) 'Rhetoric versus reality: the figure of the child and New Labour's strategic "social investment state"', *Studies in Political Economy*, vol 69, pp 43-73.

Dogra, N., Parkin, A., Gale, F. and Frake, C. (2009) *A multi-disciplinary handbook of child and adolescent mental health for frontline professionals* (2nd edn), London: Jessica Kingsley Publishers.

Donaldson, M. (1978) *Children's minds*, London: Fortuna.

Downes, D. and Rock, P. (2003) *Understanding deviance* (4th edn), Oxford: Oxford University Press.

Doyle, S. (2008) 'Sure Start', in B. Goldson (ed) *Dictionary of youth justice*, Cullompton: Willan, pp 345-7.

DrugScope (2010) *Young people's drug and alcohol treatment at the crossroads: What it's for, where it's at and how to make it even better*, London: DrugScope.

Earle, R. and Newburn, T. (2001) 'Creative tensions? Young offenders, restorative justice and the introduction of referral orders', *Youth Justice*, vol 1, no 3, pp 3-13.

Elias, N. (1978) *The civilising process: Volume 1: The history of manners*, Oxford: Blackwell.

Elias, N. (1982) *State formation and civilisation*, Oxford: Blackwell.

Erooga, M. and Masson, H. (eds) (2007a) *Children and young people who sexually abuse others* (2nd edn), Abingdon: Routledge.

Erooga, M. and Masson, H. (2007b) 'Children and young people with sexually harmful or abusive behaviours: underpinning knowledge, principles, approaches and service provision', in M. Erooga and H. Masson (eds) *Children and young people who sexually abuse others* (2nd edn), Abingdon: Routledge, pp 3-17.

Escott, K. (2012) 'Young women on the margins of the labour market', *Work, Employment & Society*, vol 26, no 3, pp 412-28.

Etzioni, A. (1993) *The spirit of community: The reinvention of American society*, New York: Touchstone.

Evans, R. (2008) 'Cautioning', in B. Goldson (ed) *Dictionary of youth*, Cullompton: Willan, p 46.

Farrington, D.P. (1986) 'Age and crime', *Crime and Justice*, vol 7, pp 189-250.

Farrington, D.P. (1989) *The origins of crime: The Cambridge Study of Delinquent Development*, Home Office Research and Planning Unit, *Research Bulletin* No 27, London: Home Office.

Farrington, D.P. (1994) 'Human development and criminal careers', in M. Maguire, R. Morgan and R. Reiner (eds) *The Oxford handbook of criminology*, Oxford: Oxford University Press, pp 511-84.

Farrington, D.P. (2000) 'Explaining and preventing crime: the globalisation of knowledge – The American Society of Criminology 1999 Presidential Address', *Criminology*, vol 8, no 1, pp 1-24.

Farrington, D.P. (2006) 'Key longitudinal-experimental studies in criminology', *Journal of Experimental Criminology*, vol 2, no 2, pp 121-41.

Farrington, D.P. (2007) 'Childhood risk factors and risk-focused intervention', in M. Maguire, R. Morgan and R. Reiner (eds) *The Oxford handbook of criminology*, Oxford: Oxford University Press, pp 602-40.

Farrow, K., Kelly, G. and Wilkinson, B. (2007) *Offenders in focus: Risk, responsivity and diversity*, Bristol: Policy Press.

Field, S. (2007) 'Practice cultures and the "new" youth justice in (England and) Wales', *British Journal of Criminology*, vol 47, pp 311-30.

Fielder, C., Hart, D. and Shaw, C. (2008) *The developing relationship between youth offending teams and children's trusts*, London: Youth Justice Board.

Feilzer, M. and Hood, R. (2004) *Differences or discrimination? Minority ethnic young people in the YJS*, London: Youth Justice Board.

Fincham, R. and Rhodes, P. (1999) *Principles of organisational behaviour*, Oxford: Oxford University Press.

Fitzpatrick, C., Abayomi, N., Kehoe, A., Devlin, N., Glacking, S., Power, L. and Guerin, S. (2011) 'Do we miss depressive disorders and suicidal behaviours in clinical practice?', *Clinical Child Psychology and Psychiatry*, vol 17, no 3, pp 449-58.

Flood-Page, C., Campbell, S., Harrington, V. and Miller, J. (2000) *Youth crime: Findings from the 1998/99 Youth Lifestyles Survey*, Home Office Research Study No 209, London: Home Office.

Foucault, M. (1977) *Discipline and punish*, London: Penguin.

France, A. (2000) 'Towards a sociological understanding of youth and their risk-taking', *Journal of Youth Studies*, vol 3, no 3, pp 317-31.

France, A. (2007) *Understanding youth in late modernity*, Maidenhead: Open University Press.

France, A. and Homel, R. (2007) 'Societal access routes and developmental pathways: putting young people's voice into the analysis of pathways into and out of crime', in A. France and R. Homel (eds) *Pathways and crime prevention: Theory, policy and practice*, Cullompton: Willan, pp 9-27.

Frost, N. and Parton, N. (2009) *Understanding children's social care: Politics, policies and practice*, London: Sage Publications.

Frost, N. and Robinson, M. (2007) 'Joining up children's services: Safeguarding children in multi-disciplinary teams', *Child Abuse Review*, vol 16, pp 184-99.

Frost, N., Robinson, M. and Anning, A. (2005) 'Social workers in multi-disciplinary teams: Issues and dilemmas for professional practice', *Child and Family Social Work*, vol 10, pp 187-96.

Furlong, A. (2006) 'Not a very NEET solution: representing problematic labour market transitions among early school leavers', *Work, Employment & Society*, vol 20, no 3, pp 553-69.

Furlong, A. and Cartmel, F. (2004) *Vulnerable young men in fragile labour markets: Employment, unemployment and the search for long-term security*, York: Joseph Rowntree Foundation.

Furlong, A. and Cartmel, F. (2007) *Young people and social change: New perspectives* (2nd edn), Maidenhead: Open University Press.

Garland, D. (2000) 'The culture of high crime societies: Some preconditions of recent law and order policies', *The British Journal of Criminology*, vol 40, no 3, pp 347-75.

Garland, D. (2001) *The culture of control: Crime and social order in contemporary society*, Oxford: Oxford University Press.

Gelsthorpe, L. and Morris, A. (1994) 'Juvenile justice 1945-1992', in M. Maguire, R. Morgan and R. Reiner (eds) *The Oxford handbook of criminology*, Oxford: Clarenden Press, pp 949-93.

Gelsthorpe, L. and Sharpe, G. (2006) 'Gender, youth and justice', in B. Goldson and J. Muncie (eds) *Youth crime and justice*, London: Sage Publications, pp 47-61.

Gelsthorpe, L. and Worrall, A. (2009) 'Looking for trouble: A recent history of girls, young women and youth justice', *Youth Justice*, vol 9, no 3, pp 209-23.

Giddens, A. (1992) *The transformation of intimacy: Sexuality, love and eroticism in modern societies*, Cambridge: Polity Press.

Gilligan, C. (1982) *In a different voice: Psychological theory and women's development*, Cambridge, MA: Harvard University Press.

Gilling, D. (2005) 'Partnership and crime prevention', in N. Tilley (ed) *The handbook of crime prevention and community safety*, Cullompton: Willan, pp 734-56.

Glueck, S. and Glueck, E. (1950) *Unravelling juvenile delinquency*, New York: Commonwealth Fund.

Glueck, S. and Glueck, E. (1968) *Delinquents and non-delinquents in perspective*, Cambridge, MA: Harvard University Press.

Goddard, C., De Bertoli, L., Saunders, J. and Tucci, J. (2005) 'The rapist's camouflage: "child prostitution"', *Child Abuse Review*, vol 14, pp 275-91.

Goldsmith, C. (2008) 'Cameras, cops and contracts: what anti-social behaviour management feels like to young people', in P. Squires (ed) *ASBO nation: The criminalisation of nuisance*, Bristol: Policy Press, pp 223-38.

Goldson, B. (2006) 'Penal custody: intolerance, irrationality and indifference', in B. Goldson and J. Munice (eds) *Youth crime and justice*, London: Sage Publications, pp 139-56.

Goldson, B. and Coles, D. (2009) 'Child deaths in the juvenile secure estate', in M. Blyth, R. Newman and C. Wright (eds) *Children and young people in custody*, Bristol: Policy Press, pp 55-68.

Goodey, J. (2005) *Victims and victimology: Research, policy and practice*, Harlow: Pearson.

Gordon, R. (2000) 'Criminal business organisations, street gangs and "wannabe" groups: a Vancouver perspective', *The Canadian Journal of Criminology and Criminal Justice*, vol 42, no 1, pp 39-60.

Gottfredson, M.R. and Hirschi, T. (1990) *A general theory of crime*, Stanford, CA: Stanford University Press.

Goulden, C. and Sondhi, A. (2001) *At the margins: Drug use by vulnerable young people in the 1998/99 Youth Lifestyles Survey*, Home Office Research Study 228, London: Home Office.

Graham, J. (2010) 'Responding to youth crime', in D. Smith (ed) *A new response to youth crime*, Abingdon: Routledge, pp 104-42.

Graham, J. and Bowling, B. (1995) *Young people and crime*, London: Home Office.

Graham, P. (2004) *The end of adolescence*, Oxford: Oxford University Press.

Grant, H. (2007) 'Assessment issues in relation to young people who have sexually abusive behaviour', in M. Erooga and H. Masson (eds) *Children and young people who sexually abuse others* (2nd edn), Abingdon: Routledge, pp 67-76.

Gray, P. (2005) 'The politics of risk and young offenders' experiences of social exclusion and restorative justice', *British Journal of Criminology*, vol 45, pp 938-57.

Gray, P. (2011) 'Youth custody, resettlement and the right to social justice', *Youth Justice*, vol 11, no 3, pp 235-49.

Green, C. (2012) 'Early intervention', in M. Blyth and E. Solomon (eds) *Effective safeguarding for children and young people: What next after Munro?*, Bristol: Policy Press, pp 9-24.

Green, E.E., Mitchell, W.A. and Bunton, R. (2000) 'Contextualising risk and danger: an analysis of young people's perceptions of risk', *Journal of Youth Studies*, vol 3, no 2, pp 109-26.

Green, H., McGennity, A., Meitzer, H., Ford, T. and Goodman, R. (2005) *Mental health of children and young people in Great Britain in 2004*, London: Office for National Statistics.

Hackett, S. (2007a) 'Towards a resilience-based intervention model for young people with sexually abusive behaviours', in M. Erooga and H. Masson (eds) *Children and young people who sexually abuse others* (2nd edn), Abingdon: Routledge, pp 103-14.

Hackett, S. (2007b) 'The personal and professional context to work with children and young people who have sexually abused', in M. Erooga and H. Masson (eds) *Children and young people who sexually abuse others* (2nd edn), Abingdon: Routledge, pp 237-48.

Hagell, A. and Hazel, N. (2001) 'Macro and micro patterns in the development of secure custodial institutions for serious and persistent young offenders in England and Wales', *Youth Justice*, vol 1, pp 3-16.

Hagell, A., Sandberg, S. and MacDonald, R. (2012a) 'Stress and mental health in adolescence: interrelationships and time trends', in A. Hagell (ed) *Changing adolescence: Social trends and mental health*, Bristol: Policy Press, pp 27-46.

Hagell, A., Aldridge, J., Meier, P., Millar, T., Symonds, J. and Donmall, M. (2012b) 'Trends in adolescent substance use and their implications for understanding trends in mental health', in A. Hagell (ed) *Changing adolescence: Social trends and mental health*, Bristol: Policy Press, pp 117-50.

Haines, K. and O'Mahoney, D. (2006) 'Restorative approaches, young people and youth justice', in B. Goldson and J. Muncie (eds) *Youth crime and justice*, London: Sage Publications, pp 110-24.

Hall, G.S. (1904) *Adolescence: Its psychology and its relationship to physiology, anthropology, sex, crime, religion and education* (2 volumes), New York: D. Appleton.

Hamilton, W. (2011) 'Young people and mental health: resilience and models of practice', in L. O'Dell and S. Leverett (eds) *Working with children and young people: Co-constructing practice*, Milton Keynes: Open University Press, pp 92-150.

Hammersley, R., Marsland, L. and Reid, M. (2003) *Substance use by young offenders: The impact of the normalisation of drug use in the early years of the 21st century*, Home Office Research Study 261, London: Home Office.

Hanvey, S., Philpott, T. and Wilson, C. (2011) *A community-based approach to the reduction of sexual offending*, London: Jessica Kingsley Publishers.

Harrington, R. and Bailey, S. with Chitsabesan, P., Kroll, L., Macdonald, W., Sneider, S., Kenning, C., Taylor, G., Byford, S. and Barratt, B. (2005) *Mental health needs and effectiveness of provision for young offenders in custody and in the community*, London: Youth Justice Board.

Harris, B. (2011) *Working with distressed young people*, Exeter: Learning Matters Ltd.

Harris, A. and Allen, T. (2011) 'Young people's views of multi-agency working', *British Educational Research Journal*, vol 37, no 3, pp 405-19.

Hart, A. and Blincow, D. with Thomas, H. (2007) *Resilient therapy: Working with children and families*, Hove: Routledge.

Hart, A. and Blincow, D. (2008) 'Resilient therapy: Strategic therapeutic engagement with children in crisis', *Child Care in Practice*, vol 14, no 2, pp 131-45.

Hart, D. and Thompson, C. (2009) *Young people's participation in the youth justice system*, London: National Children's Bureau.

Hawton, K., Rodham, K., Evans, E. and Weatherall, R. (2002) 'Deliberate self-harm in adolescents: self-report survey in schools in England', *British Medical Journal*, vol 325, pp 1207-11.

Hayes, A. (2007) 'Why early in life is not enough: timing and sustainability in prevention and early intervention', in A. France and R. Homel (eds) *Pathways and crime prevention: Theory, policy and practice*, Cullompton: Willan, pp 202-25.

Hazel, N., Hagell, A. and Brazier, L. (2002) *Young offenders: Perceptions of their experiences in the criminal justice system*, London: Policy Research Bureau.

Health Advisory Service (1995) *Together we stand: The commissioning, role and management of child and adolescent mental health services*, London: HMSO.

Healthcare Commission (2009) *Actions speak louder*, London: Healthcare Commission.

Heap, V. and Smithson, H. (2012) 'From words of action to the action of words: Politics, post-riot rhetoric and contractual governance', in D. Briggs (ed) *The English riots of 2-11: A summer of discontent*, Hook: Waterside Press, pp 257-78.

Heath, B. (2010) 'The partnership approach in drug misuse', in A. Pyecroft and D. Gough (eds) *Multi-agency working in criminal justice*, Bristol: Policy Press, pp 185-200.

Hedderman, C. and Hough, M. (2004) 'Getting tough or being effective: What matters?', in G. Mair (ed) *What matters in probation?*, Cullompton: Willan, pp 146-69.

Henderson, S., Holland, J., McGrellis, S., Sharpe, S. and Thomson, R. (2007) *Inventing adulthoods: A biographical approach to youth transitions*, London: Sage Publications.

Hendrick, H. (2006) 'Histories of youth crime and justice', in B. Goldson and J. Muncie (eds) *Youth crime and justice*, London: Sage Publications, pp 3-16.

Hill, J. (2006) 'Dreaming out of despair: A retrospective post-custody study', in D. Wilson and G. Rees (eds) *Just justice: A study into black young people's experiences of the youth justice system*, London: The Children's Society, pp 22-36.

Hill, M. (1999) 'What is the problem? Who can help? The perspectives of children and young people on their well-being and on helping professionals', *Journal of Social Work Practice*, vol 13, no 2, pp 135-45.

Hine, J. (2007) 'Young people's perspectives on final warnings', *Web Journal of Current Legal Issues*, issue 2 (http://webjcli.ncl.ac.uk/2007/issue2/hine2.html).

Hine, J. (2010) 'Young people's "voices" as evidence', in W. Taylor, R. Earle and R. Hester (eds) *Youth justice handbook: Theory, policy and practice*, Cullompton: Willan, pp 168-78.

Hirschi, T. (1969) *Causes of delinquency*, Berkeley, CA: University of California Press.

HM Government (2004) *The alcohol harm reduction strategy*, London: The Stationery Office.

HM Government (2007) *Safe, sensible, social: Next steps in the national alcohol strategy*, London: The Stationery Office.

HM Government (2008) *Youth crime action plan*, London: The Stationery Office.

HM Government (2009) *Safeguarding children and young people from sexual exploitation: Supplementary guidance to 'Working together to safeguard children'*, London: The Stationery Office.

HM Government (2010) *Drug strategy 2010: Reducing demand, restricting supply, building recovery*, London: The Stationery Office.

HM Government (2012) *Alcohol strategy*, London: The Stationery Office.

HMIP (HM Inspectorate of Prisons) (2011) *Resettlement provision for children and young people: Accommodation and education, training and employment*, London: HMIP.

Hoare, J. (2010) 'Extent and trends in illicit drug use', in J. Hoare and D. Moon (eds) *Drug misuse declared: Findings from the 2009/10 British Crime Survey*, Statistical Bulletin 13/10, London: Home Office.

Holdaway, S. (2003) 'The final warning: appearance and reality', *Criminal Justice*, vol 3, no 4, pp 351-67.

Holland, J., Reynolds, T. and Weller, S. (2007) 'Transitions, networks and communities: The significance of social capital in the lives of children and young people', *Journal of Youth Studies*, vol 10, no 1, pp 97-116.

Holland, S. (2010) 'Looked after children and the ethic of care', *British Journal of Social Work*, vol 40, pp 1664-80.

Hollingsworth, K. (2008) 'Protecting rights at the margins of youth justice in England and Wales: intensive fostering, custody and leaving custody', *Youth Justice*, vol 8, no 3, pp 229-44.

Hollway, W. and Jefferson, T. (2000) *Doing qualitative research differently: Free association, narrative and the interview method*, London: Sage Publications.

Holt, A. (2008) 'Room for resistance? Parenting orders, disciplinary power and the production of "the bad parent"', in P. Squires (ed) *ASBO nation: The criminalisation of nuisance*, Bristol: Policy Press, pp 203-22.

Home Office (1895) *Report from the Departmental Committee on Prisons (The Gladstone Report)*, Cm 7702, London: HMSO.

Home Office (1960) *Report of the Home Office departmental committees on children and young persons*, London: HMSO.

Home Office (1968) *Children in trouble*, Cmnd 3601, London: HMSO.

Home Office (1995) *Tackling drugs together: A strategy for England and Wales 1995-8*, London: Home Office.

Home Office (1997) *No more excuses*, London: Home Office.

Home Office (1998) *Tackling drugs to build a better Britain: The government's 10-year strategy for tackling drug misuse*, London: Home Office.

Home Office (2003) *Respect and responsibility: Taking a stand against anti-social behaviour*, London: Home Office.

Home Office (2004) *Paying the price: A consultation paper on prostitution*, London: Home Office.

Home Office (2011) *Statutory guidance: Injunctions to prevent gang-related violence*, London: The Stationery Office.

Home Office (2012) *Putting victims first: More effective responses to anti-social behaviour*, London: The Stationery Office.

Hopkins, M., Webb, S. and Mackie, A. (2010) *A review of YOTs and children's services interaction with young offenders and young people at risk of offending*, London: Youth Justice Board.

Hopkins-Burke, R. (2008) *Young people, crime and justice*, Cullompton: Willan.

House of Commons Justice Committee (2013) *Youth justice, Seventh report of session 2012-13: Volume 1: Report, together with formal minutes, oral and written evidence*, London: The Stationery Office.

Howard League for Penal Reform (1994) *Banged up, beaten up, cutting up: Report of the Howard League Commission of Inquiry into violence in penal institutions for teenagers under 18*, London: Howard League.

Howard League for Penal Reform (2005) *Children in custody: Promoting the legal and human rights of children*, London: Howard League.

Howe, D. (2009) *A brief introduction to social work theory*, Basingstoke: Palgrave Macmillan.

Howe, D. (2011) *Attachment across the lifecourse: A brief introduction*, Basingstoke: Palgrave Macmillan.

Hudson, A. (1988) 'Boys will be boys: Masculinism and the juvenile justice system', *Critical Social Policy*, vol 21, pp 30–48.

Hudson, B. (2003) *Justice in the risk society*, London: Sage Publications.

Hughes, G. (2007) *The politics of crime and community*, Basingstoke: Palgrave Macmillan.

Hunter, C. and Nixon, J. (2001) 'Taking the blame and losing the home: Women and anti-social behaviour', *Journal of Social Welfare and Family Law*, vol 23, no 4, pp 395–410.

Innes, M. and Fielding, N. (2002) 'From community to communicative policing: "signal crimes" and the problem of public reassurance', *Sociological Research Online* (7/2).

Jacobson, J. and Talbot, J. (2009) *Vulnerable defendants in the criminal court: A review of provision for adults and children*, London: Prison Reform Trust.

Jacobson, J., Bhardwa, B., Gyateng T., Hunter, G. and Hough, M. (2010) *Punishing disadvantage: A profile of young people in custody*, London: Prison Reform Trust.

Jamieson, J. (2005) 'New Labour, youth justice and the question of "respect"', *Youth Justice*, vol 5, pp 180-93.

Jamieson, J., McIvor, G. and Murray, C. (1999) *Understanding offending among young people*, Edinburgh: The Stationery Office.

Jamieson, L. (2000) 'Migration, place and class: Youth in a rural area', *The Sociological Review*, vol 48, no 2, pp 203-23.

Jenkins, R. (2006) *Cannabis and young people: Reviewing the evidence*, London: Jessica Kingsley Publishers.

Johnstone, G. (2002) *Restorative justice: Ideas, values, debates*, Cullompton: Willan.

Jones, D. (2001) 'Misjudged youth: a critique of the Audit Commission's reports on youth justice', *British Journal of Criminology*, vol 41, pp 362-80.

Jones, G. (2002) *The youth divide*, York: Joseph Rowntree Foundation.

Jones, G. (2009) *Youth*, Cambridge: Polity Press.

Jones, S. and Baker, K. (2009) 'Setting the scene: Risk, welfare and rights', in K. Baker and A. Sutherland (eds) *Multi-agency Public Protection Arrangements and youth justice*, Bristol: Policy Press, pp 17-24.

Kelly, L. (2012) 'Representing and preventing youth crime and disorder: intended and unintended consequences of targeted youth programmes in England', *Youth Justice*, vol 12, no 2, pp 101-17.

Kemshall, H. (2002) 'Risk, public protection and justice', in D. Ward, J. Scott and M. Lacey (eds) *Probation: Working for justice*, Oxford: Oxford University Press, pp 95-110.

Kemshall, H. (2007) 'Risk assessment and risk management: the right approach?', in M. Blyth, E. Solomon and K. Baker (eds) *Young people and 'risk'*, Bristol: Policy Press, pp 7-24.

Kemshall, H. (2008) *Understanding the community management of high risk offenders*, Maidenhead: Oxford University Press.

Kemshall, H. (2009a) 'Risk, social policy and young people', in J. Wood and J. Hine (eds) *Work with young people*, London: Sage Publications, pp 154-62.

Kemshall, H. (2009b) 'Young people and parole: risk aware or risk averse', in M. Blyth, R. Newman and C. Wright (eds) *Children and young people in custody*, Bristol: Policy Press, pp 83-96.

Kemshall, H. and Wood, J. (2009) 'MAPPA: Learning the lessons for young offenders', in K. Kaker and A. Sutherland (eds) *Multi-agency Public Protection Arrangements and youth justice,* Bristol: Policy Press, pp 25-42.

Kemshall, H., Marsland, L., Boeck, T. and Dunkerton, L. (2007) 'Young people, pathways and crime: beyond risk factors', in A. France and R. Homel (eds) *Pathways and crime prevention: Theory, policy and practice*, Cullompton: Willan, pp 87-109.

Kemshall, H., Mackenzie, G., Wood, J., Bailey, R. and Yates, J. (2005) *Strengthening Multi-agency Public Protection Arrangements (MAPPAs)*, Home Office Development and Practice Report 45, London: Home Office.

Kilbrandon Committee (1964) *Report on children and young persons, Scotland*, Edinburgh: HMSO.

Kohlberg, L. (1981) *Essays on moral development: The philosophy of moral development*, San Francisco, CA: Harper & Row.

Labour Party (1995) *A quiet life: Tough action on criminal neighbours*, London: Labour Party.

Laming (Lord) (2003) *The Victoria Climbié Inquiry: Report of an Inquiry by Lord Laming*, Cm 5730, London: The Stationery Office.

Laub, J.H. and Sampson, R. (2001) 'Understanding desistance from crime', *Crime and Justice*, vol 28, pp 1-69.

Lawrence, J. (2007) 'Taking the developmental pathways approach to understanding and preventing anti-social behaviour', in A. France and R. Homel (eds) *Pathways and crime prevention: Theory, policy and practice*, Cullompton: Willan, pp 28-50.

Levitas, R. (2005) *The inclusive society? Social exclusion and New Labour* (2nd edn), Basingstoke: Palgrave Macmillan.

Lewis, S. and Olumide, J. (2006) 'Not black and white: mixed heritage experience of criminal justice', in S. Lewis, P. Raynor, D. Smith and A. Wardak (eds) *Race and probation*, Cullompton: Willan, pp 121-42.

Lindfield, S. (2001) *Responses to questionnaire: Parenting work in the youth justice context*, Brighton: Trust for the Study of Adolescence.

Loeber, R. and Farrington, D. (2000) 'Young children who commit crime: epidemiology, developmental origins, risk factors, early interventions, and policy implications', *Development and Psychopathology*, vol 12, pp 737-62.

Losel, F. and Bender, D. (2006) 'Risk factors for serious and violent anti-social behaviour in children and youth', in A. Hagell and R. Jeyarajah-Dent (eds) *Children who commit acts of serious personal violence: Messages for best practice*, London: Jessica Kingsley Publishers, pp 42-72.

MacDonald, R. and Marsh, M. (2002) 'Crossing the Rubicon: youth transitions, poverty, drugs and social exclusion', *The International Journal of Drug Policy*, vol 13, pp 27-38.

MacDonald, R. and Marsh, J. (2005) *Disconnected youth? Growing up in Britain's poor neighbourhoods*, Basingstoke: Palgrave Macmillan.

MacDonald, R., Webster, C., Shildrick, T. and Simpson, M. (2011) 'Paths of exclusion, inclusion and desistence', in S. Farrall, R. Sparks, S. Maruna and M. Hough (eds) *Escape routes: Contemporary perspectives on life after offending*, Abingdon: Routledge, pp 135-57.

McAra, L. (2010) 'Models of youth justice', in D. Smith (ed) *A new response to youth crime*, Abingdon: Routledge, pp 287-317.

McAra, L. and McVie, S. (2005) 'The usual suspects? Street-life, young people and the police', *Criminal Justice*, vol 5, no 1, pp 5-36.

McAra, L. and McVie, S. (2007) 'The impact of system contact on patterns of desistence from offending', *European Journal of Criminology*, vol 4, no 3, pp 315-45.

McAra, L. and McVie, S. (2010) 'Youth justice and crime: Key messages from the Edinburgh Study of Youth Transitions and Crime', *Criminology and Criminal Justice*, vol 10, no 2, pp 179-209.

McCarthy, D.J. (2011) 'Classing early interventions: social class, occupational moralities and criminalisation', *Critical Social Policy*, vol 31, pp 495-516.

McCold, P. and Wachtel, T. (2003) 'In pursuit of paradigm: A theory of restorative justice', Paper presented at the XIII World Congress of Criminology, 10-15 August, Rio de Janeiro.

McGrellis, S., Henderson, S., Holland, J., Sharpe, S. and Thomson, R. (2000) *Through the moral maze: A quantitative study of young people's values*, London: The Tufnell Press.

McGuire, M. (1995) *'What works?' Reducing re-offending: Guidelines from research and practice*, Chichester: J. Wiley & Sons.

McIntosh, B. (2008) 'ASBO youth: Rhetoric and realities', in P. Squires (ed) *ASBO nation: The criminalisation of nuisance*, Bristol: Policy Press, pp 239-56.

McIvor, G., Murray, C. and Jamieson, J. (2004) 'Desistance from crime: Is it different for women and girls?', in S. Maruna and R. Immarigeon (eds) *After crime and punishment: Pathways to offender reintegration*, Cullompton: Willan, pp 181-97.

McLaughlin, J. (2003) *Feminist social and political theory: Contemporary debates and dialogues*, Basingstoke: Palgrave Macmillan.

McLeod, J. (2002) 'Working out intimacy: young people and friendships in an age of reflexivity', *Discourse: Studies in the Cultural Politics of Education*, vol 23, no 2, pp 211-26.

McNeill, F. (2003) 'Desistance-focused probation practice', in W.H. Chui and M. Nellis (eds) *Moving probation forward: Evidence, argument and practice*, Harlow: Pearson Longman, pp 146-62.

McNeill, F. (2006) 'Community supervision: context and relationships matter', in B. Goldson and J. Muncie (eds) *Youth crime and justice*, London: Sage Publications, pp 125-38.

McVie, S. (2004) 'Patterns of deviance underlying the age-crime curve: the long-term evidence', Paper for the 4th European Society of Criminology Conference, Portsmouth, 25-28 August 2004.

McVie, S. and Bradshaw, P. (2005) *Adolescent smoking, drinking and drug use*, Report No 7, Edinburgh Study of Youth Transitions and Crime, Edinburgh: University of Edinburgh.

Marshall, T. (1996) 'The evolution of restorative justice in Britain', *European Journal on Criminal Policy and Research*, vol 4, no 4, pp 21-43.

Marshall, T. (1999) *Restorative justice: An overview*, London: Home Office.

Martinson, R. (1974) 'What works? – questions and answers about prison reform', *The Public Interest*, no 35, pp 22-54.

Maruna, S. (2001) *Making good: How ex-convicts reform and rebuild their lives*, Washington, DC: American Psychological Association.

Maruna, S. and Farrall, S. (2004) 'Desistence from crime: A theoretical reformulation', *The Cologne Journal of Sociology and Social Psychology*, vol 43.

Masson, H. (2007) 'Policy, law and organisational contexts in the United Kingdom: on-going complexity and change', in M. Erooga and H. Masson (eds) *Children and young people who sexually abuse others* (2nd edn), Abingdon: Routledge, pp 18-30.

Matthews, R. (2006) 'Reintegrative shaming and restorative justice: Reconciliation or divorce?', in I. Aertsen, T. Daems and L. Robert (eds) *Institutionalising restorative justice*, Cullompton: Willan, pp 237-60.

Matthews, R. and Briggs, R. (2008) 'Lost in translation: interpreting and implementing anti-social behaviour policies', in P. Squires (ed) *ASBO nation: The criminalisation of nuisance*, Bristol: Policy Press, pp 87-100.

Matthews, S., Brasnett, L. and Smith, J. (2006) *Under-age drinking: Findings from the 2004 Offending, Crime and Justice Survey*, Research Findings 277, London: Home Office.

Measham, F., Newcombe, R. and Parker, H. (1994) 'The normalisation of recreational drug use amongst young people in North West England', *British Journal of Sociology*, vol 45, no 2, pp 287-312.

Melrose, M. (2004) 'Fractured transitions: Disadvantaged young people, drug taking and risk', *Probation Journal*, vol 51, no 4, pp 327-41.

Melrose, M. (2006) 'Young people and drugs', in R. Hughes, R. Lart and P. Higate (eds) *Drugs policy and politics*, Maidenhead: Open University Press, pp 31-44.

Mental Health Foundation (1999) *The big picture: A national survey of child mental health in Britain*, London: Mental Health Foundation.

Mental Health Foundation (2002) *The mental health needs of young offenders*, London: Mental Health Foundation.

Mental Health Foundation (2005) *Lifetime impacts: Childhood and adolescent mental health: Understanding the lifetime impacts*, London: Mental Health Foundation.

Mental Health Foundation (2006) *Truth hurts: Report of the national enquiry into self-harm among young people*, London: Mental Health Foundation.

Millie, A. (2009) *Anti-social behaviour*, Maidenhead: Open University Press.

Mind (2011) *Understanding psychotic experiences*, London: Mind.

Ministry of Justice (2010a) *Criminal statistics 2009*, London: Ministry of Justice.

Ministry of Justice (2010b) *Breaking the cycle*, London: Ministry of Justice.

Ministry of Justice (2012a) *Youth justice statistics 2010/11*, London: Ministry of Justice.

Ministry of Justice (2012b) *Punishment and reform: Effective probation services*, London: Ministry of Justice.

Ministry of Justice (2012c) *Circular No 2012/06, Legal Aid, Sentencing and Punishment of Offenders Act 2012: The new youth remand framework and amendments to adult remand provisions*, London: Ministry of Justice.

Ministry of Justice (2012d) *Further practice directions applying in the Crown Court and Magistrates' Court – Criminal Procedure rules* (www.justice.gov.uk/courts/procedure-rules/criminal/practice-direction/part3#id6328221).

Ministry of Justice (2012e) *Referral order and youth offender panels: Guidance for the courts, youth offending teams and youth offender panels*, London: Ministry of Justice.

Ministry of Justice (2013a) *Transforming rehabilitation*, London: Ministry of Justice.

Ministry of Justice (2013b) *Transforming youth custody: Putting education at the heart of detention*, London: Ministry of Justice.

Mitchell, W.A., Crawshaw, P., Bunton, R. and Green, E.E. (2001) 'Situating young people's experiences of risk and identity', *Health, Risk and Society*, vol 3, no 2, pp 217-33.

Moffitt, T. (1993) 'Adolescence-limited and life-course-persistent anti-social behaviour: a developmental taxonomy', *Psychological Review*, vol 100, no 4, pp 674-701.

Monk, D. (2009) 'Promoting public protection in youth justice', in K. Baker and A. Sutherland (eds) *Multi-agency Public Protection Arrangements and youth justice*, Bristol: Policy Press, pp 59-71.

Mooney, J. and Young, J. (2006) 'The decline in crime and the rise in anti-social behaviour', *Probation Journal*, vol 53, no 4, pp 397-407.

Moore, R., Gray, E., Roberts, C., Taylor, E. and Merrington, S. (2006) *Managing persistent and serious offenders in the community: Intensive community programmes in theory and practice*, Cullompton: Willan.

Moore, T. (2009) *Youth court guide* (3rd edn), Haywards Heath: Tottel Publishing.

Morgan, R. (2009) 'Children in custody', in M. Blyth, R. Newman and C. Wright (eds) *Children and young people in custody*, Bristol: Policy Press, pp 9-22.

Morgan, R. (2012) 'Children and young people in custody', in B. Crewe and J. Bennett (eds) *The prisoner*, London: Routledge, pp 79-91.

Morgan, R. and Newburn, T. (2007) 'Youth justice', in M. Maguire, R. Morgan and R. Reiner (eds) *The Oxford handbook of criminology* (3rd edn), Oxford: Oxford University Press, pp 1024-60.

Morgan, R. and Newburn, T. (2012) 'Youth crime and justice: Rediscovering devolution, discretion and diversion', in M. Maguire, R. Morgan and R. Reiner (eds) *The Oxford handbook of criminology* (5th edn), Oxford: Oxford University Press, pp 490-530.

Morrison, T. and Henniker, J. (2007) 'Building a comprehensive assessment and intervention system for young people who sexually harm: the AIM project', in M. Erooga and H. Masson (eds) *Children and young people who sexually abuse others* (2nd edn), Abingdon: Routledge, pp 31-50.

Morrow, G., Malin, N. and Jennings, T. (2005) 'Inter-professional teamworking for child and family referral in a Sure Start local programme', *Journal of Inter-professional Care*, vol 19, no 2, pp 93-101.

Muncie, J. (2009) *Youth and crime* (3rd edn), London: Sage Publications.

Munro, E. (2001) 'Empowering looked after children', *Child and Family Social Work*, vol 6, pp 129-37.

Munro, E. (2008) *Effective child protection*, London: Sage Publications.

Munro, E. (2010) *The Munro review of child protection, Part One: A system analysis*, London: Department for Education.

Munro, E. (2011a) *The Munro review of child protection, Interim report: The child's journey*, London: Department for Education.

Munro, E. (2011b) *The Munro review of child protection, Final report: A child-centred system*, London: Department for Education.

Murray, C. (1994) *Underclass: the crisis deepens*, London: Institute of Economic Affairs.

Nacro (2006) *Youth crime briefing: Some facts about children and young people who offend – 2004*, London: Nacro.

Nellis, M. (2001) 'Community penalties in historical perspective', in A. Bottoms, L. Gelsthorpe and S. Rex (eds) *Community penalties: Change and challenges*, Cullompton: Willan, pp 16-40.

Newburn, T. (2002) 'The contemporary politics of youth crime prevention', in J. Muncie, E. McLaughlin and G. Hughes (eds) *Youth justice: Critical readings*, Maidstone: Open University Press, pp 453-63.

Newburn, T. and Crawford, A. (2002) 'Referral orders: Some reflections on policy transfer and "what works"', *Youth Justice*, vol 2, pp 141-50.

Newburn, T., Crawford, A., Earle, R., Goldie, S., Hale, C., Hallam, A., Maters, G., Netten, A., Saunders, R., Sharpe, K. and Uglow, S. (2002) *The introduction of referral orders into the youth justice system, Final report*, Home Office Research Study 242, London: Home Office.

Newbury, A. (2011) '"I would have been able to hear what they think": Tensions in achieving restorative outcomes in the English youth justice system', *Youth Justice*, vol 11, no 3, pp 250-65.

Newman, R. and Blyth, M. (2009) 'Ten years on: Conclusions', in M. Blyth, R. Newman and C. Wright (eds) *Children and young people in custody*, Bristol: Policy Press, pp 97-102.

Nixon, J. and Parr, S. (2009) 'Family intervention projects and the efficacy of parenting interventions', in M. Blyth and E. Solomon (eds) *Prevention and youth crime: Is early intervention working?*, Bristol: Policy Press, pp 41-52.

Norris, P. and Williams, D. (2008) 'Binge-drinking, anti-social behaviour and alcohol-related disorder: Examining the 2003 Licensing Act', in P. Squires (ed) *ASBO nation: The criminalisation of nuisance*, Bristol: Policy Press, pp 257-72.

NSPCC (2012) *Statistics on children from minority ethnic backgrounds* (www.nspcc. org.uk/inform/resourcesforprofessionals/minority_ethnic_statistics_wda80509. html).

NYA (National Youth Agency) (2010) *Voice and influence in the youth justice system*, Leicester: NYA.

Ofutu, J. (2006) '"Acting strangely": Young black people and the youth justice system', in D. Wilson, D. and G. Rees (eds) *Just justice: A study into black young people's experiences of the youth justice system*, London: The Children's Society, pp 37-46.

O'Mahoney, P. (2009) 'The risk factor prevention paradigm and the causes of youth crime: a deceptively useful analysis?', *Youth Justice*, vol 9, no 2, pp 99-114.

O'Neill, M. and Campbell, R. (2001) *Working together to create change*, Stafford: Staffordshire University.

O'Neill, M. and Campbell, R. (2006) 'Street sex work and local communities: Creating discursive spaces for genuine consultation and inclusion', in R. Campbell and M. O'Neill (eds) *Sex work now*, Cullompton: Willan, pp 33-61.

ONS (Office for National Statistics) (2008) *Social Trends*, London: ONS.

ONS (2011) *Social Trends 41: Households and families*, London: ONS.

O'Reilly, M., Vostanis, P., Taylor, H., Day, C., Street, C. and Wolpert, M. (2012) 'Service user perspectives of multi-agency working: a qualitative study with children with educational and mental health difficulties and their parents', *Child and Adolescent Mental Health* (doi 10.1111/j.1475-3588.2012.00674.x).

Parker, H., Aldridge, J. and Measham, F. (1998) *Illegal leisure: The normalisation of adolescent recreational drug use*, London: Routledge.

Parker, H., Williams, L. and Aldridge, J. (2002) 'The normalisation of "sensible" recreational drug use: Further evidence from the North West England Longitudinal Study', *Sociology*, vol 36, no 4, pp 941-64.

Parr, S. and Nixon, J. (2008) 'Rationalising family intervention projects', in P. Squires (ed) *ASBO nation: The criminalisation of nuisance*, Bristol: Policy Press, pp 161-78.

Paylor, I., Measham, F. and Asher, H. (2012) *Social work and drug use*, Maidenhead: Open University Press.

Payne, M. (2000) *Teamwork in multi-professional care*, Basingstoke: Palgrave Macmillan.

Pearce, J. (2006) 'Finding the "I" in sexual exploitation: Young people's voices within policy and practice', R. Campbell and M. O'Neill (eds) *Sex work now*, Cullompton: Willan, pp 190-211.

Pearce, J. (2009) 'Beyond child protection: young people, social exclusion and sexual exploitation', in J. Phoenix (ed) *Regulating sex for sale: Prostitution policy reform in the UK*, Bristol: Policy Press, pp 121-36.

Pearce, J. with Williams, M. and Galvin, C. (2002) *'It's someone taking a part of you': a study of young women and sexual exploitation*, London: National Children's Bureau for Joseph Rowntree Foundation.

Phoenix, J. (2002) 'Youth prostitution policy reforms: New discourse, same old story', in P. Carlen (ed) *Women and punishment: A struggle for justice*, Cullompton: Willan, pp 76-95.

Phoenix, J. (2003) 'Rethinking youth prostitution: national provision at the margins of child protection and youth justice', *Youth Justice*, vol 3, no 3, pp 152-68.

Phoenix, J. (2006) 'Regulating prostitution: Controlling women's lives', in F. Heidensohn (ed) *Gender and justice: New concepts and approaches*, Cullompton: Willan, pp 76-95.

Phoenix, J. (2009) 'Beyond risk assessment: the return of repressive welfarism?', in M. Barry and F. McNeill (eds) *Youth offending and youth justice*, London: Jessica Kingsley Publishers, pp 113-31.

Phoenix, J. (2010a) 'Whose account counts? Politics and research in youth justice', in W. Taylor, R. Earle and R. Hester (eds) *Youth justice handbook: Theory, policy and practice*, Cullompton: Willan, pp 73-82.

Phoenix, J. (2010b) 'Pre-sentence reports, magisterial discourse and agency in the youth courts in England and Wales', *Punishment and Society*, vol 12, no 3, pp 348-66.

Piaget, J. (1932) *The moral development of the child*, London: Routledge & Kegan Paul.

Piaget, J. (1958) *The child's construction of reality*, London: Routledge & Kegan Paul.

Pinchbeck, I. and Hewitt, M. (1973) *Children in English society, Vol 2*, London: Routledge.

Piquero, A. (2001) 'Testing Moffitt's neuropsychological variation hypothesis for the prediction of life-course persistent offending', *Psychology, Crime & Law*, vol 7, nos 1-4, pp 193-215.

Pitts, J. (2008) *Reluctant gangsters: The changing face of youth crime*, Cullompton: Willan.

Plant, M.A. and Plant, M. (2006) *Binge Britain: Alcohol and the national response*, Oxford: Oxford University Press.

Plotnikoff, J. and Woolfson, R. (2002) *Young defendants' pack: Scoping study for the Youth Justice Board*, London: Youth Justice Board.

Pratt, J. (1989) 'Corporatism: the third model of juvenile justice', *British Journal of Criminology*, vol 29, no 3, pp 236-54.

Preston-Shoot, M. (2012) 'Safeguarding Children Boards: faith, hope and evidence', in M. Blyth and E. Solomon (eds) *Effective safeguarding for children and young people: What next after Munro?*, Bristol: Policy Press, pp 25-50.

Prior, D., Farrow, K., Hughes, N., Kelly, G., Manders, G., White, S. and Wilkinson, B. (2011) *Maturity, young adults and criminal justice: A literature review*, Birmingham: University of Birmingham.

Prison Reform Trust (2011) *Bromley briefings*, London: Prison Reform Trust.

Putnam, R. (2000) *Bowling alone: The collapse and revival of American community*, New York: Simon & Schuster.

Radzinowicz, L. and Hood, A. (1986) *A history of English criminal law, Vol 5*, London: Stevens and Sons.

Raffo, C. and Reeves, M. (2000) 'Youth transitions and social exclusion: Developments in social capital theory', *Journal of Youth Studies*, vol 3, no 2, pp 147-66.

Raine, A., Moffitt, T., Caspi, A., Loeber, R., Loeber, M.S. and Lynam, D. (2005) 'Neurocognitive impairments on boys on the life-course persistent anti-social path', *Journal of Abnormal Psychology*, vol 114, no 1, pp 38-49.

Ray, K., Hoggart, L., Vegeris, S. and Taylor, R. (2010) *Better off working? Work, poverty and benefit cycling*, York: Joseph Rowntree Foundation.

Rees, G. and Stein, M. (2012) 'Older children and the child protection system', in M. Blyth, M. and E. Solomon (eds) *Effective safeguarding for children and young people: What next after Munro?*, Bristol: Policy Press, pp 107-26.

Rex, S. (1999) 'Desistance from offending: Experiences of probation', *The Howard Journal*, vol 38, no 4, pp 366-83.

Rixon, A. (2007) 'Practitioners', in M. Robb (ed) *Youth in context: Frameworks, settings and encounters*, London: Sage Publications, pp 15-52.

Robb, M. (2007) 'Relating', in M.J. Kehily (ed) *Understanding youth: Perspectives, identities and practices*, London: Sage Publications, pp 313-46.

Robinson, A. (2011) *Foundations for offender management: Theory, law and policy for contemporary practice*, Bristol: Policy Press.

Robinson, A. (2013) 'What's valued, what's valuable in today's youth justice?', in M. Cowburn, M. Duggan, A. Robinson and P. Senior (eds) *Values in criminology and criminal justice*, Bristol: Policy Press, pp 295–312.

Robinson, G. and McNeill, F. (2008) 'Exploring the dynamics of compliance with community penalties', *Theoretical Criminology*, vol 12, pp 431-49.

Robinson, M. and Cottrell, D. (2005) 'Health professionals in multi-disciplinary and multi-agency teams: Changing professional practice', *The Journal of Inter-professional Care*, vol 19, no 6, pp 547-60.

Rodger, J.J. (2008) *Criminalising social policy: Anti-social behaviour and welfare in a de-civilised society*, Cullompton: Willan.

Rodham, K., Hawton, K., Evans, E. and Weatherall, R. (2005) 'Ethnic and gender differences in drinking, smoking and drug taking among adolescents in England: a self-report school-based survey of 15 and 16 year olds', *Journal of Adolescence*, vol 28, pp 63-73.

Roe, S. and Ashe, J. (2008) *Young people and crime: Findings from the 2006 Offending, Crime and Justice Survey*, Home Office Statistical Bulletin 09/08, London: Home Office.

Rumgay, J. (2003) 'Partnerships in the probation service', in W.H. Chui and M. Nellis (eds) *Moving probation forward: Evidence, arguments and practice*, Harlow: Pearson Education, pp 195-213.

Salmon, G. and Rapport, F. (2005) 'Multi-agency voices: a thematic analysis of multi-agency working practices within the setting of a child and adolescent mental health service', *Journal of Inter-professional Care*, vol 19, no 5, pp 429-43.

Sampson, R.J. and Laub, J.H. (1993) *Crime in the making: Pathways and turning points through life*, Cambridge, MA: Harvard University Press.

Sampson, R.J and Laub, J.H. (2005) 'A life course view of the development of crime', *The Annals of the American Academy of Political and Social Science*, vol 602, pp 12-45.

Sanders, R. and Mace, S. (2006) 'Agency policy and participation of children and young people in the child protection process', *Child Abuse Review*, vol 15, pp 89-109.

Sanders, T., O'Neill, M. and Pitcher, J. (2009) *Prostitution: Sex work, policy and politics*, London: Sage Publications.

Scott, J. and Telford, P. (2007) 'Similarities and differences in working with girls and boys who display sexually harmful behaviours: the journey continues', in M. Erooga and H. Masson (eds) *Children and young people who sexually abuse others* (2nd edn), Abingdon: Routledge, pp 174-84.

Sentencing Guidelines Council (2009) *Over-arching principles – Sentencing youths*, London: Sentencing Guidelines Council.

SEU (Social Exclusion Unit) (1998) *Bringing Britain together: A national strategy for neighbourhood renewal*, London: SEU.

SEU (1999) *Bridging the gap: New opportunities for 16-18 year olds not in education, employment or training*, London: SEU.

Seymour, M. (2013) *Youth justice in context: Community, compliance and young people*, Abingdon: Routledge.

Sharpe, G. (2012) *Offending girls: Young women and youth justice*, Abingdon: Routledge.

Sharpe, S. (2001) *More than just a piece of paper: young people's views on marriage and relationships*, London: National Children's Bureau.

Shildrick, T., MacDonald, R., Webster, C. and Garthwaite, K. (2012) *Poverty and insecurity: Life in low-pay, no-pay Britain*, Bristol: Policy Press.

Shiner, M. (2006) 'Drugs, law and the regulation of harm', in R. Hughes, R. Lart and P. Higate (eds) *Drugs: Policy and politics*, Maidenhead: Open University Press, pp 59-74.

Silvestri, M. and Crowther-Dowey, C. (2008) *Gender and crime*, London: Sage Publications.

Slapper, G. and Kelly, D. (2009) *The English legal system* (10th edn), Abingdon: Routledge.

Smith, D.J. (2007) 'Crime and the life-course', in M. Maguire, R. Morgan and R. Reiner (eds) *The Oxford handbook of criminology* (4th edn), Oxford: Oxford University Press, pp 641-83.

Smith, D.J. and Bradshaw, P. (2005) *Gang membership and teenage offending*, Edinburgh: Edinburgh Study of Youth Transitions and Crime.

Smith, L. and Foxcroft, D. (2009) *Drinking in the UK: An exploration of trends*, York: Joseph Rowntree Foundation.

Smith, M. (2009) *Rethinking residential childcare: Positive perspectives*, Bristol: Policy Press.

Smith, M., Fulcher, L. and Doran, P. (2013) *Residential childcare in practice: Making a difference*, Bristol: Policy Press.

Smith, R. (2003) *Youth justice: Ideas, policy, practice*, Cullompton: Willan.

Smith, R. (2006) 'Actuarialism and early intervention in contemporary youth justice', in B. Goldson and J. Muncie (eds) *Youth crime and justice*, London: Sage Publications, pp 92-109.

Smith, R. (2007) *Youth justice: Ideas, policy, practice* (2nd edn), Cullompton: Willan.

Smith, R. (2009) 'Childhood, agency and youth justice', *Children & Society*, vol 23, pp 252-64.

Smith, R. (2011) *Doing justice to young people: Youth crime and social justice*, Abingdon: Willan.

Solomon, E. and Blyth, M. (2009) 'Introduction', in M. Blyth and E. Solomon (eds) *Prevention and youth crime: Is early intervention working?*, Bristol: Policy Press, pp 1-7.

Solomon, E. and Blyth, M. (2012) 'Conclusion', in M. Blyth and E. Solomon (eds) *Effective safeguarding for children and young people: What next after Munro?*, Bristol: Policy Press, pp 145-54.

Sommers, L., Baskin, D. and Fagan, J. (1994) 'Getting out of the life: crime desistence by female street offenders', *Deviant Behaviour: An Interdisciplinary Journal*, vol 15, pp 125-49.

Soothill, K., Fitzpatrick, C. and Francis, B. (2009) *Understanding criminal careers*, Cullompton: Willan.

Souhami, A. (2007) *Transforming youth justice: Occupational identity and cultural change*, Cullompton: Willan.

Souhami, A. (2008) 'Multi-agency practice: experiences in the youth justice system', in S. Green, E. Lancaster and S. Feasey (eds) *Addressing offending behaviour: Context, practice and values*, Cullompton: Willan, pp 208-25.

Souhami, A. (2009) 'Doing youth justice beyond boundaries?', in M. Barry and F. McNeill (eds) *Youth offending and youth justice*, London: Jessica Kingsley Publishers, pp 113-31.

Spencer, G. (2013) 'Young people's perspectives on health: empowerment or risk?', *Health Education*, vol 113, no 2, pp 115-31.

Squires, P. and Silvestri, A. (2008) *Street weapons commission: Guns, knives and street violence*, London: Centre for Crime and Justice Studies.

Squires, P. and Stephen, D. (2005) *Rough justice: ASB and young people*, Cullompton: Willan.

Stafford, A., Parton, N., Vincent, S. and Smith, C. (2012) *Child protection systems in the United Kingdom: A comparative analysis*, London: Jessica Kingsley Publishers.

Stein, M. (2005) *Resilience and young people leaving care: Overcoming the odds*, York: Joseph Rowntree Foundation.

Stein, M. (2006) 'Research review: young people leaving care', *Child and Family Social Work*, vol 11, no 3, pp 273-9.

Steinberg, L. (2010) 'A dual systems model of adolescent risk-taking', *Developmental Psychology*, vol 55, pp 216-24.

Stephen, D.E. and Squires, P.A. (2003) '"Adults don't realise how sheltered they are". A contribution to the debate on youth transitions from some voices on the margins', *Journal of Youth Studies*, vol 6, no 2, pp 145-64.

Stephenson, M. (2007) *Young people and offending: Education, youth justice and social inclusion*, Cullompton: Willan.

Stephenson, M., Giler, H. and Brown, S. (2011) *Effective practice in youth justice* (2nd edn), Abingdon: Routledge.

Stretesky, P.B. and Pogrebin, M.R. (2007) 'Gun-related gang violence: socialisation, identity and self', *Journal of Contemporary Ethnography*, vol 36, pp 85-114.

Summerfield, A. (2011) *Children and young people in custody 2010-11*, London: HM Inspectorate of Prisons.

Sutherland, A. (2009) 'Youth offending teams and MAPPA: past problems, current challenges and future prospects', in K. Baler and A. Sutherland (eds) *Multi-agency Public Protection Arrangements and youth justice*, Bristol: Policy Press, pp 43-58.

Sylva, K. and Lunt, I. (1982) *Child development: A first course*, Oxford: Blackwell.

Taylor, C. (2006) *Young people in care and criminal behaviour*, London: Jessica Kingsley Publishers.

Thomas, M. (2009) 'Youth offending teams', in B. Goldson (ed) *Dictionary of youth justice*, Cullompton: Willan, pp 388-9.

Thomson, R. (2007a) 'A biographical perspective', in M.J. Kehily (ed) *Understanding youth: Perspectives, identities and practices*, London: Sage Publications, pp 73-106.

Thomson, R. (2007b) 'The qualitative longitudinal case history: Practical, methodological and ethical reflections', *Social Policy and Society*, vol 6, no 4, pp 571-82.

Thomson, R. (2011) *Unfolding lives: Youth, gender and change*, Bristol: Policy Press.

Thomson, R. and Taylor, R. (2005) 'Between cosmopolitanism and the locals: Mobility as a resource in the transition to adulthood', *Young*, vol 13, no 4, pp 327-42.

Thomson, R., Henderson, S. and Holland, J. (2003) 'Making the most of what you've got? Resources, values and inequalities in young women's transitions to adulthood', *Educational Review*, vol 55, no 1, pp 33-46.

Thomson, R., Bell, R., Holland, J., Henderson, S., McGrellis, S. and Sharpe, S. (2002) 'Critical moments: Choice, chance and opportunity in young people's narratives of transition', *Sociology*, vol 36, no 2, pp 335-54.

Thomson, R., Holland, J., McGrellis, S., Bell, R., Henderson, S. and Sharpe, S. (2004) 'Inventing adulthoods: A biographical approach to understanding youth citizenship', *The Sociological Review*, vol 52, no 2, pp 218-39.

Thornberry, T., Krohn, M., Lizotte, A. and Chard-Wierschem, D. (1993) 'The role of juvenile gangs in facilitating delinquent behaviour', *Journal of Research in Crime and Delinquency*, vol 30, pp 75-85.

Tierney, J. (2006) *Criminology: Theory and context*, Harlow: Longman.

Tolonen, T. (2005) 'Locality and gendered capital in working class youth', *Young*, vol 13, no 4, pp 343-61.

Trevithick, P. (2012) *Social work skills and knowledge: A practice handbook*, Maidenhead: Open University Press.

Trotter, C. (2006) *Working with involuntary clients: A guide to practice*, London: Sage Publications.

Tuckman, R.W. (1965) 'Developmental sequences in small groups', *Psychological Bulletin*, vol 63, no 6, pp 384-99.

Tunstall, R., Lupton, R., Watmough, S. and Bates, K. (2012) *Disadvantaged young people looking for work: A job in itself?*, York: Joseph Rowntree Foundation.

UK Commission for Employment and Skills (2011) *Youth inquiry evidence base* (www.ukces.org.uk/publications/youth-inquiry).

Ungar, M. and Teram, E. (2000) 'Drifting towards mental health: High risk adolescents and the process of empowerment', *Youth & Society*, vol 32, no 2, pp 228-52.

Uprichard, E. (2008) 'Children as "beings" and "becomings": Children, childhood and temporality', *Children & Society*, vol 22, pp 303-13.

User Voice (2011a) *Young people's views on restraint in the secure estate*, London: User Voice.

User Voice (2011b) *The user voice of young people in the secure estate on safeguarding*, London: User Voice.

van Ness, D. and Strong, K.H. (1997) *Restoring justice*, Cincinnati, OH: Anderson Publishing.

Vanstone, M. (2004) *Supervising offenders in the community: A history of probation theory and practice*, Aldershot: Ashgate.

Vaughan, K. (2003) 'Changing lanes: Young people making sense of pathways', Paper presented at the New Zealand Council for Educational Research Annual Conference 'Educating for the 21st century', 8 August (http://nzcer/pdfs/12223.pdf).

Vaughan, K. and Roberts, J. (2007) 'Developing a "productive" account of young people's transition perspectives', *Journal of Education and Work*, vol 20, no 2, pp 91–105.

Walker, J., Thompson, C., Laing, K., Raybould, S., Coombes, M., Proctor, S. and Wren, C. (2007) *Youth inclusion and support panels: Preventing crime and anti-social behaviour*, London: Department for Children, Schools and Families.

Walker, S. (2011) *The social worker's guide to child and adolescent mental health*, London: Jessica Kingsley Publishers.

Walsh, J., Scaife, V., Notley, C., Dodsworth, J. and Schofield, G. (2011) 'Perception of need and barriers to access: the mental health needs of young people attending a youth offending team in the UK', *Health and Social Care in the Community*, vol 19, no 4, pp 420–8.

Walvoord, E.C. (2010) 'The timing of puberty: Is it changing? Does it matter?', *Journal of Adolescent Health*, vol 47, no 5, pp 433–9.

Way, I. (2002) 'Childhood maltreatment histories of male adolescents with sexually offending behaviours: a review of the literature', in M.C. Calder (ed) *Young people who sexually abuse: Building the evidence base for your practice*, Lyme Regis: Russell House Publishing, pp 26–55.

Webster, C., Simpson, D., MacDonald, R., Abbas, A., Cieslik, M., Shildrick, T. and Simpson, M. (2004) *Poor transitions: Social exclusion and young adults*, Bristol: Policy Press.

Wenger, E. (1998) *Communities of practice*, Cambridge: Cambridge University Press.

White, M. and Grove, D. (2003) *Towards an understanding of partnership*, London: NCCVCO.

White, R.C.A. (1999) *The English legal system in action*, Oxford: Oxford University Press.

White, R.C.A. and Graham, H. (2010) *Working with offenders: A guide to concepts and practices*, Cullompton: Willan.

Whittle, N., Bailey, S. and Kurtz, Z. (2006) *The needs and effective treatment of young people who sexually abuse: Current evidence*, London: Department of Health.

Whyte, B. (2009) *Youth justice in practice: Making a difference*, Bristol: Policy Press.

Williams, I. (2009) 'Offender health and social care: a review of the evidence on inter-agency collaboration', *Health and Social Care in the Community*, vol 17, no 6, pp 573–80.

Williams, J. (2008) *Child law for social work*, London: Sage Publications.

Williamson, H. (2009) 'Integrated or targeted youth support services: an essay on "prevention"', in M. Blyth and E. Solomon (eds) *Prevention and youth crime: Is early intervention working?*, Bristol: Policy Press, pp 9-20.

Wilson, D. (2006) 'Playing the game the experiences of young black men in custody', in D. Wilson and G. Rees (eds) *Just justice: A study into black young people's experiences of the youth justice system*, London: The Children's Society, pp 14-21.

Wilson, D. and Rees, G. (eds) (2006) *Just justice: A study in black young people's experiences of the youth justice system*, London: The Children's Society.

Wilson, J.Q. and Kelling, G. (1982) 'Broken windows', *Atlantic Monthly*, March, pp 29-38.

Wolf, A. (2011) *Review of vocational education: The Wolf report*, London: Department for Education.

Woodman, D. (2009) 'The mysterious case of the pervasive choice biography: Ulrich Beck, structure/agency and the middling state of theory in the sociology of youth', *Journal of Youth Studies*, vol 12, no 3, pp 243-56.

Worrall, A. and Hoy, C. (2005) *Punishment in the community: Managing offenders, making choices*, Cullompton: Willan.

Wortley, R. (2011) *Psychological criminology: An integrative approach*, Abingdon: Routledge.

Wright, B.E.W., Caspi, A., Moffitt, T. and Silva, P.A. (2001) 'The effects of social ties on crime vary by criminal propensity: a life-course model of interdependence', *Criminology*, vol 39, no 2, pp 321-52.

Yates, S. (2009) 'Good practice in guidance: lessons from Connexions', in J. Wood and J. Hine (eds) *Work with young people*, London: Sage Publications, pp 163-75..

Young, J. (1986) 'The failure of criminology: The need for a radical realism', in J. Young and R. Matthews (eds) *Confronting crime*, London: Sage Publications, pp 4-30.

YJB (Youth Justice Board) (2004a) *Report on resources for young women*, London: YJB.

YJB (2004b) *ISSP: The final report*, London: YJB.

YJB (2006a) *Anti-social Behaviour Orders*, London: YJB.

YJB (2006b) *Youth justice annual statistics 2005/6*, London: YJB.

YJB (2010) *Youth justice statistics 2009/10 England and Wales*, London: YJB.

YJB (2011) *Assessment and planning interventions: Review and redesign project*, London: YJB.

YJB (2013a) *Assetplus – Assessment and planning interventions framework* (www.yjb.gov.uk).

YJB (2013b) *Youth out-of-court disposals: Guide for police and youth offending services*, London: YJB.

Zehr, H. (2013) 'Retributive justice, restorative justice', in G. Johnstone (ed) *A restorative justice reader* (2nd edn), Abingdon: Routledge, pp 23-35.

Index

Ward, T. 62
Warren, M. 4
Webster, C. 80
welfarism 6, 7
  court system 231, 233
  dependency and 77, 80, 81, 151
  female offenders 46
  historical background 37, 38–40, 41, 43,
    44–5
  'repressive' 54
  social investment state 78
well-being *see* mental health and well-being
White, M. 209
White, R.C.A 202
Williams, I. 208–9
Williamson, H. 227
Wilson, D. 47–8, 292
Wilson, J.Q. 152
witnesses 238
Wolf report (2011) 74, 83
Woolfson, R. 232, 233
work *see* employment
Working together to safeguard children: A guide to
  inter-agency working to safeguard and promote
  the welfare of children (Department of
  Health) 185–6
Working together to safeguard children
  (Department for Education) 192, 199
working-classes 6–7, 9, 11, 16, 42, 157
  dependency 85–6
  economic marginalisation 79–82
  opportunities 73
  probation service 37, 38
  sex and relationships 92
  substance use 144
Worrall, A. 45

Y

YCAP *see* Youth crime action plan
YISPs *see* Youth Inclusion and Support
  Projects
Young, J. 152
young men *see* boys and young men
Young Offender Institution (YOI) 109, 280,
  281*f*, 290, 291, 294, 295
young women *see* girls and young women
'youth conditional caution' 56–7, 219, 220,
  284
Youth Contract 83, 84
Youth Court Panel 229
youth courts 40, 217, 229, 232, 271–2
Youth crime action plan (YCAP) (HM
  Government) 56, 222
youth groups 160
Youth Inclusion Projects (YIPs) 163, 221, 222
Youth Inclusion and Support Projects (YISPs)
  172, 213, 222, 223
Youth Justice Board 35, 43, 51–2, 53, 177, 203,
  204

community sentences 270
court system 232, 239
criteria and targets 56
imprisonment 278, 281, 291
prevention/intervention 219, 221, 222
Youth Justice and Criminal Evidence Act
  (1999) 238, 243, 250
youth justice plans 125
Youth Justice System (YJS) 34
  Coalition Government and 57–8
  court system 241
  critiques of New Labour reforms 55–7
  diversion from formal processing 60
  future developments 59–60
  mental health and well-being 113–17
  New Labour reforms 42–3, 51–2, 233, 234
  restorative justice 255–7
  risk behaviours and 172–5
  welfare issues and 53–5
  youth-centred practice 61*f*, 62–5
Youth Lifestyles Survey (1998/99) 20, 137
youth movements 160
Youth Offender Panel (YOP) 59, 250, 251–2,
  253, 254, 255
Youth Offending Teams (YOTs) 43–4, 48, 54,
  56, 172
  anti-social behaviour 165
  collaboration/multi-agency working 201,
    203, 204*f*, 205, 208–9, 213, 214
  community sentences 259, 262*t*, 263, 269–70
  Connexions Service and 79
  court system 229, 234, 236, 238, 239, 241
  development of 203, 204*f*, 205–8
  imprisonment 287–8, 293–4
  mental health and well-being 101, 105, 112,
    113, 114
  prevention/intervention 221–2
  restorative justice 251–2, 253, 254–5, 257
  risk-taking 175, 177, 179–82
  women and 46–7
  see also collaborative working
'youth problem' 19–20
youth rehabilitation order (YRO) 39, 57–8,
  146, 234
  breach proceedings 240
  practitioners and 261, 262*t*, 263
  risk and 175, 176
  see also community sentences
youth secure estate 279, 281, 291
Youth Transitions and Social Change' 13
'Youth Values: Identity, Diversity and Social
  Change' (Economic and Social Research
  Council) 13
youth-centred practice 17, 20, 49, 61*f*, 62–5,
  84
  anti-social behaviour 164–5
  collaborative/multi-agency work 206, 214
  community sentences 261, 262*t*, 263
  court system 229, 231–2, 240–2